DATE DUE

893069			

PRINTED IN U.S.A.

3-04

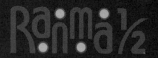

Ranma 1/2

VOL. 23
Action Edition

Story and Art by
RUMIKO TAKAHASHI

English Adaptation/Gerard Jones and Matt Thorn
Touch-Up Art & Lettering/Wayne Truman
Cover Design/Hidemi Sahara
Graphics & Design/Sean Lee
Editor/Julie Davis

Managing Editor/Annette Roman
Editor in Chief/William Flanagan
Dir. of Licensing & Acquisitions/Rika Inouye
VP of Sales & Marketing/Liza Coppola
Sr. VP of Editorial/Hyoe Narita
Publisher/Seiji Horibuchi

RANMA 1/2 is rated "T+" for Older Teens. It may contain violence, language, alcohol or tobacco use, or suggestive situations.

The stories, characters and incidents mentioned in this publication are entirely fictional. For the purposes of publication in English, the artwork in this publication is printed in reverse from the original Japanese version.

Printed in Canada.

Published by VIZ, LLC
P.O. Box 77010
San Francisco, CA 94107

Action Edition
10 9 8 7 6 5 4 3 2 1
First printing, August 2003

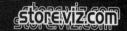

Ranma 1/2

VOL. 23   Action Edition

STORY & ART BY
RUMIKO TAKAHASHI

STORY THUS FAR

The Tendos are an average, run-of-the-mill Japanese family—at least on the surface, that is. Soun Tendo is the owner and proprietor of the Tendo Dojo, where "Anything-Goes Martial Arts" is practiced. Like the name says, anything goes, and usually does.

When Soun's old friend Genma Saotome comes to visit, Soun's three lovely young daughters—Akane, Nabiki, and Kasumi—are told that it's time for one of them to become the fiancée of Genma's teenage son, as per an agreement made between the two fathers years ago. Youngest daughter Akane—who says she hates boys—is quickly nominated for bridal duty by her sisters.

Unfortunately, Ranma and his father have suffered a strange accident. While training in China, both plunged into one of many "accursed" springs at the legendary martial arts training ground of Jusenkyo. These springs transform the unlucky dunkee into whoever—or whatever—drowned there hundreds of years ago.

From now on, a splash of cold water turns Ranma's father into a giant panda, and Ranma becomes a beautiful, busty young woman. Hot water reverses the effect...but only until next time.

Ranma and Genma weren't the only ones to take the Jusenkyo plunge—it isn't long before they meet several other members of the "cursed." And although their parents are still determined to see Ranma and Akane marry and carry on the training hall, Ranma seems to have a strange talent for accumulating extra fiancées, and Akane has a few suitors of her own. Will the two ever work out their differences, get rid of all these extra people, or just call the whole thing off? And will Ranma ever get rid of his curse?

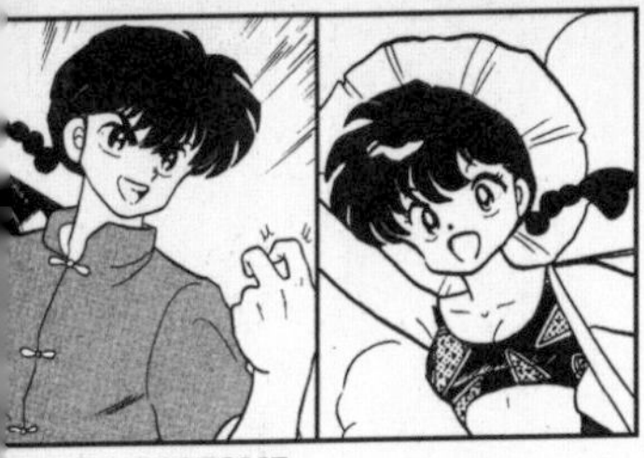

RANMA SAOTOME
Martial artist with far too many finacées, and an ego that won't let him take defeat easily. He changes into a girl when splashed with cold water.

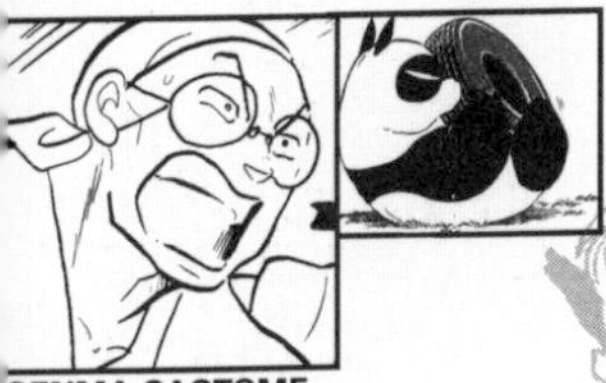

GENMA SAOTOME
Ranma's lazy father, who left his home and wife years ago with his young son to train in the martial arts. He changes into a panda.

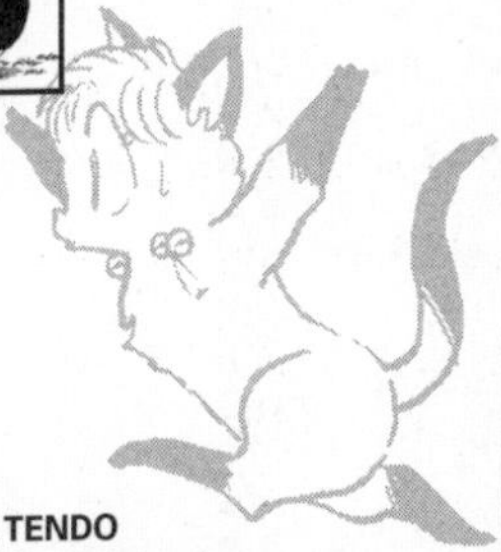

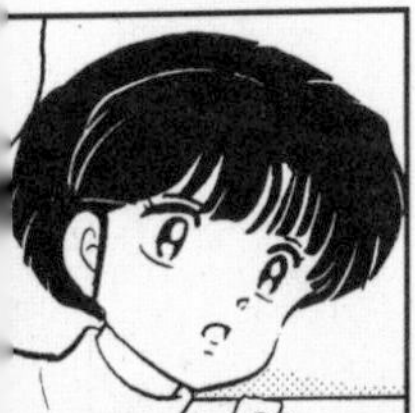

AKANE TENDO
A martial artist, tomboy, and Ranma's fiancée by parental arrangement. She has no clue how much Ryoga likes her, or what relation he has to her pet black pig, P-chan.

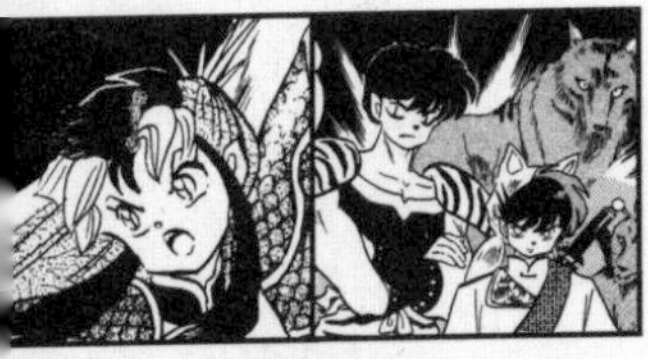

HERB, MINT, AND LIME
A trio of Chinese martial arts with special powers.

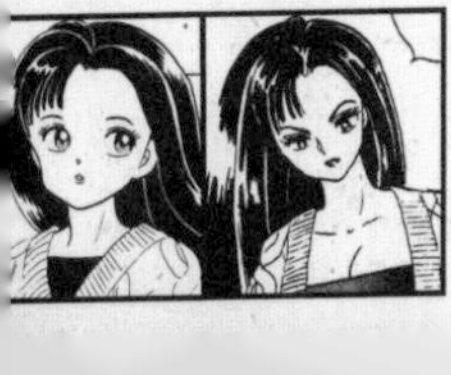

HINAKO NINOMIYA
A new high school teacher with a reputation for dealing with delinquents.

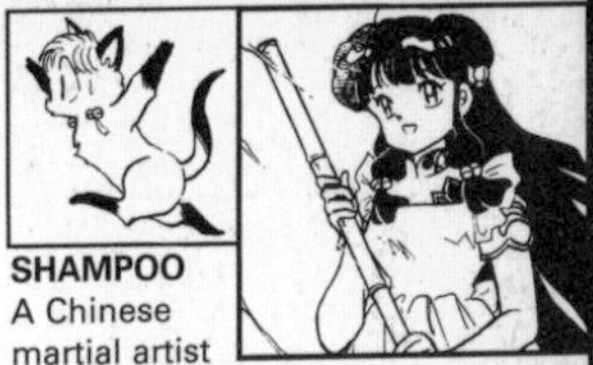

SHAMPOO
A Chinese martial artist from a village of amazons who is in love with Ranma and claims that he must marry her due to village law. She changes into a cat.

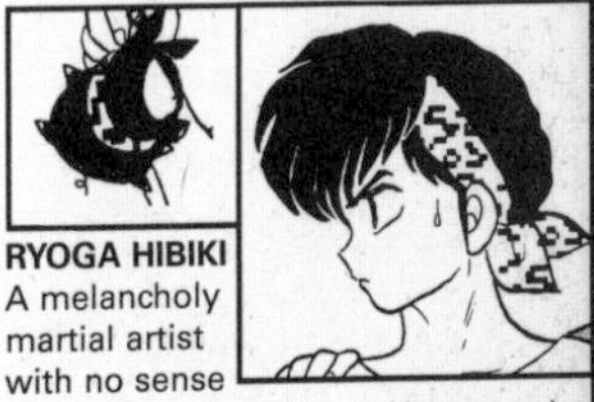

RYOGA HIBIKI
A melancholy martial artist with no sense of direction, a crush on Akane, and a grudge against Ranma. He changes into a small, black pig Akane calls "P-chan."

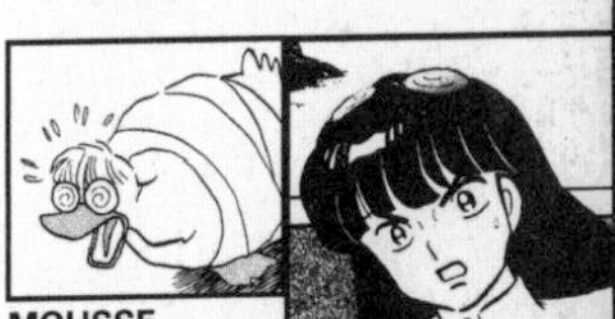

MOUSSE
A nearsighted Chinese martial artist whose specialty is hidden weapons, Mousse has been Shampoo's suitor since childhood. He changes into a duck.

COLOGNE
Great-grandmother to Shampoo who's looking forward to getting a new grandson-in-law in Ranma.

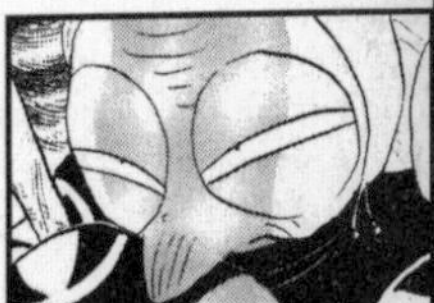

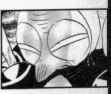

UKYO KUONJI
Another of Ranma's fianceés, Ukyo is both a martial artist and *okonomiyaki* chef.

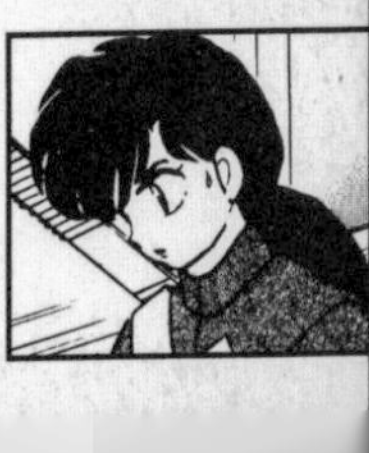

CONTENTS

Part 1

A MAN AGAIN!

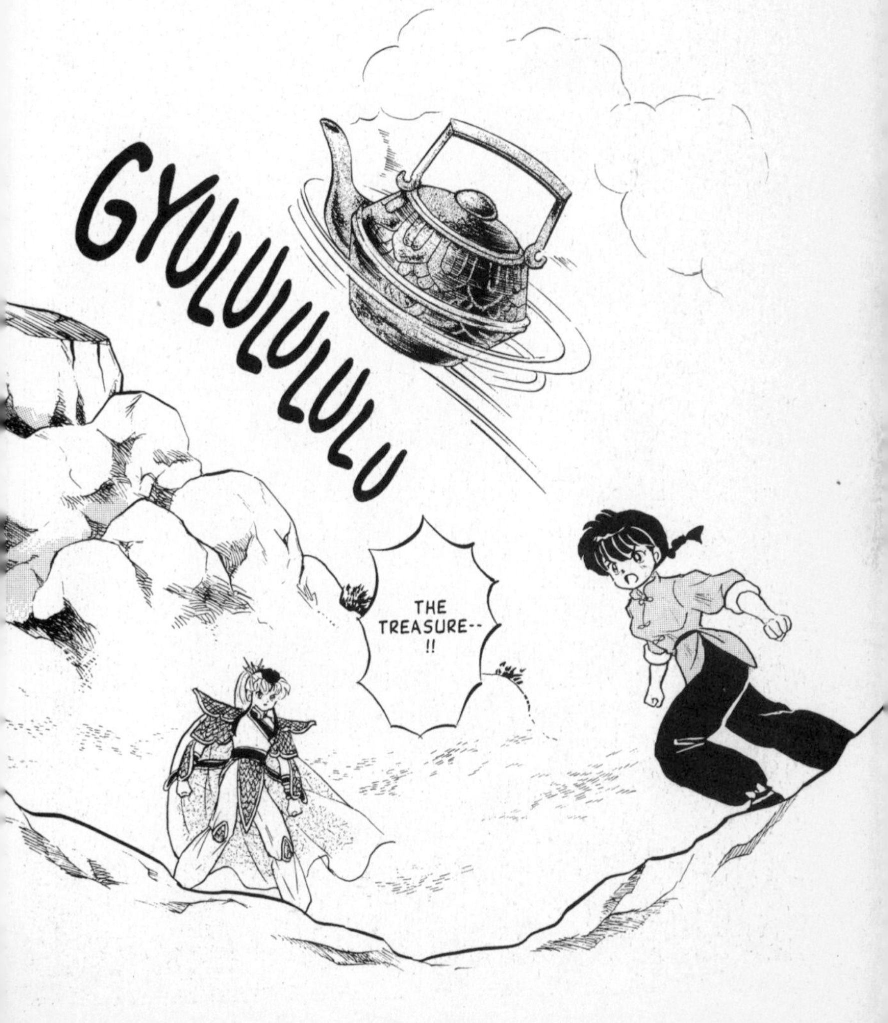
GYULULULULU
THE TREASURE--!!

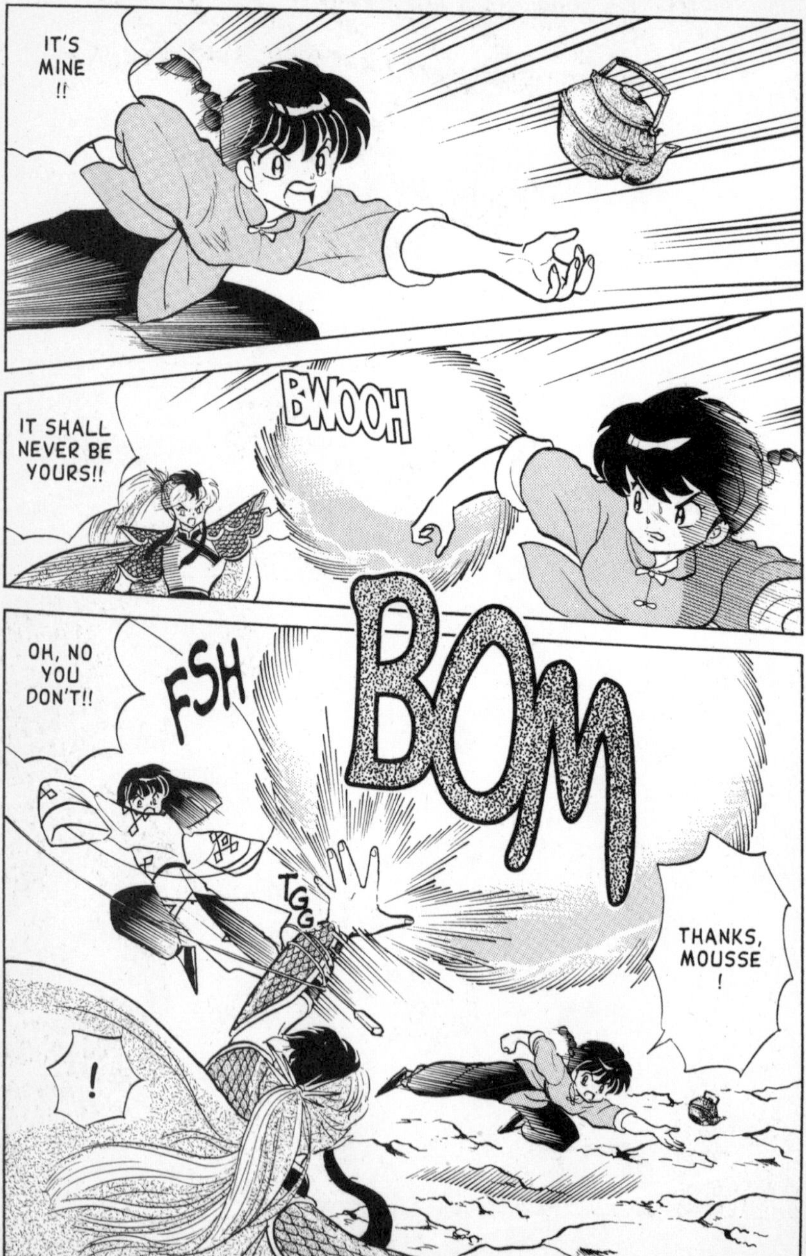
IT'S MINE !!
IT SHALL NEVER BE YOURS!!
BWOOH
OH, NO YOU DON'T!!
FSH
BOM
TGG
THANKS, MOUSSE !
!

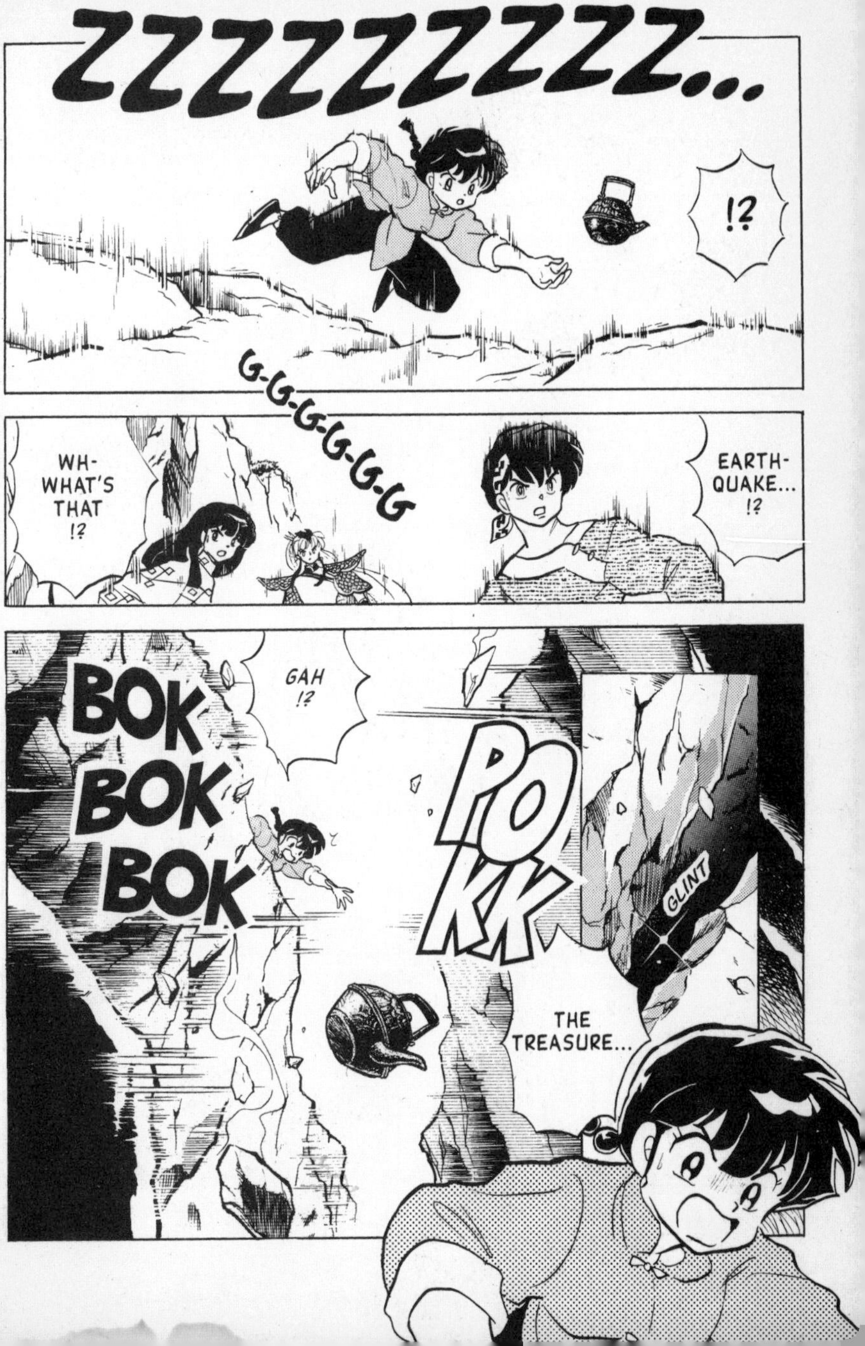
ZZZZZZZZZZ...
!?
G-G-G-G-G-G-G
WH- WHAT'S THAT !?
EARTH- QUAKE... !?
BOK BOK BOK
GAH !?
POKK
GLINT
THE TREASURE...

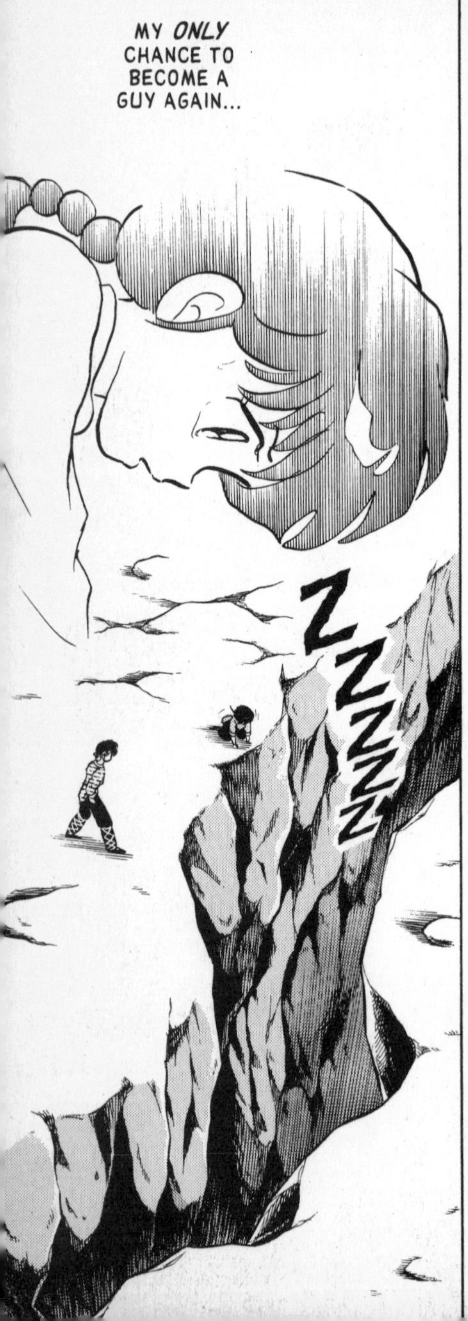
MY *ONLY* CHANCE TO BECOME A GUY AGAIN...
ZZZZZZ
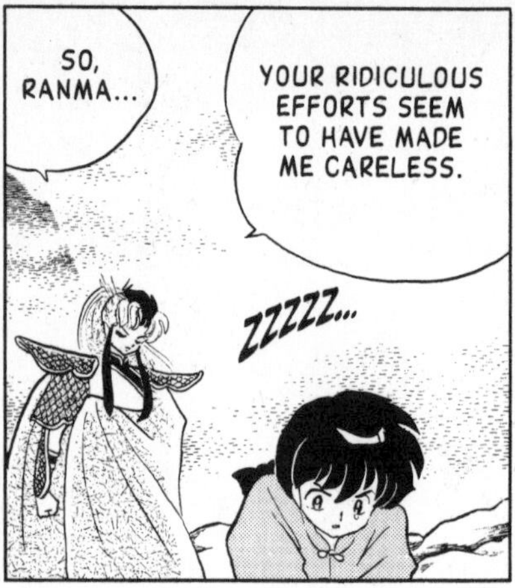
SO, RANMA...
YOUR RIDICULOUS EFFORTS SEEM TO HAVE MADE ME CARELESS.
ZZZZZ...
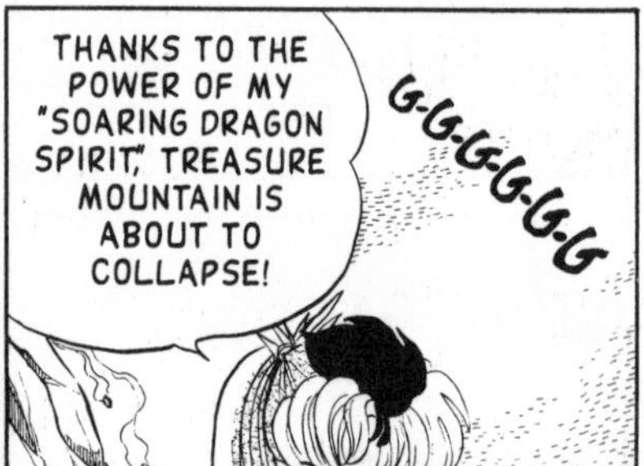
THANKS TO THE POWER OF MY "SOARING DRAGON SPIRIT," TREASURE MOUNTAIN IS ABOUT TO COLLAPSE!
G-G-G-G-G-G-G
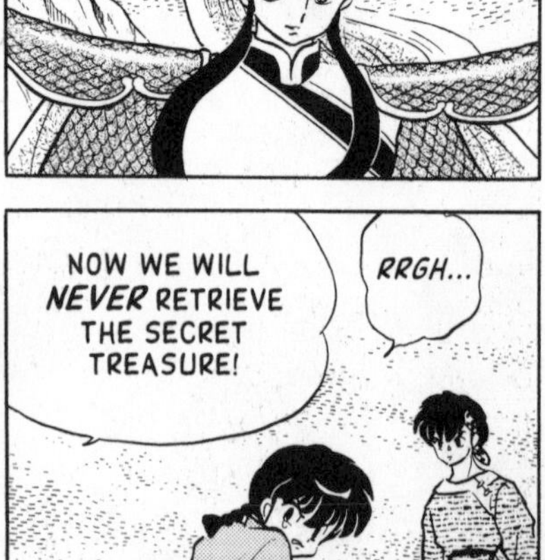
NOW WE WILL *NEVER* RETRIEVE THE SECRET TREASURE!
RRGH...

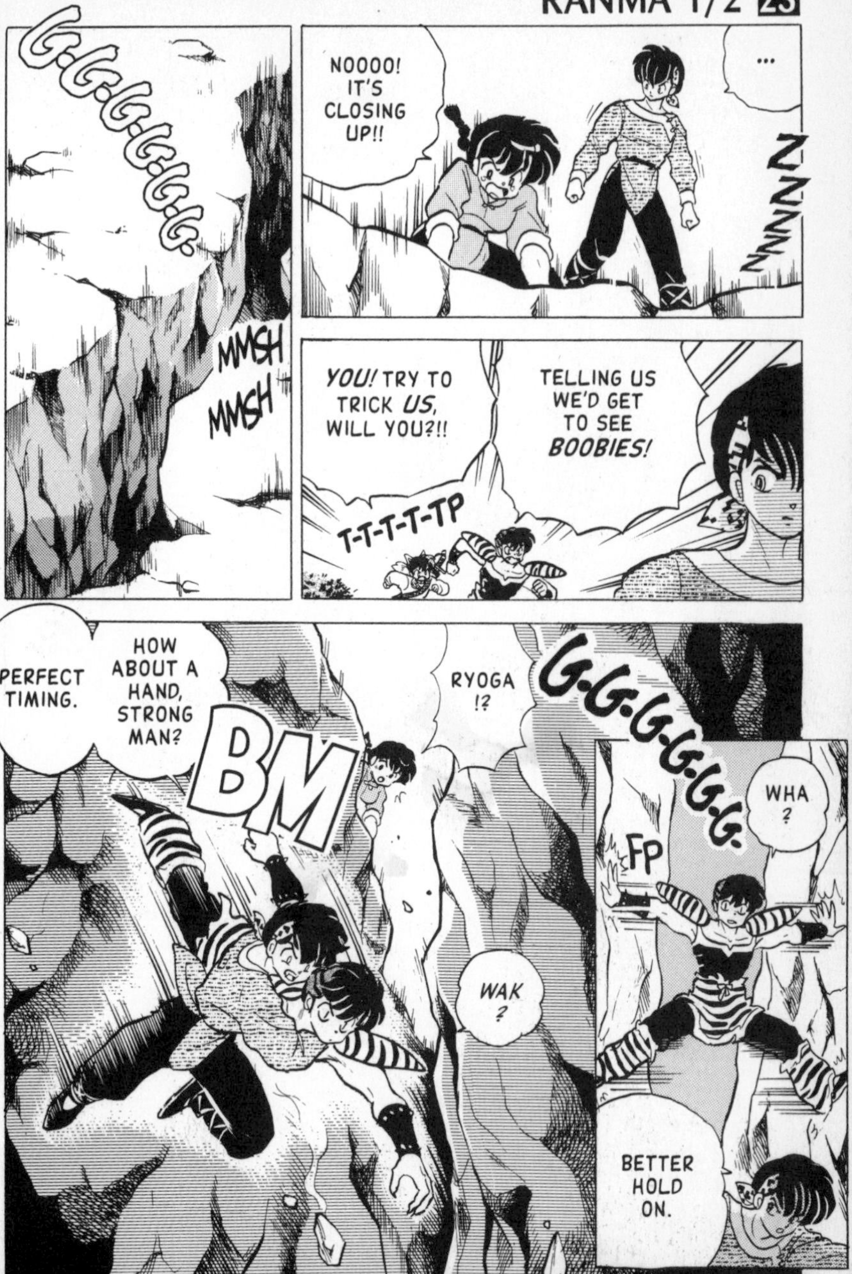
G-G-G-G-G-G-G
MMSH
MMSH
NOOOO! IT'S CLOSING UP!!
...
ZZZZNNNNN
YOU! TRY TO TRICK US, WILL YOU?!!
TELLING US WE'D GET TO SEE BOOBIES!
T-T-T-T-TP
PERFECT TIMING.
HOW ABOUT A HAND, STRONG MAN?
BM
RYOGA !?
WAK ?
G-G-G-G-G-G-G
FP
WHA ?
BETTER HOLD ON.

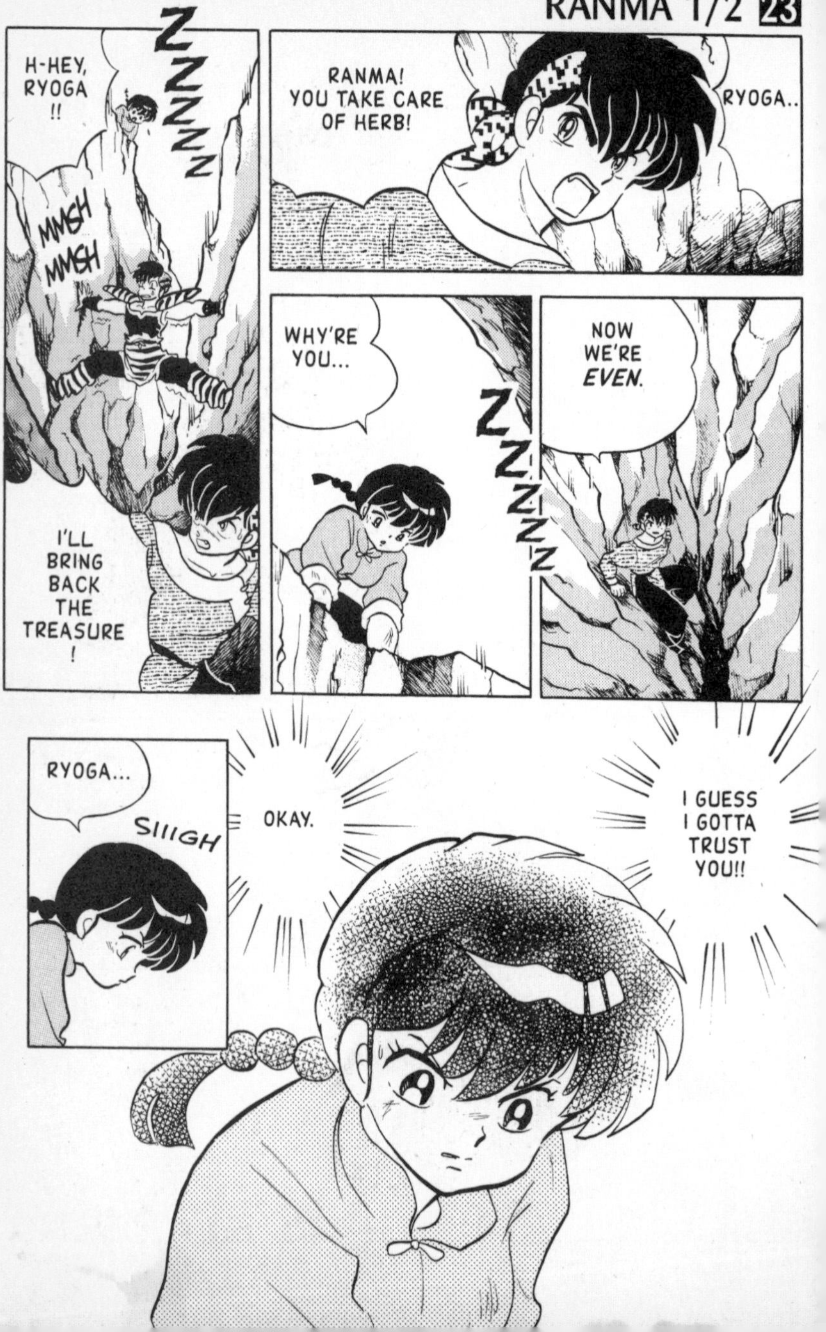
H-HEY, RYOGA !!
ZZZZZ
MMSH MMSH
I'LL BRING BACK THE TREASURE !
RANMA! YOU TAKE CARE OF HERB!
RYOGA..
WHY'RE YOU...
ZZZZZ
NOW WE'RE *EVEN*.
RYOGA...
SIIIGH
OKAY.
I GUESS I GOTTA TRUST YOU!!

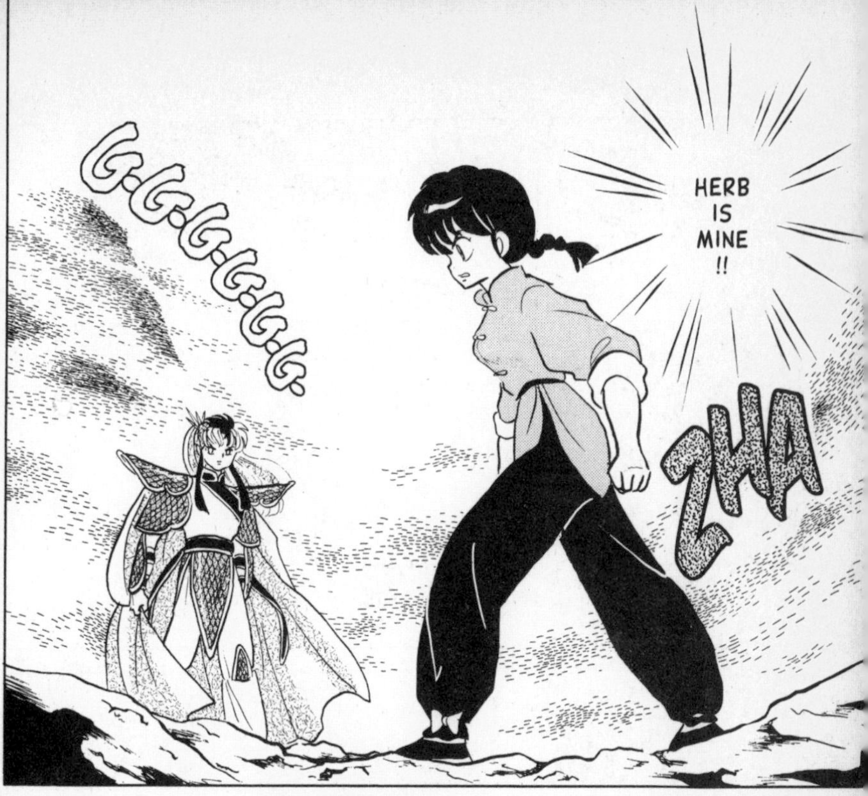
G-G-G-G-G-G-G
HERB IS MINE !!
ZHA
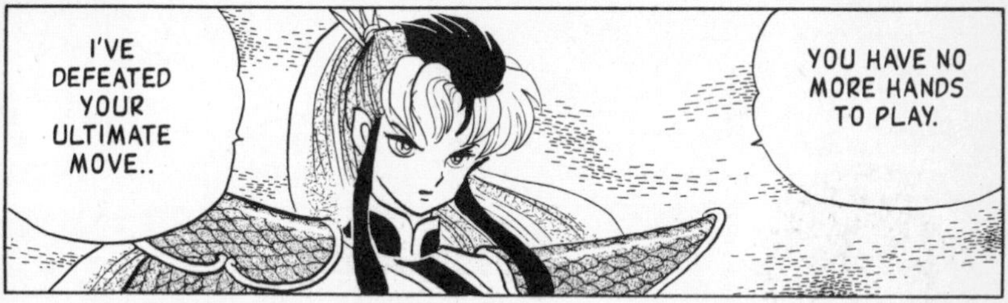
I'VE DEFEATED YOUR ULTIMATE MOVE..
YOU HAVE NO MORE HANDS TO PLAY.
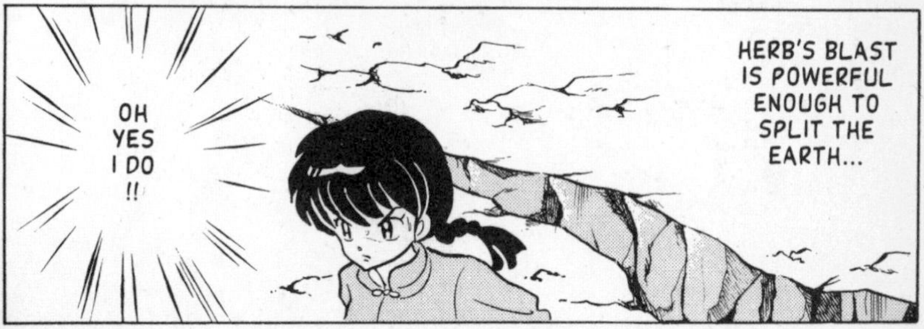
OH YES I DO !!
HERB'S BLAST IS POWERFUL ENOUGH TO SPLIT THE EARTH...

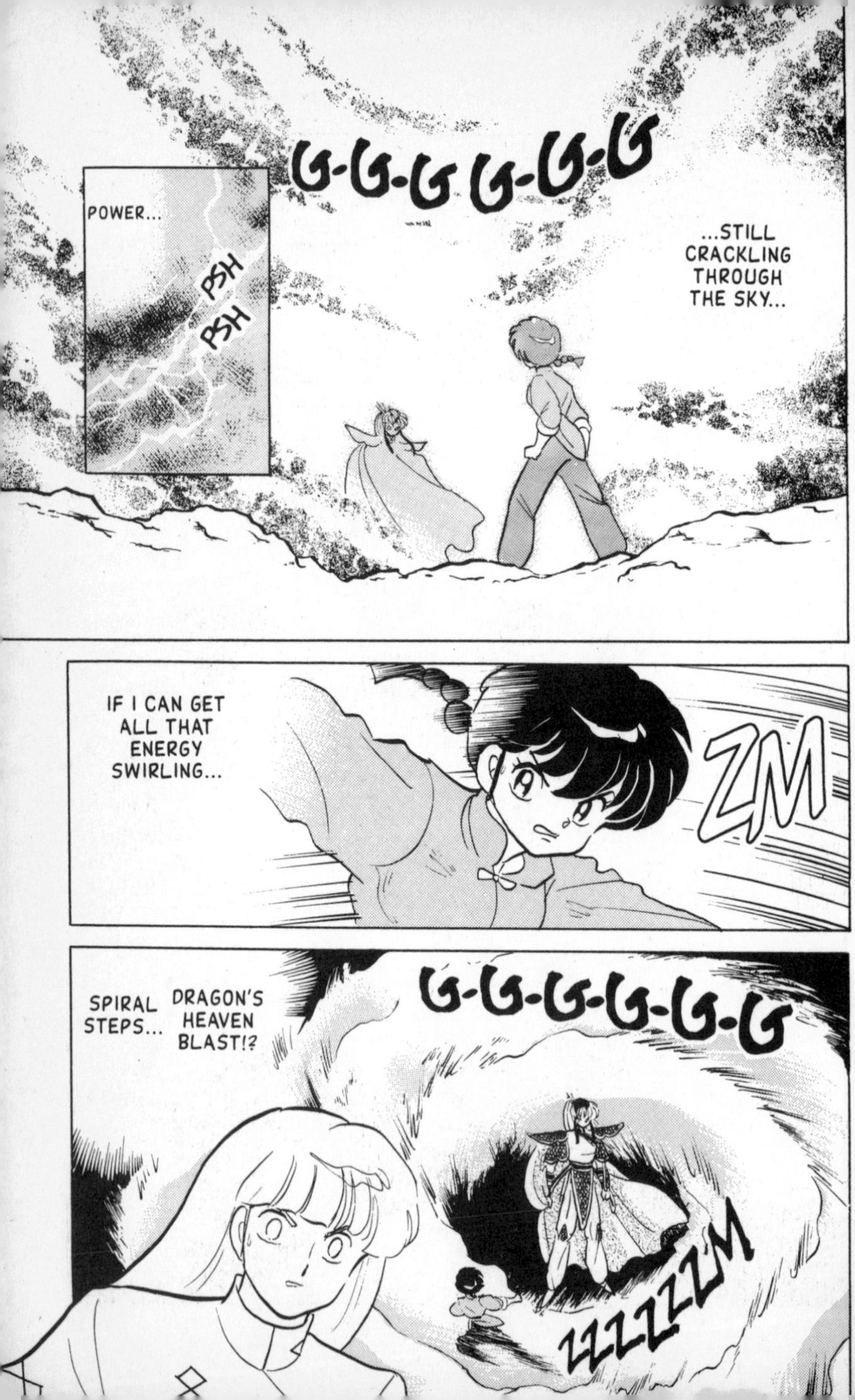
POWER...
PSH
PSH
G-G-G G-G-G
...STILL CRACKLING THROUGH THE SKY...
IF I CAN GET ALL THAT ENERGY SWIRLING...
ZM
SPIRAL STEPS...
DRAGON'S HEAVEN BLAST!?
G-G-G-G-G-G
ZZZZZZM

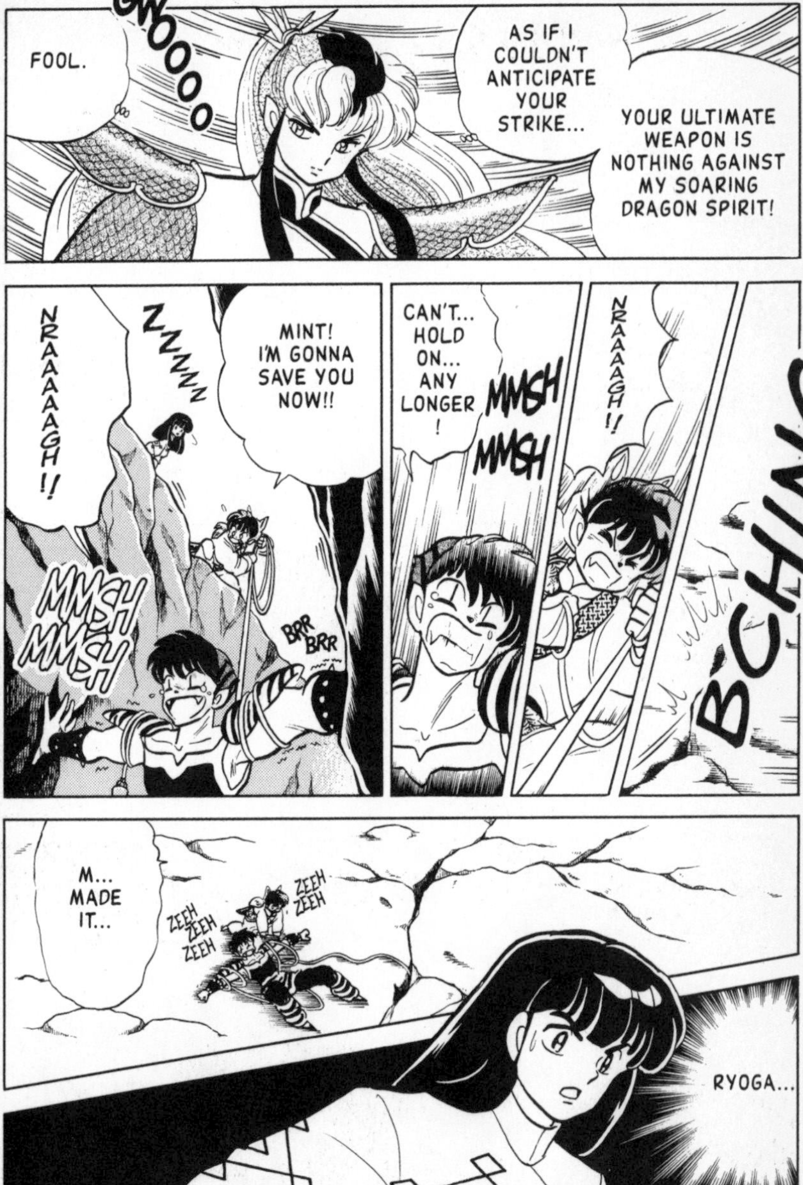
GWOOOOO
FOOL.
AS IF I COULDN'T ANTICIPATE YOUR STRIKE...
YOUR ULTIMATE WEAPON IS NOTHING AGAINST MY SOARING DRAGON SPIRIT!
NRAAAAAAGH!!
ZZZZZ
MINT! I'M GONNA SAVE YOU NOW!!
MMSH MMSH
BRR BRR
CAN'T... HOLD ON... ANY LONGER!
MMSH
MMSH
NRAAAAAGH!!
B'CHING
M... MADE IT...
ZEEH ZEEH ZEEH
ZEEH ZEEH
RYOGA...

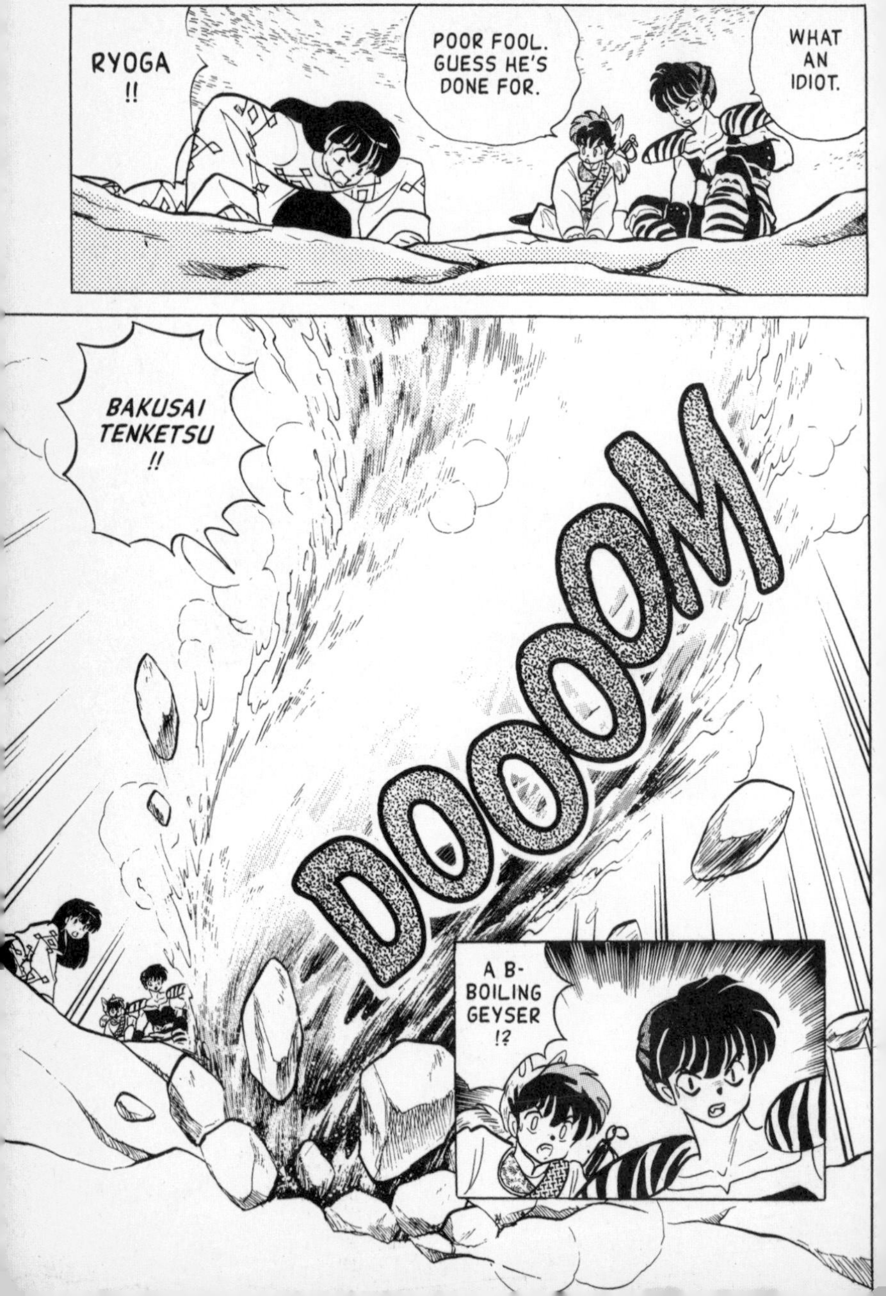
RYOGA !!
POOR FOOL. GUESS HE'S DONE FOR.
WHAT AN IDIOT.
BAKUSAI TENKETSU !!
DOOOOOM
A B-BOILING GEYSER !?

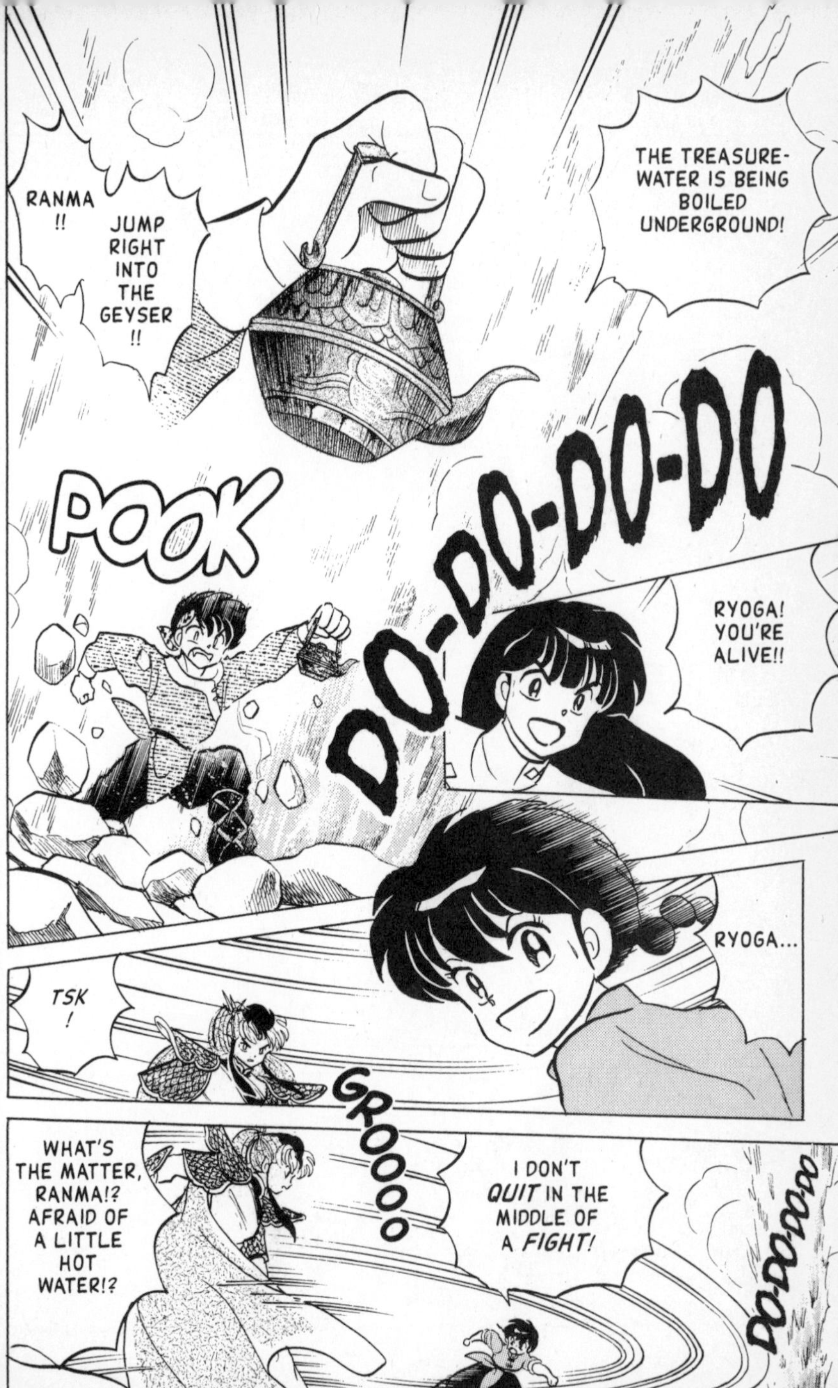
RANMA!!
JUMP RIGHT INTO THE GEYSER!!
THE TREASURE-WATER IS BEING BOILED UNDERGROUND!
POOK
DO-DO-DO-DO-DO
RYOGA! YOU'RE ALIVE!!
RYOGA...
TSK!
GROOOOO
WHAT'S THE MATTER, RANMA!? AFRAID OF A LITTLE HOT WATER!?
I DON'T *QUIT* IN THE MIDDLE OF A *FIGHT*!
DO-DO-DO-DO

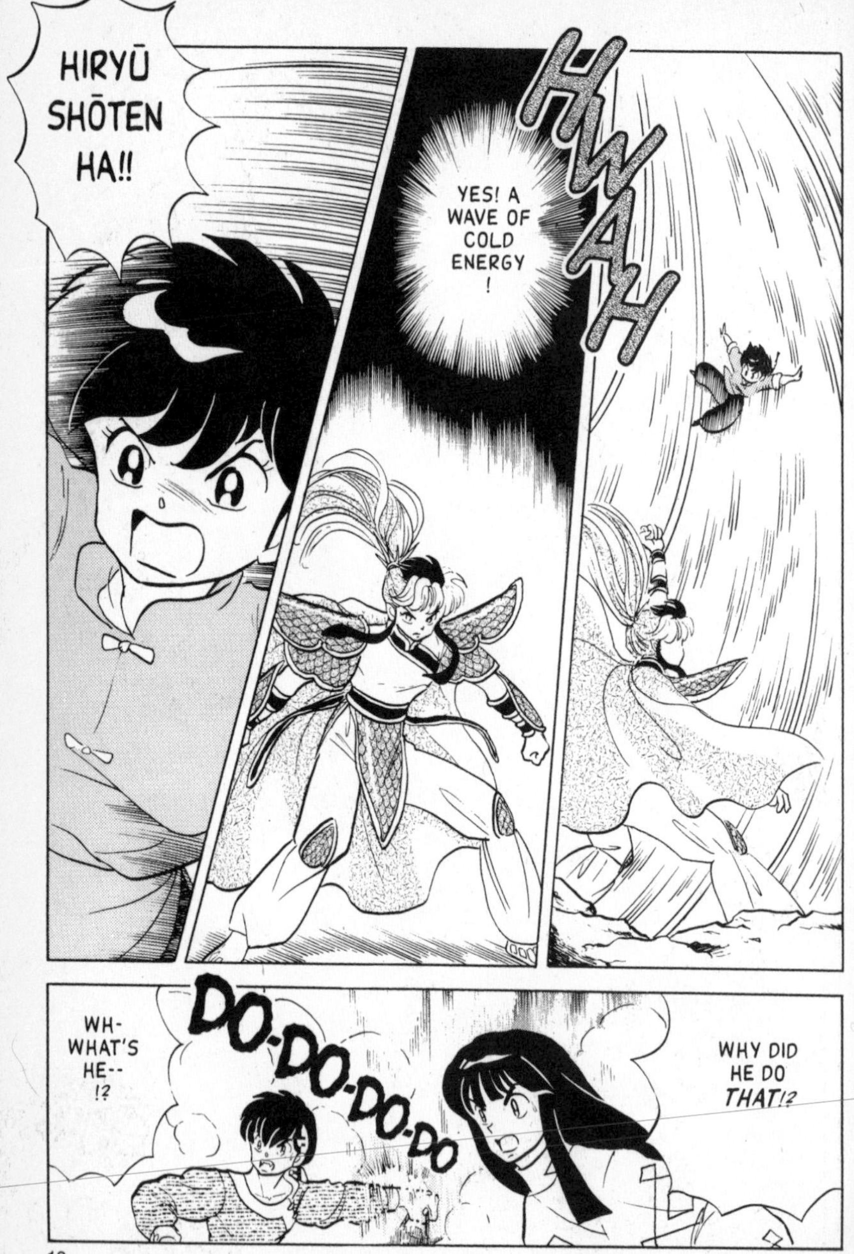

HIRYŪ SHŌTEN HA!!
YES! A WAVE OF COLD ENERGY !
HWAH
WH- WHAT'S HE-- !?
DO-DO-DO-DO-DO
WHY DID HE DO *THAT*!?

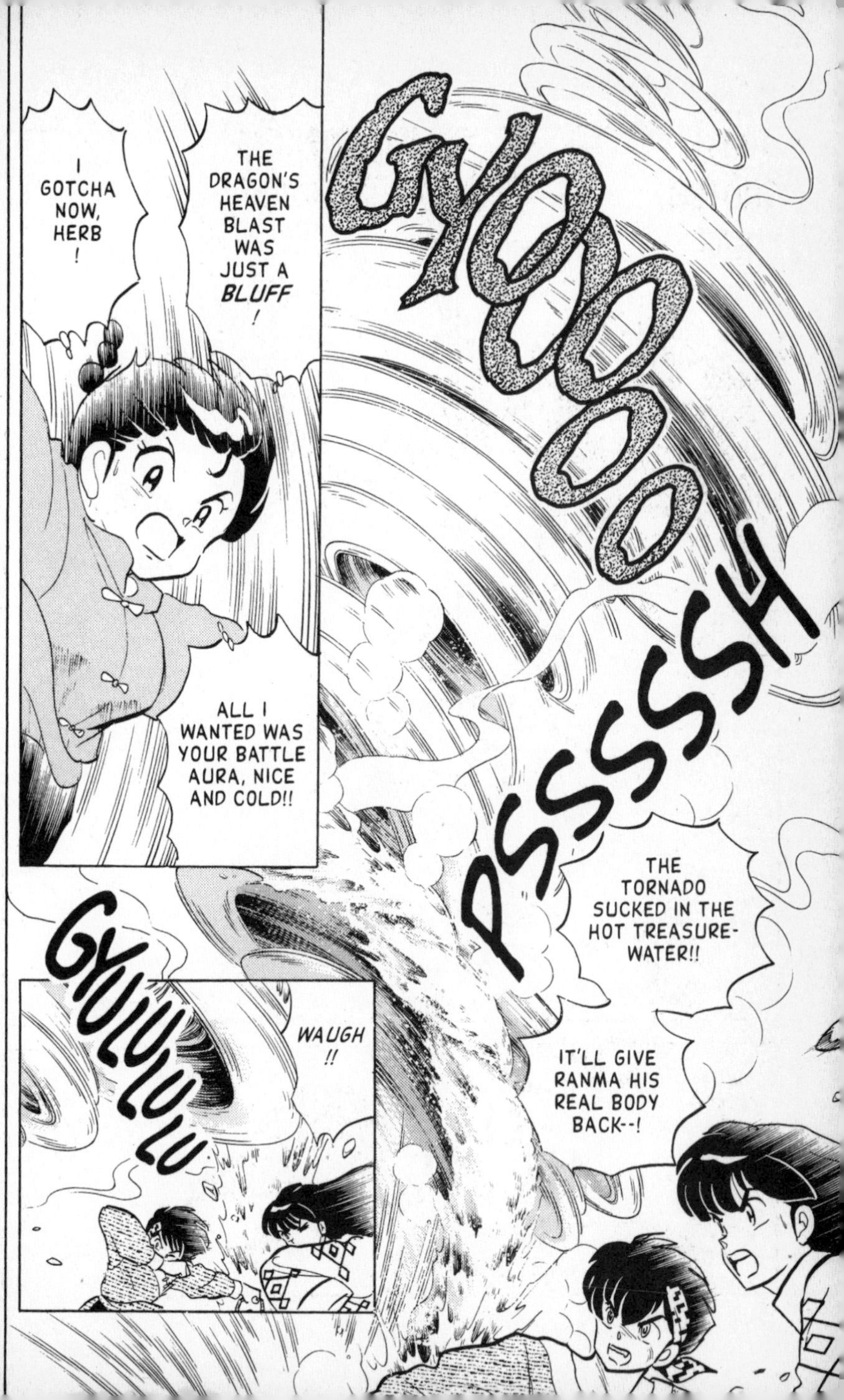
I GOTCHA NOW, HERB!
THE DRAGON'S HEAVEN BLAST WAS JUST A *BLUFF*!
ALL I WANTED WAS YOUR BATTLE AURA, NICE AND COLD!!
GYULULULU
WAUGH!!
GYOOOOO
PSSSSSH
THE TORNADO SUCKED IN THE HOT TREASURE-WATER!!
IT'LL GIVE RANMA HIS REAL BODY BACK--!

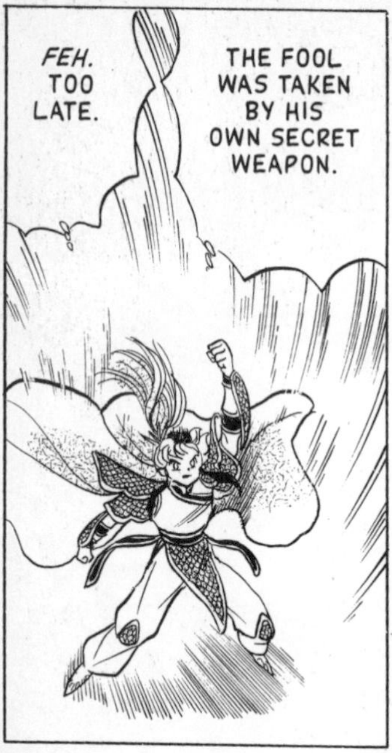
FEH. TOO LATE.
THE FOOL WAS TAKEN BY HIS OWN SECRET WEAPON.

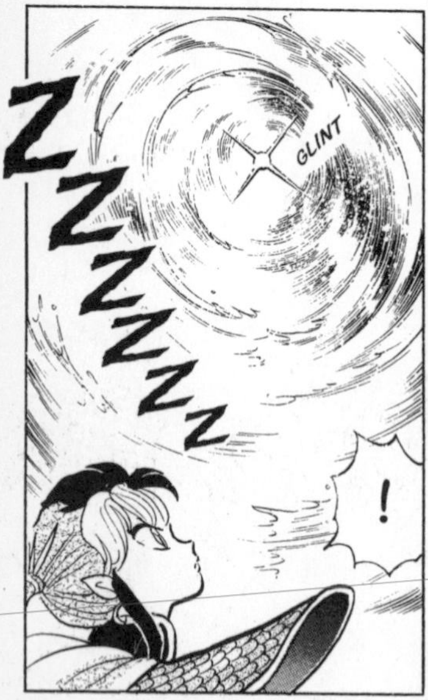
ZZZZZZZ
GLINT
!

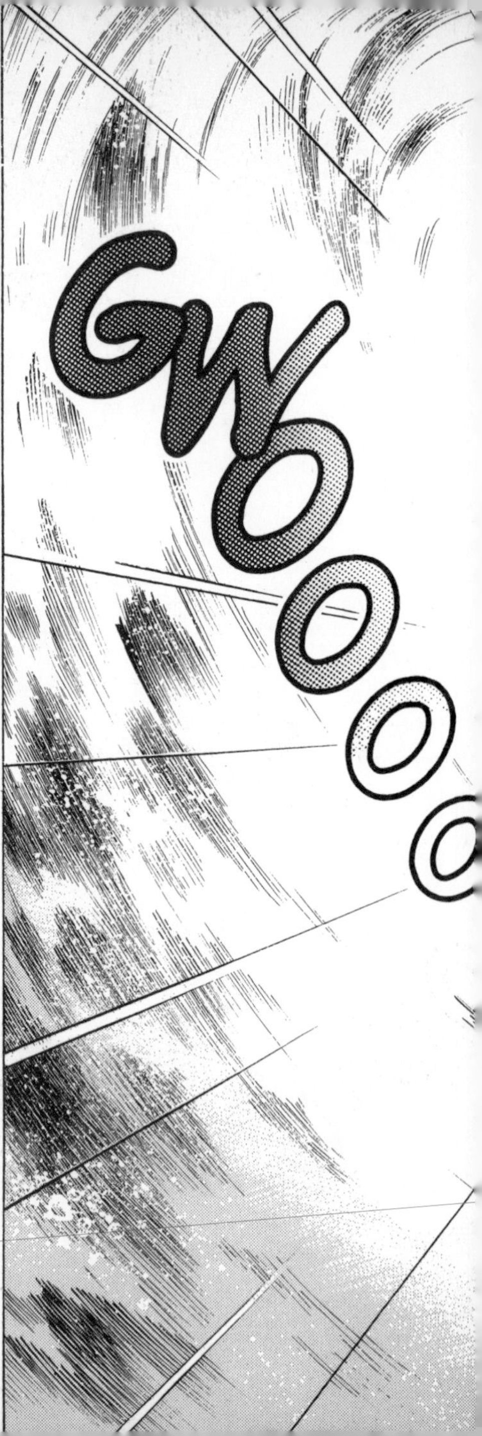
GWOOOOO

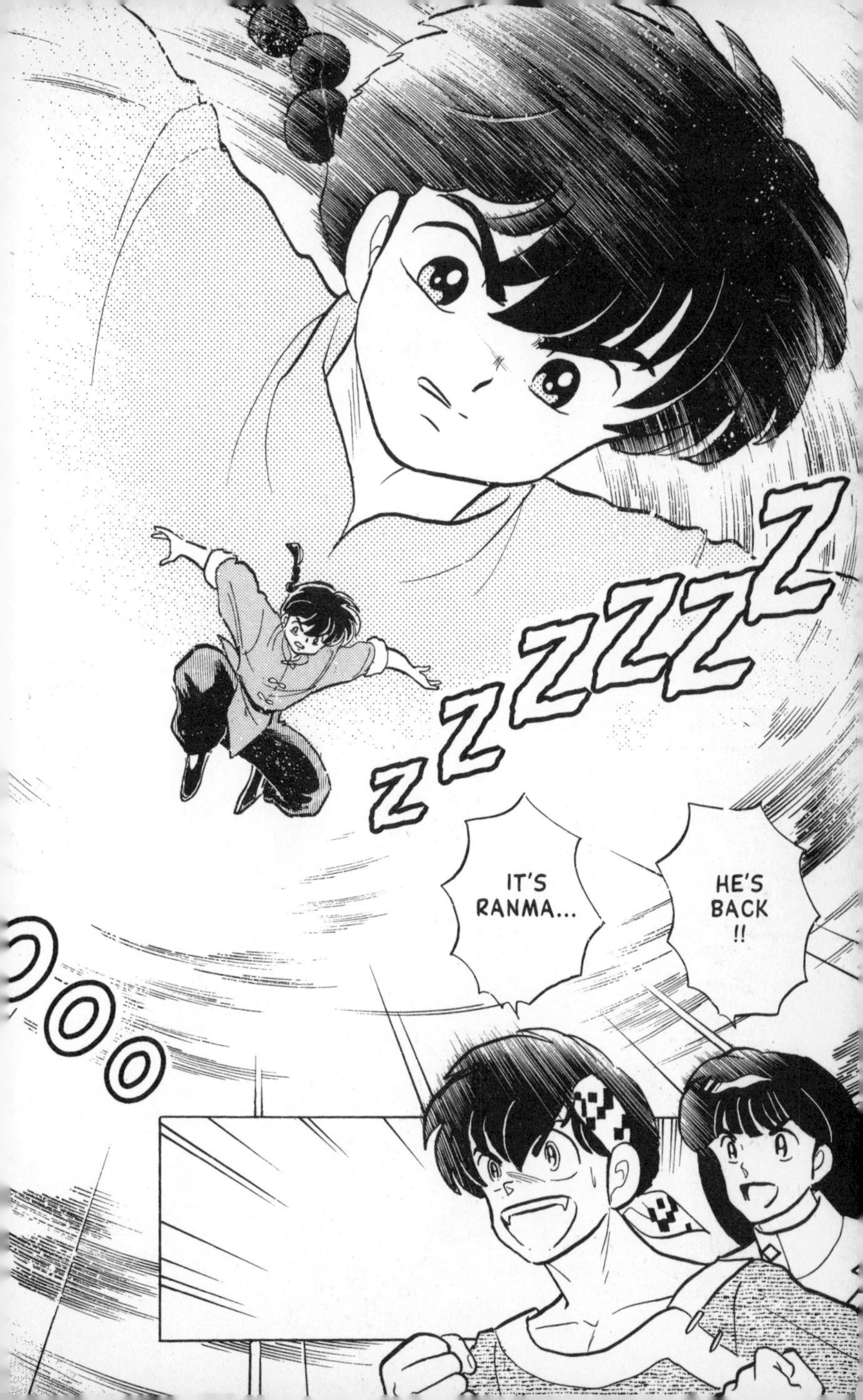

zZZZZZZ
IT'S RANMA...
HE'S BACK !!

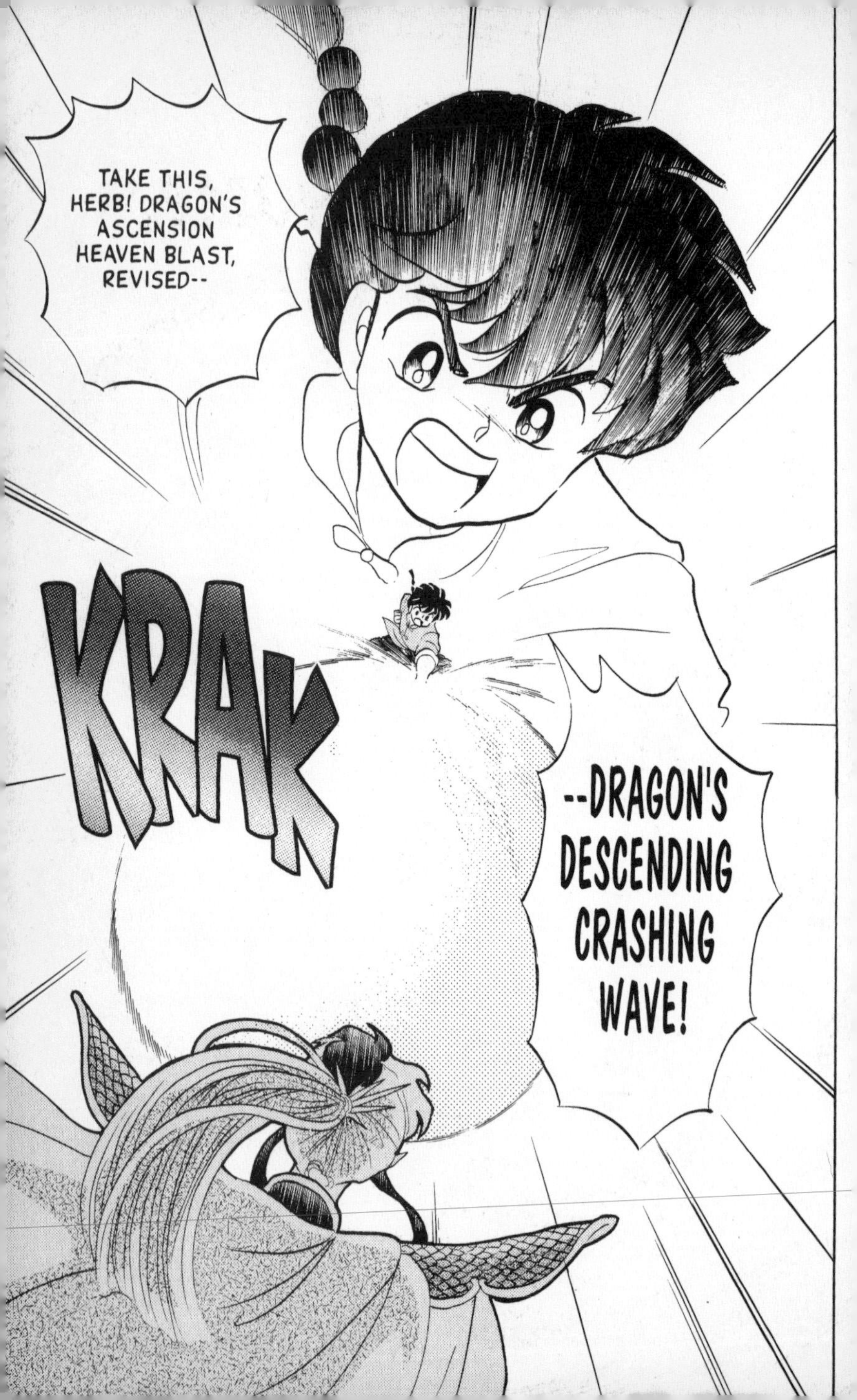
TAKE THIS, HERB! DRAGON'S ASCENSION HEAVEN BLAST, REVISED--
KRAK
--DRAGON'S DESCENDING CRASHING WAVE!

Part 2
WELCOME HOME, RANMA!

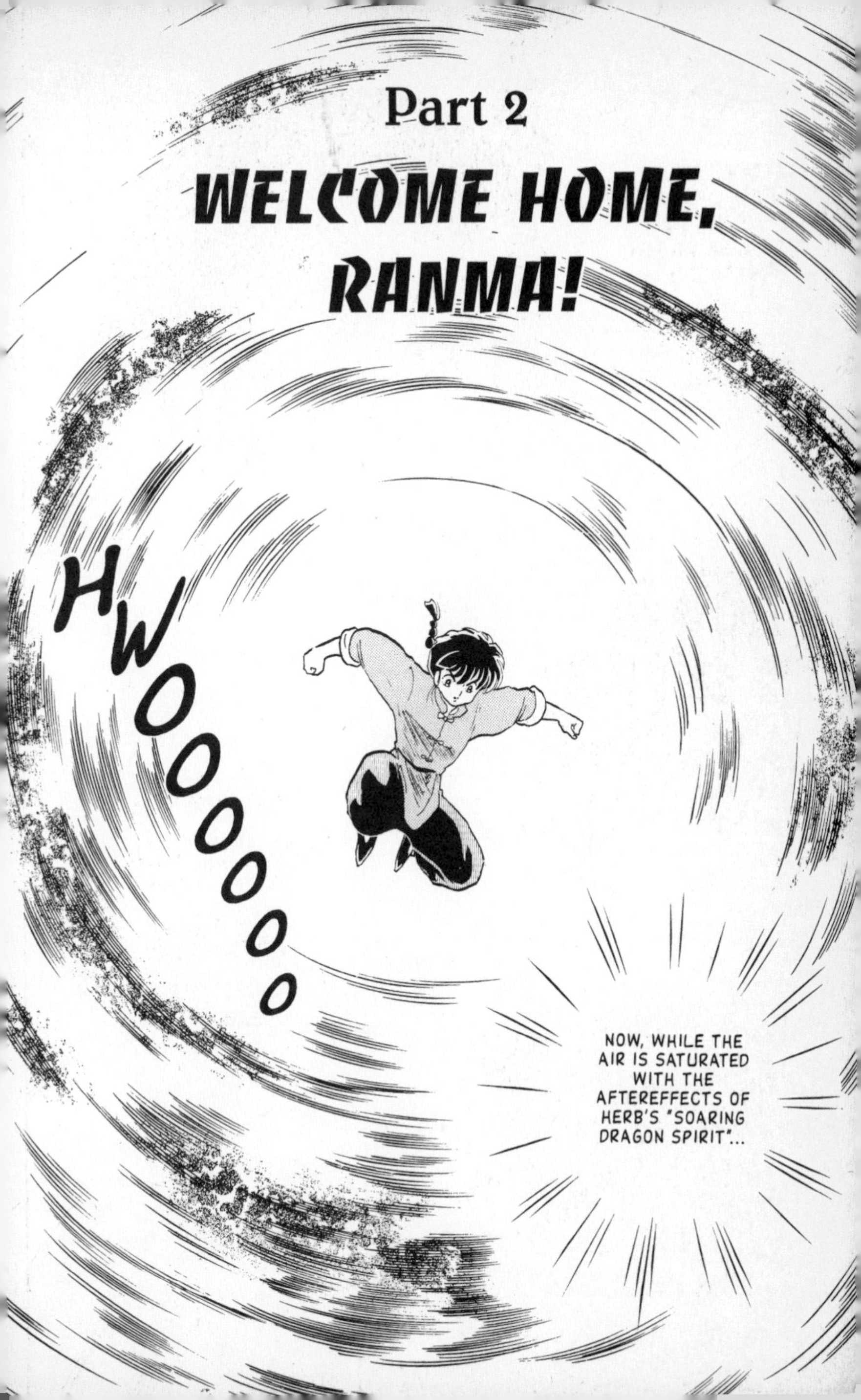
HWOOOOOO
NOW, WHILE THE AIR IS SATURATED WITH THE AFTEREFFECTS OF HERB'S "SOARING DRAGON SPIRIT"...

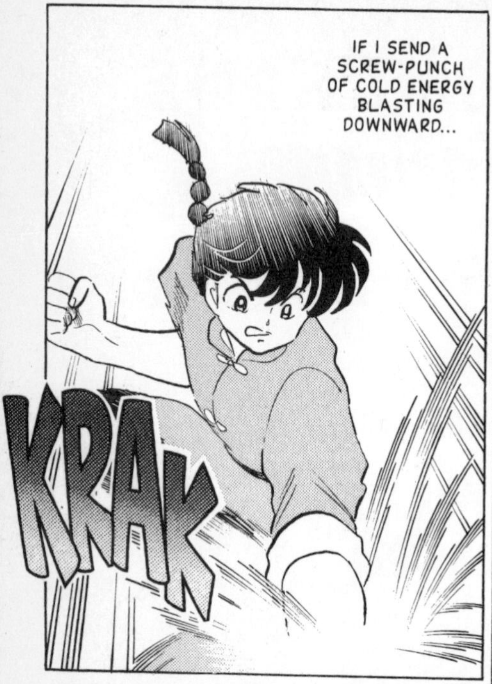
IF I SEND A SCREW-PUNCH OF COLD ENERGY BLASTING DOWNWARD...
KRAK

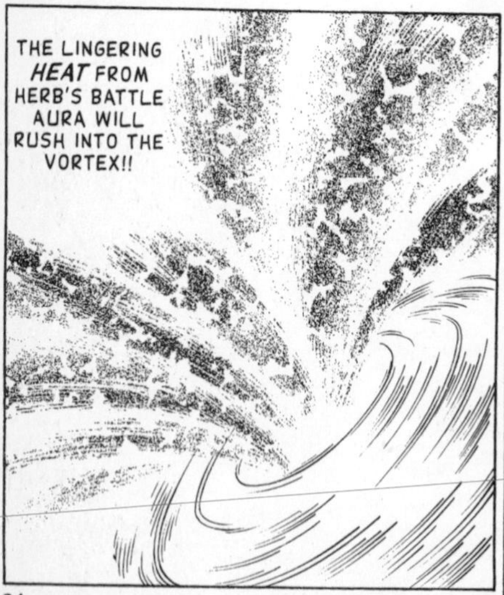
THE LINGERING *HEAT* FROM HERB'S BATTLE AURA WILL RUSH INTO THE VORTEX!!

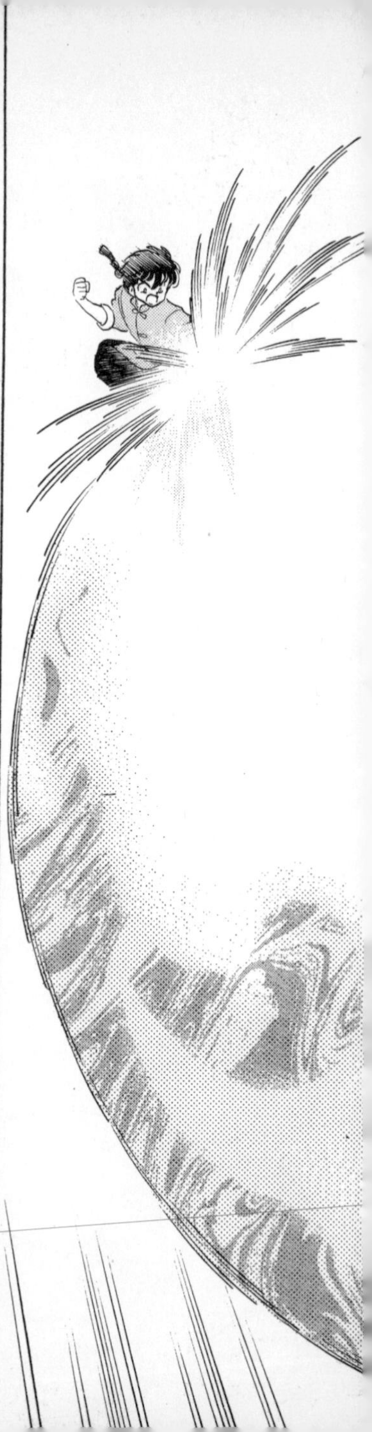

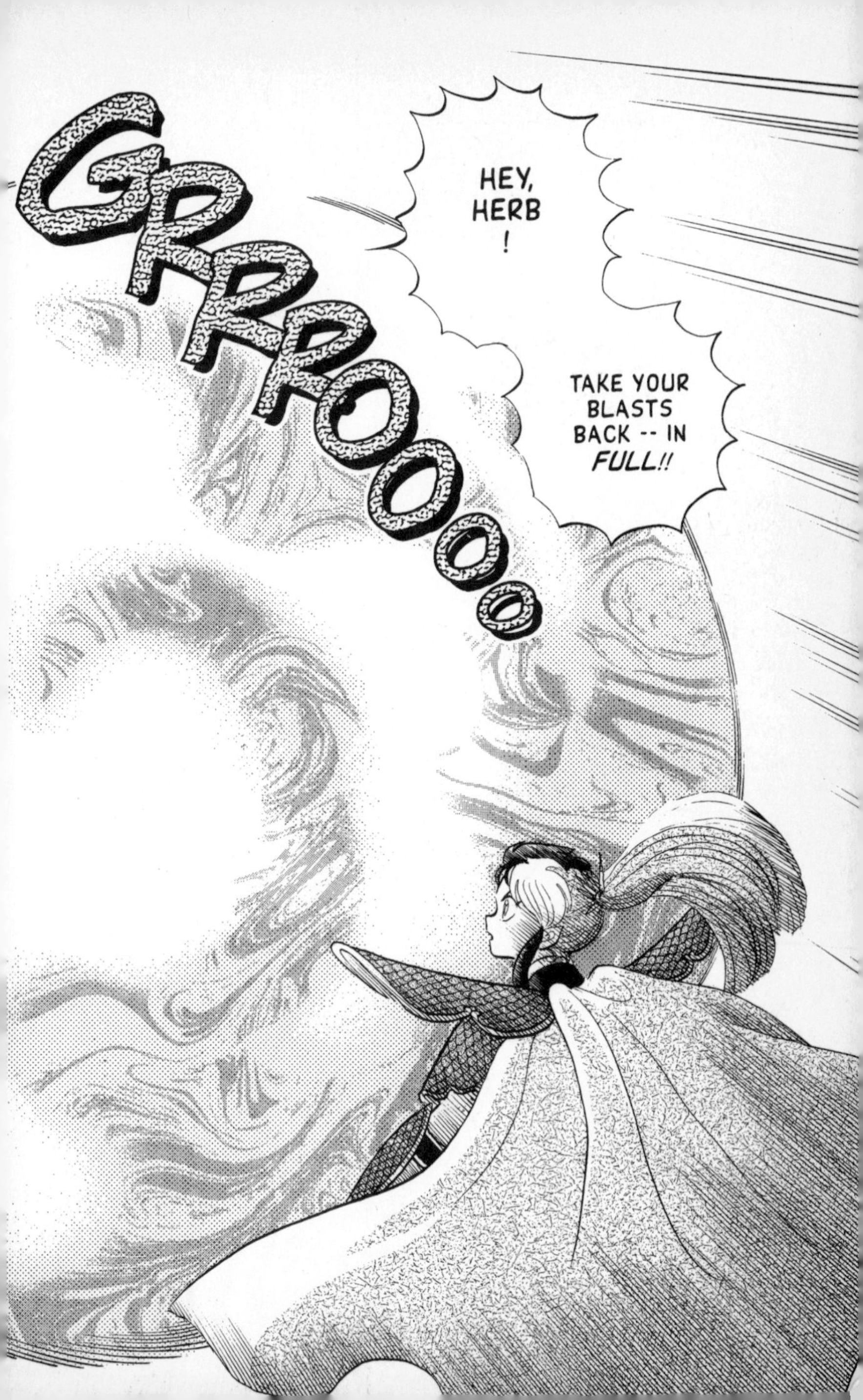
GRRROOOOOO
HEY, HERB!
TAKE YOUR BLASTS BACK -- IN *FULL!!*

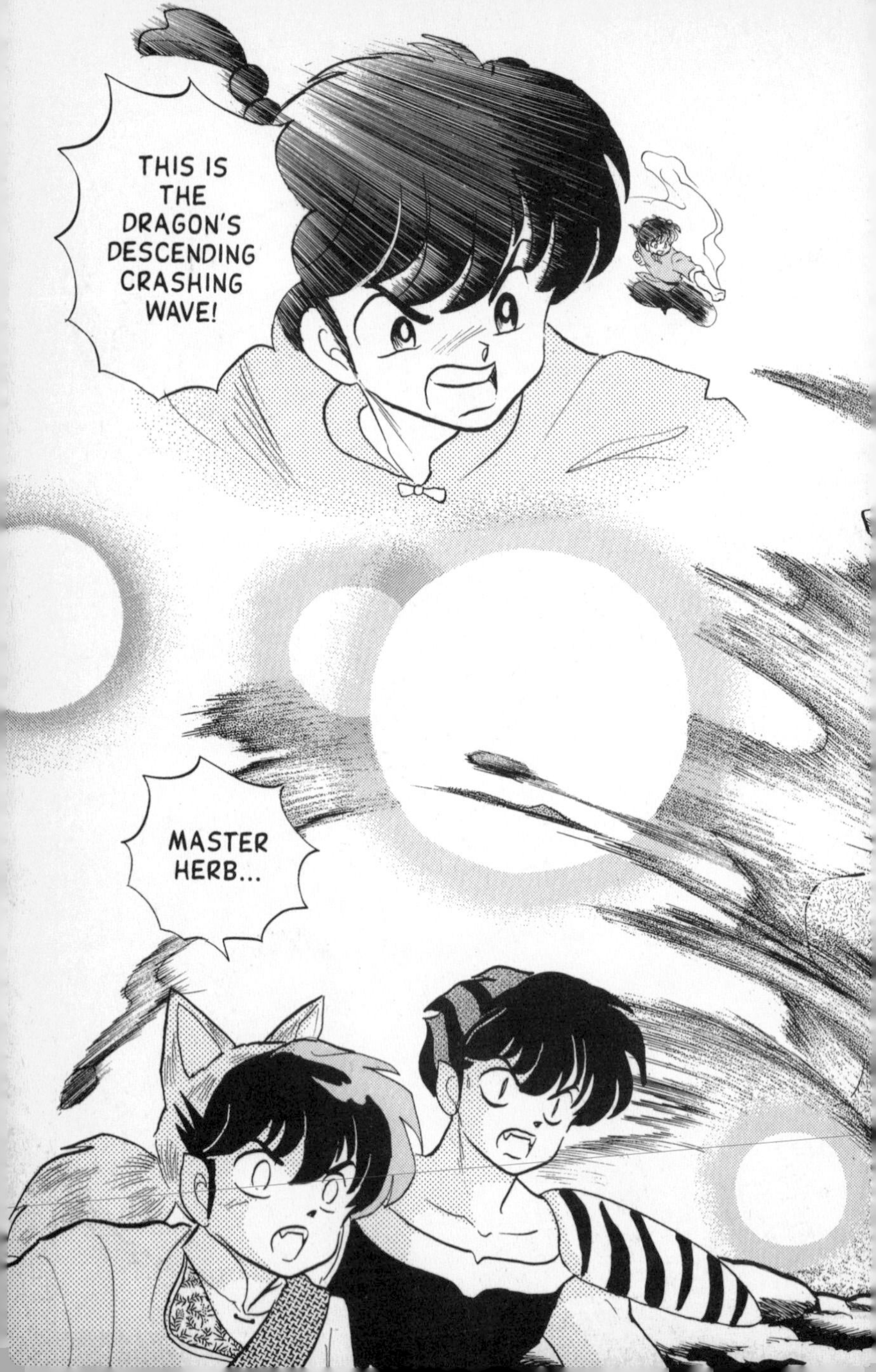
THIS IS THE DRAGON'S DESCENDING CRASHING WAVE!
MASTER HERB...

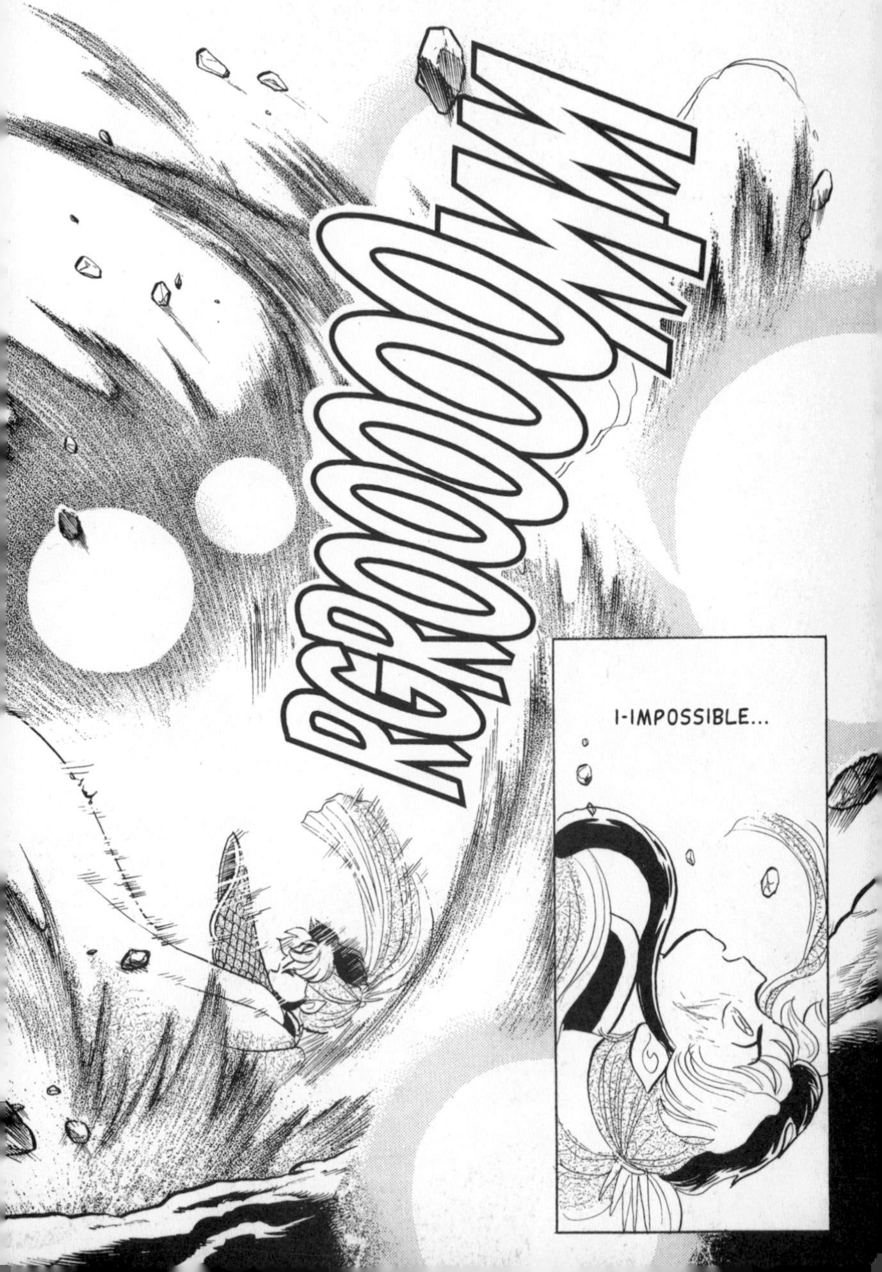
BGDOOOOOOM!!
I-IMPOSSIBLE...

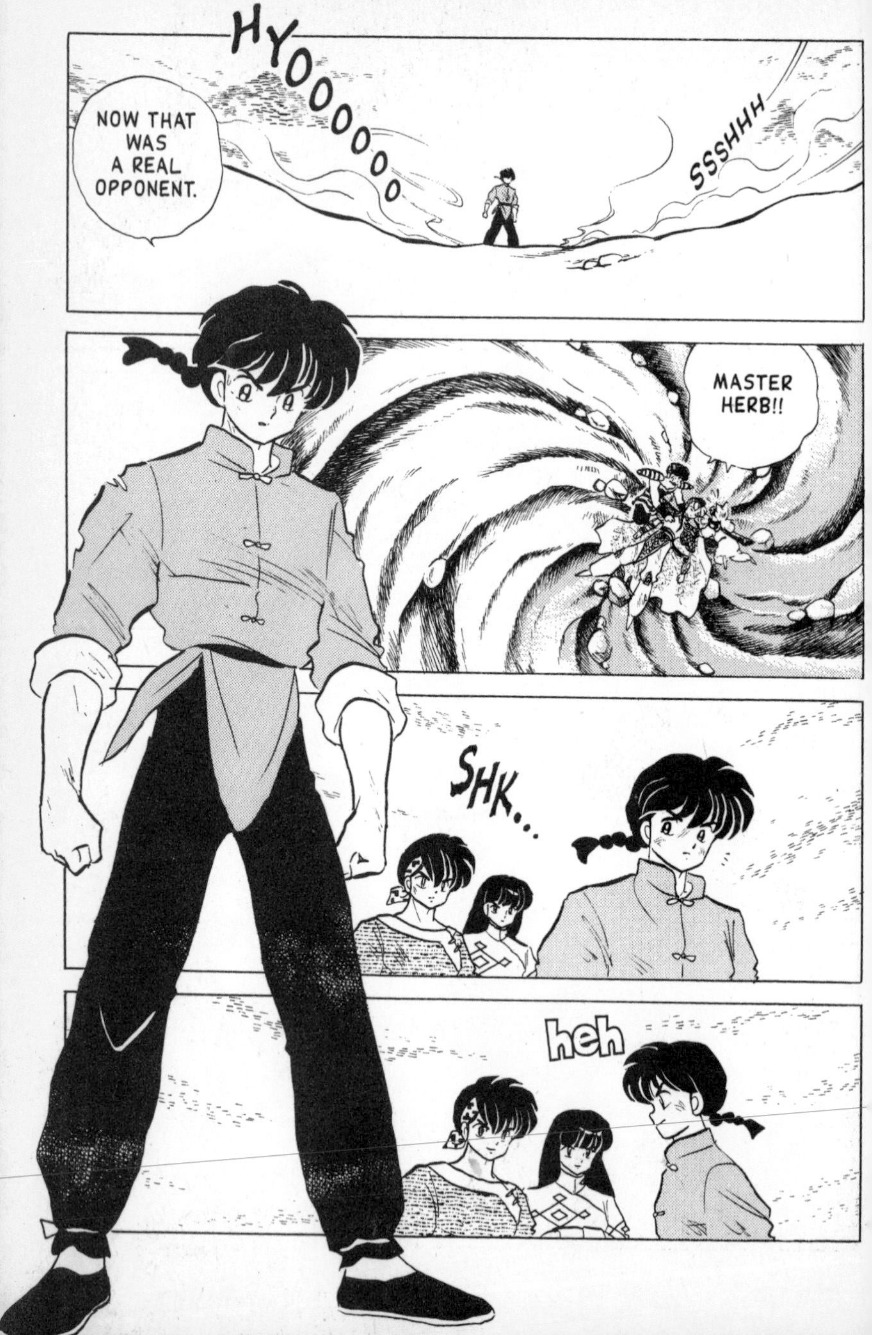
HYOOOOOOO
NOW THAT WAS A REAL OPPONENT.
SSSHHH
MASTER HERB!!
SHK...
heh

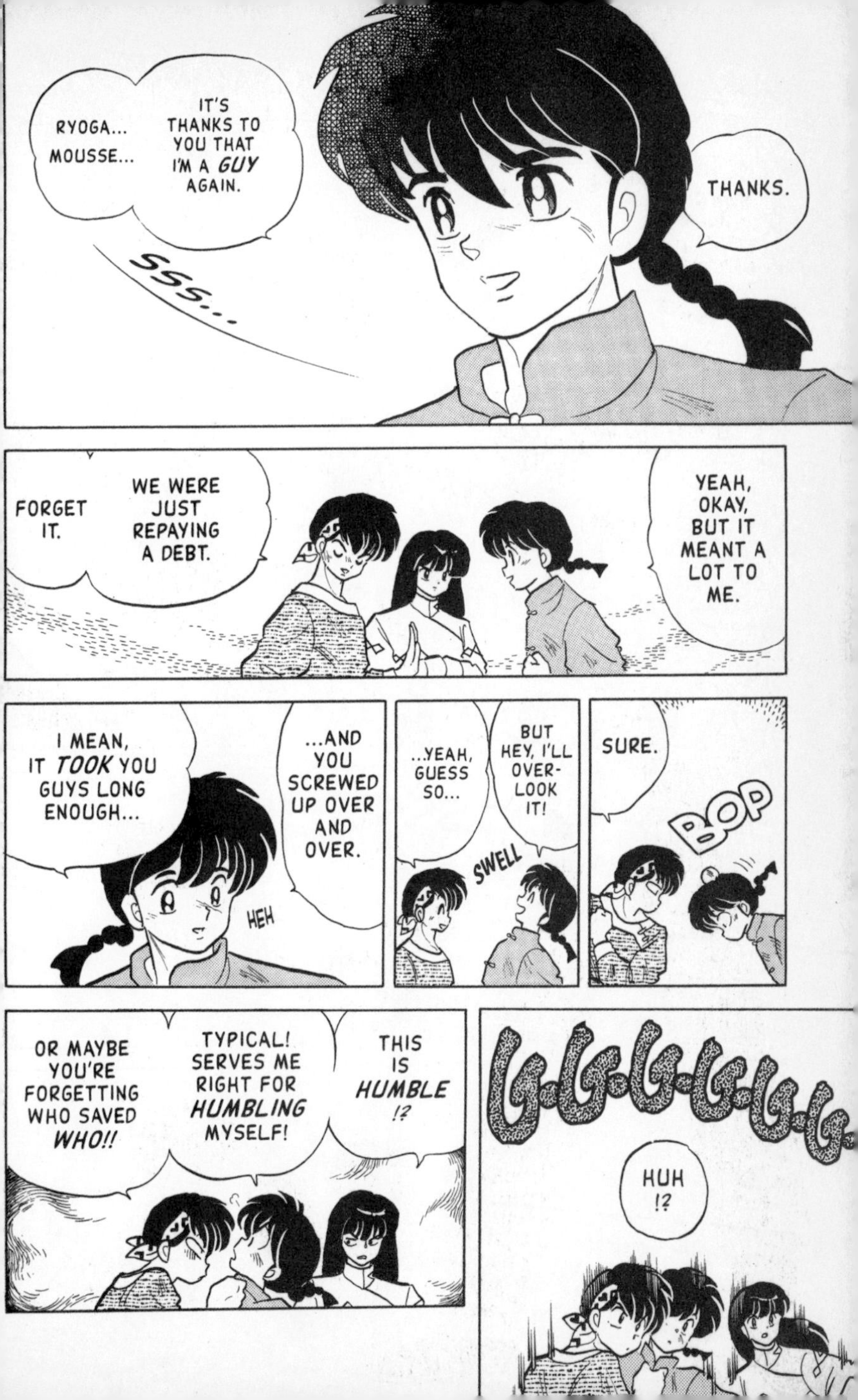
RYOGA... MOUSSE...
IT'S THANKS TO YOU THAT I'M A GUY AGAIN.
THANKS.
SSS...
FORGET IT.
WE WERE JUST REPAYING A DEBT.
YEAH, OKAY, BUT IT MEANT A LOT TO ME.
I MEAN, IT TOOK YOU GUYS LONG ENOUGH...
...AND YOU SCREWED UP OVER AND OVER.
HEH
...YEAH, GUESS SO...
BUT HEY, I'LL OVER-LOOK IT!
SWELL
SURE.
BOP
OR MAYBE YOU'RE FORGETTING WHO SAVED WHO!!
TYPICAL! SERVES ME RIGHT FOR HUMBLING MYSELF!
THIS IS HUMBLE !?
G-G-G-G-G-G-G-
HUH !?

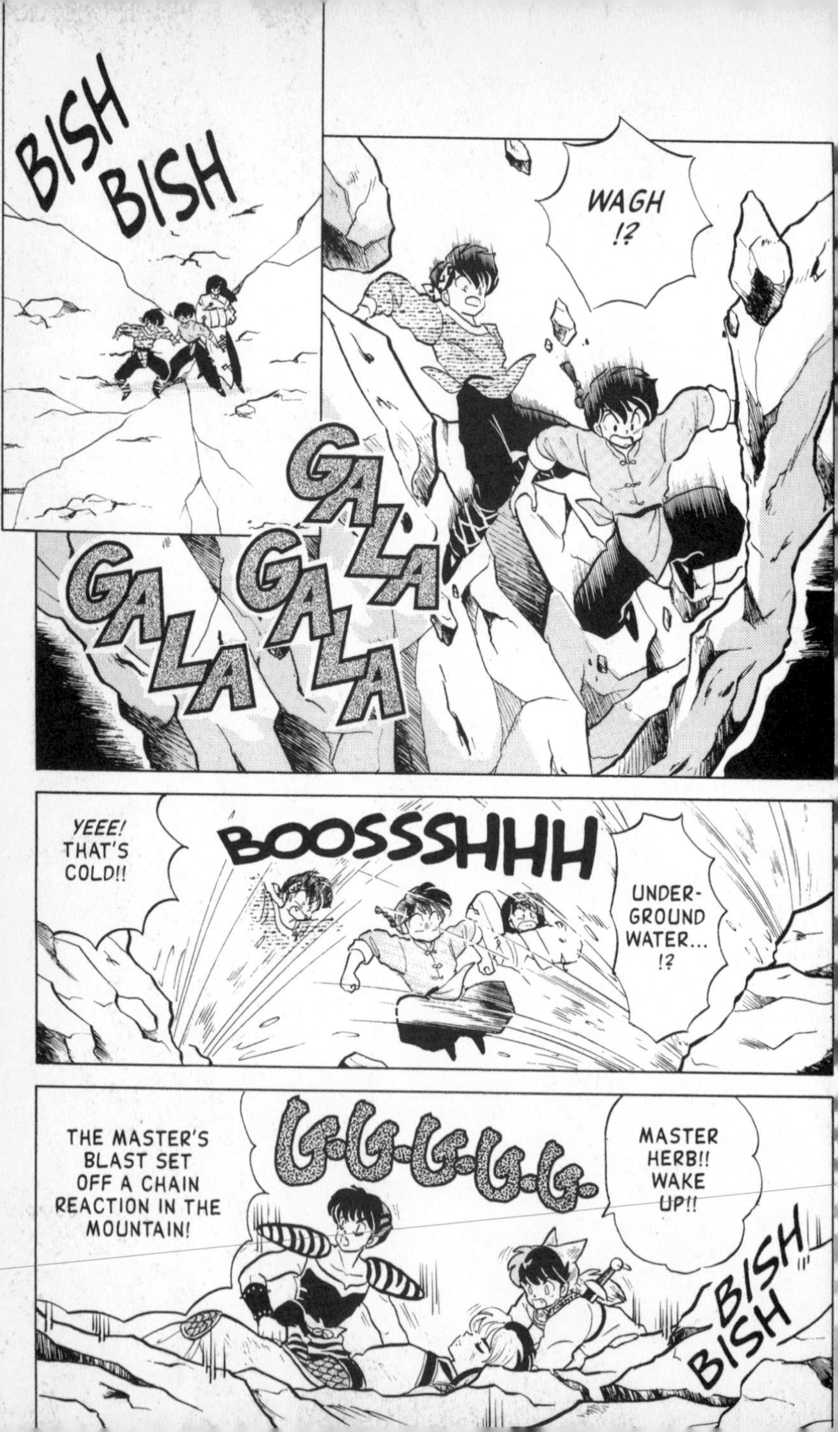
BISH
BISH
WAGH !?
GALA
GALA
GALA
YEEE! THAT'S COLD!!
BOOSSHHH
UNDER-GROUND WATER... !?
THE MASTER'S BLAST SET OFF A CHAIN REACTION IN THE MOUNTAIN!
G-G-G-G-G-G
MASTER HERB!! WAKE UP!!
BISH BISH

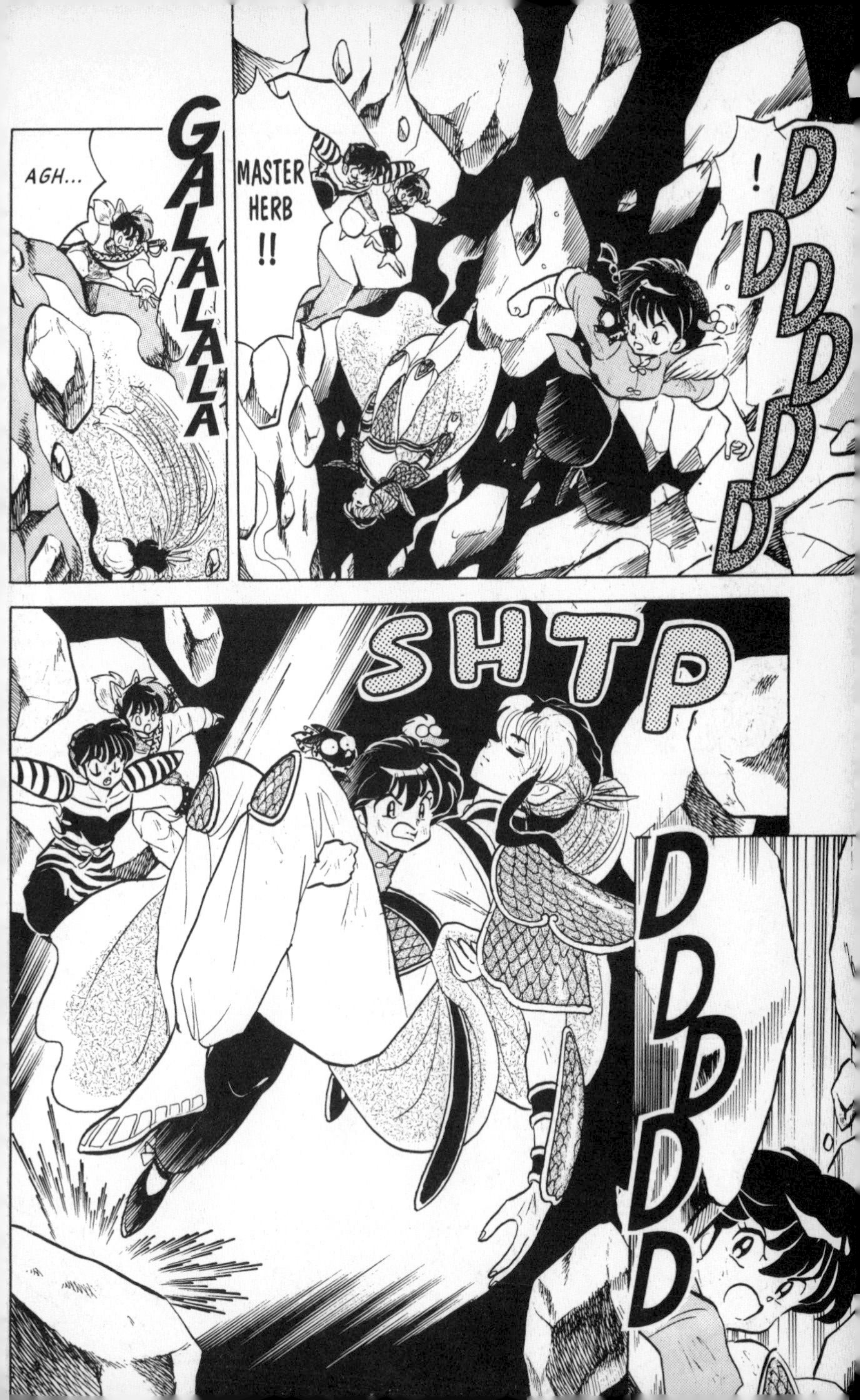
AGH...
GALALALA
MASTER HERB !!
!
DDDDDDD
SHTP
DDDDDDD

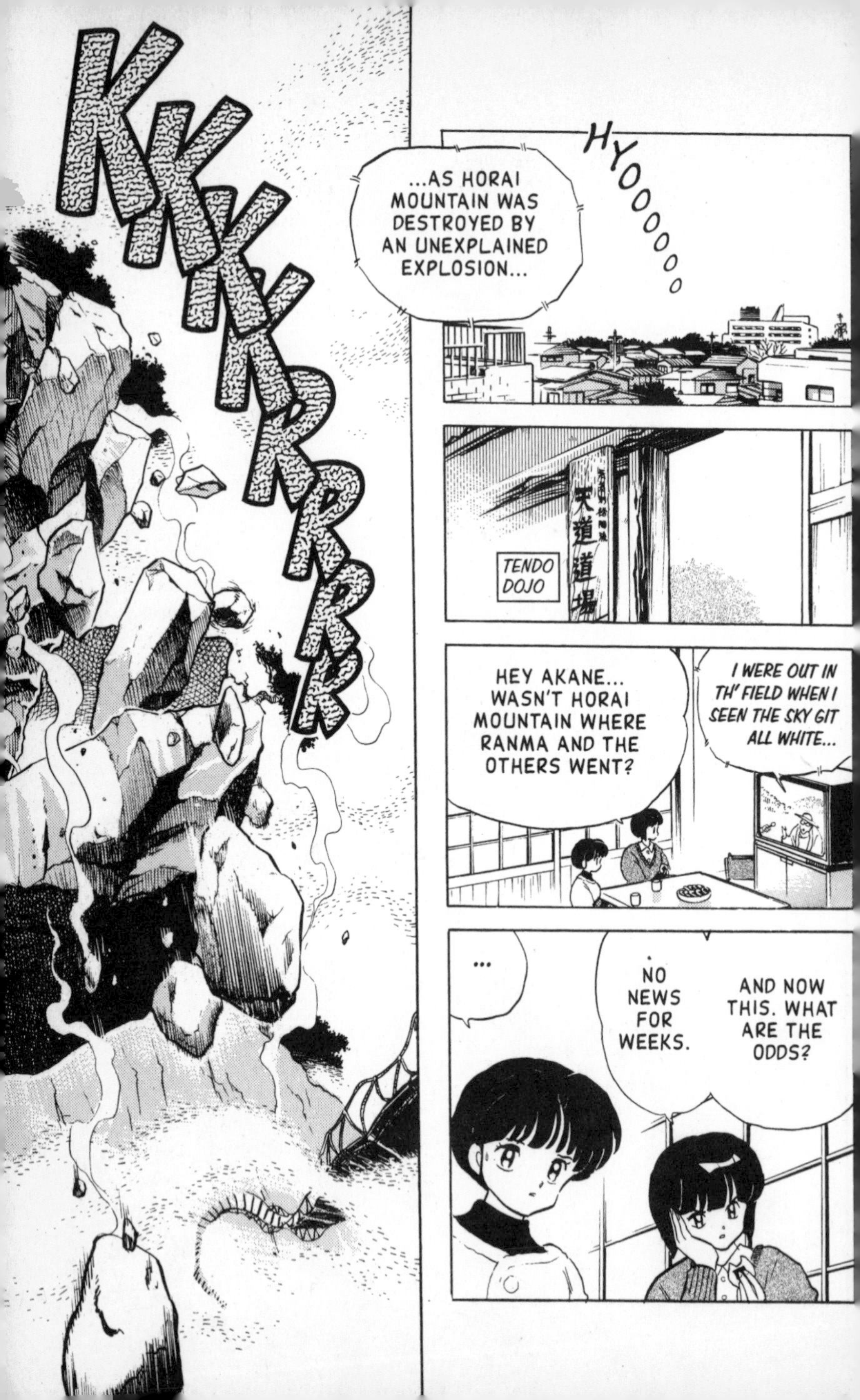
KKKKRRRR
...AS HORAI MOUNTAIN WAS DESTROYED BY AN UNEXPLAINED EXPLOSION...
HYOOOOOO
TENDO DOJO
天道道場
HEY AKANE... WASN'T HORAI MOUNTAIN WHERE RANMA AND THE OTHERS WENT?
I WERE OUT IN TH' FIELD WHEN I SEEN THE SKY GIT ALL WHITE...
...
NO NEWS FOR WEEKS.
AND NOW THIS. WHAT ARE THE ODDS?

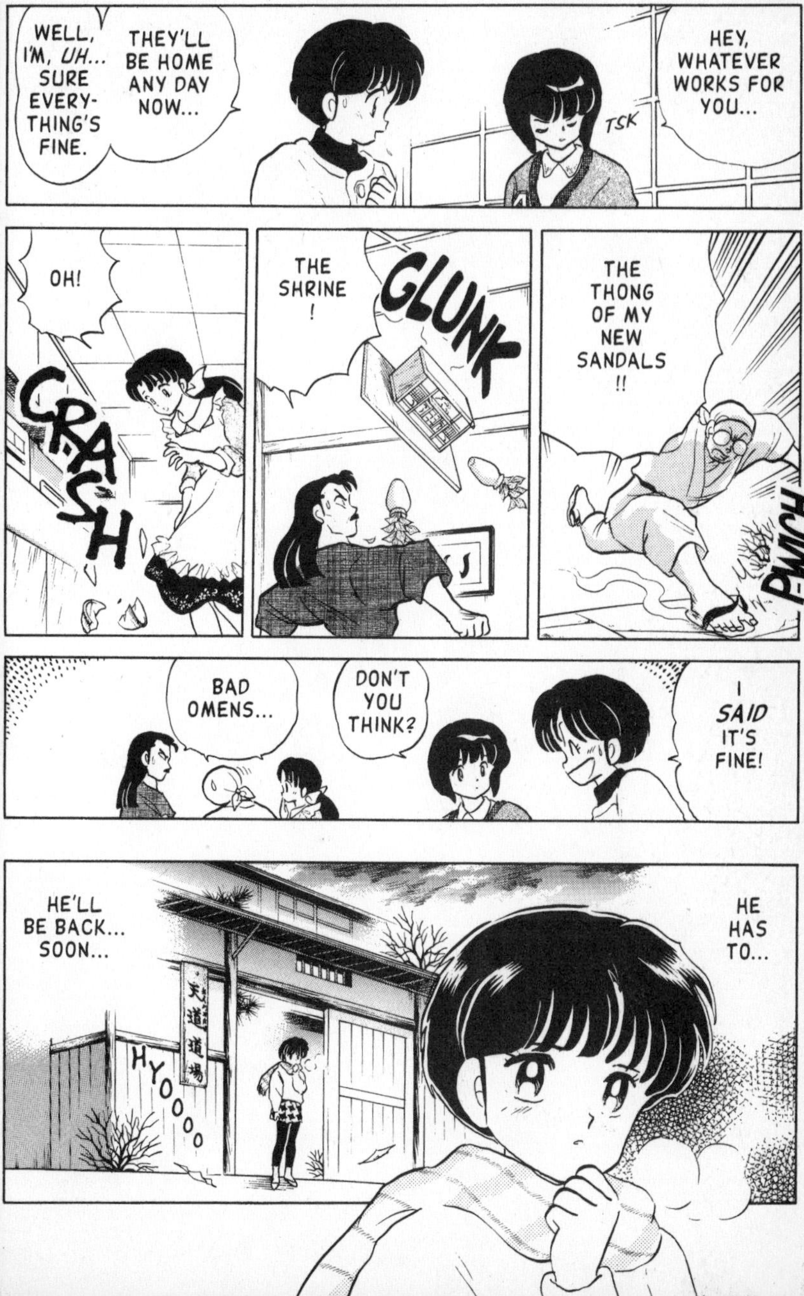
WELL, I'M, *UH*... SURE EVERYTHING'S FINE.
THEY'LL BE HOME ANY DAY NOW...
TSK
HEY, WHATEVER WORKS FOR YOU...
OH!
CRASH
THE SHRINE!
GLUNK
THE THONG OF MY NEW SANDALS!!
P-WICH
BAD OMENS...
DON'T YOU THINK?
I *SAID* IT'S FINE!
HE'LL BE BACK... SOON...
HYOOOOO
HE HAS TO...

AKANE, PLEASE COME INDOORS.

I'M SURE RANMA IS ALL RIGHT. WE'LL SEE HIM IN NO TIME.

...YEAH....

YOU'RE CHILLED TO THE BONE. A NICE BATH WILL WARM YOU UP.

...

MAYBE... SOMETHING DID HAPPEN...

CHK

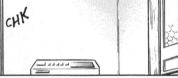

HM ?

SPLSSH

SHOOOP

STARE

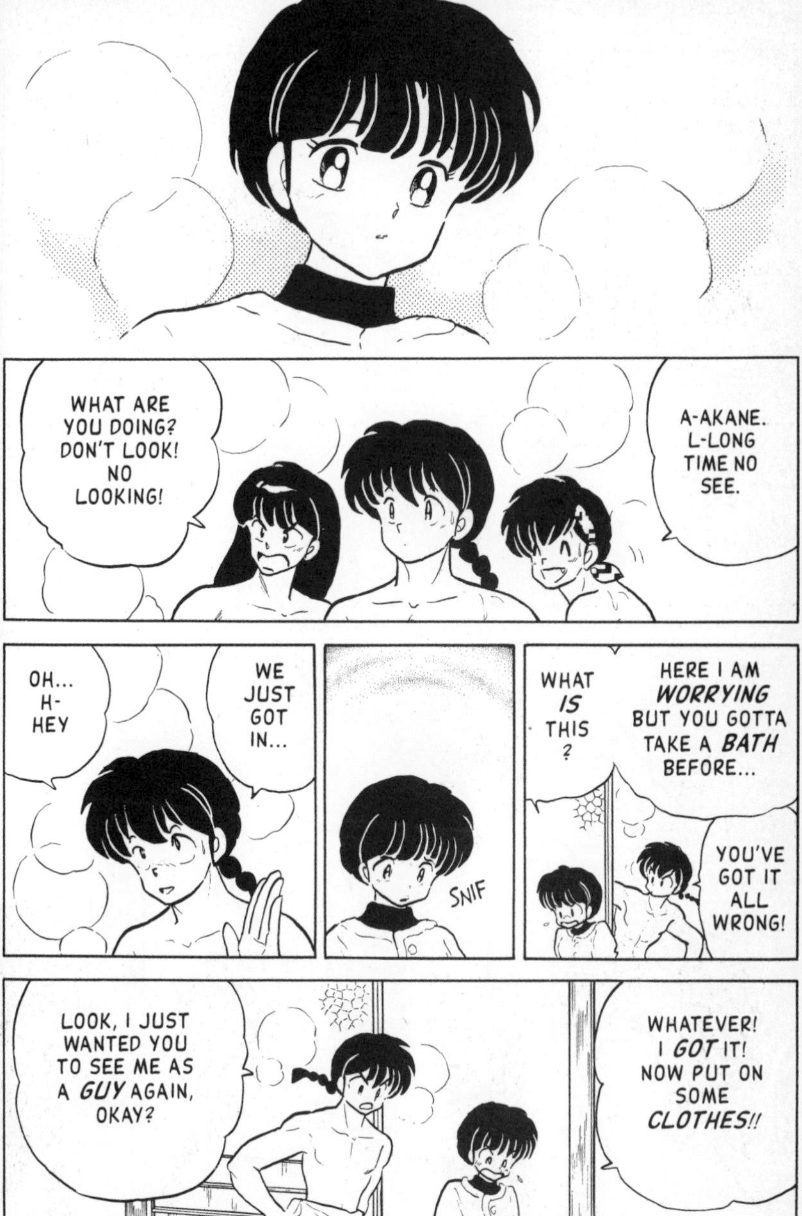
WHAT ARE YOU DOING? DON'T LOOK! NO LOOKING!
A-AKANE. L-LONG TIME NO SEE.
OH... H- HEY
WE JUST GOT IN...
SNIF
WHAT IS THIS?
HERE I AM WORRYING BUT YOU GOTTA TAKE A BATH BEFORE...
YOU'VE GOT IT ALL WRONG!
LOOK, I JUST WANTED YOU TO SEE ME AS A GUY AGAIN, OKAY?
WHATEVER! I GOT IT! NOW PUT ON SOME CLOTHES!!

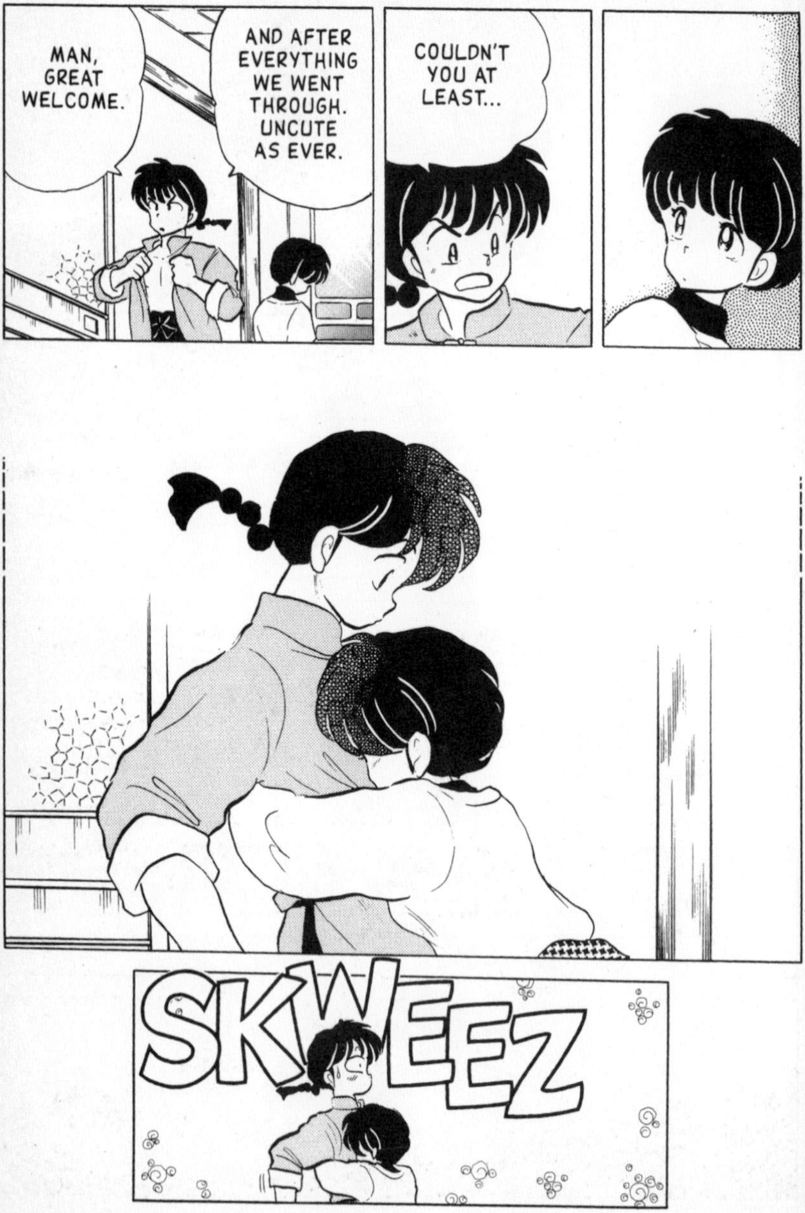
MAN, GREAT WELCOME.
AND AFTER EVERYTHING WE WENT THROUGH. UNCUTE AS EVER.
COULDN'T YOU AT LEAST...
SKWEEZ

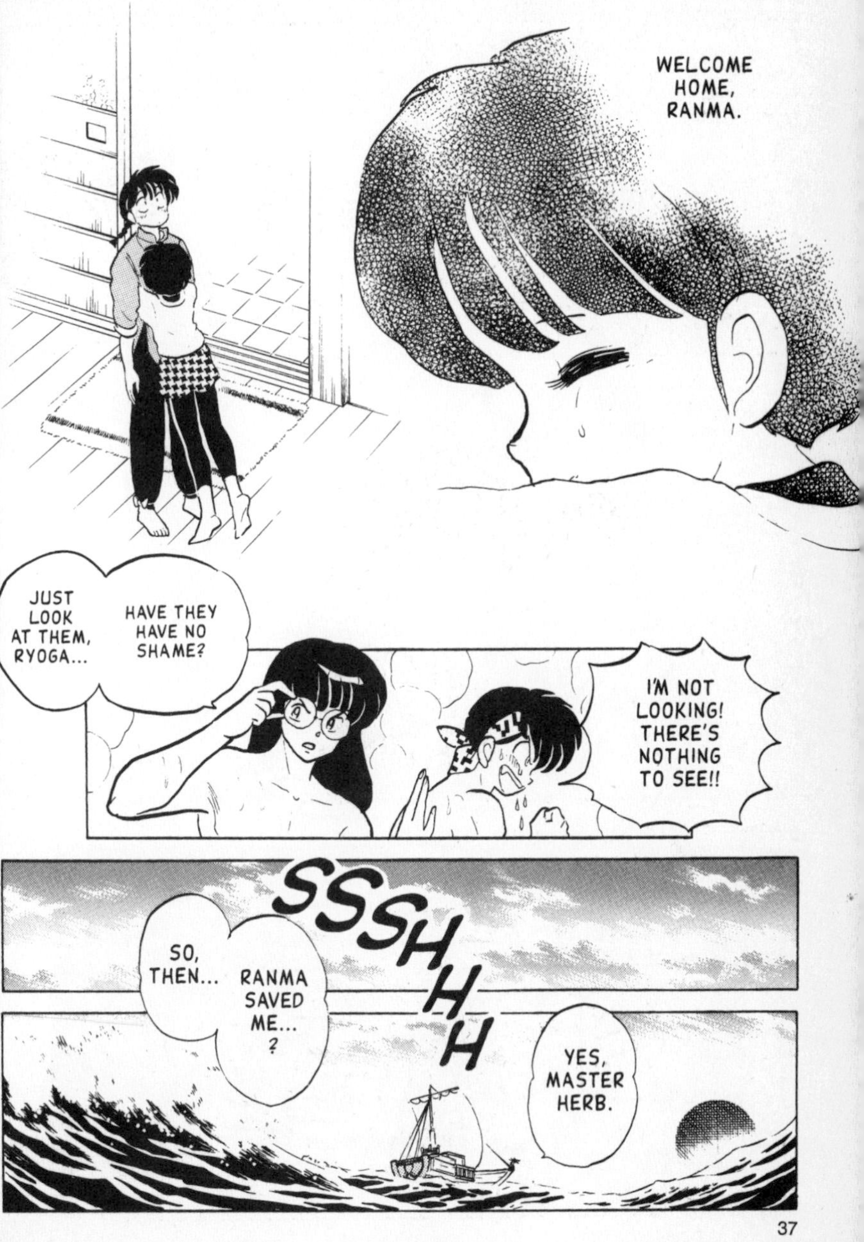
WELCOME HOME, RANMA.
JUST LOOK AT THEM, RYOGA...
HAVE THEY HAVE NO SHAME?
I'M NOT LOOKING! THERE'S NOTHING TO SEE!!
SSSHHHH
SO, THEN...
RANMA SAVED ME...?
YES, MASTER HERB.

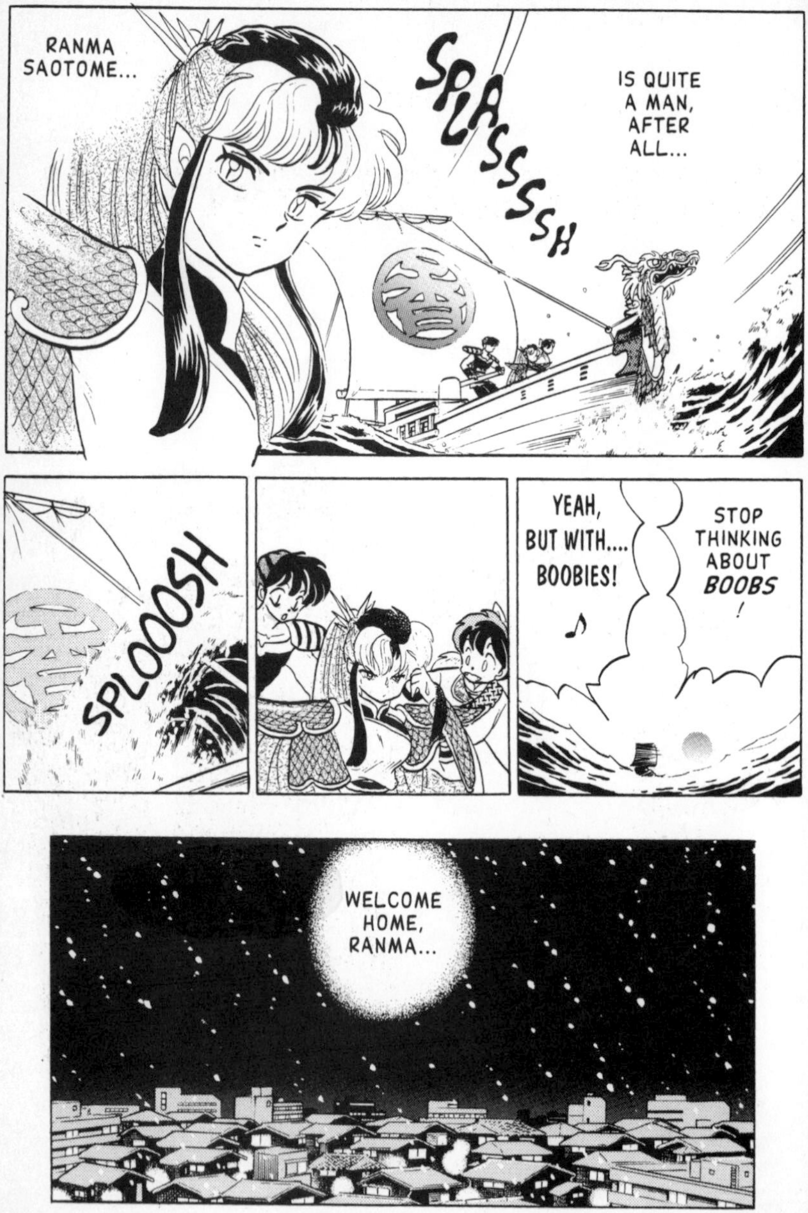

RANMA SAOTOME...
SPLASSSSSH
IS QUITE A MAN, AFTER ALL...
SPLOOOSH
YEAH, BUT WITH.... BOOBIES! ♪
STOP THINKING ABOUT BOOBS!
WELCOME HOME, RANMA...

Part 3

THE ULTIMATE TEACHER!

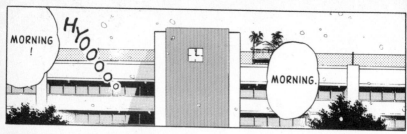

MORNING!

HYOOOOO

MORNING.

HEY, DID YOU HEAR?

THEY SAY THIS MONSTER OF A TEACHER IS COMING.

BLAH BLAH

WHAT? A NEW TEACHER?

YADA YADA

THEY SAY BEFORE COMING HERE...

THIS TEACHER CONQUERED *THREE SCHOOLS* FULL OF DELINQUENTS!

THE CONQUEST.

HEY... BUT *WE'RE* NOT DELINQUENTS, ARE WE?

SO WHY WOULD THIS TEACHER BE *HERE*...?

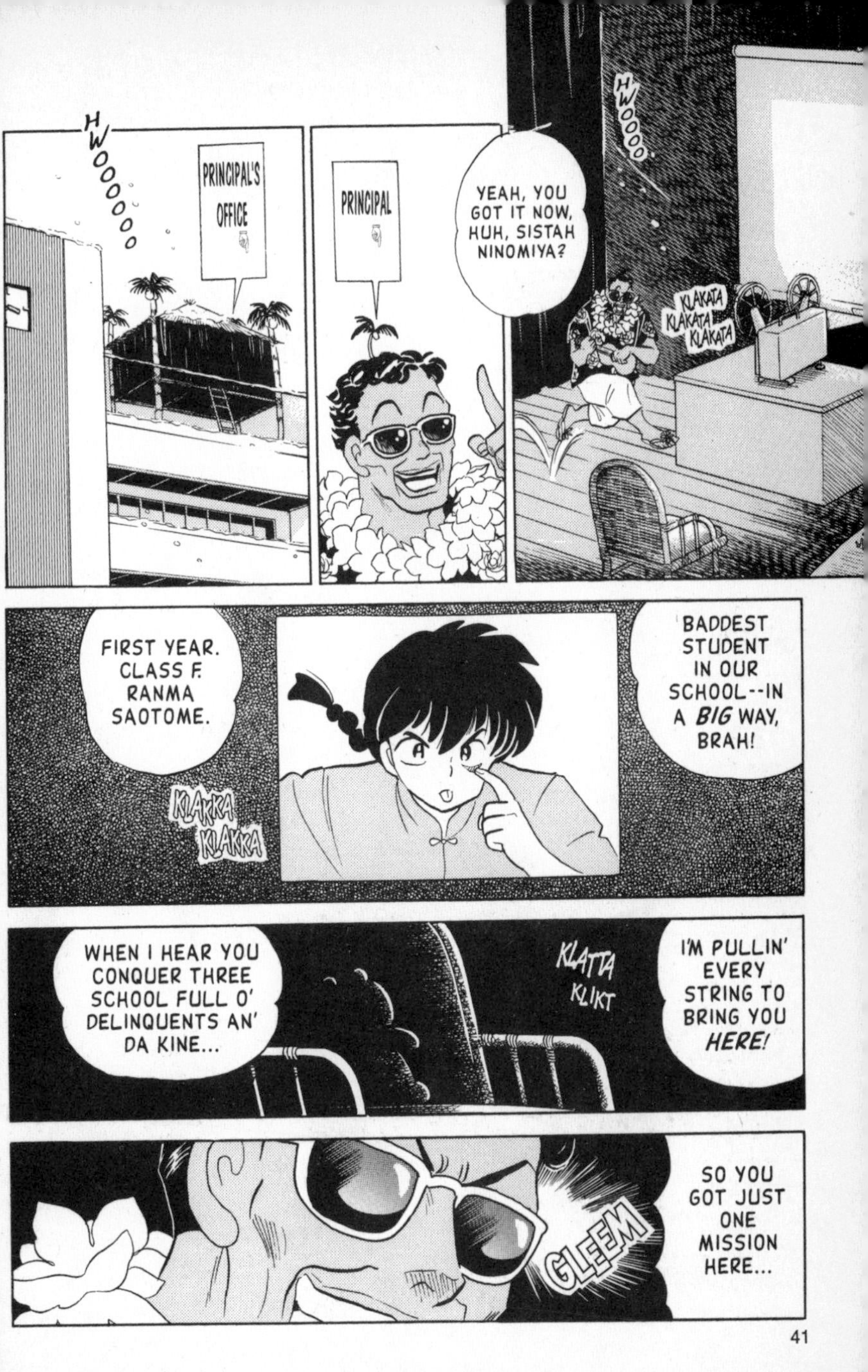
HWOOOOOOO
PRINCIPAL'S OFFICE
PRINCIPAL
YEAH, YOU GOT IT NOW, HUH, SISTAH NINOMIYA?
HWOOOO
KLAKATA KLAKATA KLAKATA
FIRST YEAR. CLASS F. RANMA SAOTOME.
KLAKKA KLAKKA
BADDEST STUDENT IN OUR SCHOOL--IN A BIG WAY, BRAH!
WHEN I HEAR YOU CONQUER THREE SCHOOL FULL O' DELINQUENTS AN' DA KINE...
KLATTA KLIKT
I'M PULLIN' EVERY STRING TO BRING YOU HERE!
GLEEM
SO YOU GOT JUST ONE MISSION HERE...

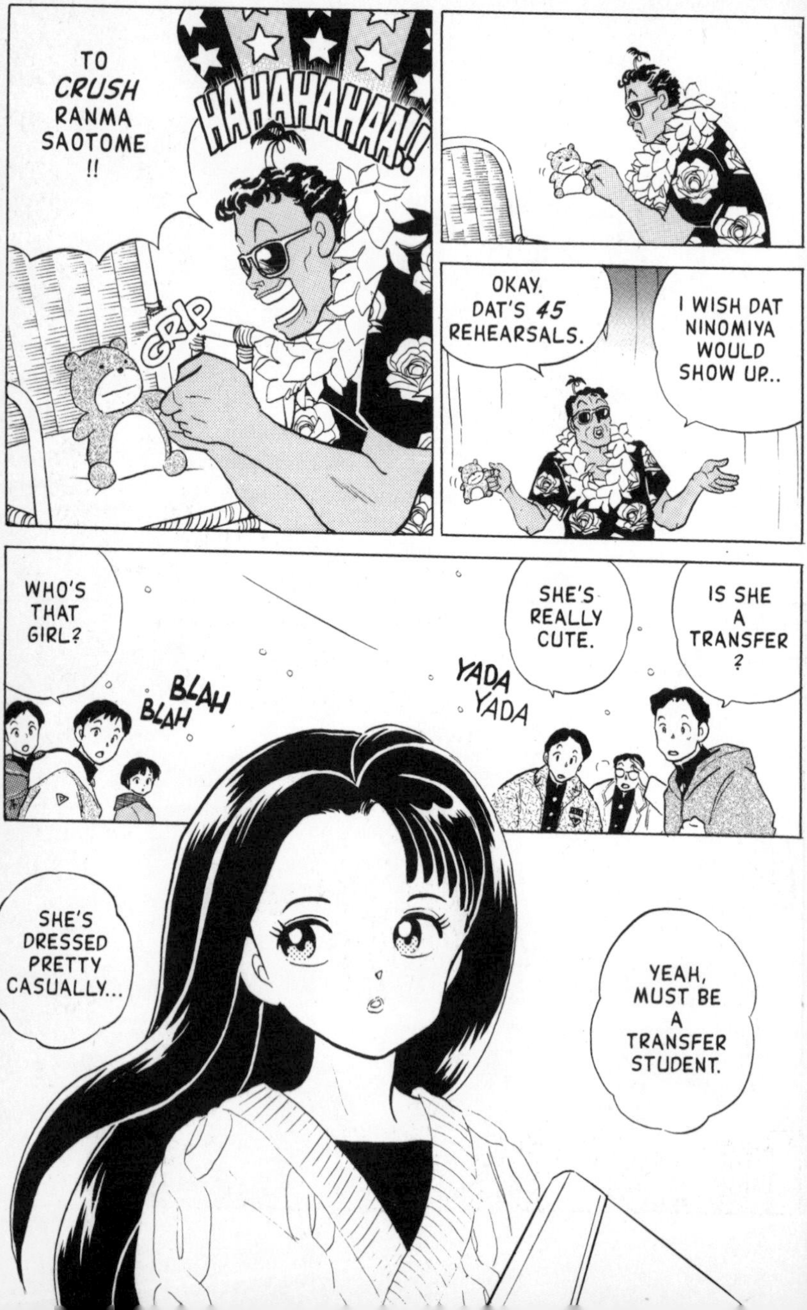
TO CRUSH RANMA SAOTOME !!
HAHAHAHAHAA!!
GRIP
OKAY. DAT'S 45 REHEARSALS.
I WISH DAT NINOMIYA WOULD SHOW UP...
WHO'S THAT GIRL?
BLAH BLAH
YADA YADA
SHE'S REALLY CUTE.
IS SHE A TRANSFER ?
SHE'S DRESSED PRETTY CASUALLY...
YEAH, MUST BE A TRANSFER STUDENT.

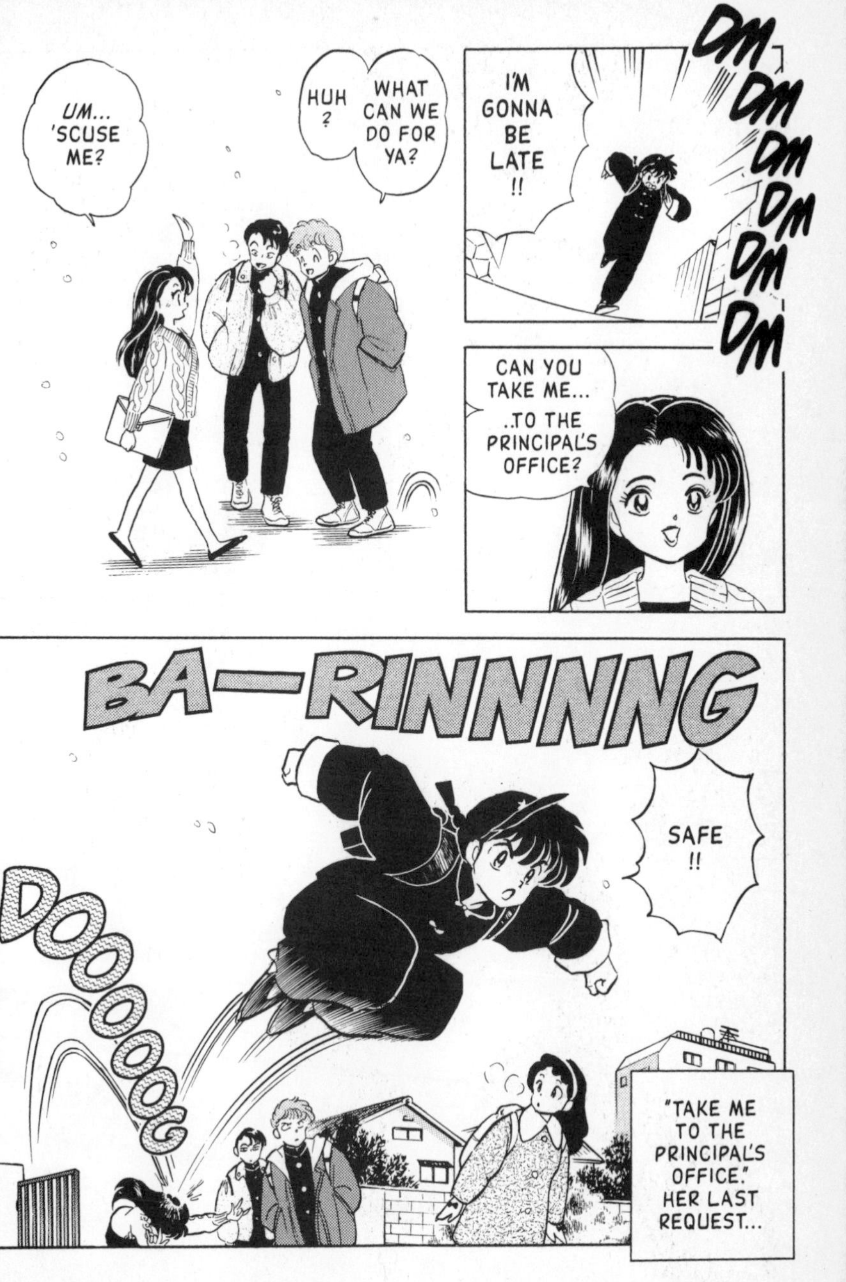

UM... 'SCUSE ME?
HUH?
WHAT CAN WE DO FOR YA?
DM DM DM DM DM DM
I'M GONNA BE LATE !!
CAN YOU TAKE ME...
..TO THE PRINCIPAL'S OFFICE?
BA-RINNNNG
SAFE !!
DOOOOOOG
"TAKE ME TO THE PRINCIPAL'S OFFICE." HER LAST REQUEST...

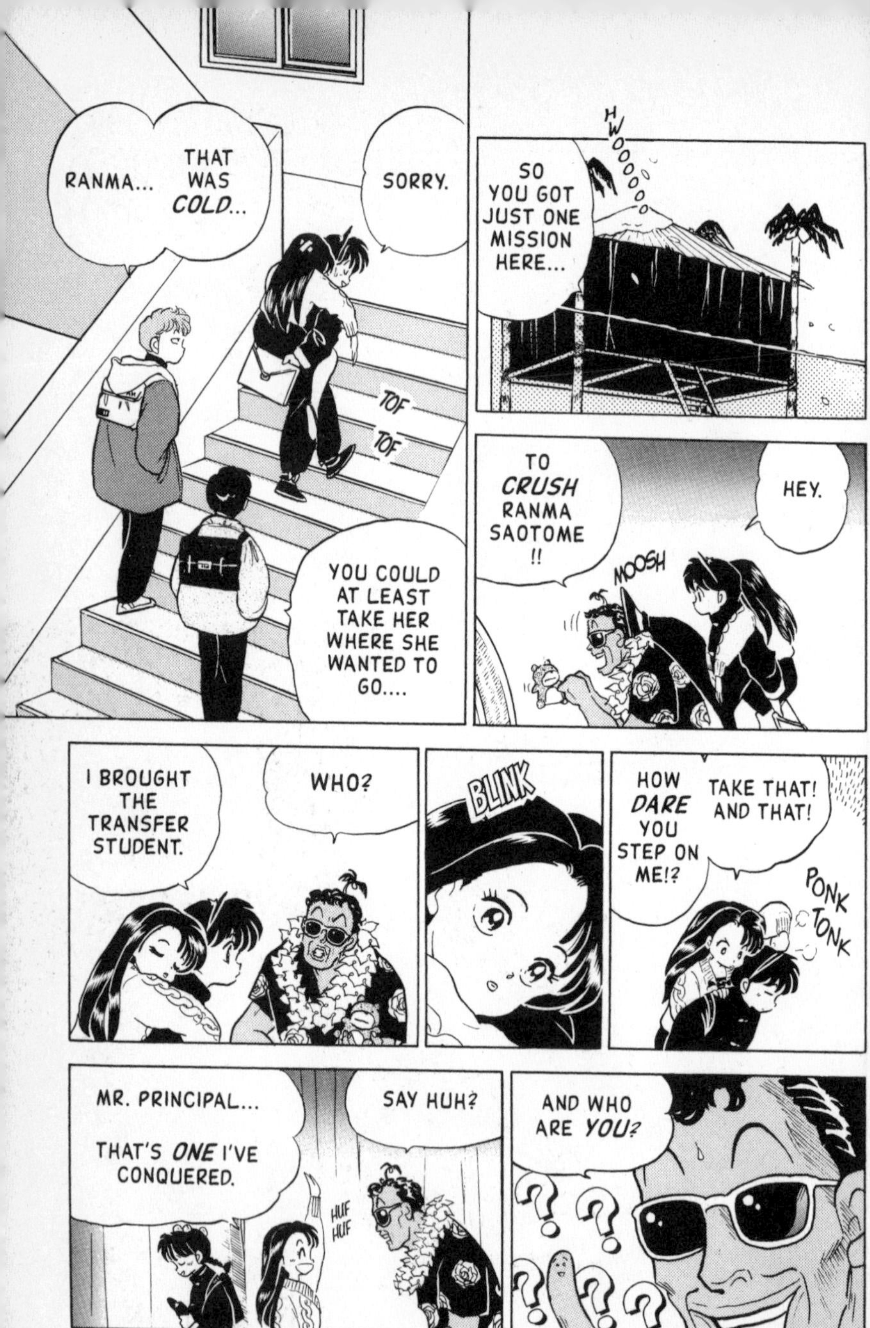
RANMA... THAT WAS COLD...
SORRY.
TOF TOF
YOU COULD AT LEAST TAKE HER WHERE SHE WANTED TO GO....
HWOOOOOOO
SO YOU GOT JUST ONE MISSION HERE...
TO CRUSH RANMA SAOTOME !!
HEY.
MOOSH
I BROUGHT THE TRANSFER STUDENT.
WHO?
BLINK
HOW DARE YOU STEP ON ME!?
TAKE THAT! AND THAT!
PONK TONK
MR. PRINCIPAL...
THAT'S ONE I'VE CONQUERED.
SAY HUH?
HUF HUF
AND WHO ARE YOU?

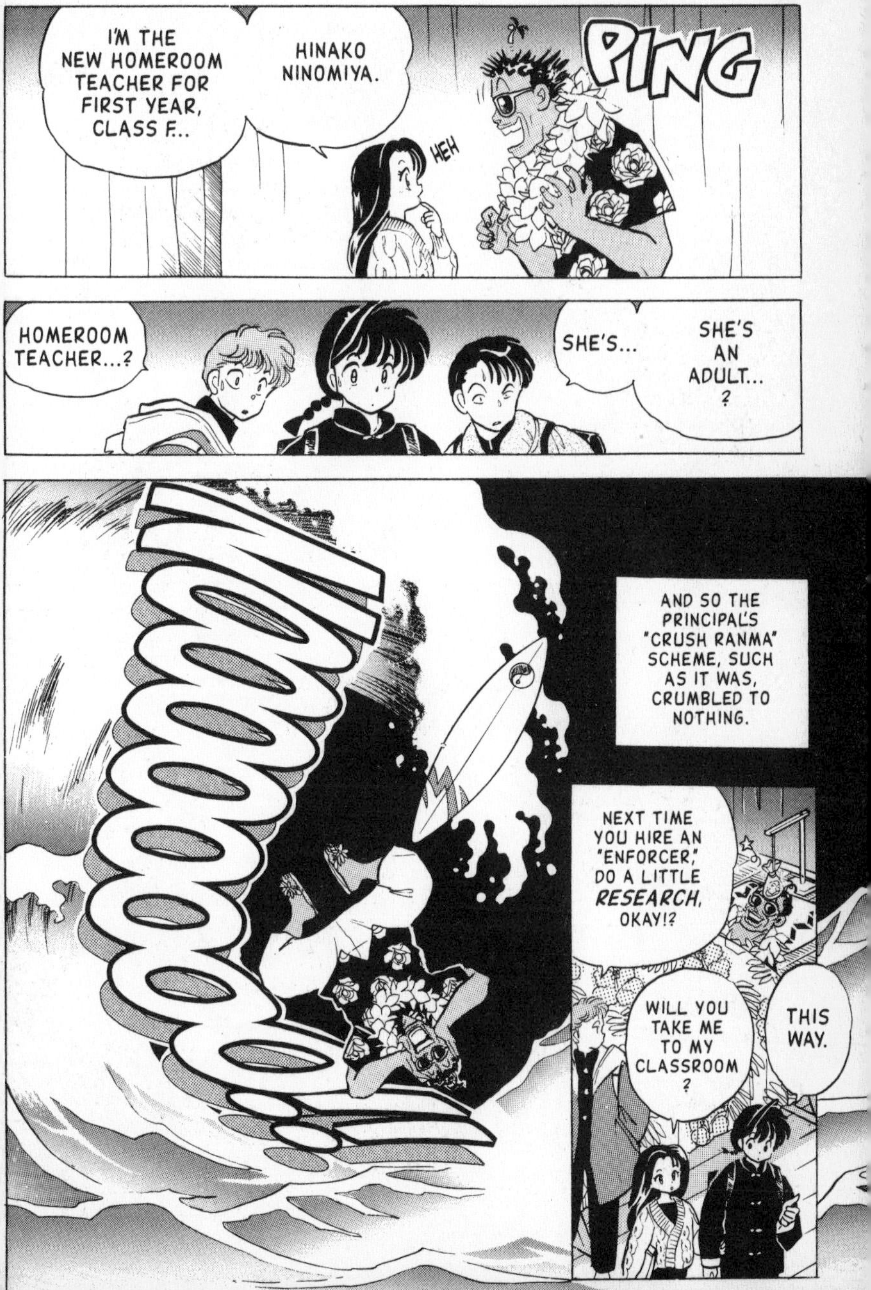
I'M THE NEW HOMEROOM TEACHER FOR FIRST YEAR, CLASS F...
HINAKO NINOMIYA.
HEH
PING
HOMEROOM TEACHER...?
SHE'S...
SHE'S AN ADULT...?
AND SO THE PRINCIPAL'S "CRUSH RANMA" SCHEME, SUCH AS IT WAS, CRUMBLED TO NOTHING.
NEXT TIME YOU HIRE AN "ENFORCER," DO A LITTLE *RESEARCH*, OKAY!?
WILL YOU TAKE ME TO MY CLASSROOM?
THIS WAY.

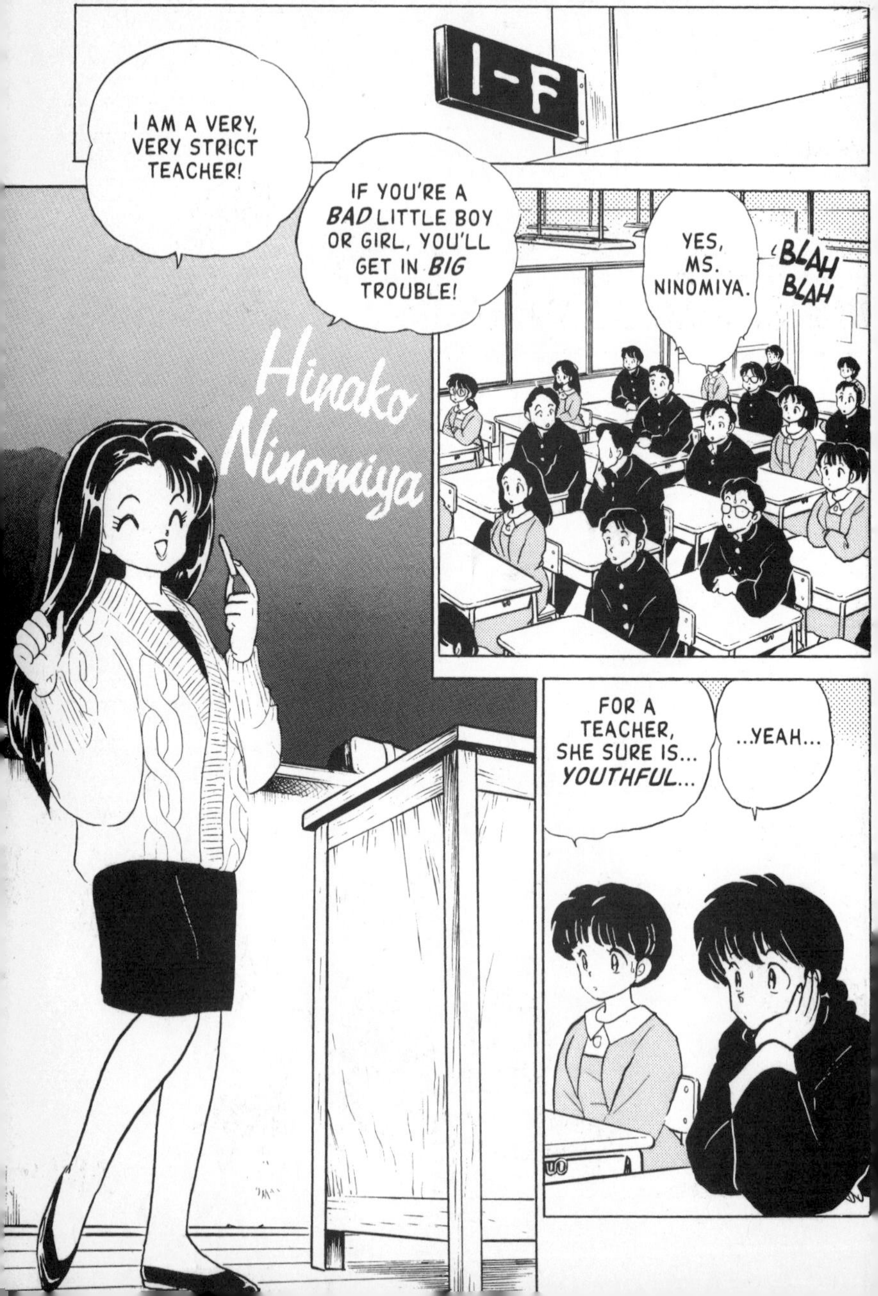
1-F
I AM A VERY, VERY STRICT TEACHER!
IF YOU'RE A *BAD* LITTLE BOY OR GIRL, YOU'LL GET IN *BIG* TROUBLE!
Hinako Ninomiya
YES, MS. NINOMIYA.
BLAH BLAH
FOR A TEACHER, SHE SURE IS... *YOUTHFUL*...
...YEAH...

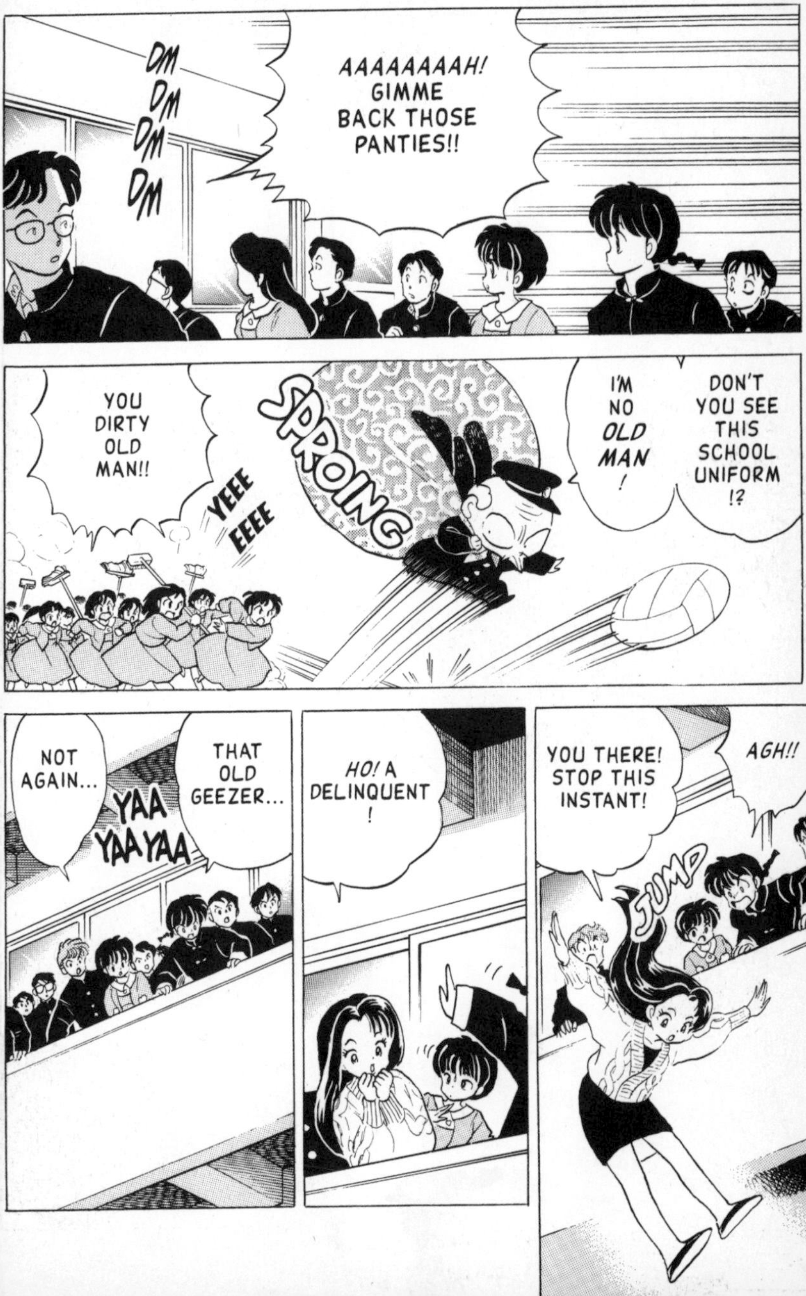
DM DM DM DM
AAAAAAAAH! GIMME BACK THOSE PANTIES!!
YOU DIRTY OLD MAN!!
SPROING
YEEE EEEE
I'M NO OLD MAN!
DON'T YOU SEE THIS SCHOOL UNIFORM !?
NOT AGAIN...
YAA YAA YAA
THAT OLD GEEZER...
HO! A DELINQUENT!
YOU THERE! STOP THIS INSTANT!
AGH!!
JUMP

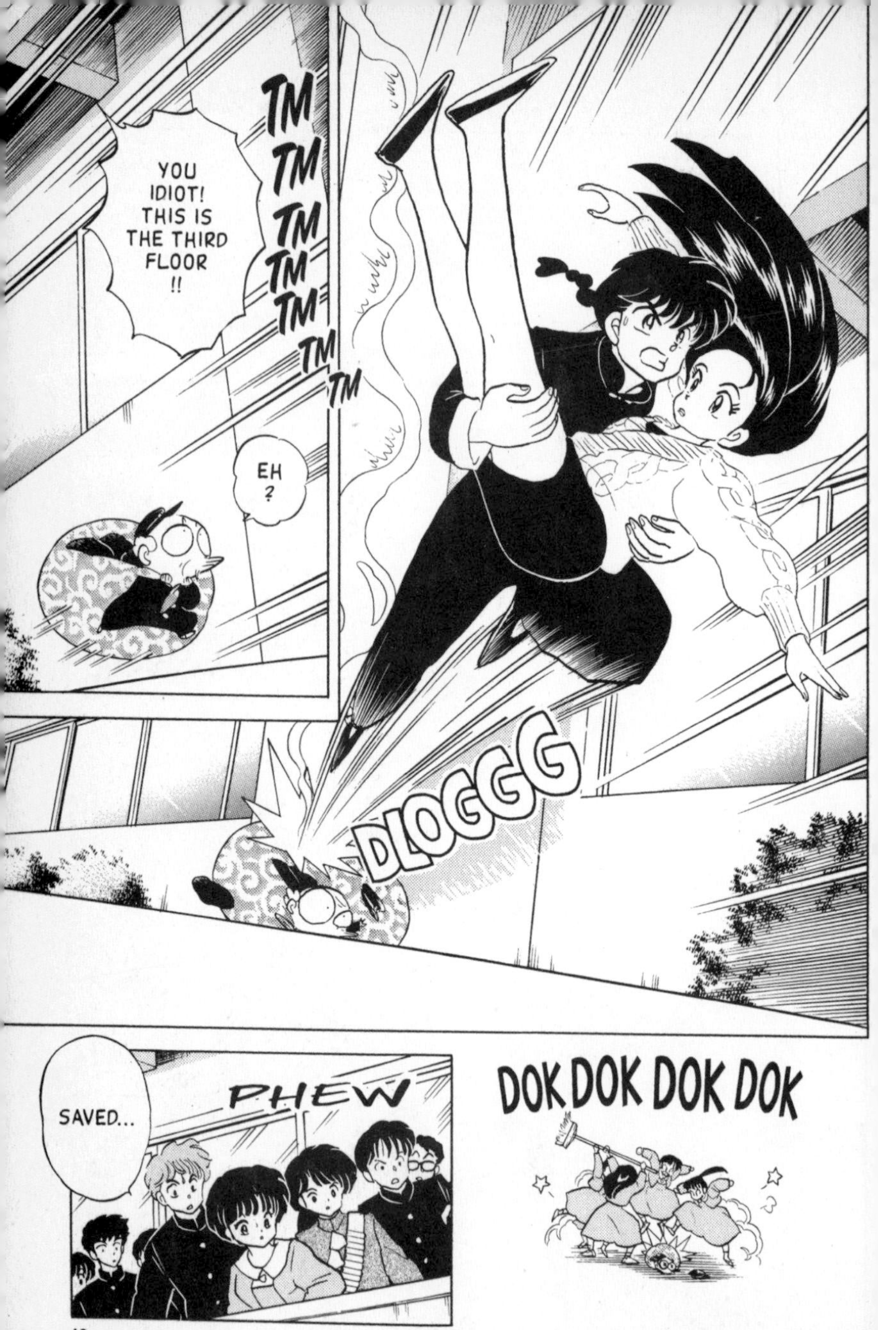
YOU IDIOT! THIS IS THE THIRD FLOOR !!
TM TM TM TM TM TM TM
EH ?
DLOGGG
SAVED...
PHEW
DOK DOK DOK DOK

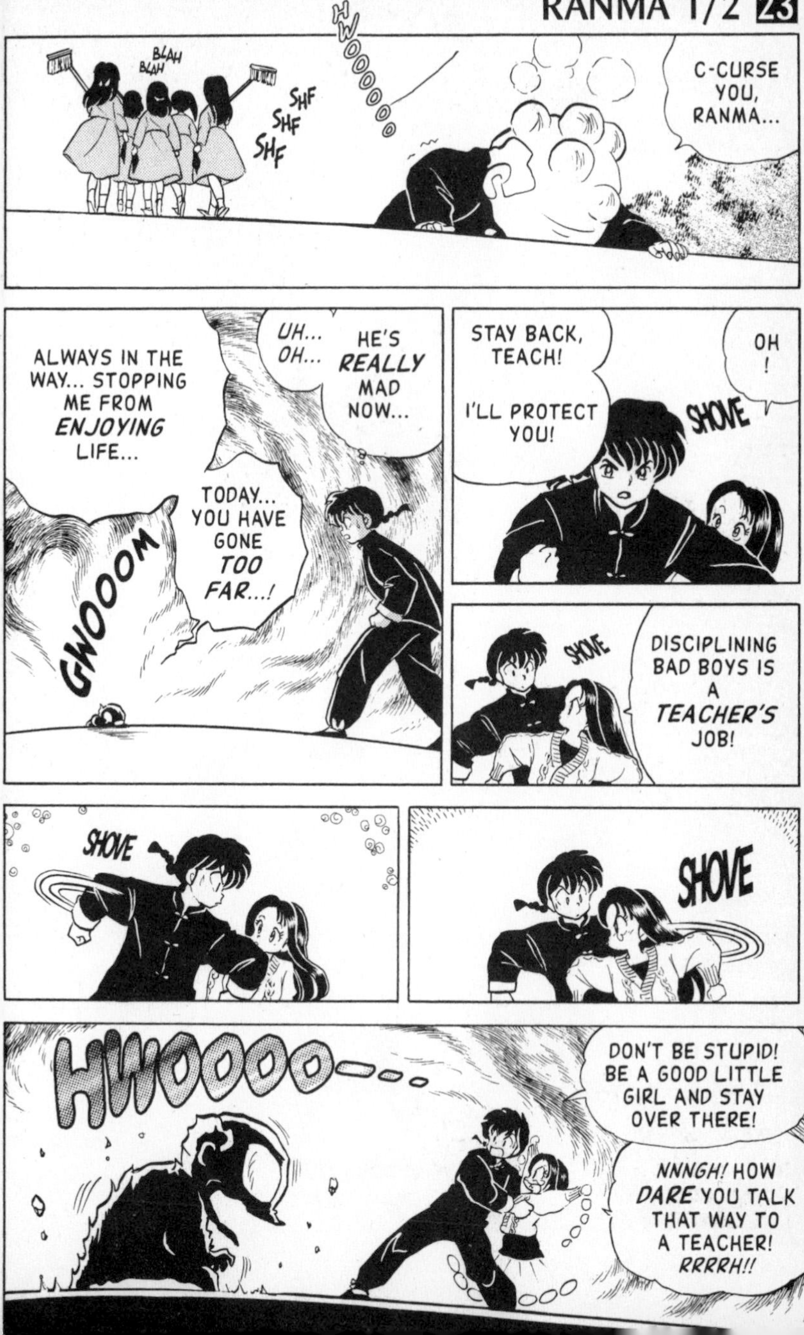
BLAH
BLAH
SHF
SHF
SHF
HWOOOOOO
C-CURSE YOU, RANMA...
ALWAYS IN THE WAY... STOPPING ME FROM ENJOYING LIFE...
UH... OH...
HE'S REALLY MAD NOW...
TODAY... YOU HAVE GONE TOO FAR...!
GWOOOM
STAY BACK, TEACH!
I'LL PROTECT YOU!
OH!
SHOVE
SHOVE
DISCIPLINING BAD BOYS IS A TEACHER'S JOB!
SHOVE
SHOVE
HWOOOO---
DON'T BE STUPID! BE A GOOD LITTLE GIRL AND STAY OVER THERE!
NNNGH! HOW DARE YOU TALK THAT WAY TO A TEACHER! RRRRH!!

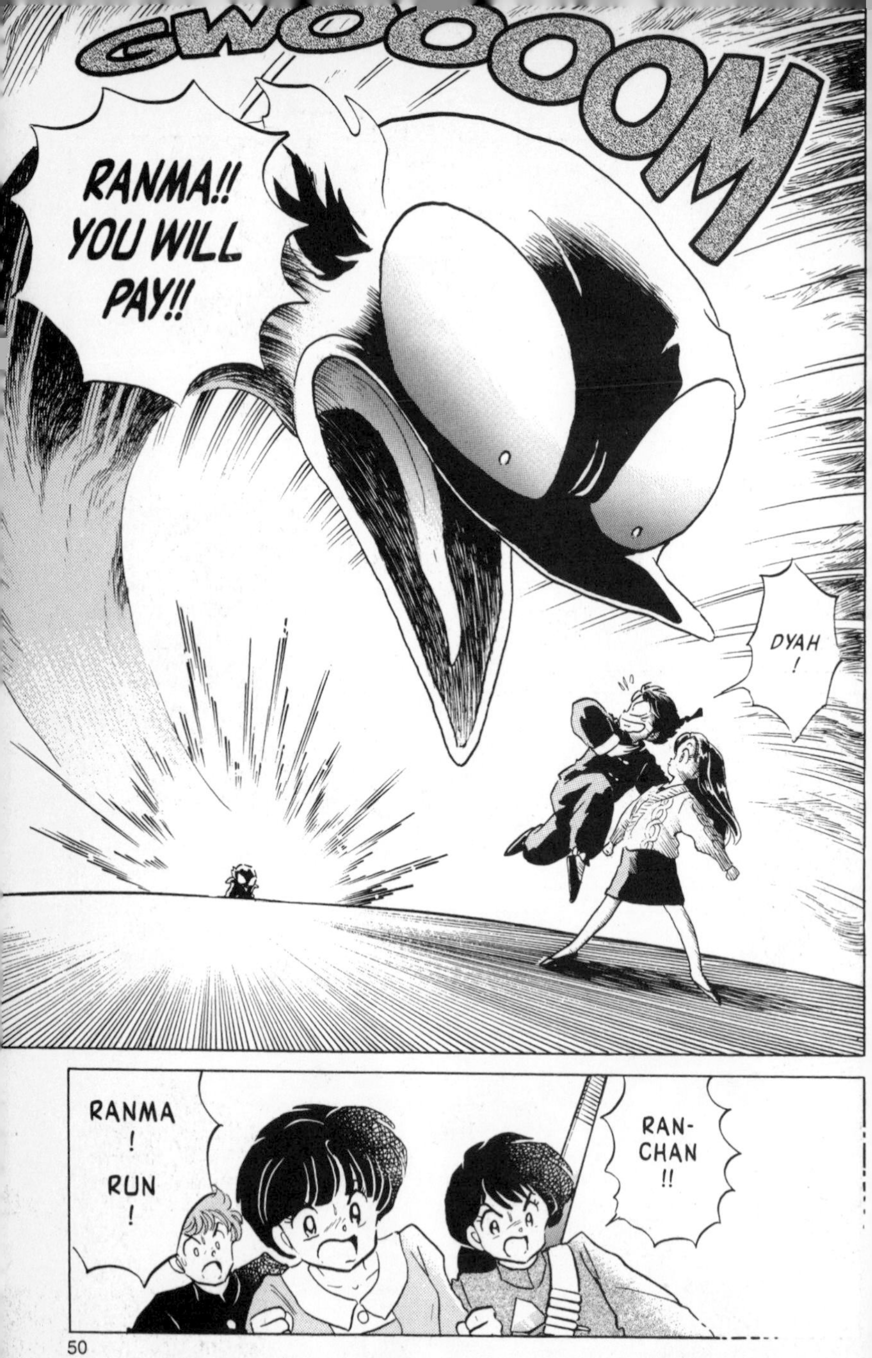
GWOOOOOM
RANMA!! YOU WILL PAY!!
DYAH!
RANMA! RUN!
RAN-CHAN!!

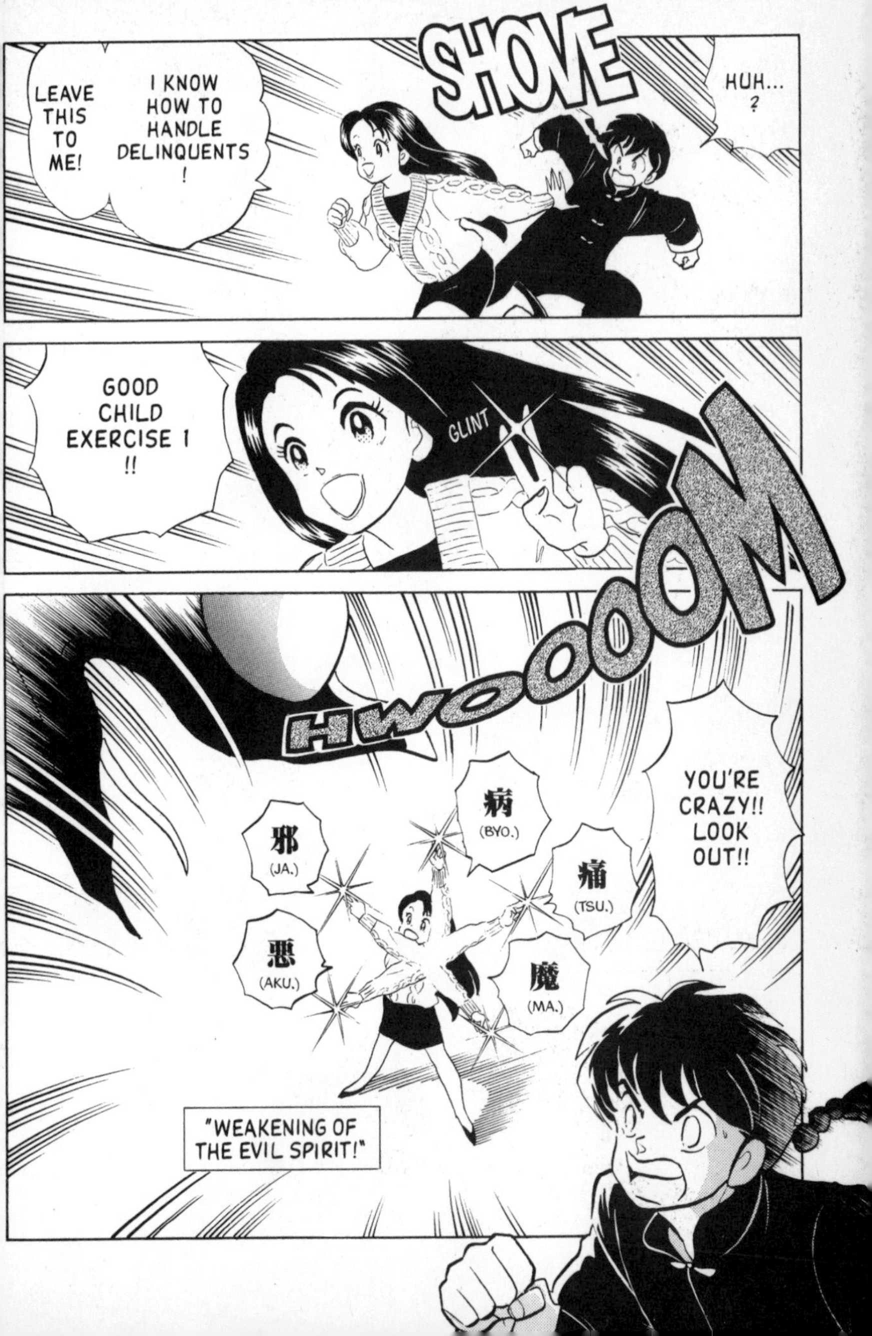
LEAVE THIS TO ME!
I KNOW HOW TO HANDLE DELINQUENTS!
SHOVE
HUH...?
GOOD CHILD EXERCISE 1!!
GLINT
HWOOOOOM
邪 (JA.)
病 (BYO.)
痛 (TSU.)
悪 (AKU.)
魔 (MA.)
YOU'RE CRAZY!! LOOK OUT!!
"WEAKENING OF THE EVIL SPIRIT!"

KRAK

SSHHHHH...

OH...
POOR
TEACHER...

SHE NEVER
HAD A CHANCE
AGAINST THAT
OLD GEEZER'S
ENORMOUS
WICKED BATTLE
AURA...

GAH...

SSHHHHH...

HUH...
?

WHAT...
?

SSHHHHH...

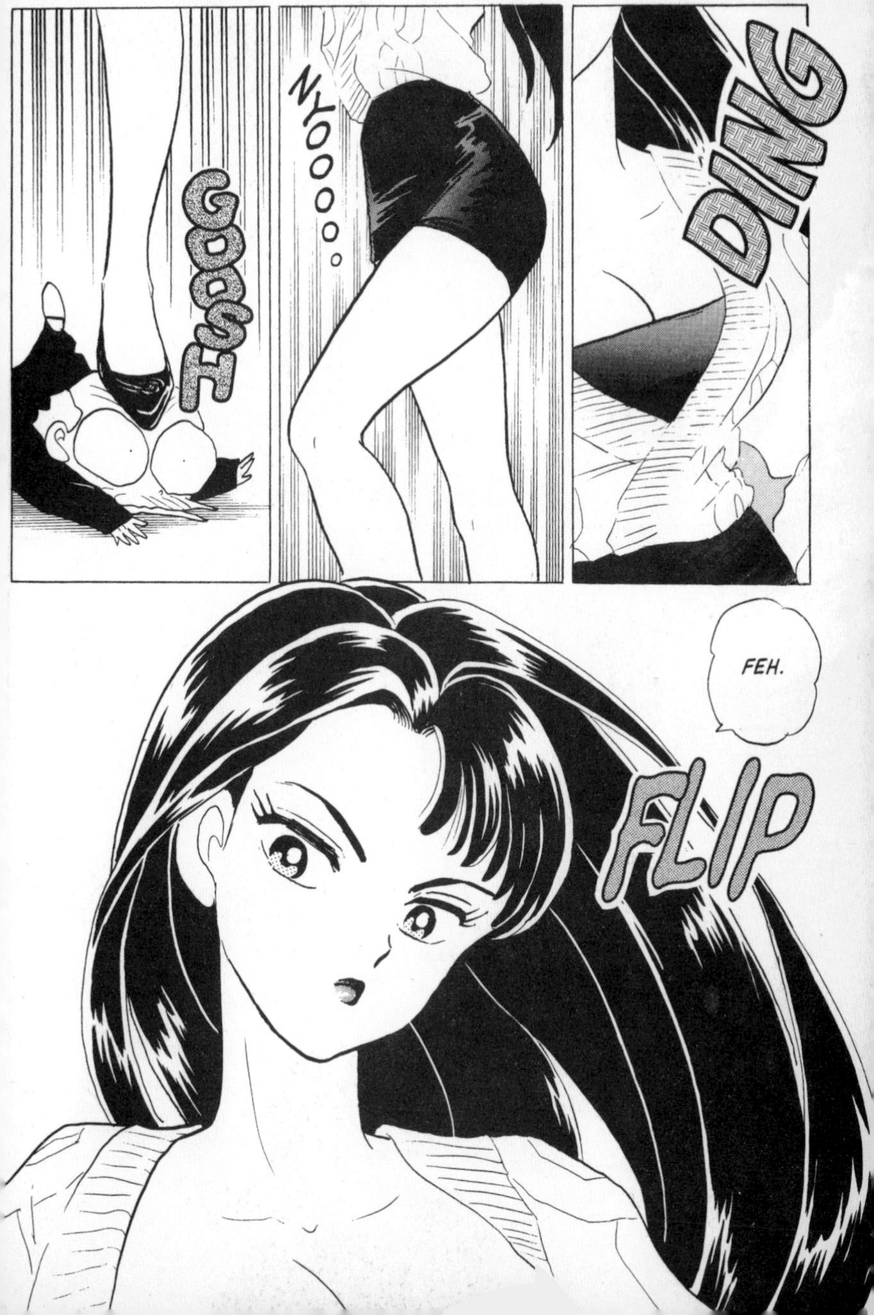
GOOSH
NYOOOOOo
DING
FEH.
FLIP

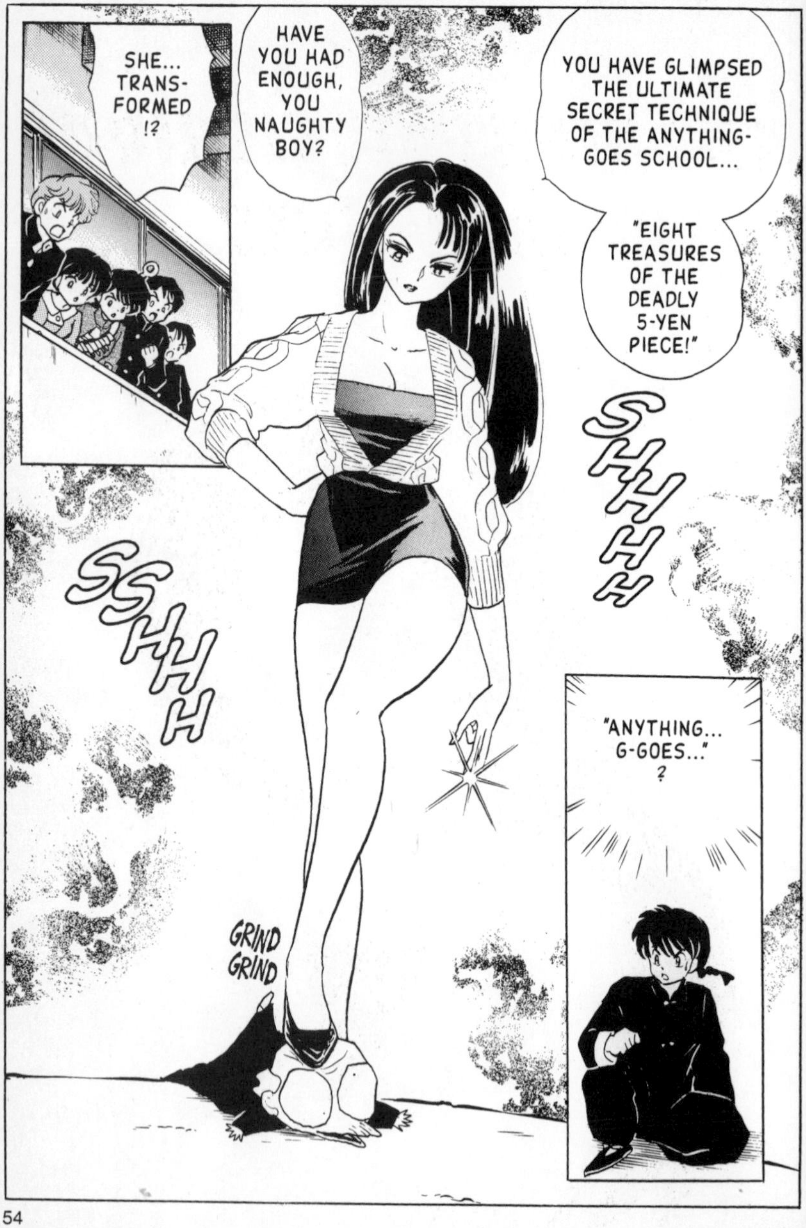
SHE... TRANS-FORMED !?
HAVE YOU HAD ENOUGH, YOU NAUGHTY BOY?
YOU HAVE GLIMPSED THE ULTIMATE SECRET TECHNIQUE OF THE ANYTHING-GOES SCHOOL...
"EIGHT TREASURES OF THE DEADLY 5-YEN PIECE!"
SSHHHH
SHHHHH
GRIND GRIND
"ANYTHING... G-GOES..." ?

Part 4

THE EIGHT MYSTERIOUS TREASURES

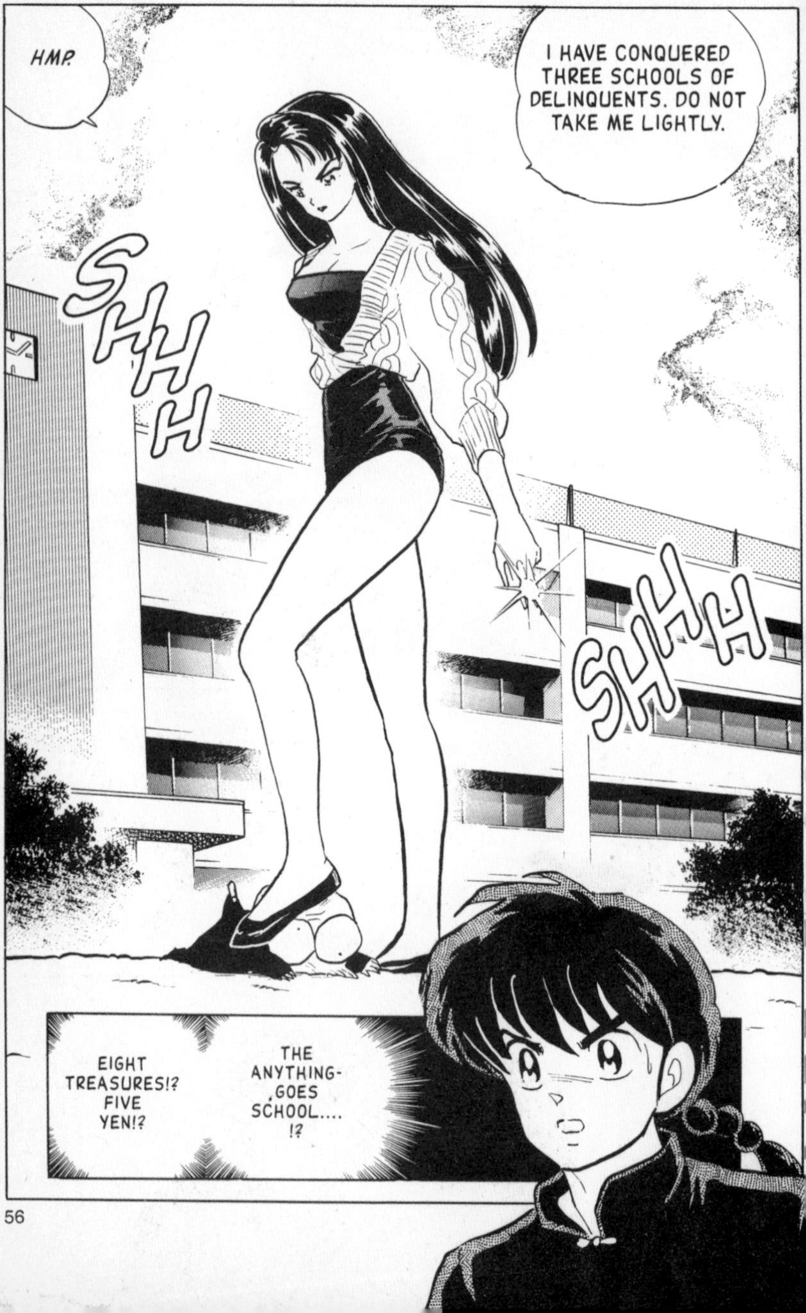
HMP.
I HAVE CONQUERED THREE SCHOOLS OF DELINQUENTS. DO NOT TAKE ME LIGHTLY.
SHHHH
SHHHH
EIGHT TREASURES!? FIVE YEN!?
THE ANYTHING-GOES SCHOOL.... !?

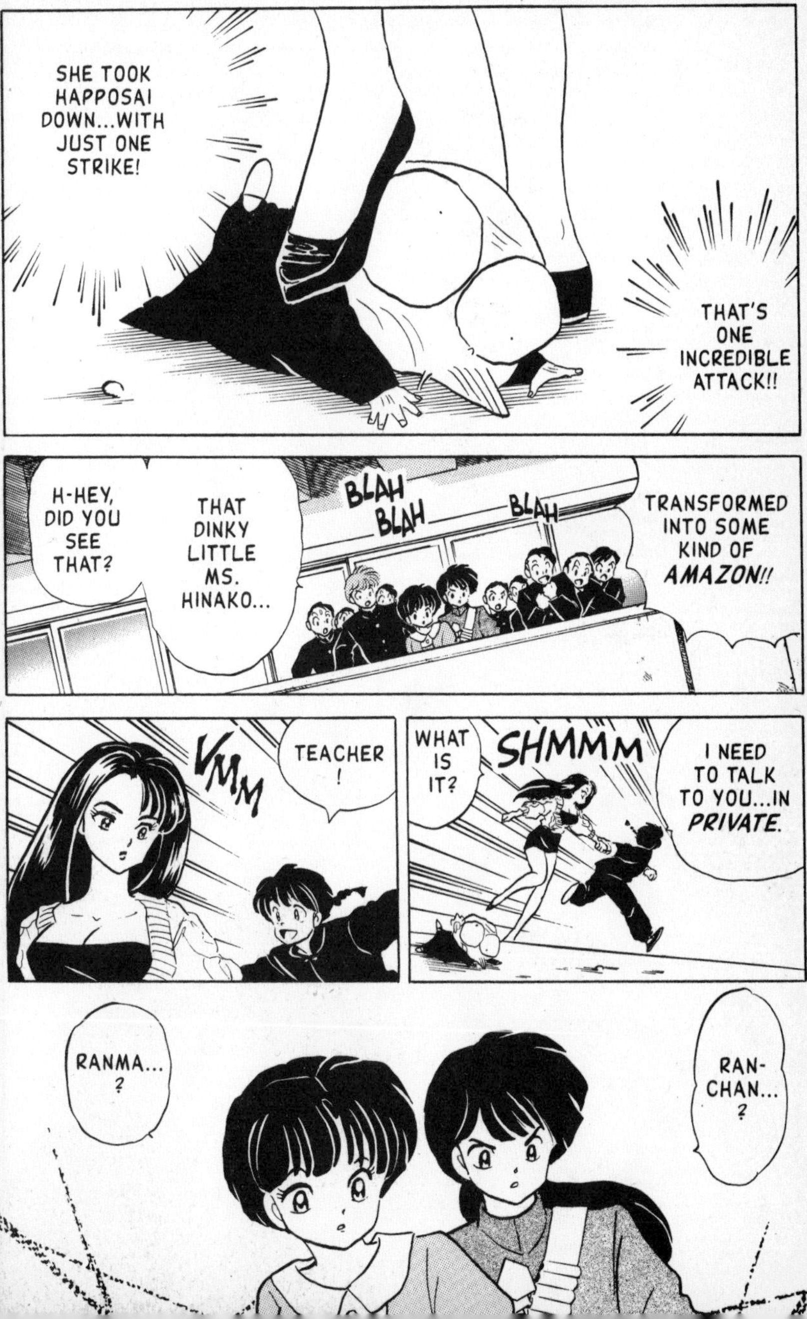
SHE TOOK HAPPOSAI DOWN...WITH JUST ONE STRIKE!
THAT'S ONE INCREDIBLE ATTACK!!
H-HEY, DID YOU SEE THAT?
THAT DINKY LITTLE MS. HINAKO...
BLAH BLAH
BLAH
TRANSFORMED INTO SOME KIND OF AMAZON!!
VMM
TEACHER!
WHAT IS IT?
SHMMM
I NEED TO TALK TO YOU...IN PRIVATE.
RANMA...?
RAN-CHAN...?

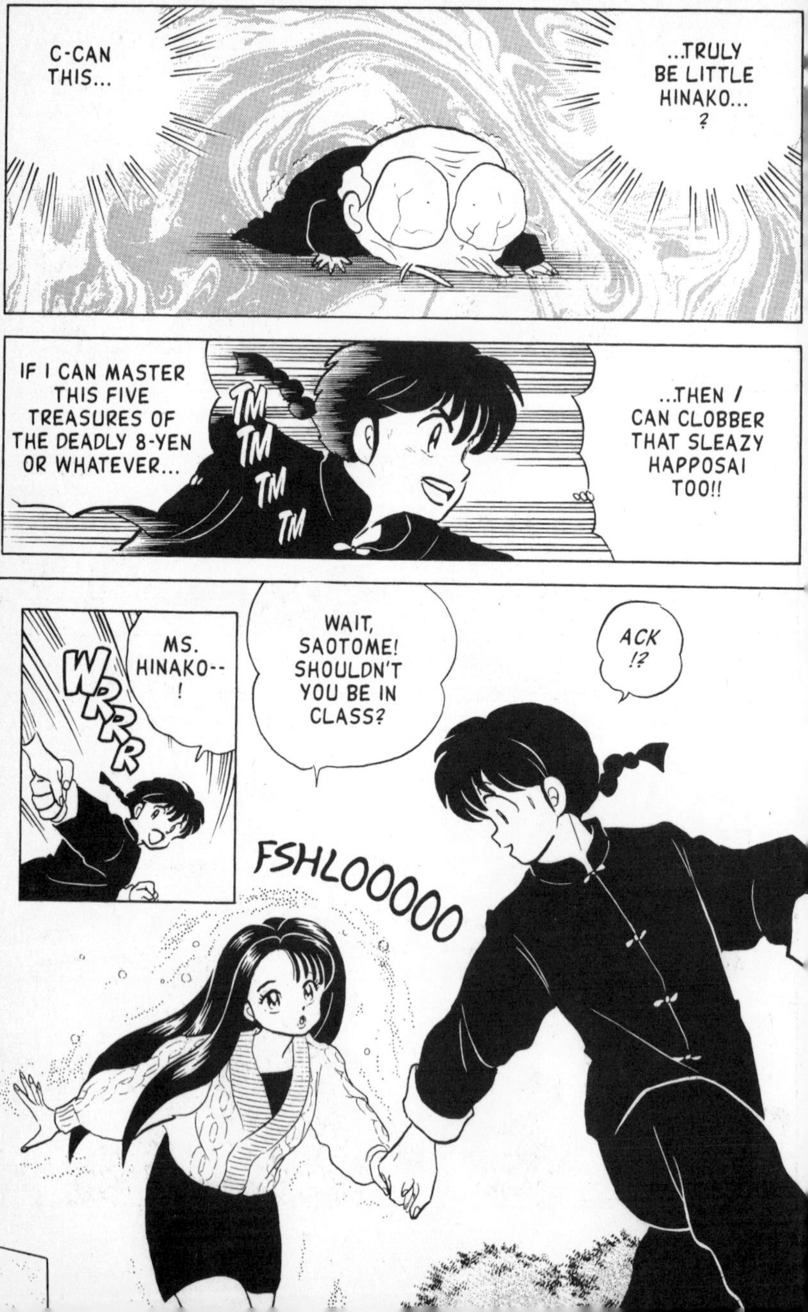
C-CAN THIS...
...TRULY BE LITTLE HINAKO...?
IF I CAN MASTER THIS FIVE TREASURES OF THE DEADLY 8-YEN OR WHATEVER...
TM TM TM TM
...THEN I CAN CLOBBER THAT SLEAZY HAPPOSAI TOO!!
WRRRR
MS. HINAKO--!
WAIT, SAOTOME! SHOULDN'T YOU BE IN CLASS?
ACK!?
FSHLOOOOOO

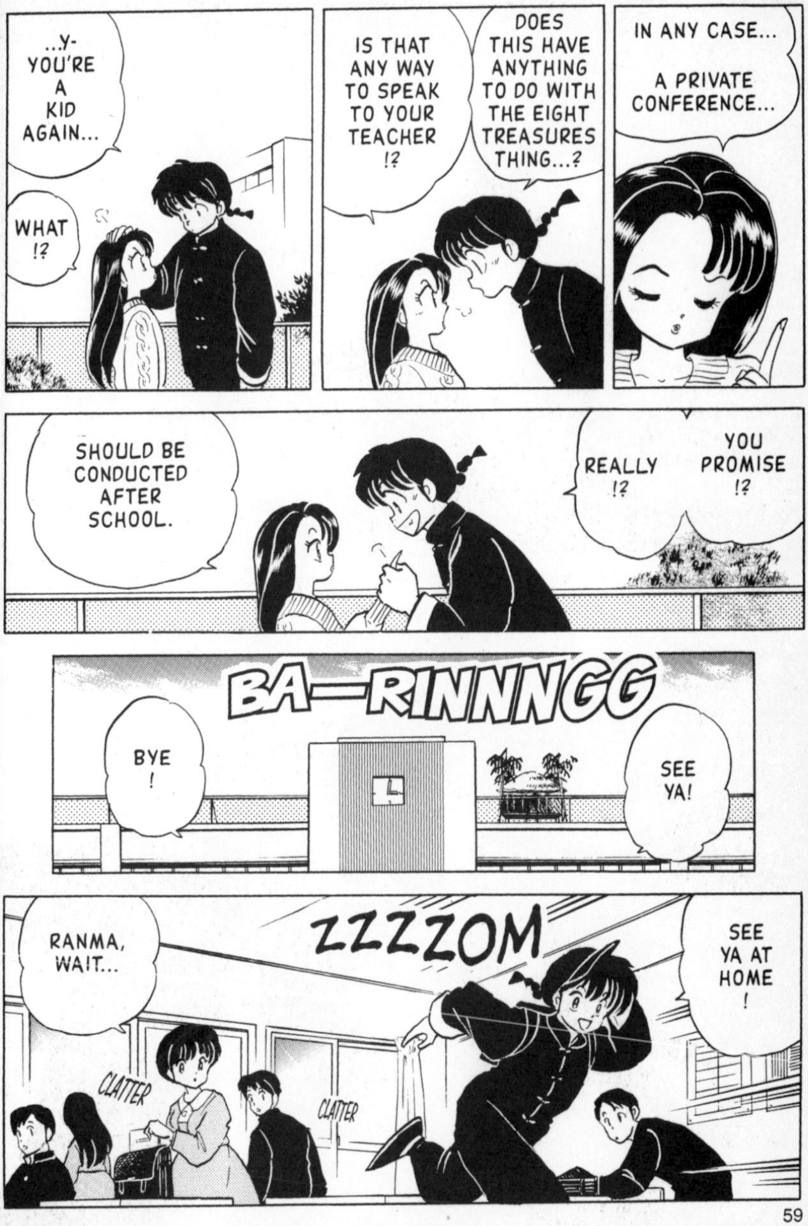
...Y- YOU'RE A KID AGAIN...
WHAT !?
IS THAT ANY WAY TO SPEAK TO YOUR TEACHER !?
DOES THIS HAVE ANYTHING TO DO WITH THE EIGHT TREASURES THING...?
IN ANY CASE...
A PRIVATE CONFERENCE...
SHOULD BE CONDUCTED AFTER SCHOOL.
REALLY !?
YOU PROMISE !?
BA-RINNNGG
BYE !
SEE YA!
RANMA, WAIT...
ZZZZOM
SEE YA AT HOME !
CLATTER
CLATTER

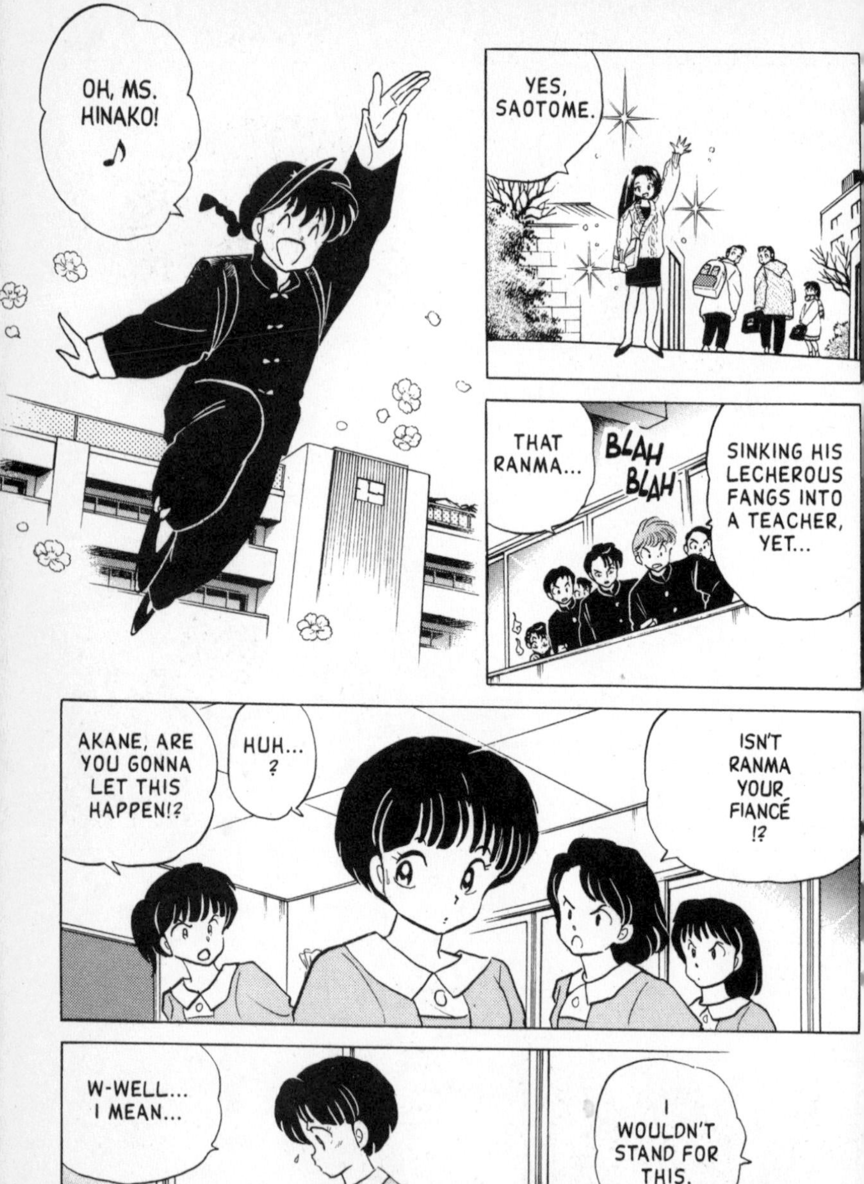
OH, MS. HINAKO! ♪
YES, SAOTOME.
THAT RANMA...
BLAH BLAH
SINKING HIS LECHEROUS FANGS INTO A TEACHER, YET...
AKANE, ARE YOU GONNA LET THIS HAPPEN!?
HUH...?
ISN'T RANMA YOUR FIANCÉ!?
W-WELL... I MEAN...
I WOULDN'T STAND FOR THIS.

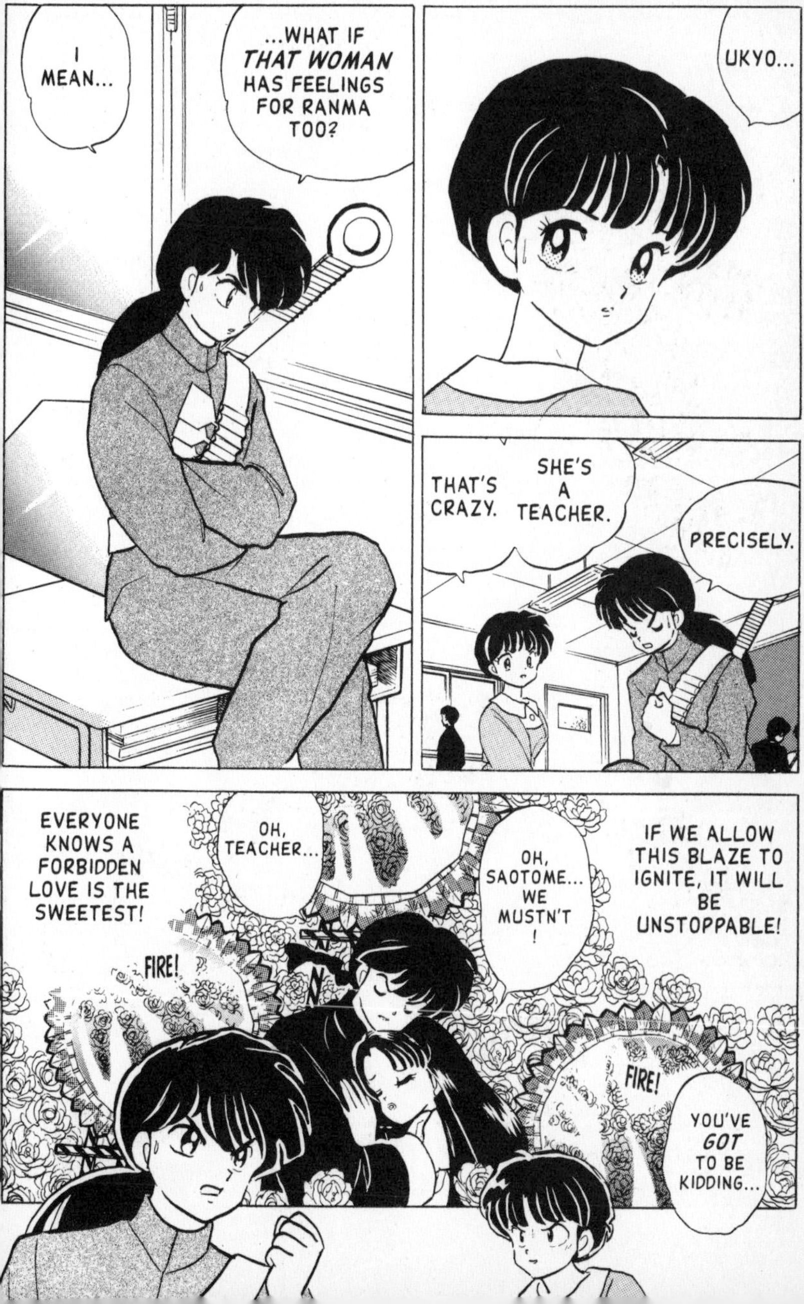
I MEAN...
...WHAT IF *THAT WOMAN* HAS FEELINGS FOR RANMA TOO?
UKYO...
THAT'S CRAZY.
SHE'S A TEACHER.
PRECISELY.
EVERYONE KNOWS A FORBIDDEN LOVE IS THE SWEETEST!
OH, TEACHER...
OH, SAOTOME... WE MUSTN'T!
IF WE ALLOW THIS BLAZE TO IGNITE, IT WILL BE UNSTOPPABLE!
FIRE!
FIRE!
YOU'VE *GOT* TO BE KIDDING...

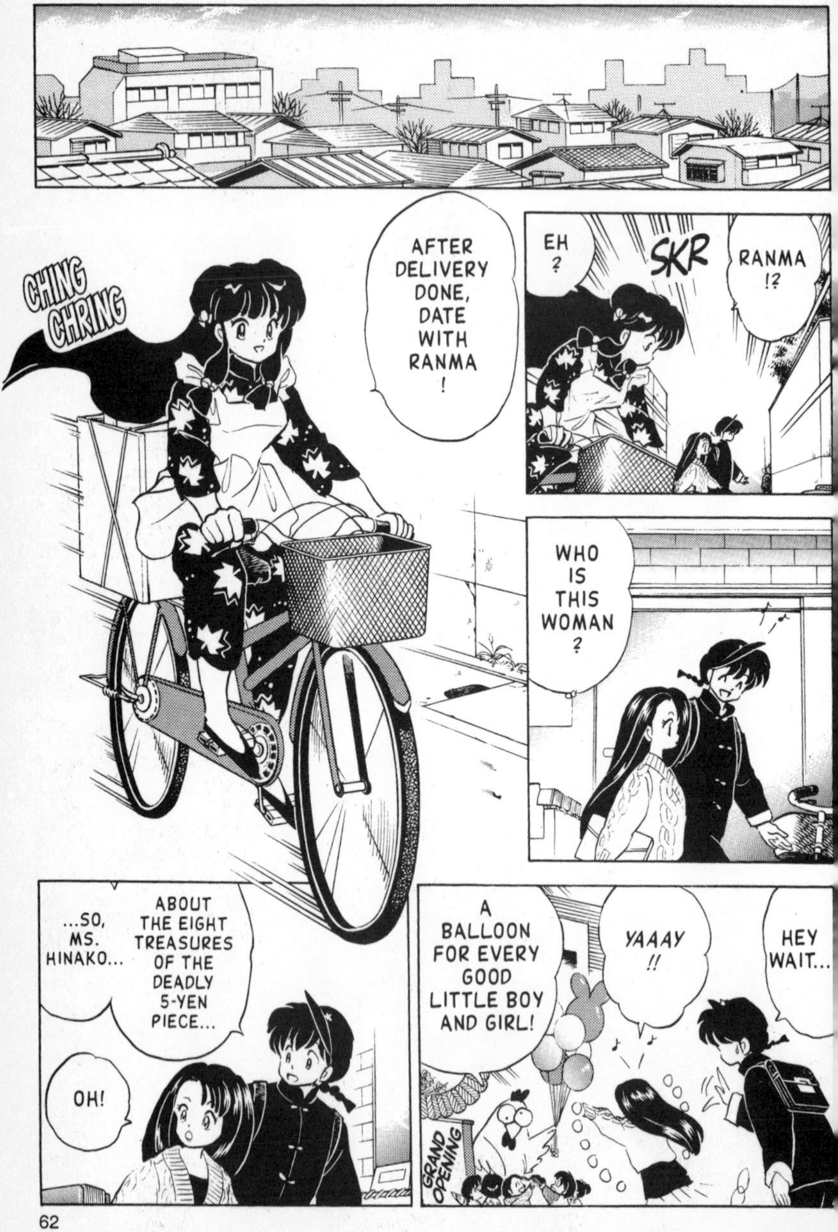
CHING CHRING
AFTER DELIVERY DONE, DATE WITH RANMA!
EH?
SKR
RANMA!?
WHO IS THIS WOMAN?
...SO, MS. HINAKO...
ABOUT THE EIGHT TREASURES OF THE DEADLY 5-YEN PIECE...
OH!
A BALLOON FOR EVERY GOOD LITTLE BOY AND GIRL!
YAAAY!!
HEY WAIT...
GRAND OPENING

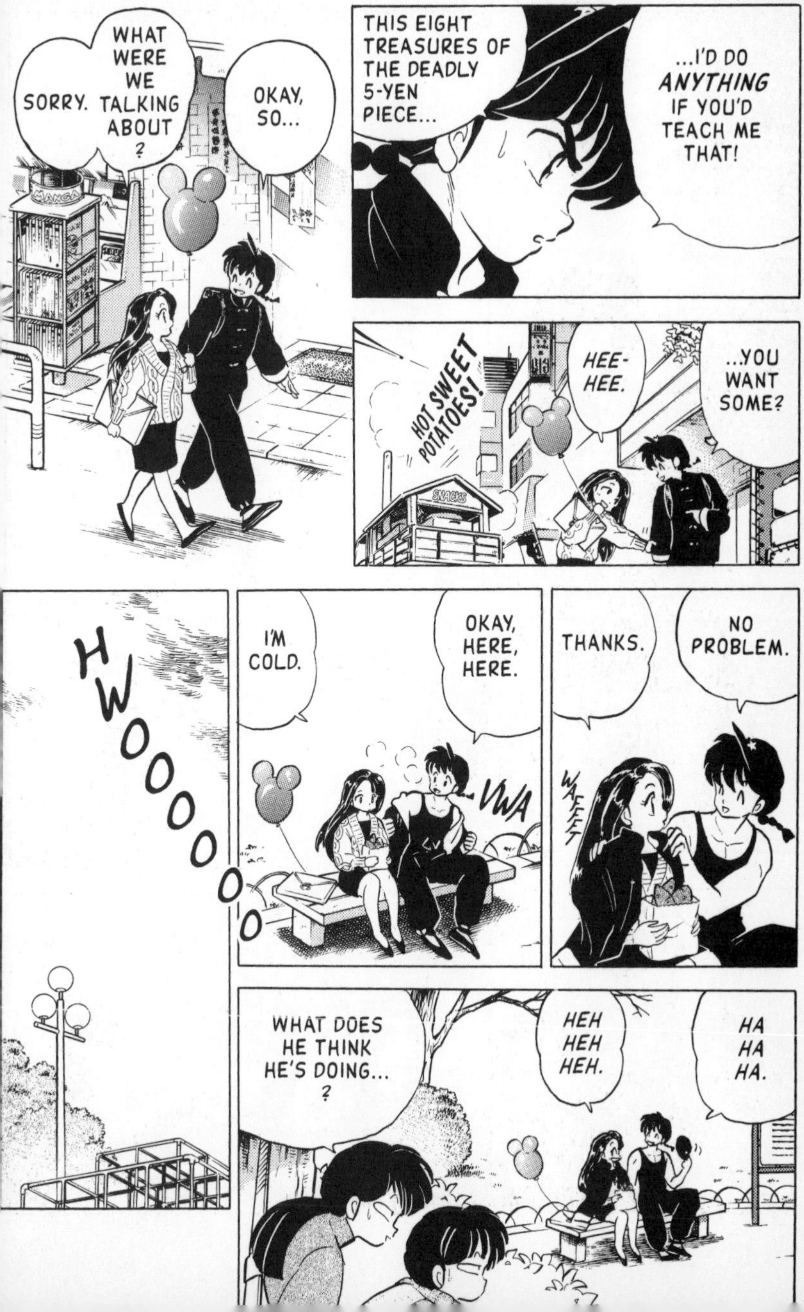
SORRY.
WHAT WERE WE TALKING ABOUT ?
OKAY, SO...
MANGA
THIS EIGHT TREASURES OF THE DEADLY 5-YEN PIECE...
...I'D DO *ANYTHING* IF YOU'D TEACH ME THAT!
HOT SWEET POTATOES!
SNACKS
HEE-HEE.
...YOU WANT SOME?
HWOOOOOOO
I'M COLD.
OKAY, HERE, HERE.
VWA
THANKS.
NO PROBLEM.
WAFFFT
WHAT DOES HE THINK HE'S DOING... ?
HEH HEH HEH.
HA HA HA.

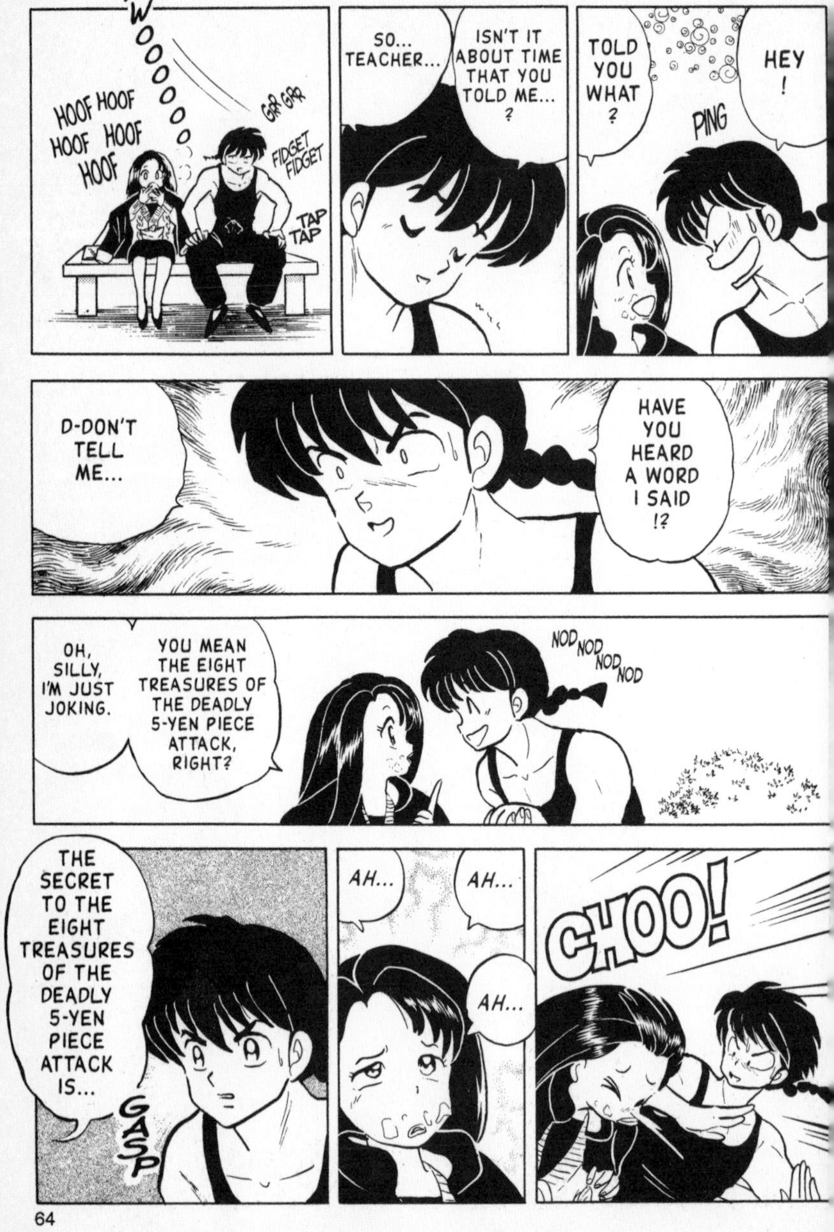
HWOOOOOOO
HOOF HOOF HOOF HOOF HOOF
GRR GRR
FIDGET FIDGET
TAP TAP
SO... TEACHER...
ISN'T IT ABOUT TIME THAT YOU TOLD ME...?
TOLD YOU WHAT?
HEY!
PING
D-DON'T TELL ME...
HAVE YOU HEARD A WORD I SAID!?
OH, SILLY, I'M JUST JOKING.
YOU MEAN THE EIGHT TREASURES OF THE DEADLY 5-YEN PIECE ATTACK, RIGHT?
NOD NOD NOD NOD
THE SECRET TO THE EIGHT TREASURES OF THE DEADLY 5-YEN PIECE ATTACK IS...
GASP
AH...
AH...
AH...
CHOO!

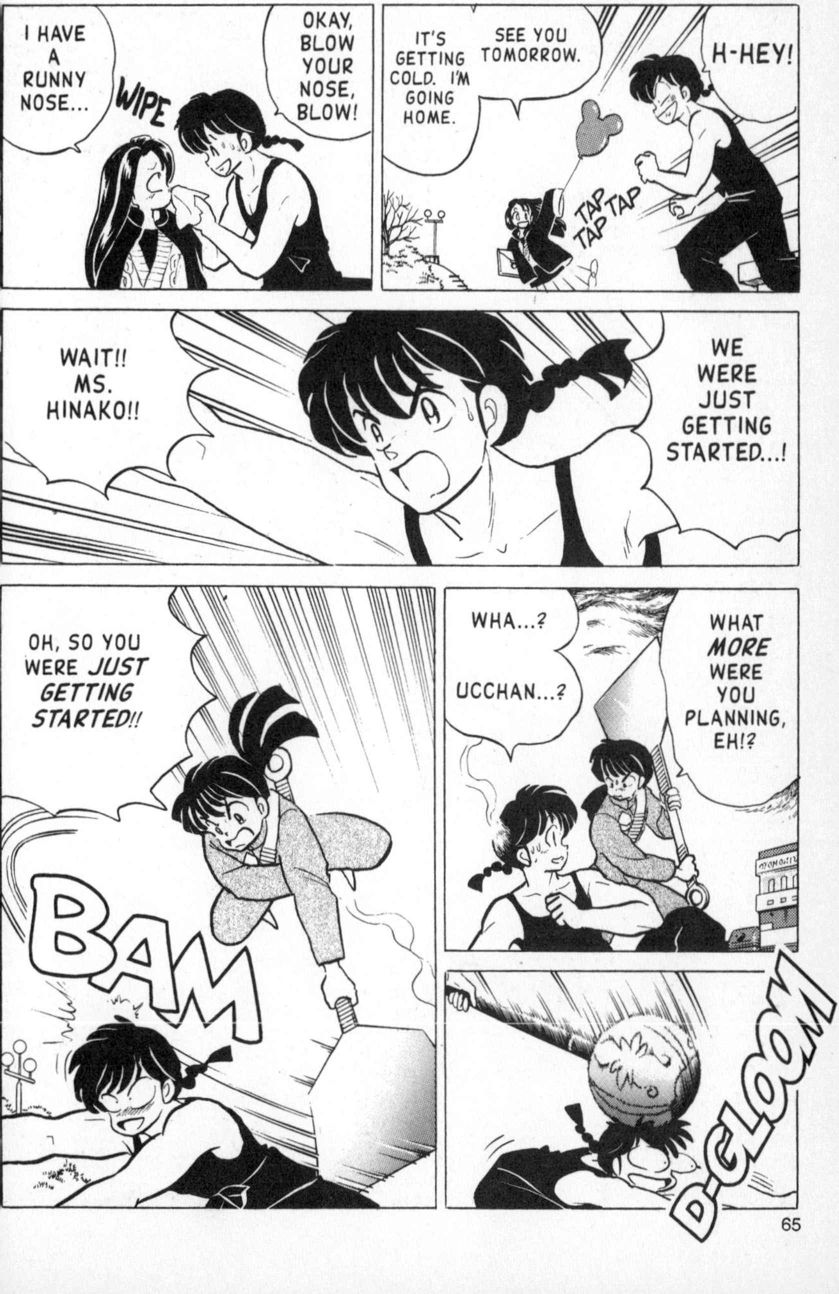
I HAVE A RUNNY NOSE...
WIPE
OKAY, BLOW YOUR NOSE, BLOW!
IT'S GETTING COLD. I'M GOING HOME.
SEE YOU TOMORROW.
TAP TAP TAP TAP
H-HEY!
WAIT!! MS. HINAKO!!
WE WERE JUST GETTING STARTED...!
OH, SO YOU WERE *JUST GETTING STARTED*!!
BAM
WHA...?
UCCHAN...?
WHAT *MORE* WERE YOU PLANNING, EH!?
D-CLOOM

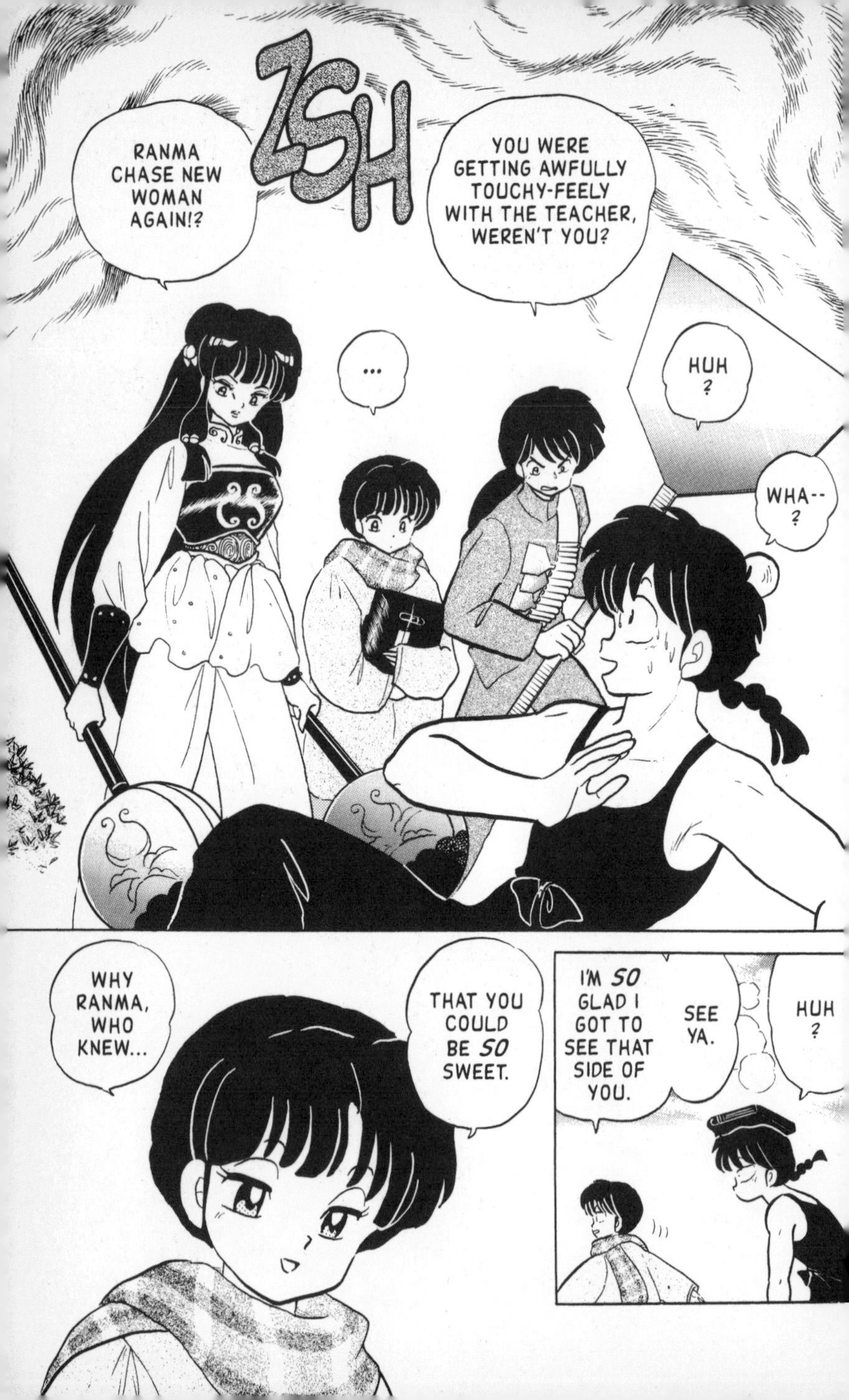
RANMA CHASE NEW WOMAN AGAIN!?
ZSH
YOU WERE GETTING AWFULLY TOUCHY-FEELY WITH THE TEACHER, WEREN'T YOU?
...
HUH?
WHA--?
WHY RANMA, WHO KNEW...
THAT YOU COULD BE *SO* SWEET.
I'M *SO* GLAD I GOT TO SEE THAT SIDE OF YOU.
SEE YA.
HUH?

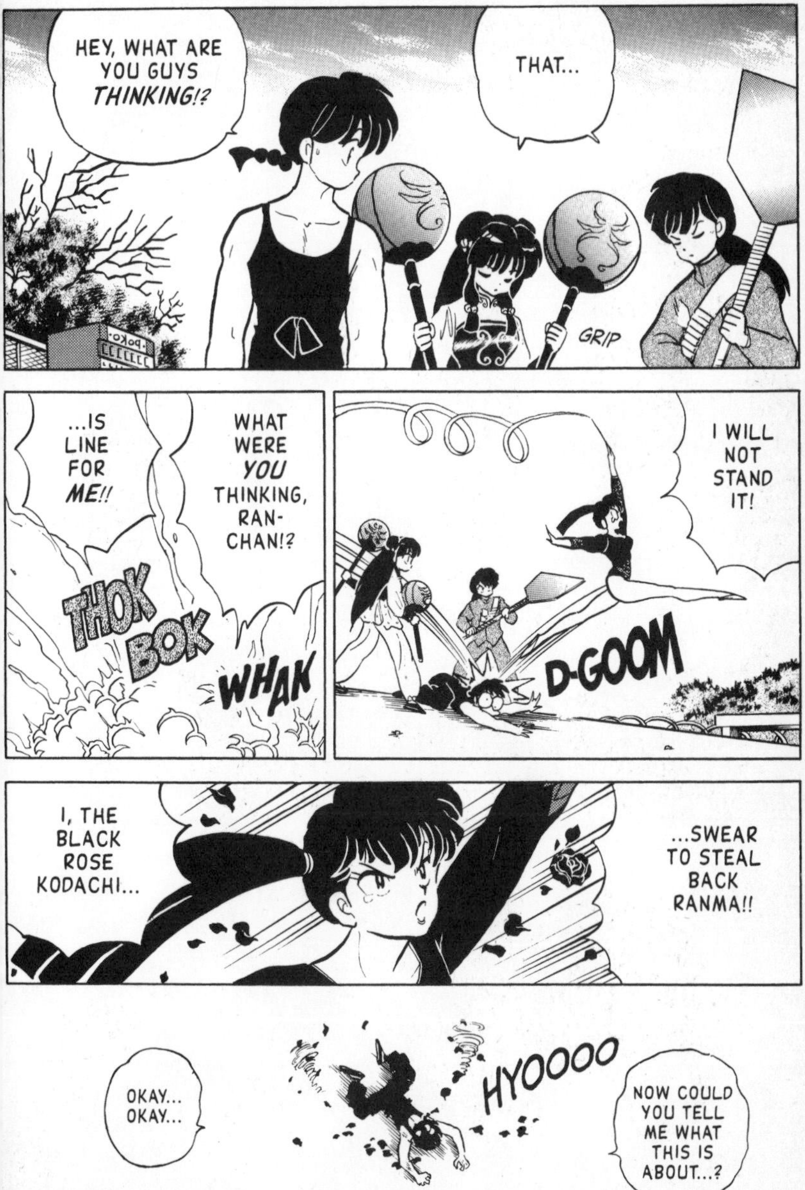
HEY, WHAT ARE YOU GUYS THINKING!?
THAT...
GRIP
...IS LINE FOR ME!!
WHAT WERE YOU THINKING, RAN-CHAN!?
THOK
BOK
WHAK
I WILL NOT STAND IT!
D-GOOM
I, THE BLACK ROSE KODACHI...
...SWEAR TO STEAL BACK RANMA!!
OKAY... OKAY...
HYOOOO
NOW COULD YOU TELL ME WHAT THIS IS ABOUT...?

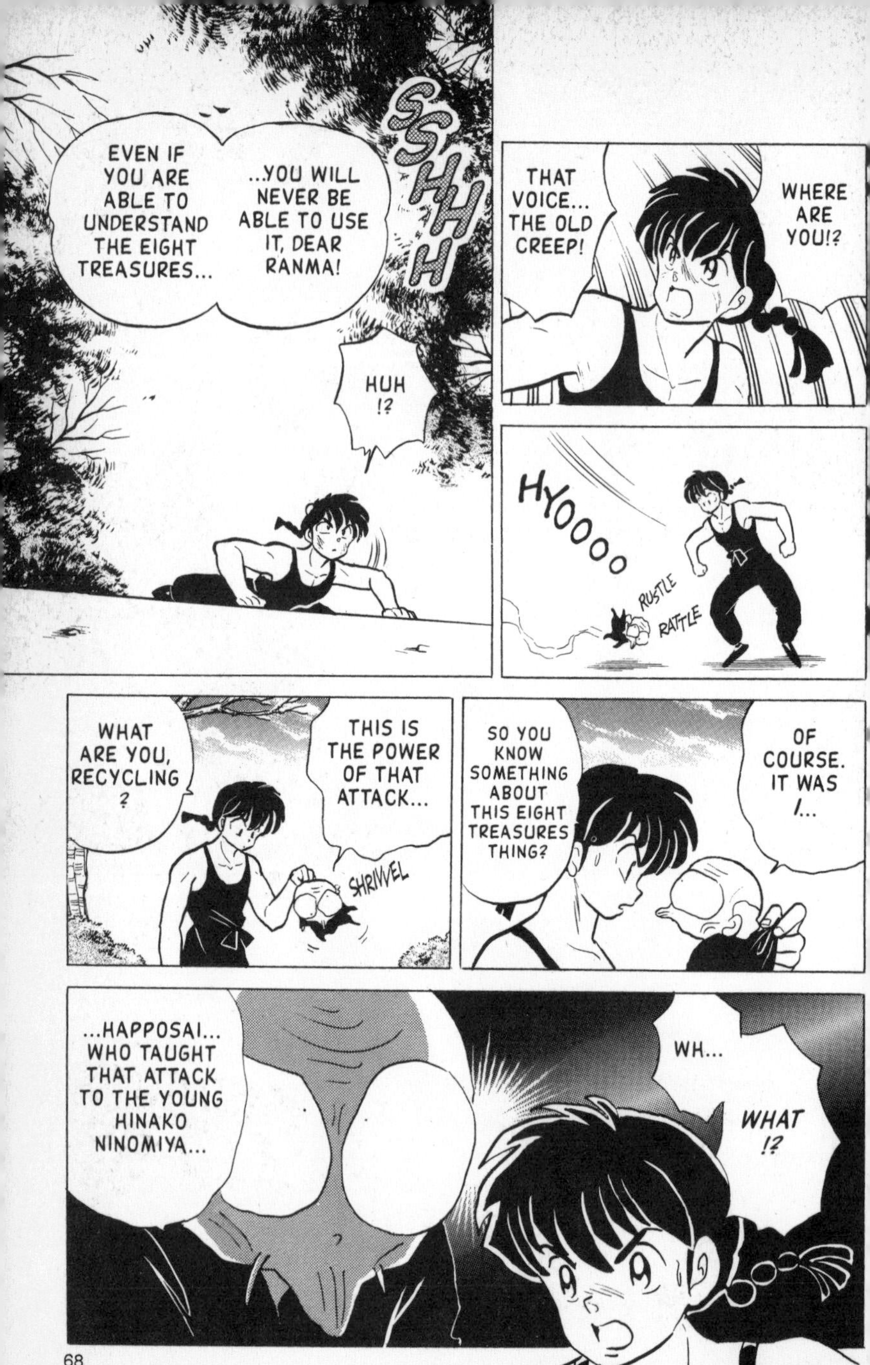
EVEN IF YOU ARE ABLE TO UNDERSTAND THE EIGHT TREASURES...
...YOU WILL NEVER BE ABLE TO USE IT, DEAR RANMA!
SSHHH
HUH !?
THAT VOICE... THE OLD CREEP!
WHERE ARE YOU!?
HYOOOO
RUSTLE
RATTLE
WHAT ARE YOU, RECYCLING ?
THIS IS THE POWER OF THAT ATTACK...
SHRIVVEL
SO YOU KNOW SOMETHING ABOUT THIS EIGHT TREASURES THING?
OF COURSE. IT WAS I...
...HAPPOSAI... WHO TAUGHT THAT ATTACK TO THE YOUNG HINAKO NINOMIYA...
WH...
WHAT !?

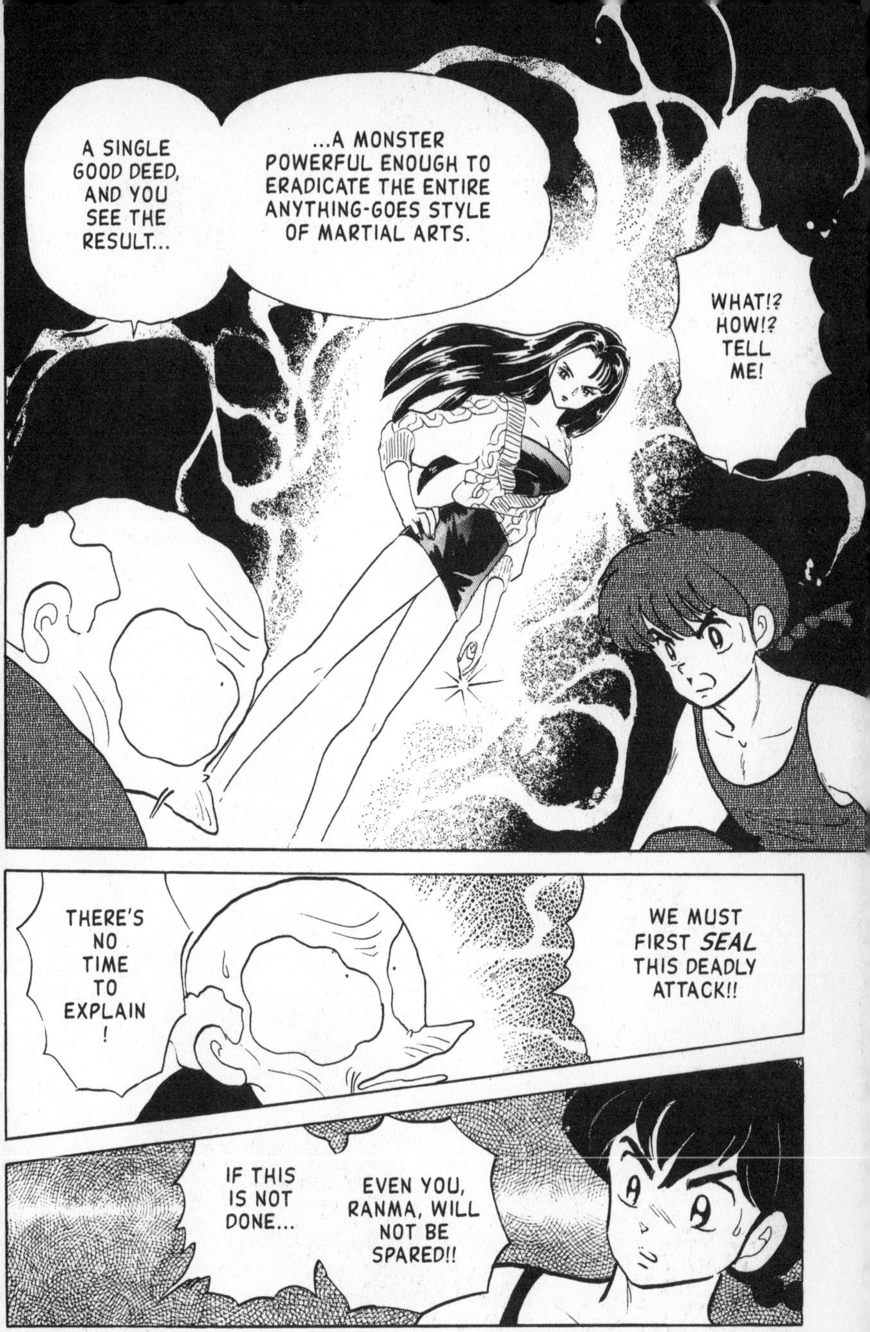
A SINGLE GOOD DEED, AND YOU SEE THE RESULT...
...A MONSTER POWERFUL ENOUGH TO ERADICATE THE ENTIRE ANYTHING-GOES STYLE OF MARTIAL ARTS.
WHAT!? HOW!? TELL ME!
THERE'S NO TIME TO EXPLAIN!
WE MUST FIRST SEAL THIS DEADLY ATTACK!!
IF THIS IS NOT DONE...
EVEN YOU, RANMA, WILL NOT BE SPARED!!

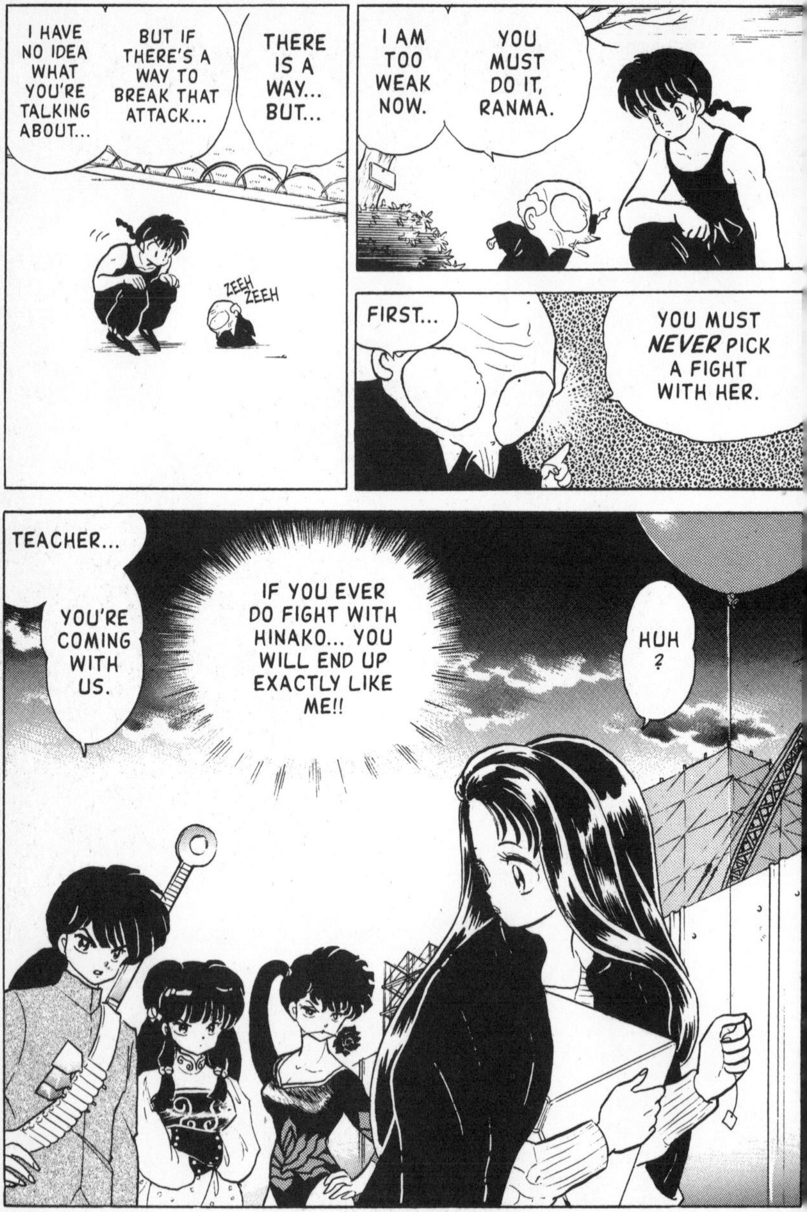
I HAVE NO IDEA WHAT YOU'RE TALKING ABOUT...
BUT IF THERE'S A WAY TO BREAK THAT ATTACK...
THERE IS A WAY... BUT...
ZEEH ZEEH
I AM TOO WEAK NOW.
YOU MUST DO IT, RANMA.
FIRST...
YOU MUST *NEVER* PICK A FIGHT WITH HER.
TEACHER...
YOU'RE COMING WITH US.
IF YOU EVER DO FIGHT WITH HINAKO... YOU WILL END UP EXACTLY LIKE ME!!
HUH?

Part 5

THE WORLD'S MOST POWERFUL WOMAN

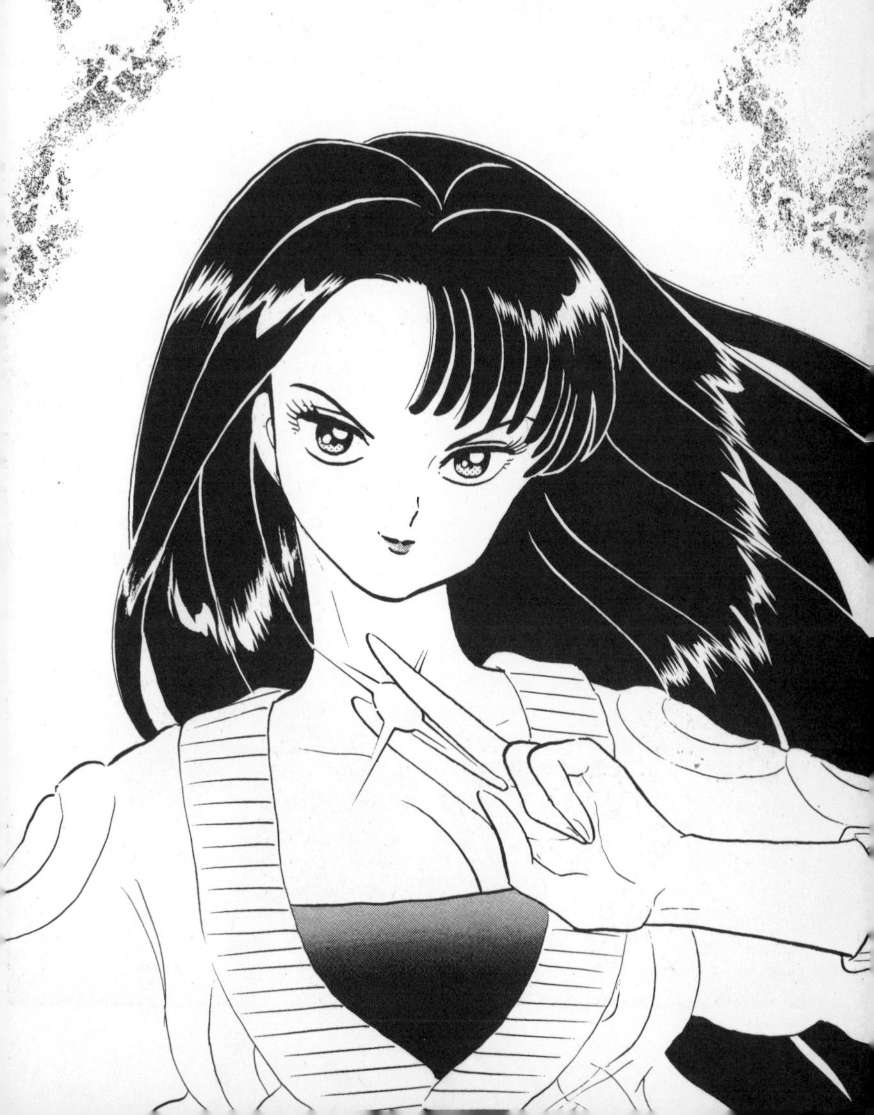

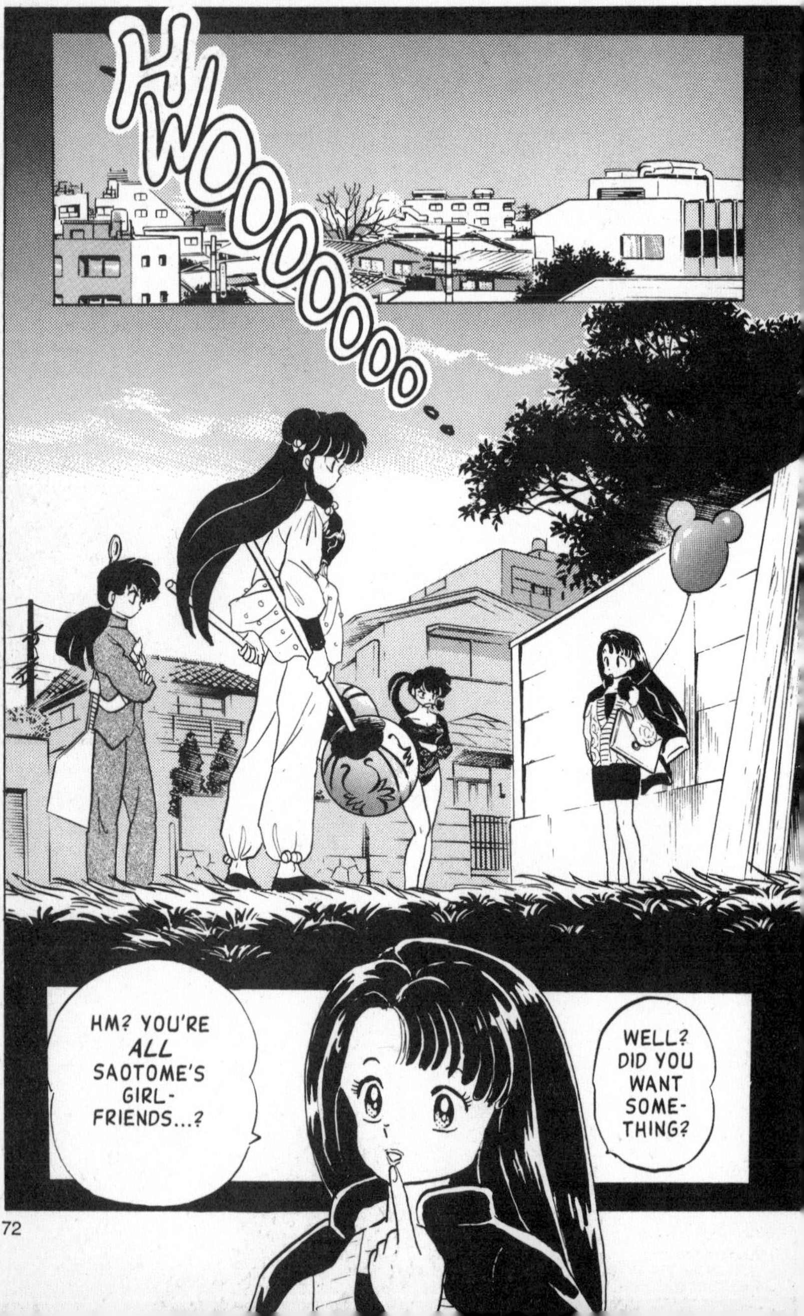
HWOOOOOOO...
HM? YOU'RE ALL SAOTOME'S GIRL-FRIENDS...?
WELL? DID YOU WANT SOME-THING?

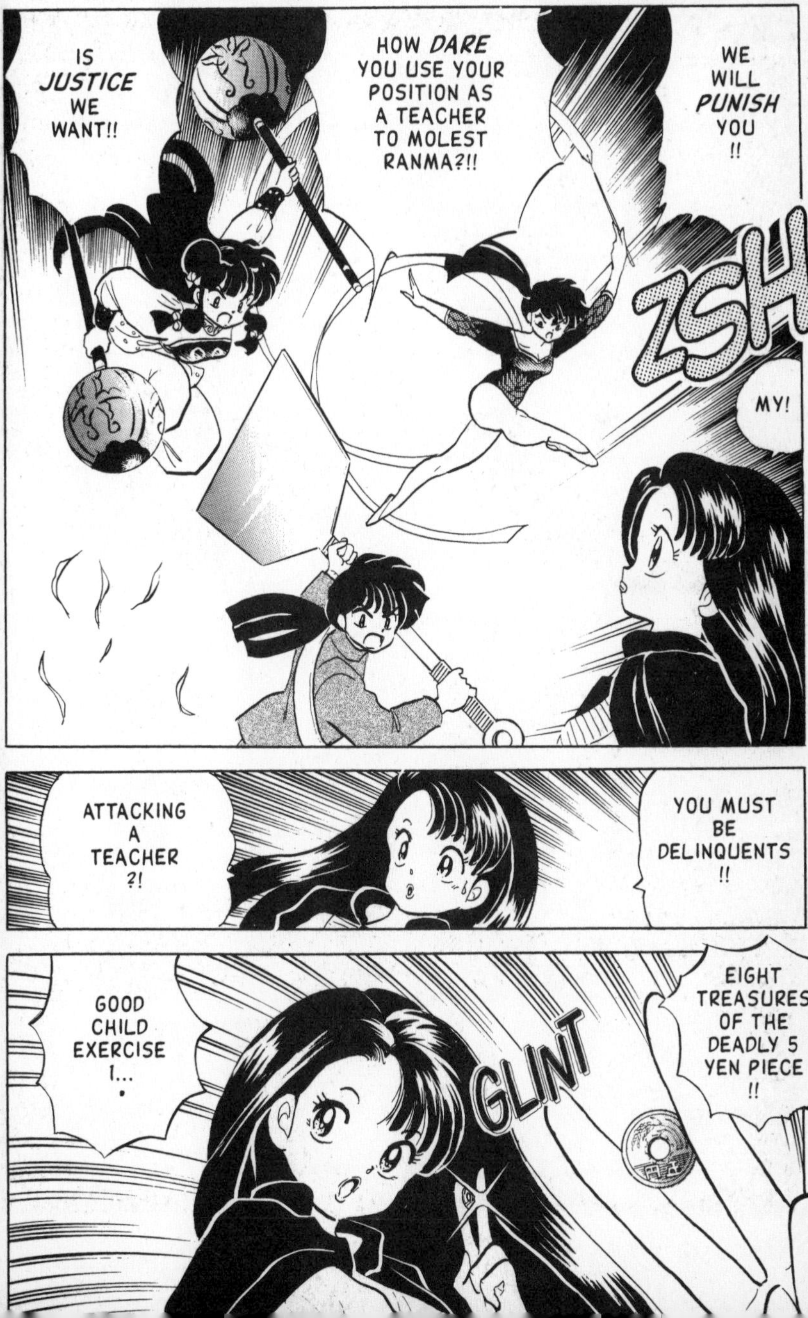
IS JUSTICE WE WANT!!
HOW DARE YOU USE YOUR POSITION AS A TEACHER TO MOLEST RANMA?!!
WE WILL PUNISH YOU !!
ZSH
MY!
ATTACKING A TEACHER ?!
YOU MUST BE DELINQUENTS !!
GOOD CHILD EXERCISE 1...
GLINT
EIGHT TREASURES OF THE DEADLY 5 YEN PIECE !!

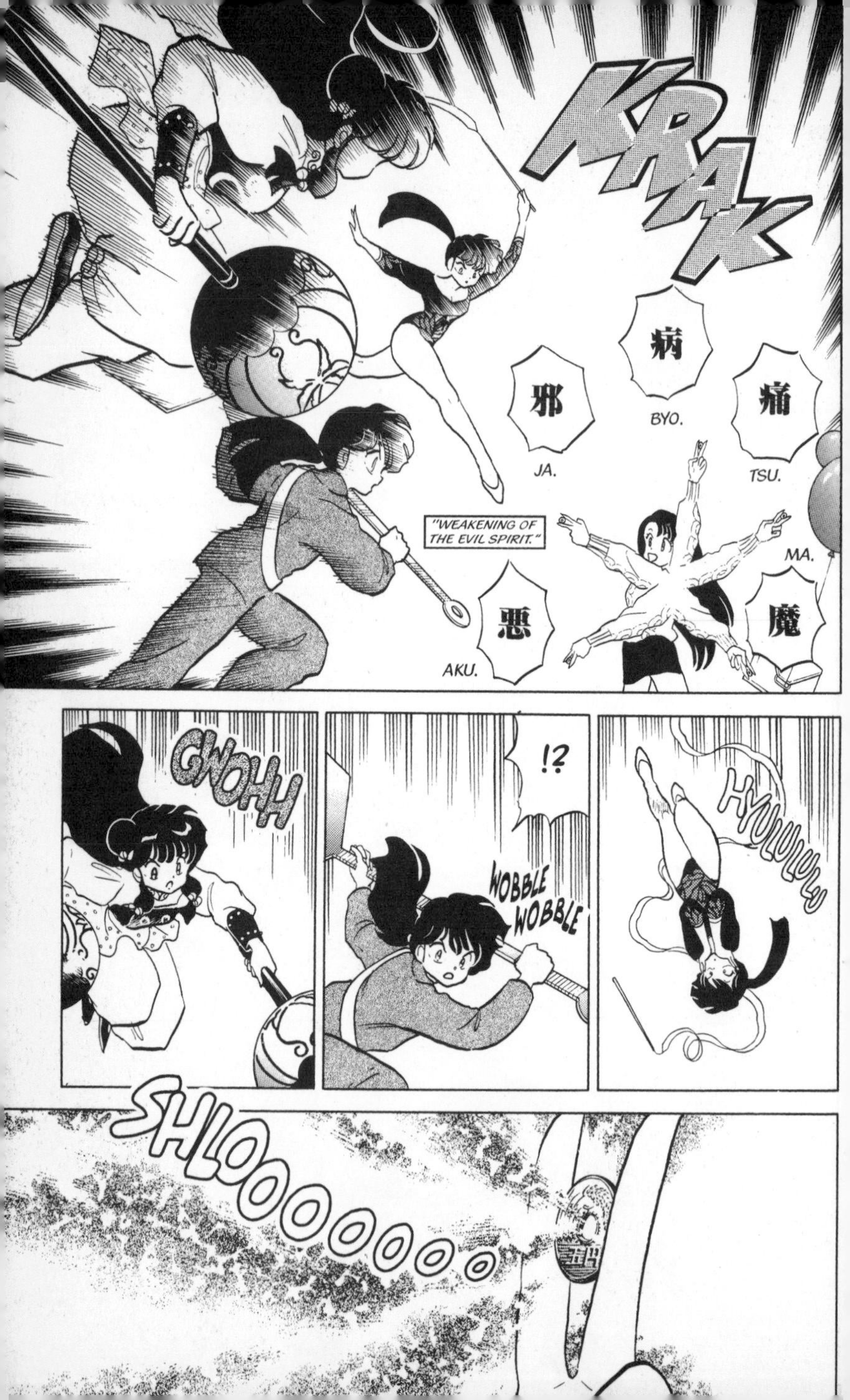
KRAK
邪
JA.
病
BYO.
痛
TSU.
"WEAKENING OF THE EVIL SPIRIT."
悪
AKU.
MA.
魔
GWOHH
!?
WOBBLE WOBBLE
HYULULULU
SHLOOOOOOO

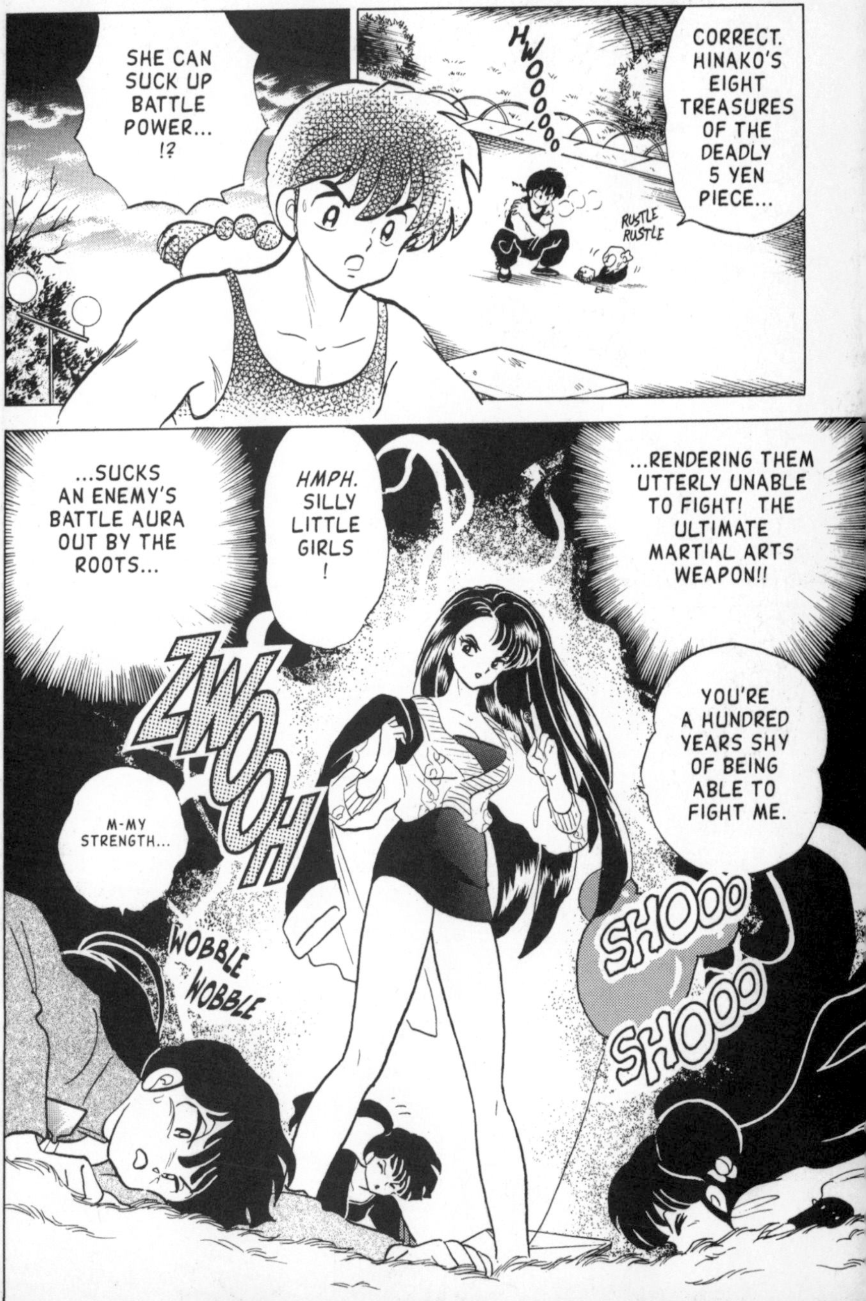
SHE CAN SUCK UP BATTLE POWER... !?
HWOOOOOOO
CORRECT. HINAKO'S EIGHT TREASURES OF THE DEADLY 5 YEN PIECE...
RUSTLE RUSTLE
...SUCKS AN ENEMY'S BATTLE AURA OUT BY THE ROOTS...
HMPH. SILLY LITTLE GIRLS !
...RENDERING THEM UTTERLY UNABLE TO FIGHT! THE ULTIMATE MARTIAL ARTS WEAPON!!
ZWOOOH
M-MY STRENGTH...
YOU'RE A HUNDRED YEARS SHY OF BEING ABLE TO FIGHT ME.
WOBBLE WOBBLE
SHOOO SHOOO

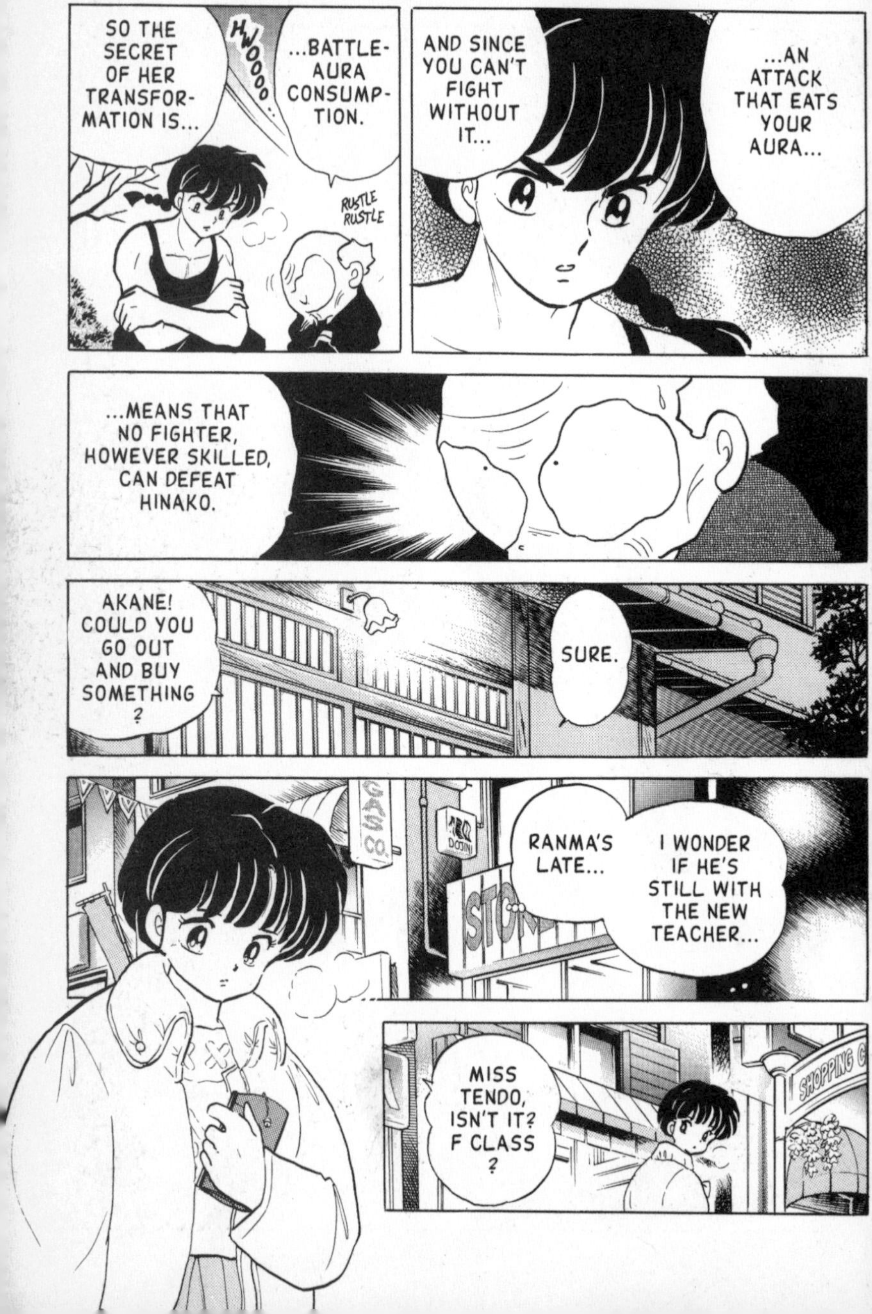
SO THE SECRET OF HER TRANSFORMATION IS...
HWOOOOO
...BATTLE-AURA CONSUMPTION.
RUSTLE RUSTLE
AND SINCE YOU CAN'T FIGHT WITHOUT IT...
...AN ATTACK THAT EATS YOUR AURA...
...MEANS THAT NO FIGHTER, HOWEVER SKILLED, CAN DEFEAT HINAKO.
AKANE! COULD YOU GO OUT AND BUY SOMETHING?
SURE.
GAS CO.
DOJIN
STO
RANMA'S LATE...
I WONDER IF HE'S STILL WITH THE NEW TEACHER...
MISS TENDO, ISN'T IT? F CLASS?
SHOPPING C

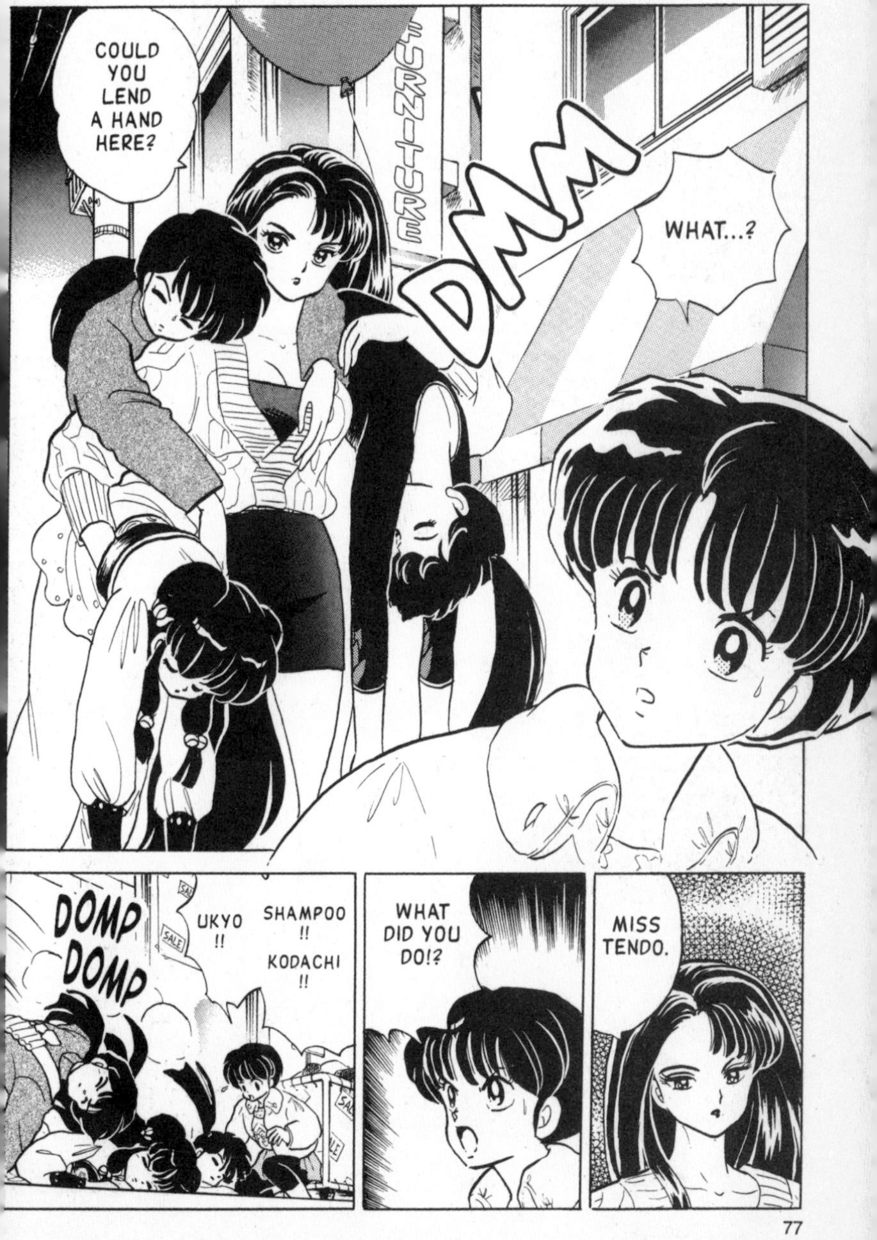
COULD YOU LEND A HAND HERE?
FURNITURE
DMM
WHAT...?
DOMP DOMP
UKYO !!
SHAMPOO !!
KODACHI !!
WHAT DID YOU DO!?
MISS TENDO.

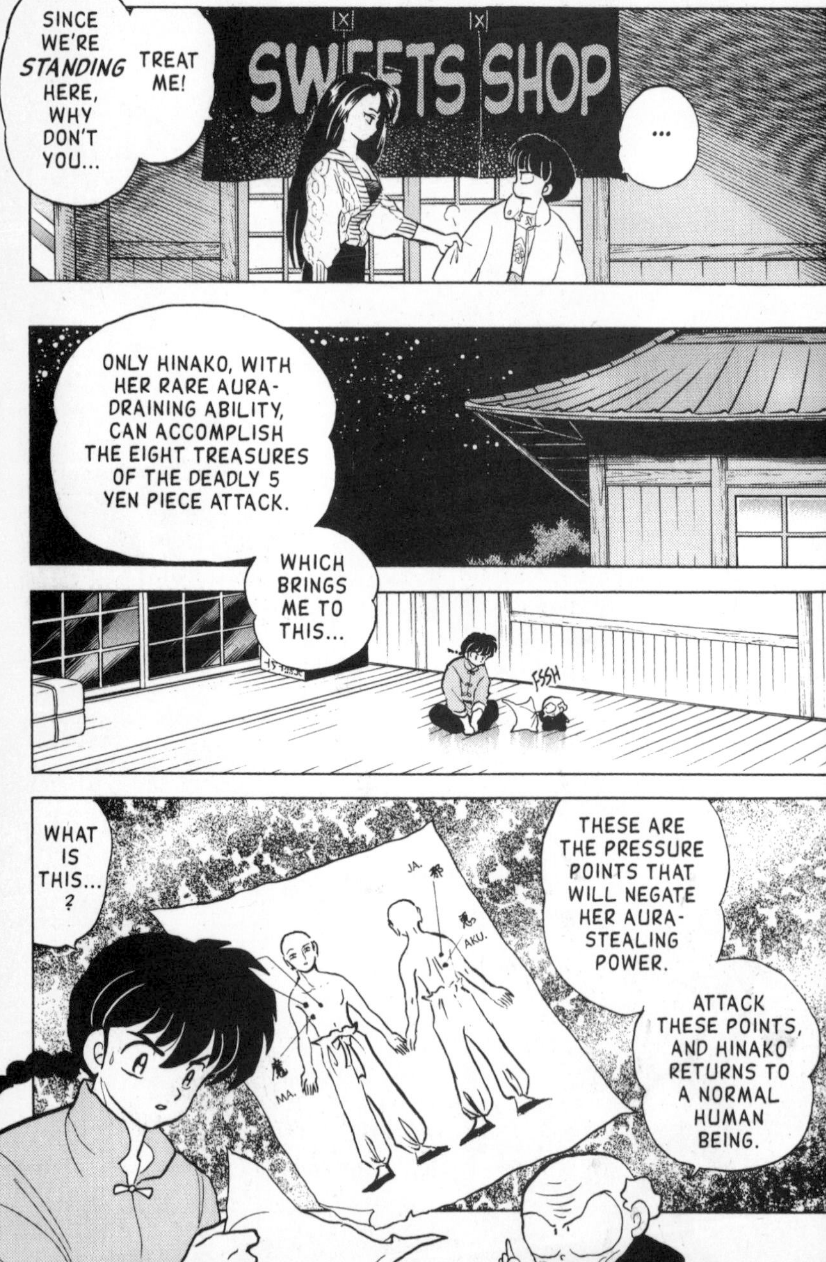

SINCE WE'RE *STANDING* HERE, WHY DON'T YOU...
TREAT ME!
SWEETS SHOP
...
ONLY HINAKO, WITH HER RARE AURA-DRAINING ABILITY, CAN ACCOMPLISH THE EIGHT TREASURES OF THE DEADLY 5 YEN PIECE ATTACK.
WHICH BRINGS ME TO THIS...
FSSH
WHAT IS THIS...?
JA.
AKU.
MA.
THESE ARE THE PRESSURE POINTS THAT WILL NEGATE HER AURA-STEALING POWER.
ATTACK THESE POINTS, AND HINAKO RETURNS TO A NORMAL HUMAN BEING.

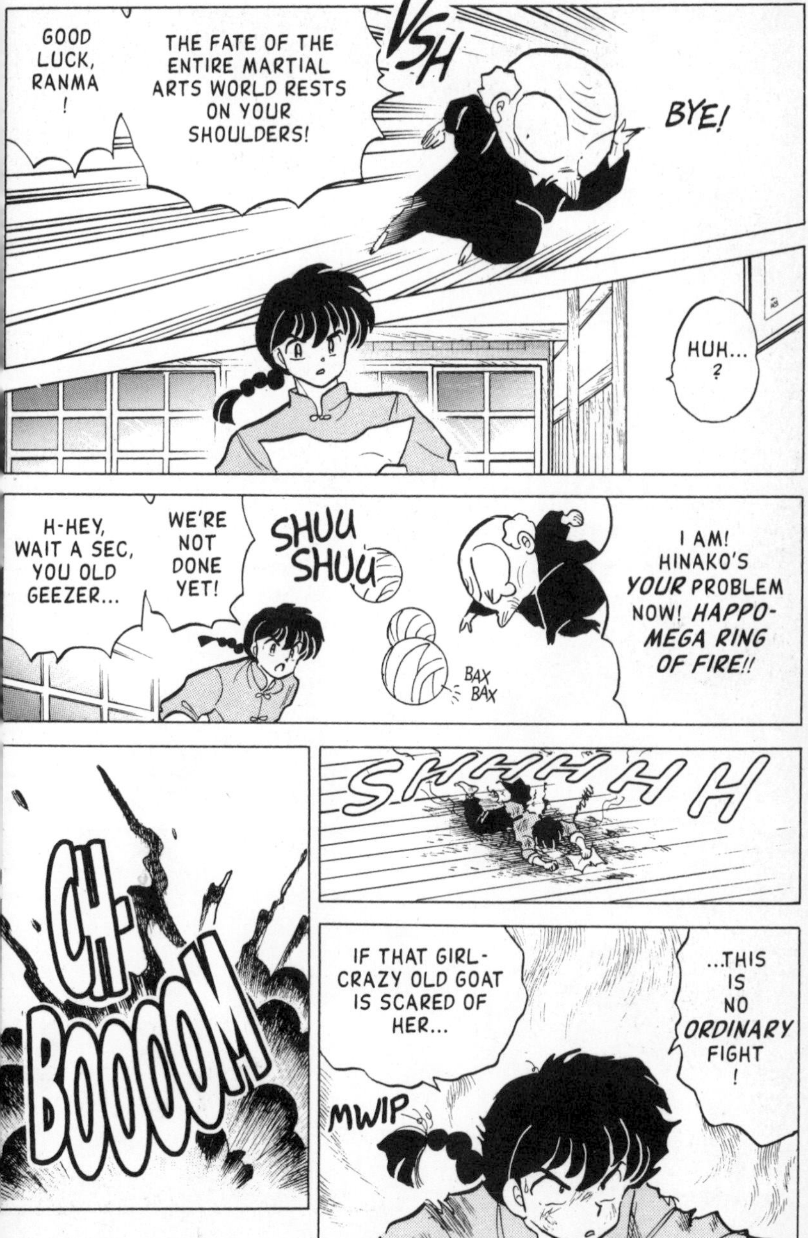
GOOD LUCK, RANMA !
THE FATE OF THE ENTIRE MARTIAL ARTS WORLD RESTS ON YOUR SHOULDERS!
VSH
BYE!
HUH... ?
H-HEY, WAIT A SEC, YOU OLD GEEZER...
WE'RE NOT DONE YET!
SHUU SHUU
BAX BAX
I AM! HINAKO'S YOUR PROBLEM NOW! HAPPO-MEGA RING OF FIRE!!
CH-BOOOOM
SHHHHHH
IF THAT GIRL-CRAZY OLD GOAT IS SCARED OF HER...
...THIS IS NO ORDINARY FIGHT !
MWIP

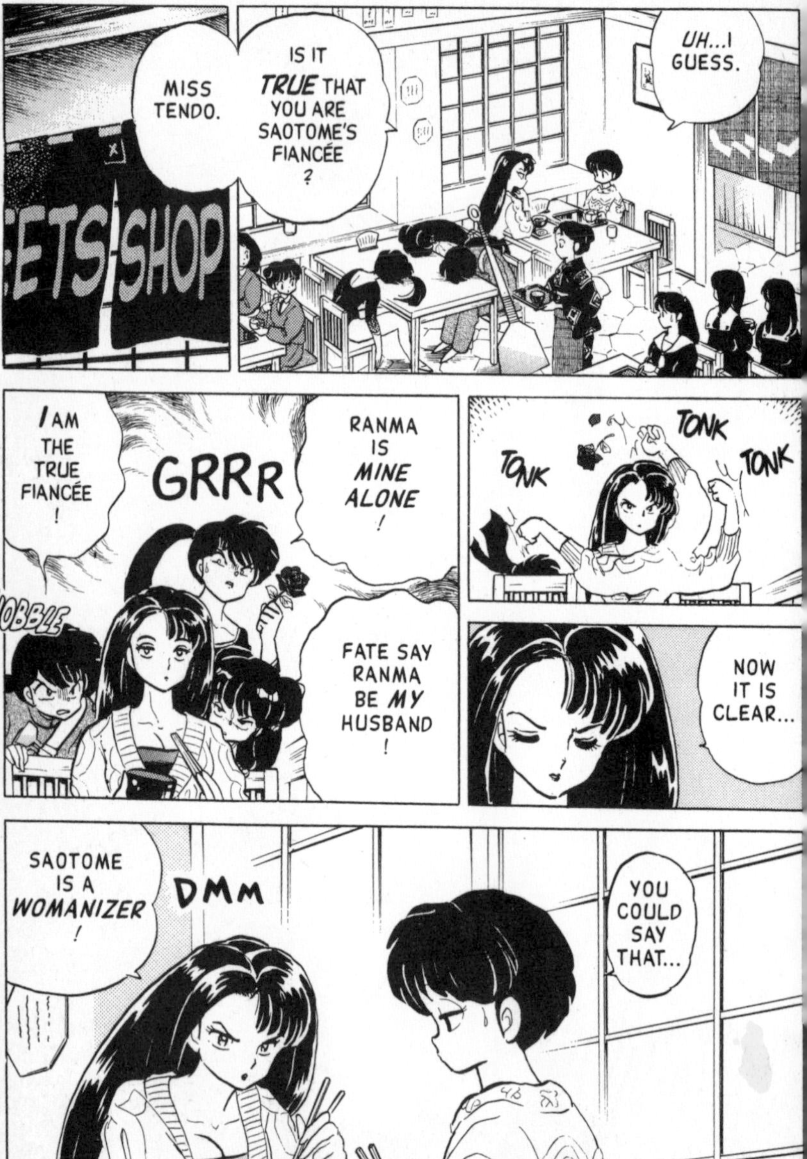

ETS SHOP
MISS TENDO.
IS IT TRUE THAT YOU ARE SAOTOME'S FIANCÉE ?
UH...I GUESS.
I AM THE TRUE FIANCÉE !
GRRR
RANMA IS MINE ALONE !
WOBBLE
FATE SAY RANMA BE MY HUSBAND !
TONK
TONK
TONK
NOW IT IS CLEAR...
SAOTOME IS A WOMANIZER !
DMM
YOU COULD SAY THAT...

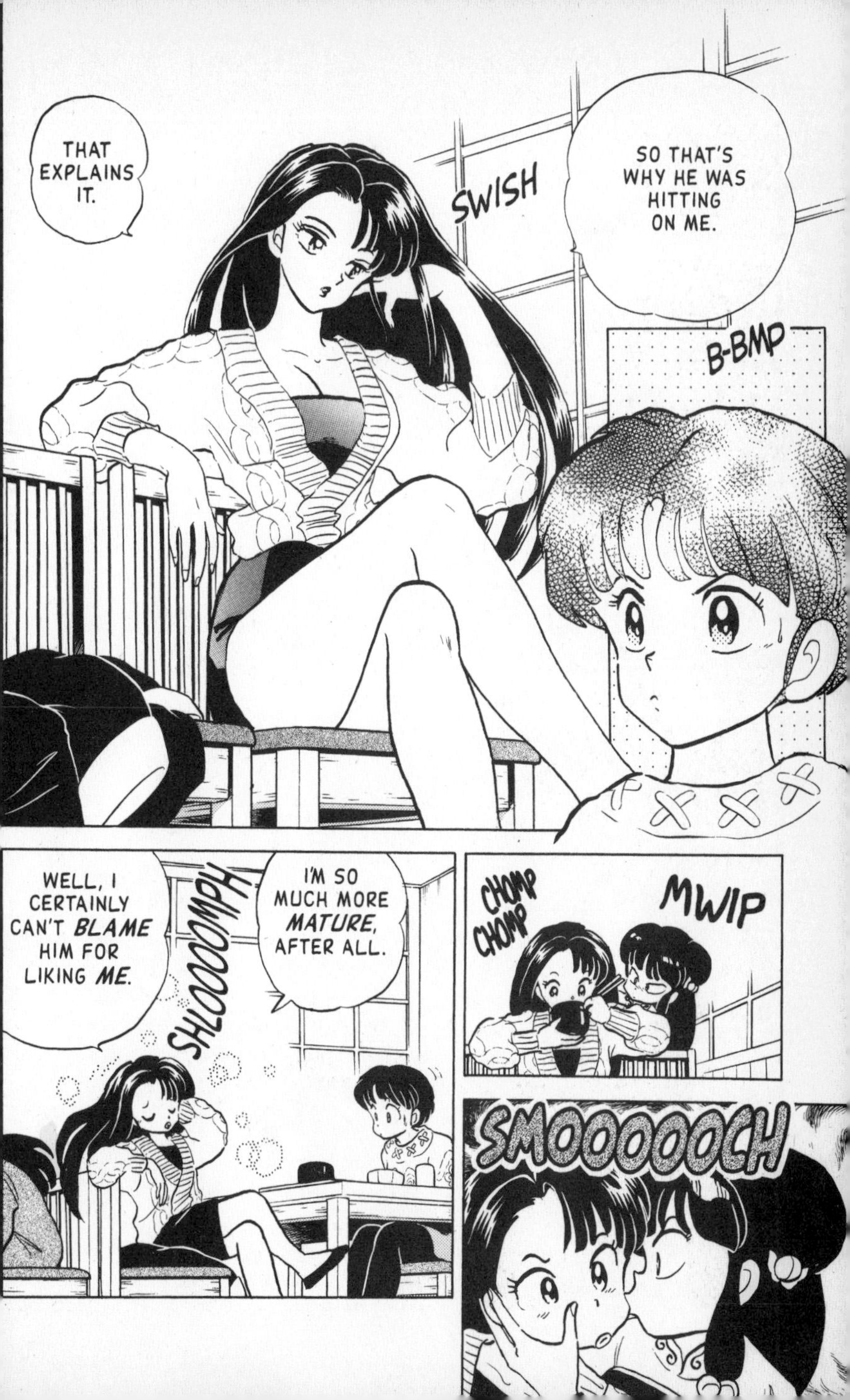
THAT EXPLAINS IT.
SWISH
SO THAT'S WHY HE WAS HITTING ON ME.
B-BMP
WELL, I CERTAINLY CAN'T *BLAME* HIM FOR LIKING *ME*.
SHLOOOOOMPH
I'M SO MUCH MORE *MATURE*, AFTER ALL.
CHOMP CHOMP
MWIP
SMOOOOOCH

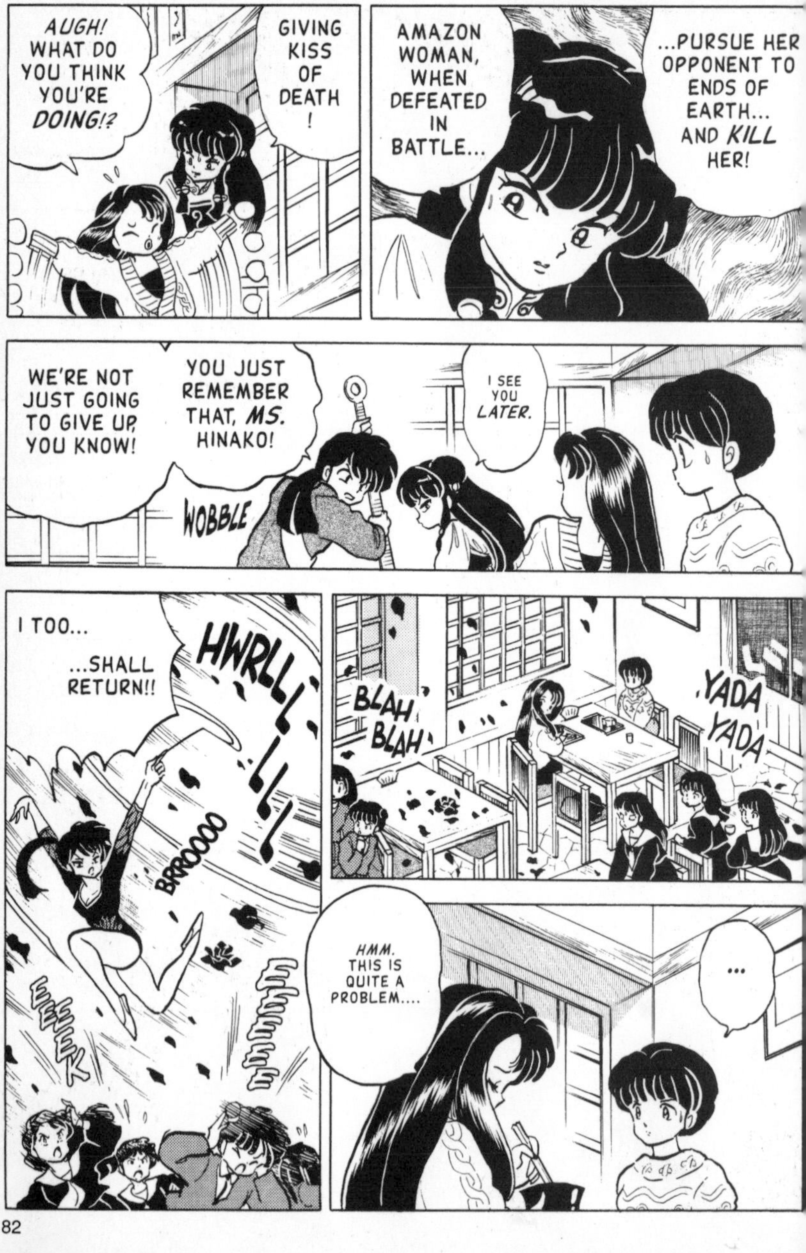
AUGH! WHAT DO YOU THINK YOU'RE DOING!?
GIVING KISS OF DEATH!
AMAZON WOMAN, WHEN DEFEATED IN BATTLE...
...PURSUE HER OPPONENT TO ENDS OF EARTH... AND KILL HER!
WE'RE NOT JUST GOING TO GIVE UP, YOU KNOW!
YOU JUST REMEMBER THAT, MS. HINAKO!
WOBBLE
I SEE YOU LATER.
I TOO...
...SHALL RETURN!!
HWRLLL
BRROOOO
EEEEK
BLAH BLAH
YADA YADA
HMM. THIS IS QUITE A PROBLEM....
...

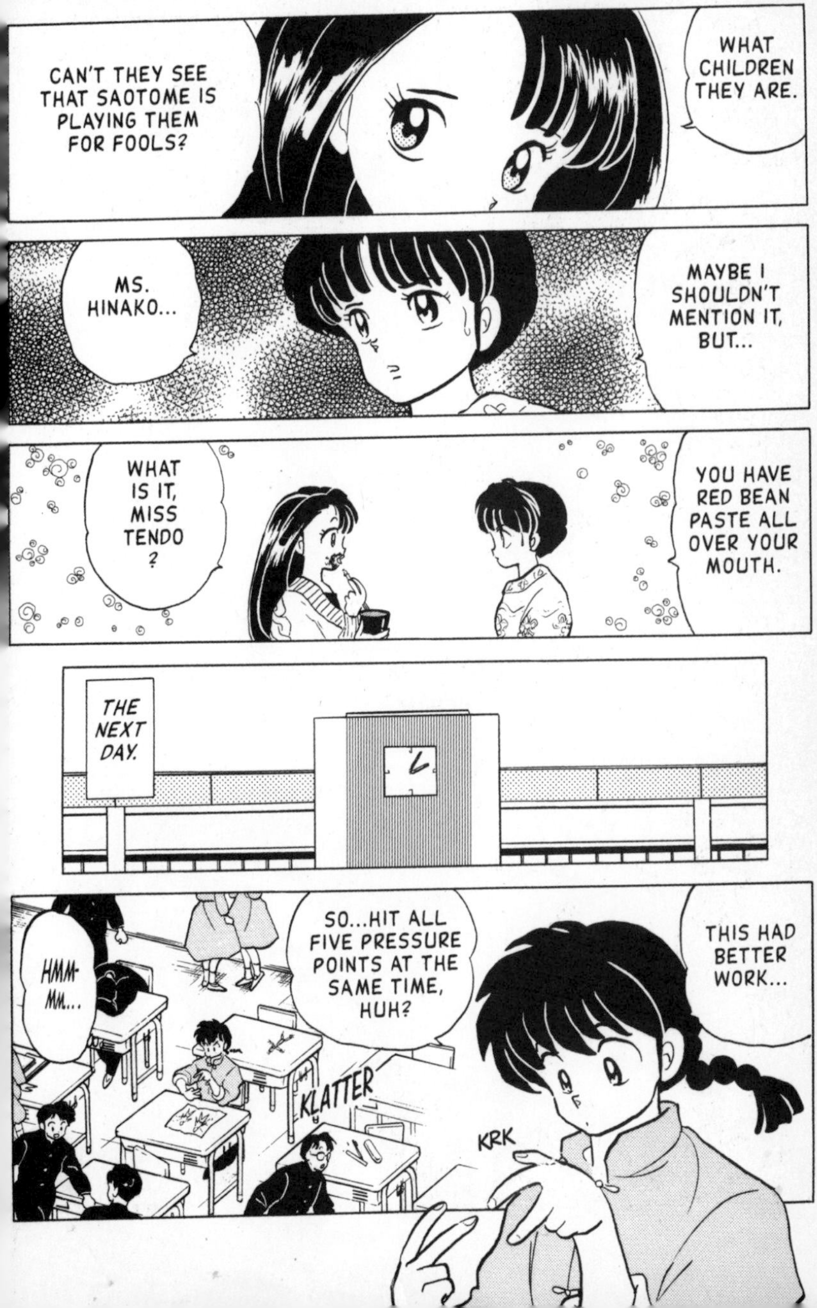
CAN'T THEY SEE THAT SAOTOME IS PLAYING THEM FOR FOOLS?
WHAT CHILDREN THEY ARE.
MS. HINAKO...
MAYBE I SHOULDN'T MENTION IT, BUT...
WHAT IS IT, MISS TENDO?
YOU HAVE RED BEAN PASTE ALL OVER YOUR MOUTH.
THE NEXT DAY.
HMM-MM...
SO...HIT ALL FIVE PRESSURE POINTS AT THE SAME TIME, HUH?
KLATTER
KRK
THIS HAD BETTER WORK...

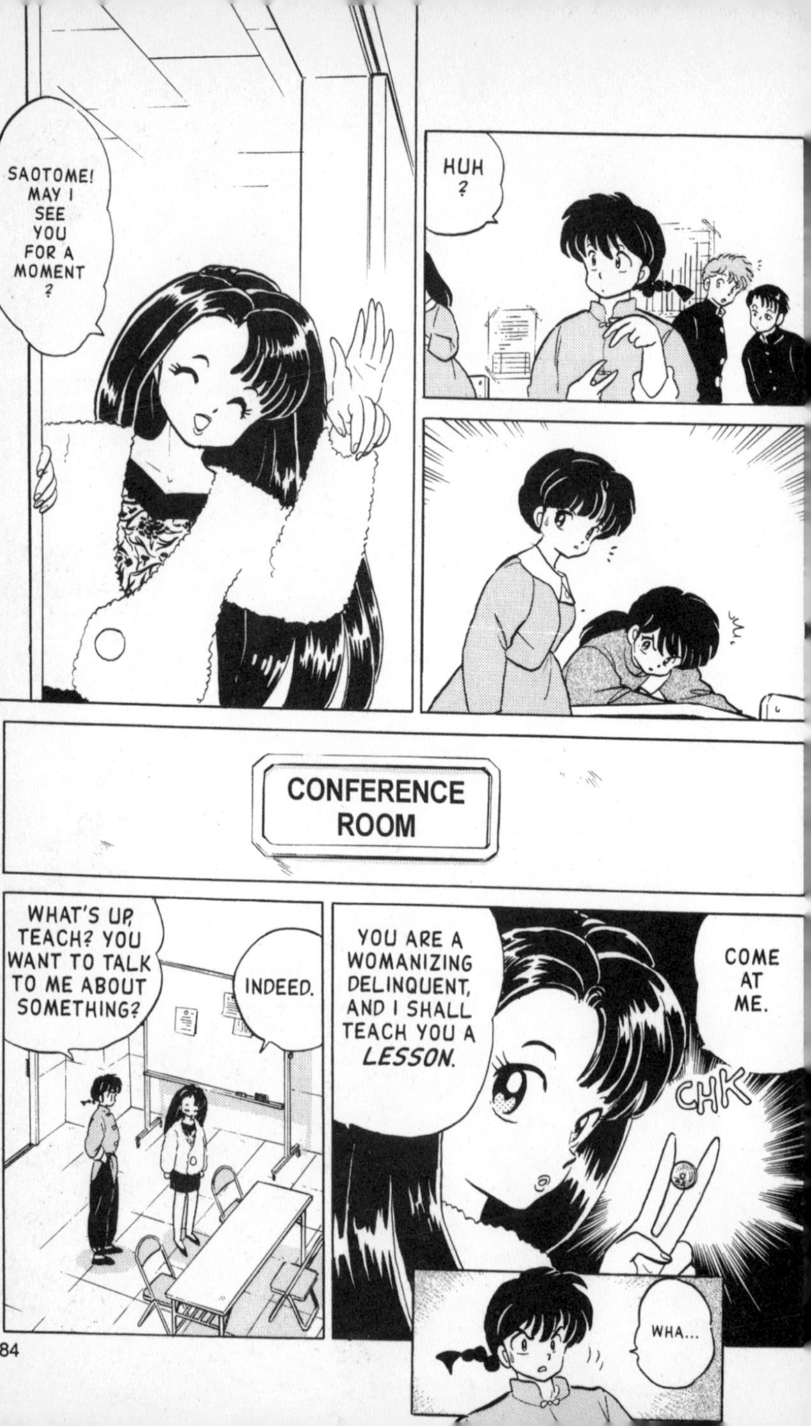
SAOTOME! MAY I SEE YOU FOR A MOMENT?
HUH?
CONFERENCE ROOM
WHAT'S UP, TEACH? YOU WANT TO TALK TO ME ABOUT SOMETHING?
INDEED.
YOU ARE A WOMANIZING DELINQUENT, AND I SHALL TEACH YOU A *LESSON*.
COME AT ME.
CHK
WHA...

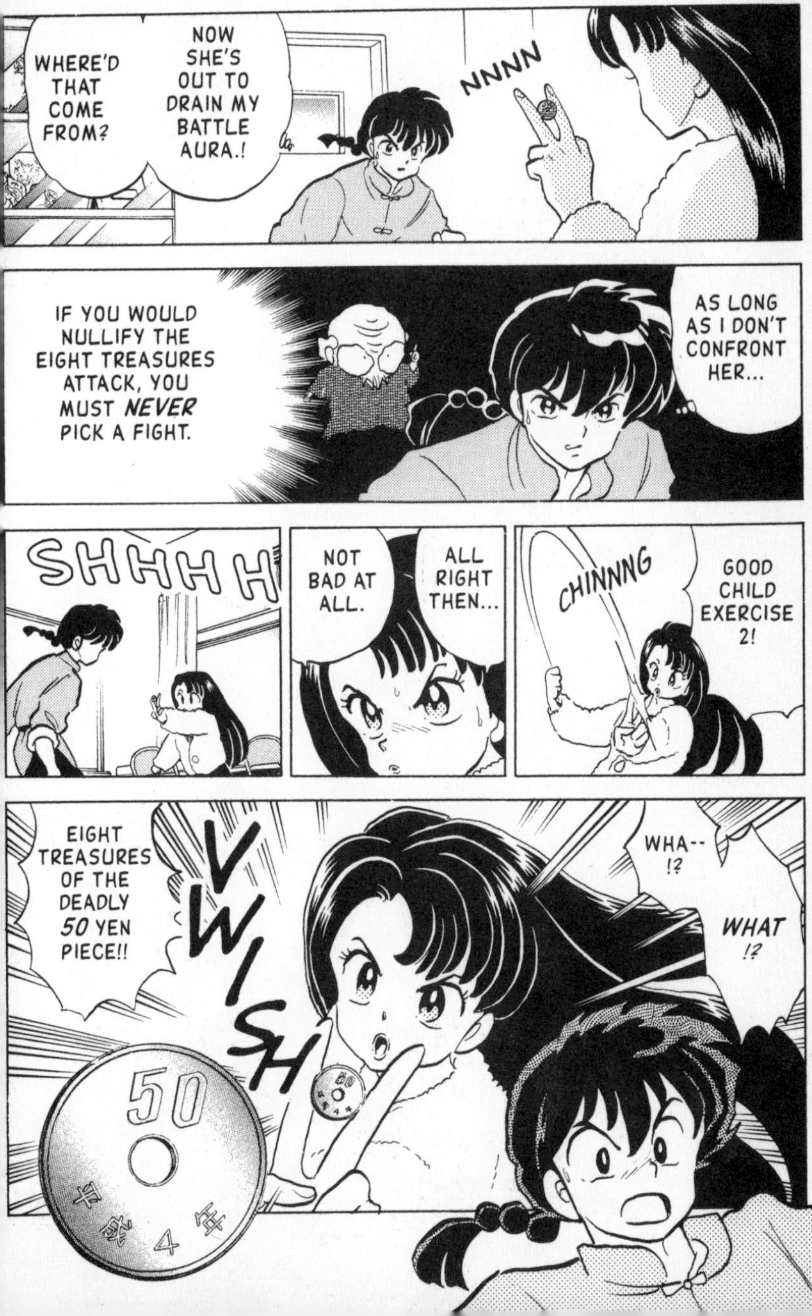
WHERE'D THAT COME FROM?
NOW SHE'S OUT TO DRAIN MY BATTLE AURA.!
NNNN
IF YOU WOULD NULLIFY THE EIGHT TREASURES ATTACK, YOU MUST *NEVER* PICK A FIGHT.
AS LONG AS I DON'T CONFRONT HER...
SHHHHH
NOT BAD AT ALL.
ALL RIGHT THEN...
CHINNNG
GOOD CHILD EXERCISE 2!
EIGHT TREASURES OF THE DEADLY *50* YEN PIECE!!
VWISH
WHA-- !?
WHAT !?
50
平成4年

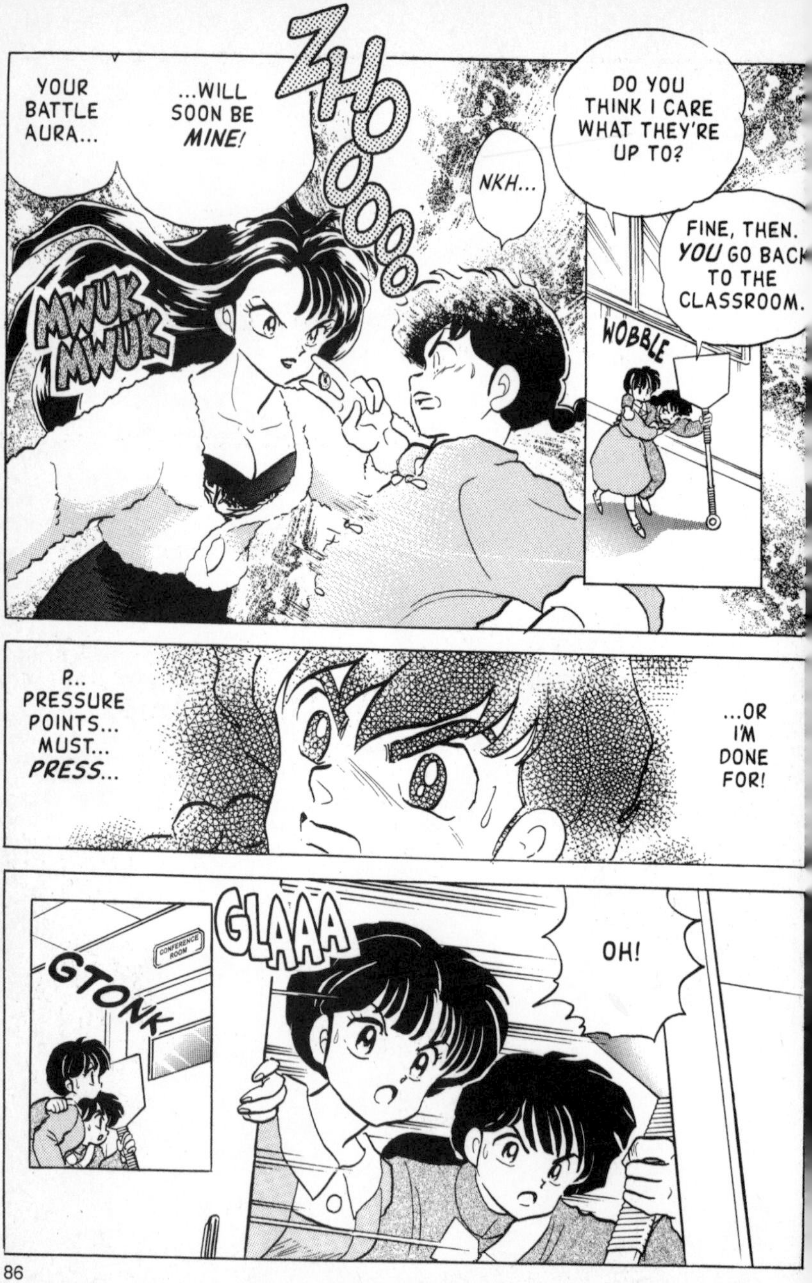
YOUR BATTLE AURA...
...WILL SOON BE *MINE!*
ZHOOOOOO
MWUK MWUK
NKH...
DO YOU THINK I CARE WHAT THEY'RE UP TO?
FINE, THEN. *YOU* GO BACK TO THE CLASSROOM.
WOBBLE
P... PRESSURE POINTS... MUST... *PRESS*...
...OR I'M DONE FOR!
CONFERENCE ROOM
GTONK
GLAAA
OH!

Part 6

GO FOR THE PRESSURE POINTS!

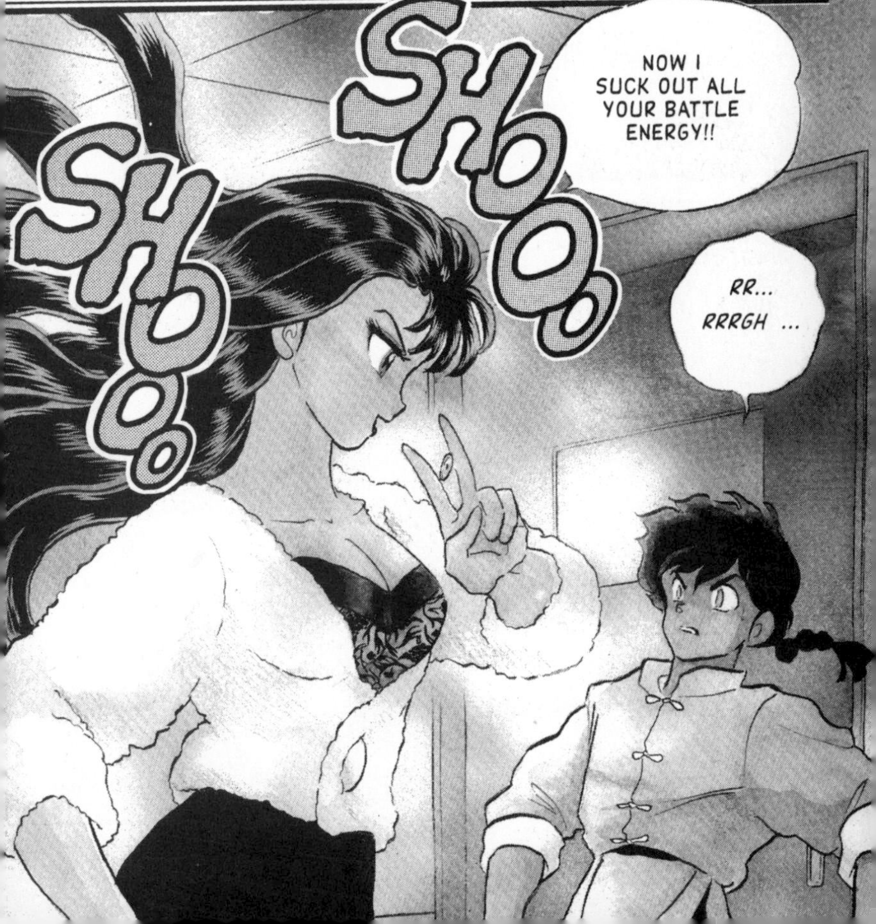
SHOOO
SHOOO
NOW I SUCK OUT ALL YOUR BATTLE ENERGY!!
RR... RRRGH ...

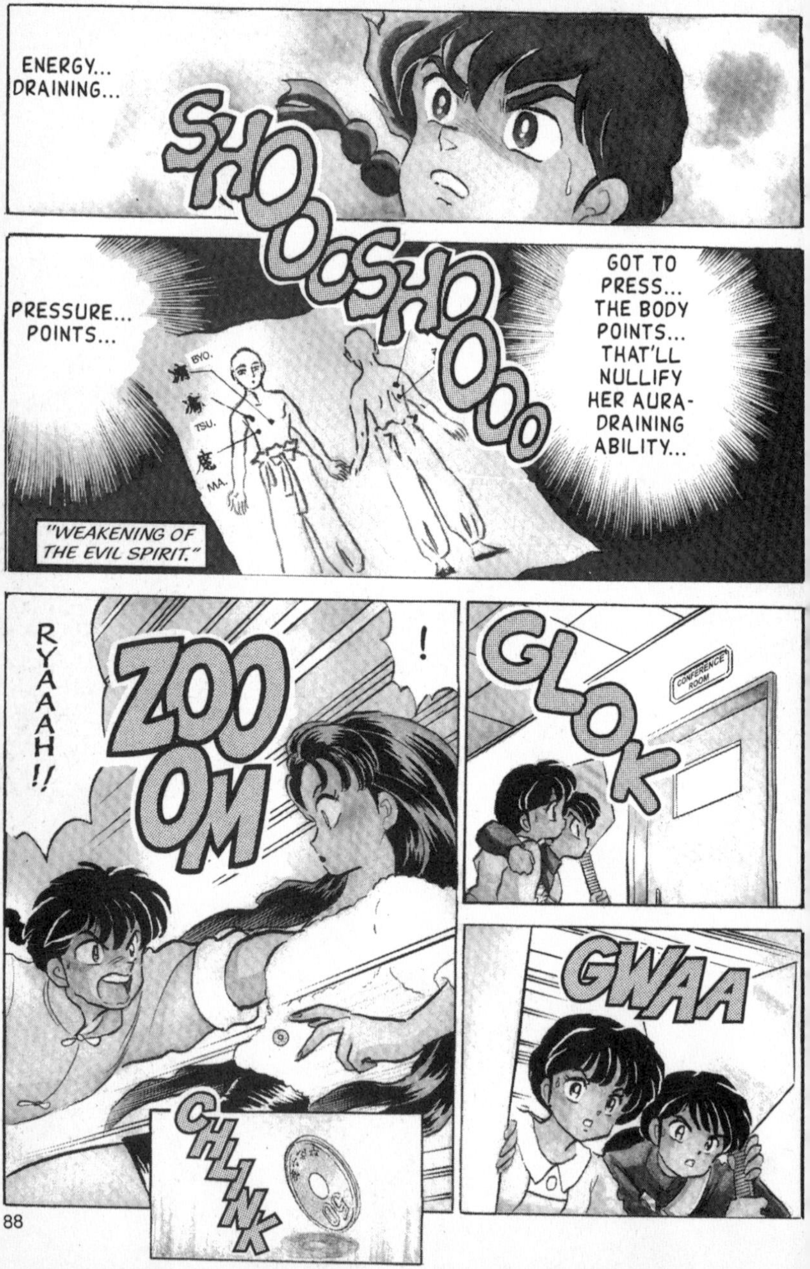

ENERGY... DRAINING...
SHOOOSHOOOOOO
PRESSURE... POINTS...
BYO.
TSU.
MA.
GOT TO PRESS... THE BODY POINTS... THAT'LL NULLIFY HER AURA-DRAINING ABILITY...
"WEAKENING OF THE EVIL SPIRIT."
RYAAAAH!!
ZOOOM
!
CHLINK
GLOK
CONFERENCE ROOM
GWAA

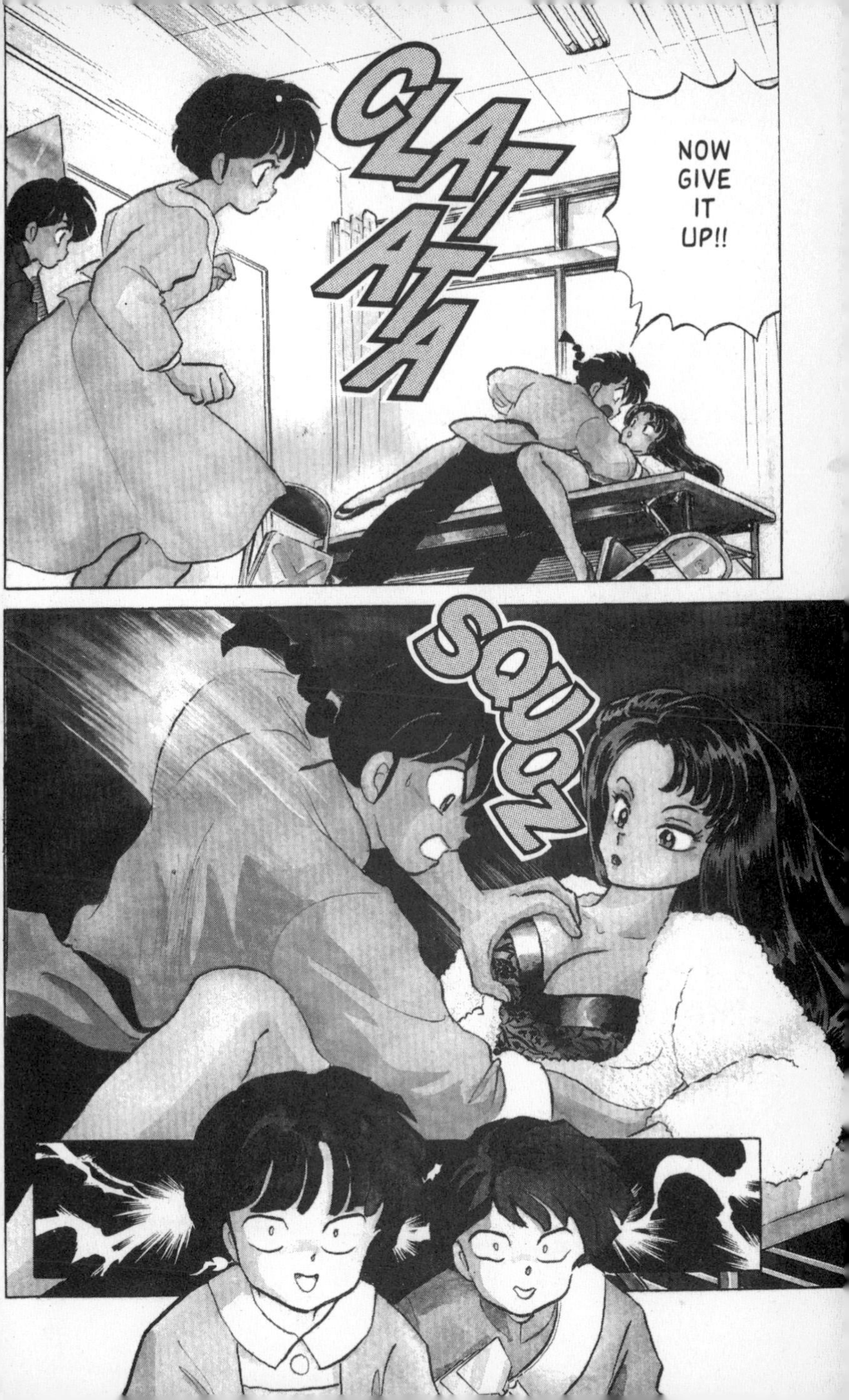
CLATATA
NOW GIVE IT UP!!
SQUOZ

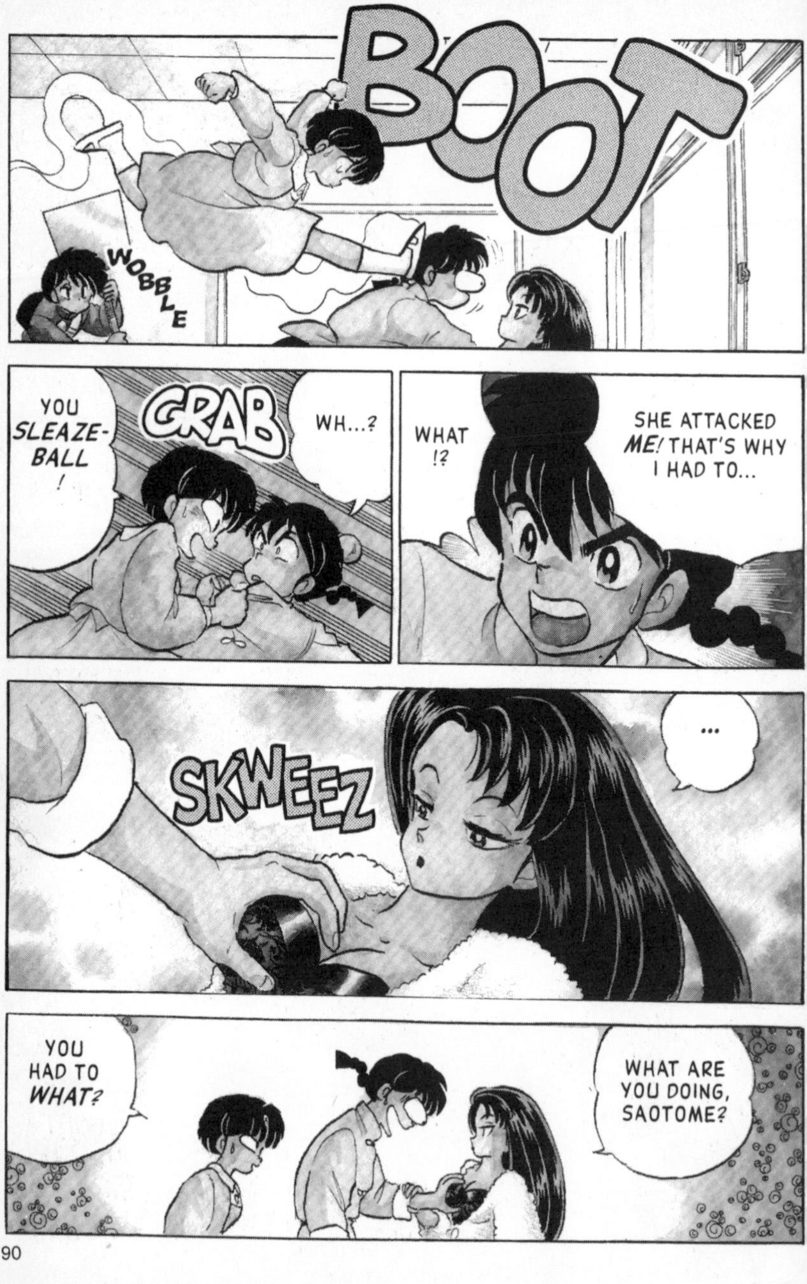
BOOT
WOBBLE
YOU SLEAZE-BALL!
GRAB
WH...?
WHAT !?
SHE ATTACKED ME! THAT'S WHY I HAD TO...
SKWEEZ
...
YOU HAD TO WHAT?
WHAT ARE YOU DOING, SAOTOME?

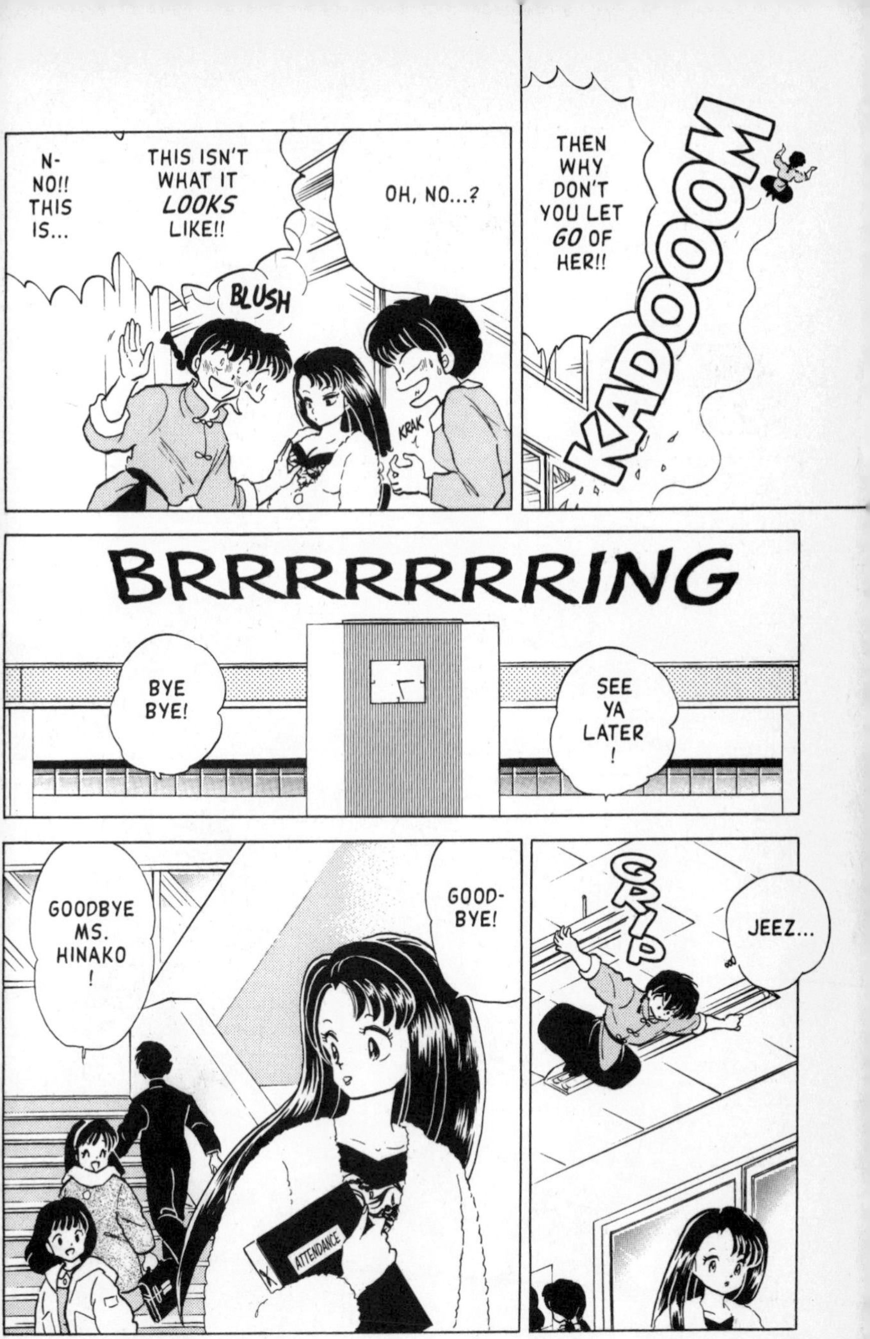
N-
NO!! THIS IS...
THIS ISN'T WHAT IT *LOOKS* LIKE!!
OH, NO...?
BLUSH
KRAK
THEN WHY DON'T YOU LET *GO* OF HER!!
KADOOOM
BRRRRRRRRING
BYE BYE!
SEE YA LATER!
GOODBYE MS. HINAKO!
GOOD-BYE!
ATTENDANCE
GRIP
JEEZ...

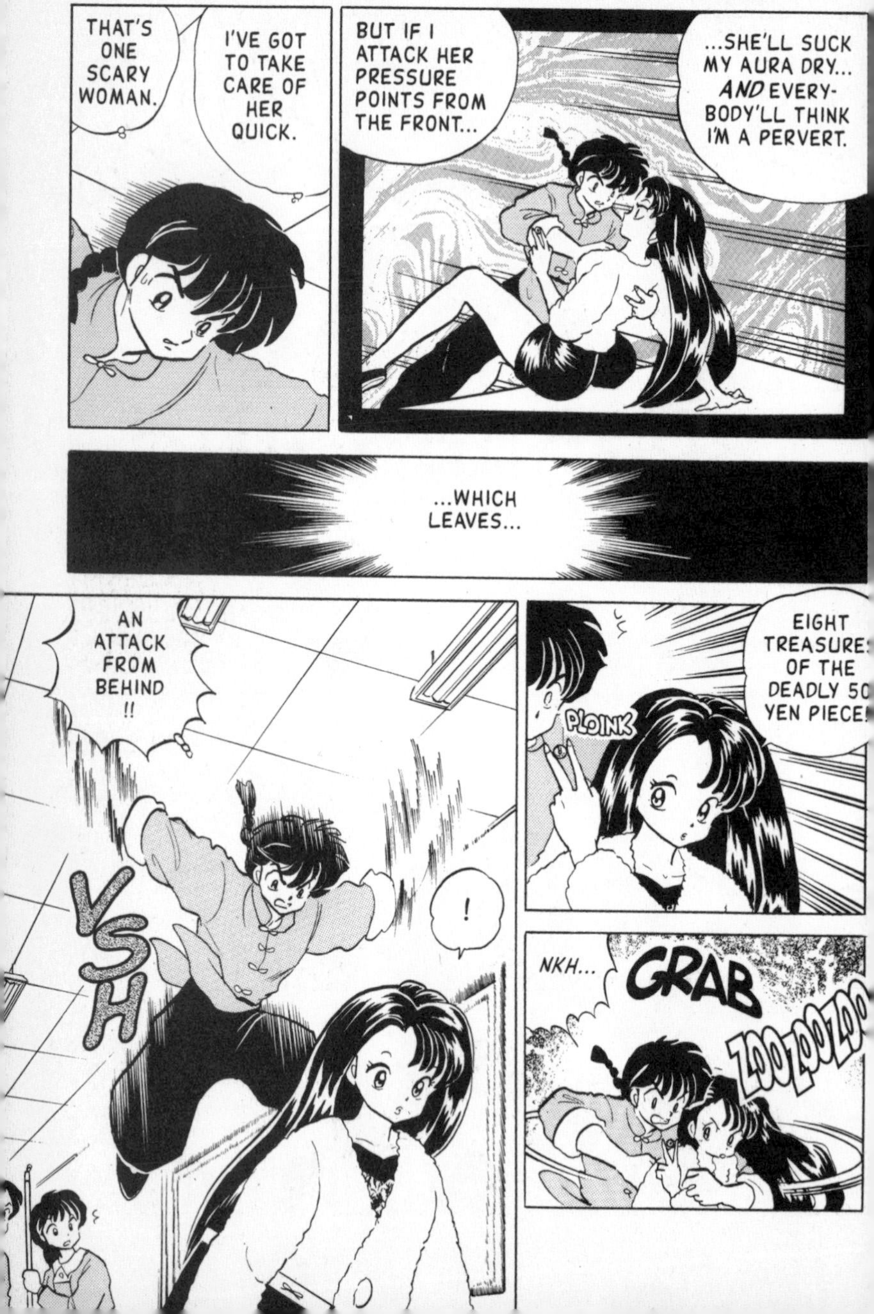
THAT'S ONE SCARY WOMAN.
I'VE GOT TO TAKE CARE OF HER QUICK.
BUT IF I ATTACK HER PRESSURE POINTS FROM THE FRONT...
...SHE'LL SUCK MY AURA DRY... AND EVERY-BODY'LL THINK I'M A PERVERT.
...WHICH LEAVES...
AN ATTACK FROM BEHIND !!
VSH
!
EIGHT TREASURE: OF THE DEADLY 50 YEN PIECE!
PLOINK
NKH...
GRAB
ZOOZOOZOO

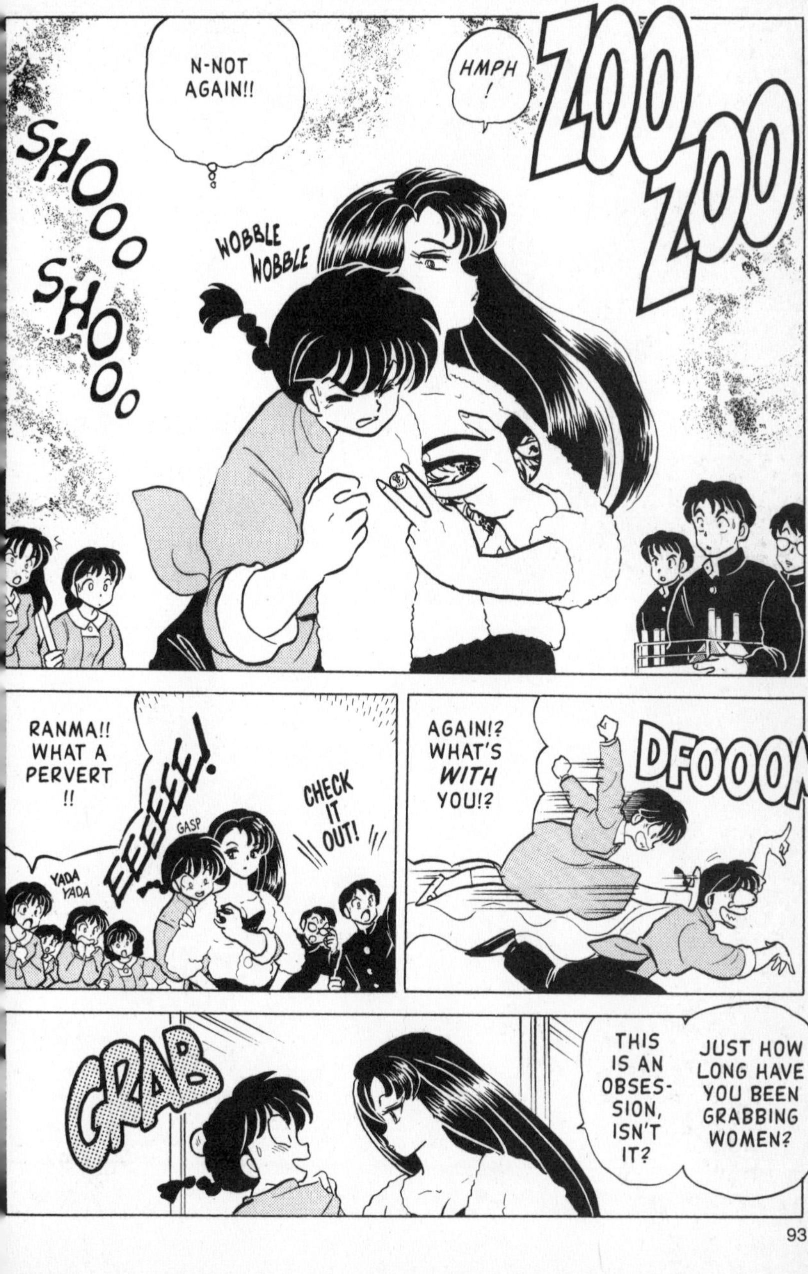

N-NOT AGAIN!!
HMPH !
ZOO ZOO
SHOOO SHOOO
WOBBLE WOBBLE
RANMA!! WHAT A PERVERT !!
EEEEEE!
GASP
CHECK IT OUT!
YADA YADA
AGAIN!? WHAT'S *WITH* YOU!?
DFOOOM
GRAB
THIS IS AN OBSES-SION, ISN'T IT?
JUST HOW LONG HAVE YOU BEEN GRABBING WOMEN?

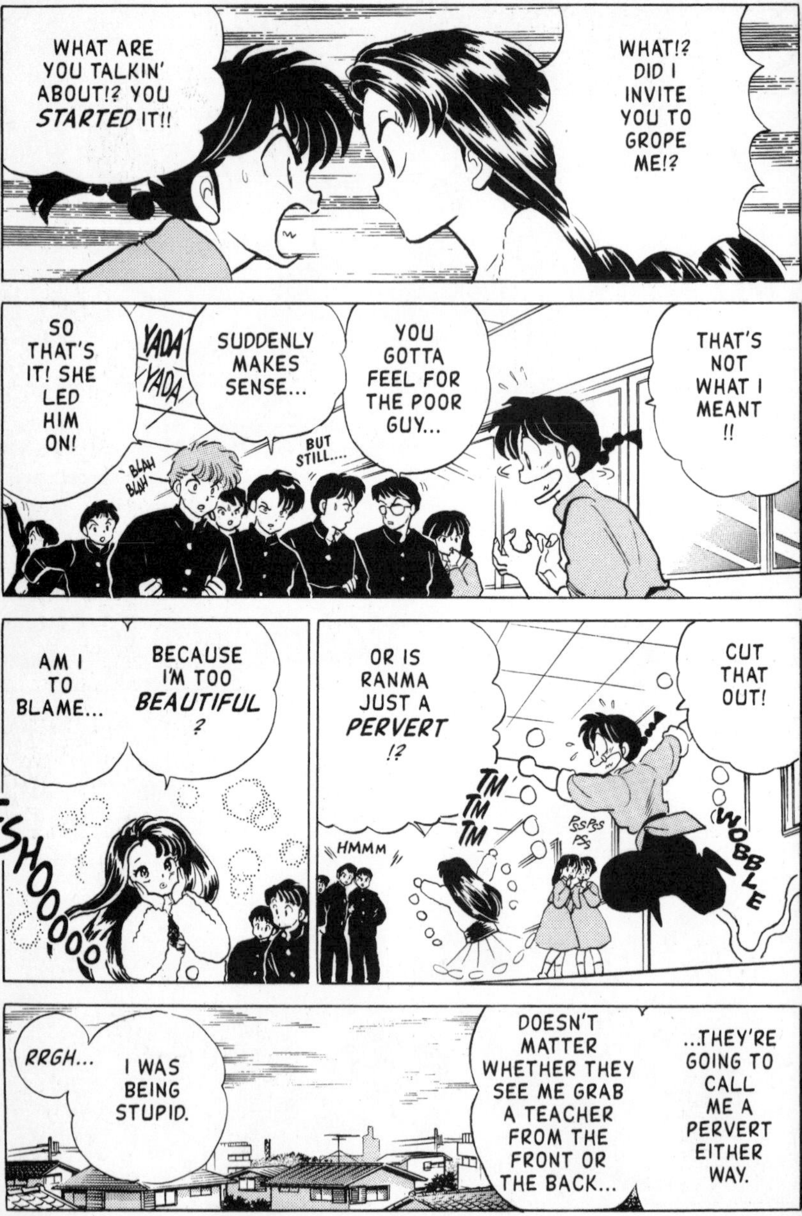
WHAT ARE YOU TALKIN' ABOUT!? YOU *STARTED* IT!!
WHAT!? DID I INVITE YOU TO GROPE ME!?
SO THAT'S IT! SHE LED HIM ON!
YADA YADA
BLAH BLAH
SUDDENLY MAKES SENSE...
BUT STILL....
YOU GOTTA FEEL FOR THE POOR GUY...
THAT'S NOT WHAT I MEANT !!
AM I TO BLAME...
BECAUSE I'M TOO *BEAUTIFUL* ?
FSHOOOOOO
OR IS RANMA JUST A *PERVERT* !?
TM TM TM
HMMM
PSPSS PSS
CUT THAT OUT!
WOBBLE
RRGH...
I WAS BEING STUPID.
DOESN'T MATTER WHETHER THEY SEE ME GRAB A TEACHER FROM THE FRONT OR THE BACK...
...THEY'RE GOING TO CALL ME A PERVERT EITHER WAY.

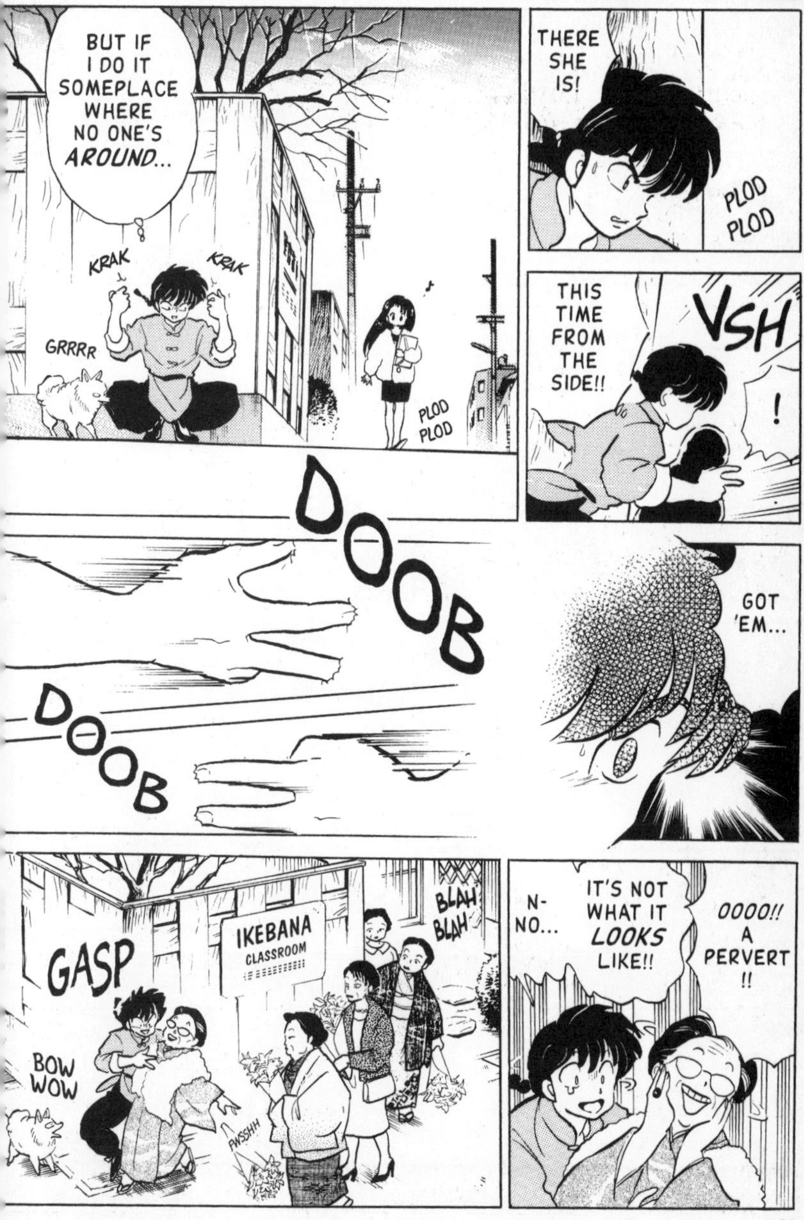
BUT IF I DO IT SOMEPLACE WHERE NO ONE'S *AROUND*...
KRAK
KRAK
GRRRR
PLOD PLOD
THERE SHE IS!
PLOD PLOD
THIS TIME FROM THE SIDE!!
VSH
!
DOOB
DOOB
GOT 'EM...
GASP
IKEBANA CLASSROOM
BLAH BLAH
BOW WOW
FWSSHH
N-NO...
IT'S NOT WHAT IT *LOOKS* LIKE!!
OOOO!! A PERVERT !!

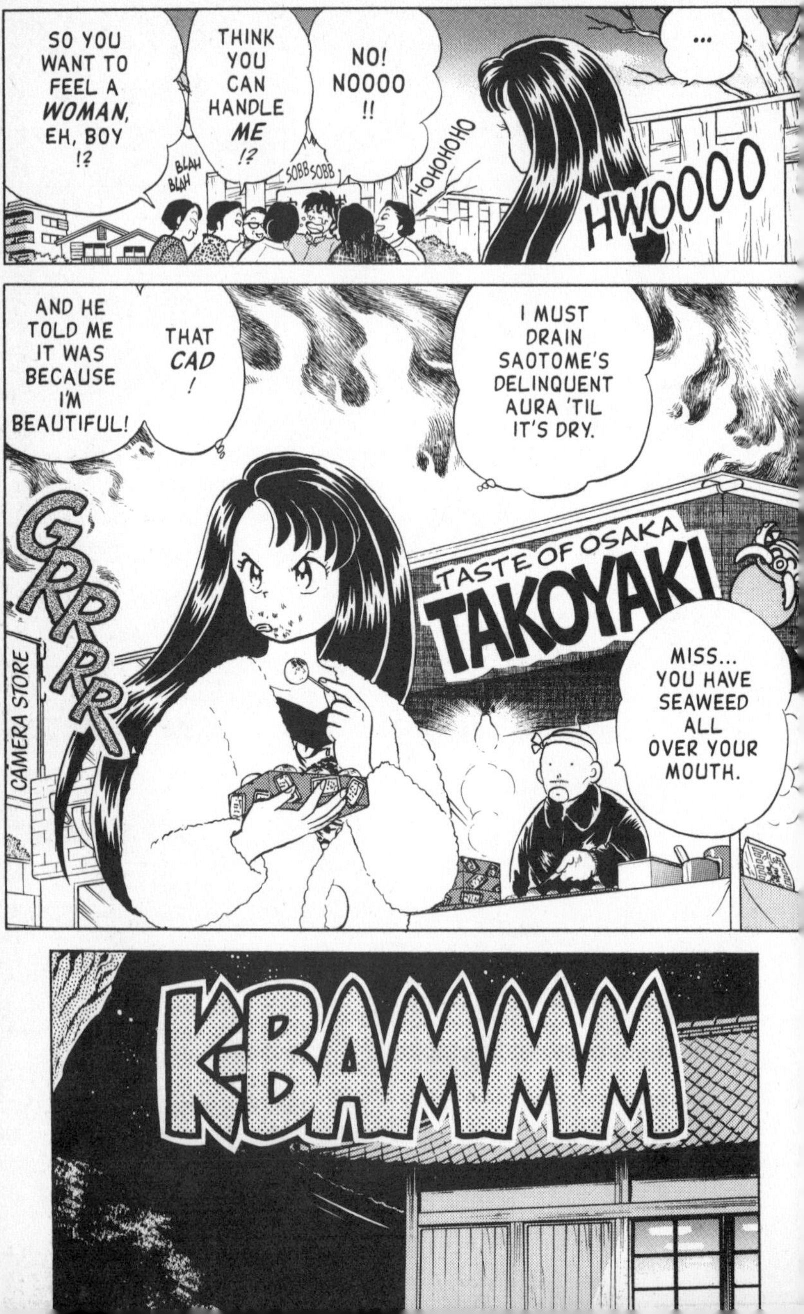
SO YOU WANT TO FEEL A WOMAN, EH, BOY !?
BLAH BLAH
THINK YOU CAN HANDLE ME !?
SOBB SOBB
NO! NOOOO !!
HOHOHOHO
...
HWOOOO
AND HE TOLD ME IT WAS BECAUSE I'M BEAUTIFUL!
THAT CAD !
I MUST DRAIN SAOTOME'S DELINQUENT AURA 'TIL IT'S DRY.
GRRRR
CAMERA STORE
TASTE OF OSAKA
TAKOYAKI
MISS... YOU HAVE SEAWEED ALL OVER YOUR MOUTH.
KBAMMM

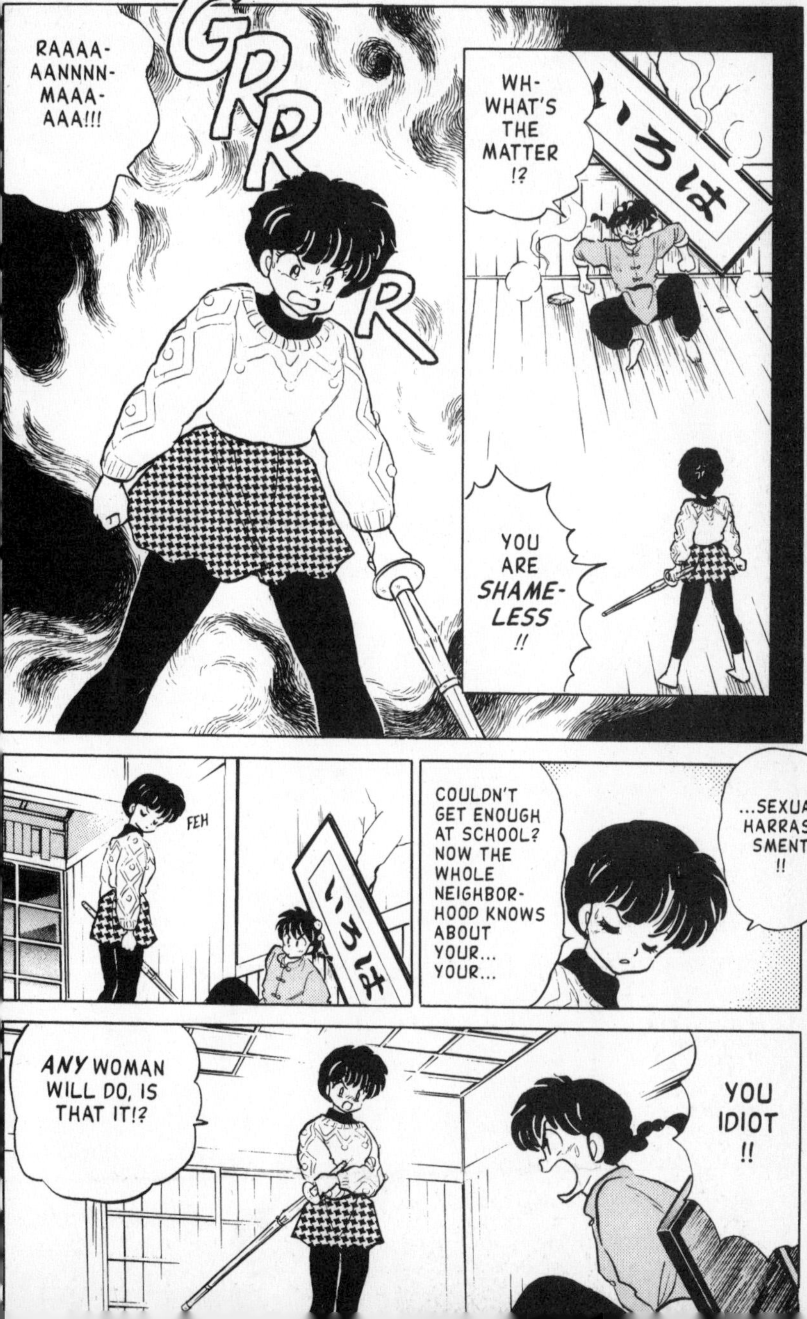
RAAAA-AANNNN-MAAA-AAA!!!
GRRR
WH-WHAT'S THE MATTER !?
いろは
YOU ARE *SHAME-LESS* !!
FEH
いろは
COULDN'T GET ENOUGH AT SCHOOL? NOW THE WHOLE NEIGHBOR-HOOD KNOWS ABOUT YOUR... YOUR...
...SEXUAL HARRAS-SMENT !!
ANY WOMAN WILL DO, IS THAT IT!?
YOU IDIOT !!

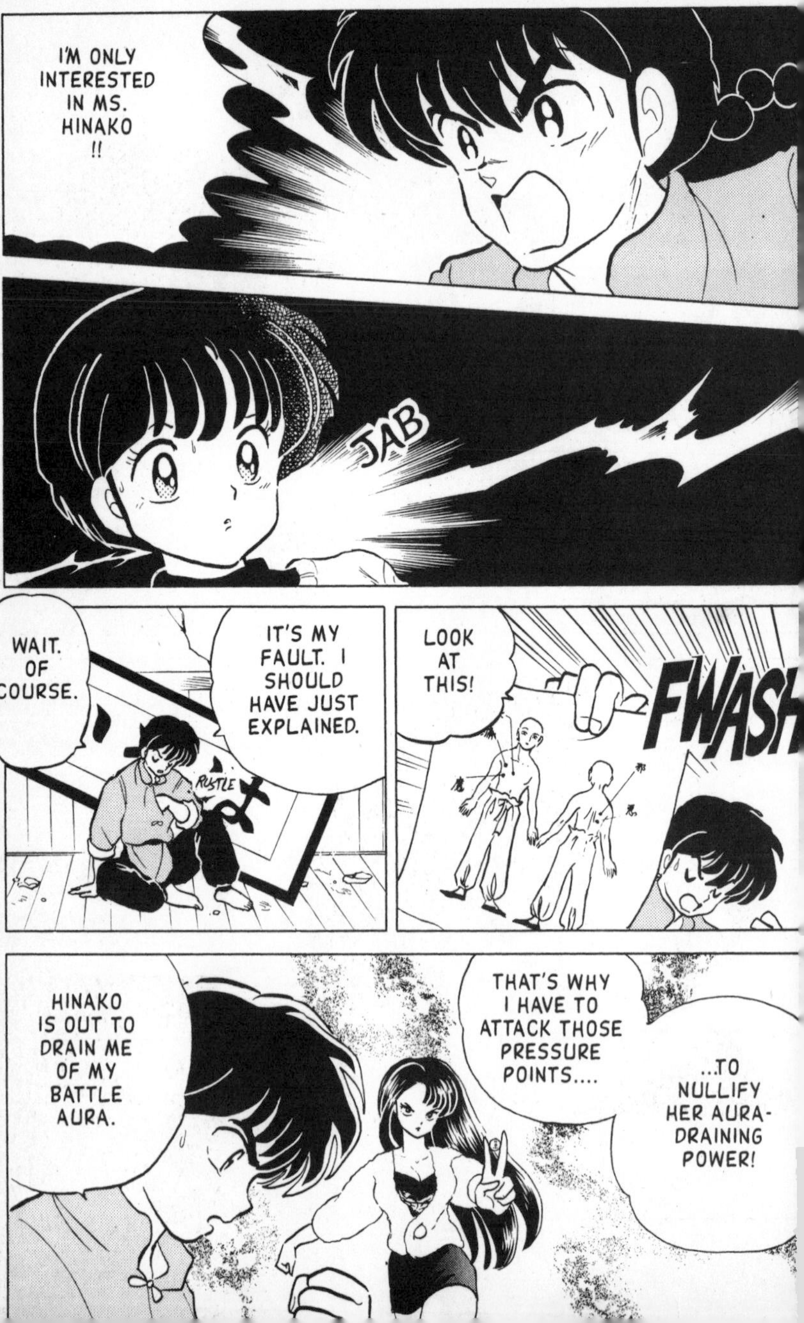
I'M ONLY INTERESTED IN MS. HINAKO !!
JAB
WAIT. OF COURSE.
IT'S MY FAULT. I SHOULD HAVE JUST EXPLAINED.
RUSTLE
LOOK AT THIS!
FWASH
HINAKO IS OUT TO DRAIN ME OF MY BATTLE AURA.
THAT'S WHY I HAVE TO ATTACK THOSE PRESSURE POINTS....
...TO NULLIFY HER AURA-DRAINING POWER!

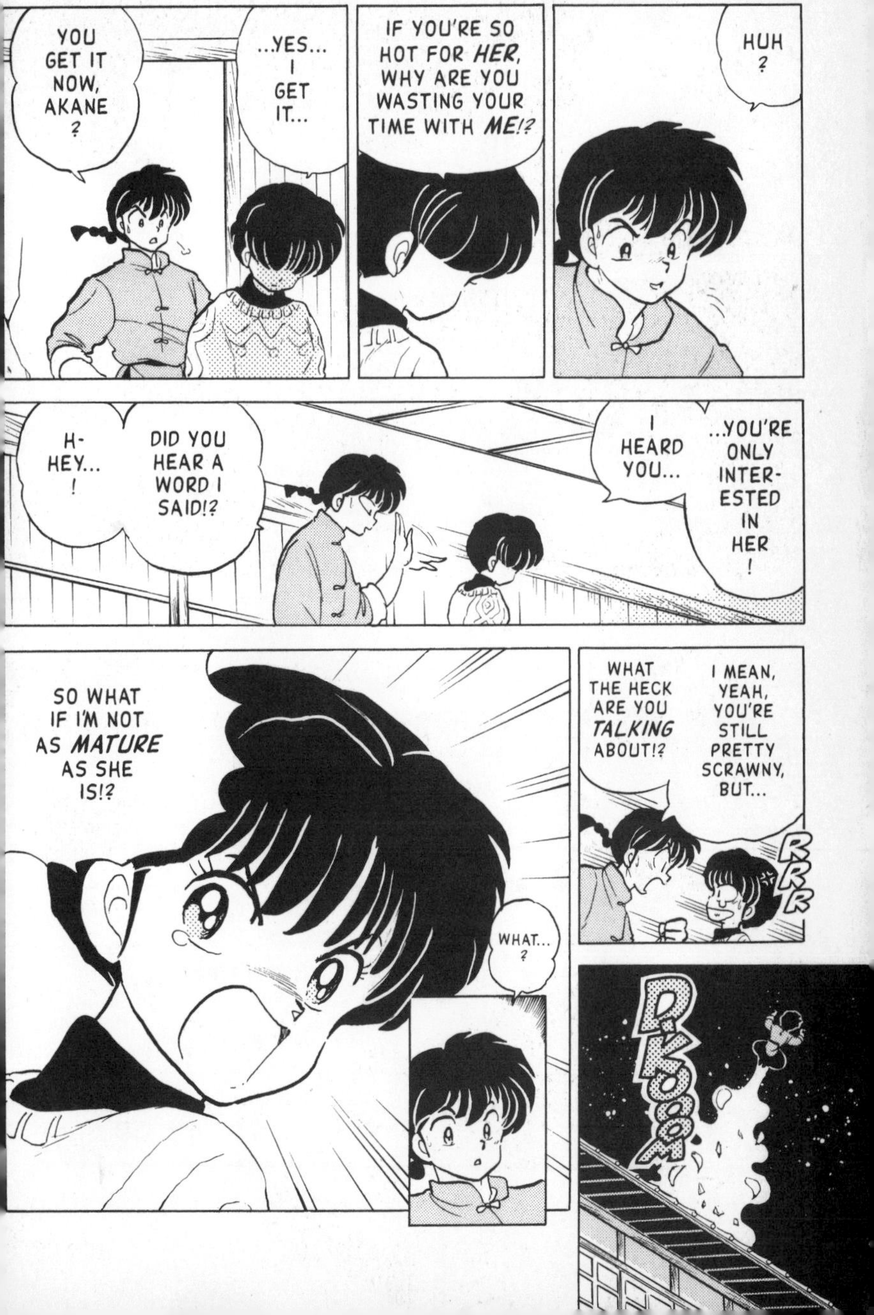
YOU GET IT NOW, AKANE?
...YES... I GET IT...
IF YOU'RE SO HOT FOR *HER*, WHY ARE YOU WASTING YOUR TIME WITH *ME!?*
HUH?
H-HEY...!
DID YOU HEAR A WORD I SAID!?
I HEARD YOU...
...YOU'RE ONLY INTERESTED IN HER!
SO WHAT IF I'M NOT AS *MATURE* AS SHE IS!?
WHAT...?
WHAT THE HECK ARE YOU *TALKING* ABOUT!?
I MEAN, YEAH, YOU'RE STILL PRETTY SCRAWNY, BUT...
RRR
DKOOOM

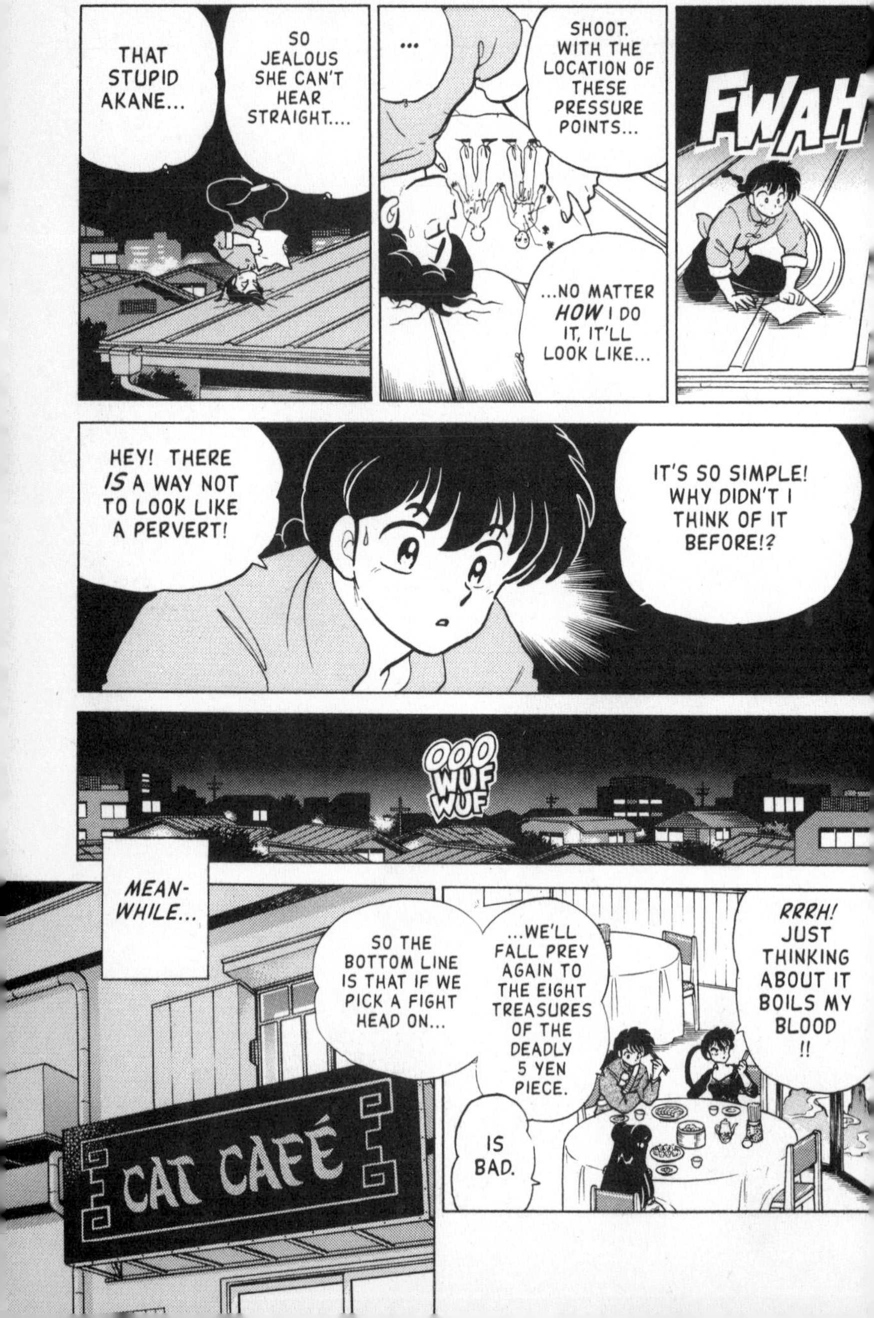
THAT STUPID AKANE...
SO JEALOUS SHE CAN'T HEAR STRAIGHT....
...
SHOOT. WITH THE LOCATION OF THESE PRESSURE POINTS...
...NO MATTER *HOW* I DO IT, IT'LL LOOK LIKE...
FWAH
HEY! THERE *IS* A WAY NOT TO LOOK LIKE A PERVERT!
IT'S SO SIMPLE! WHY DIDN'T I THINK OF IT BEFORE!?
OOO WUF WUF
MEAN-WHILE...
CAT CAFÉ
SO THE BOTTOM LINE IS THAT IF WE PICK A FIGHT HEAD ON...
...WE'LL FALL PREY AGAIN TO THE EIGHT TREASURES OF THE DEADLY 5 YEN PIECE.
IS BAD.
RRRH! JUST THINKING ABOUT IT BOILS MY BLOOD !!

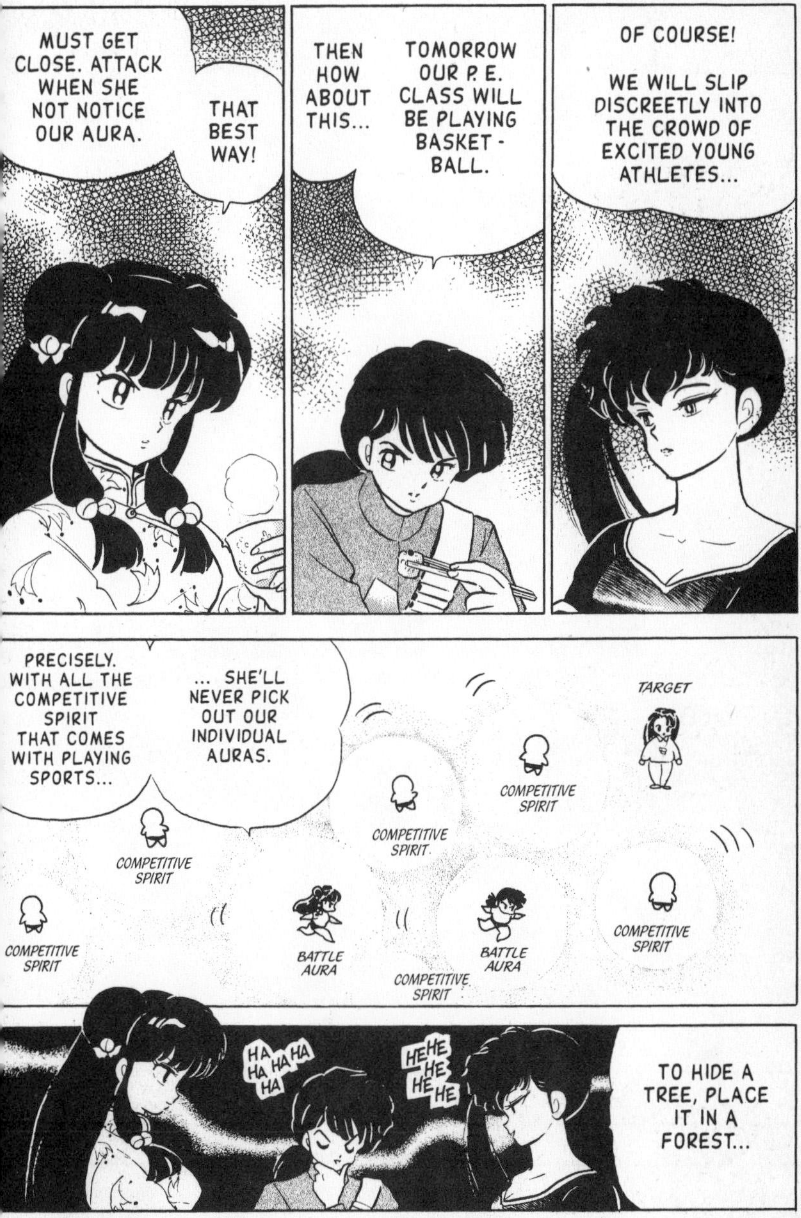
MUST GET CLOSE. ATTACK WHEN SHE NOT NOTICE OUR AURA.
THAT BEST WAY!
THEN HOW ABOUT THIS...
TOMORROW OUR P. E. CLASS WILL BE PLAYING BASKET - BALL.
OF COURSE!
WE WILL SLIP DISCREETLY INTO THE CROWD OF EXCITED YOUNG ATHLETES...
PRECISELY. WITH ALL THE COMPETITIVE SPIRIT THAT COMES WITH PLAYING SPORTS...
... SHE'LL NEVER PICK OUT OUR INDIVIDUAL AURAS.
TARGET
COMPETITIVE SPIRIT
COMPETITIVE SPIRIT
COMPETITIVE SPIRIT
COMPETITIVE SPIRIT
BATTLE AURA
BATTLE AURA
COMPETITIVE SPIRIT
COMPETITIVE SPIRIT
HA HA HA HA HA
HE HE HE HE HE
TO HIDE A TREE, PLACE IT IN A FOREST...

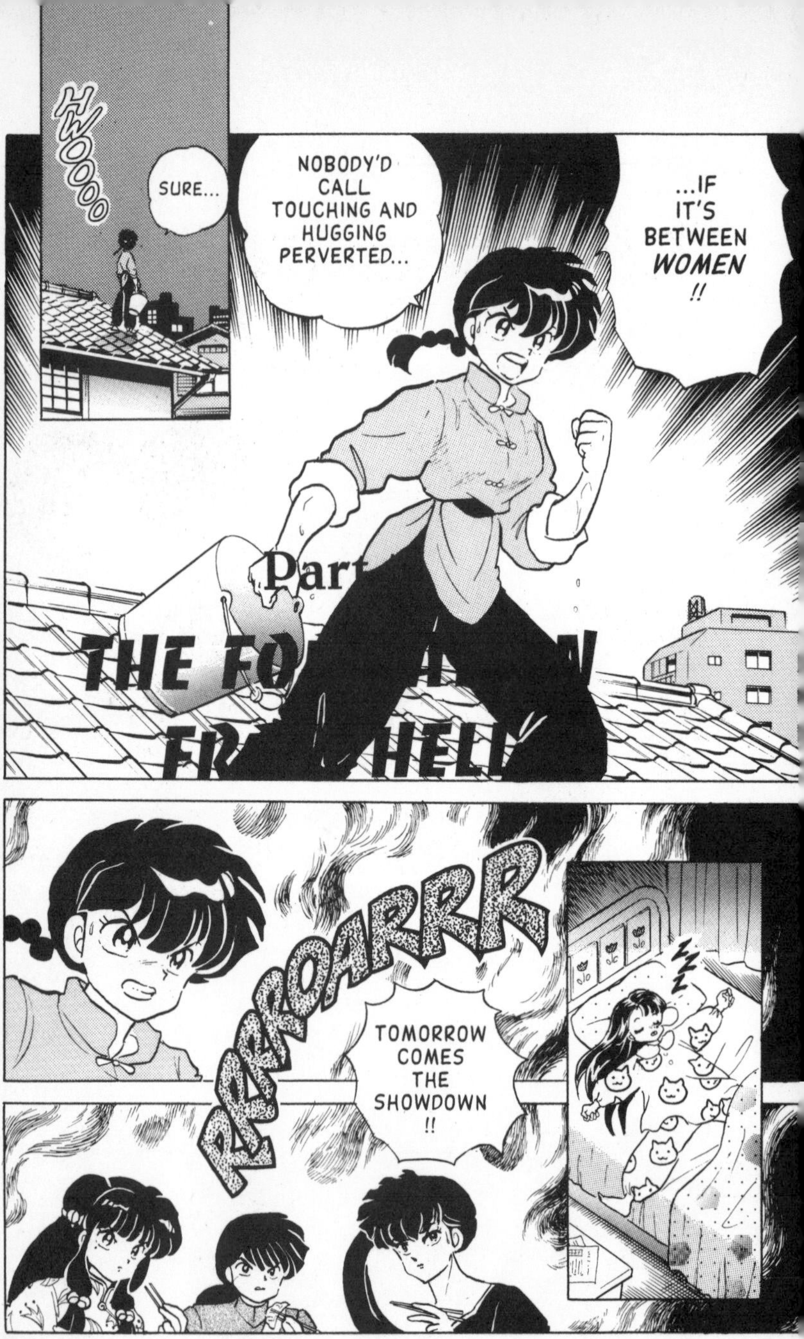
HWOOOO
SURE...
NOBODY'D CALL TOUCHING AND HUGGING PERVERTED...
...IF IT'S BETWEEN WOMEN !!
Part
RRROARRRR
TOMORROW COMES THE SHOWDOWN !!
ZZZ

Part 7

THE FORMATION FROM HELL

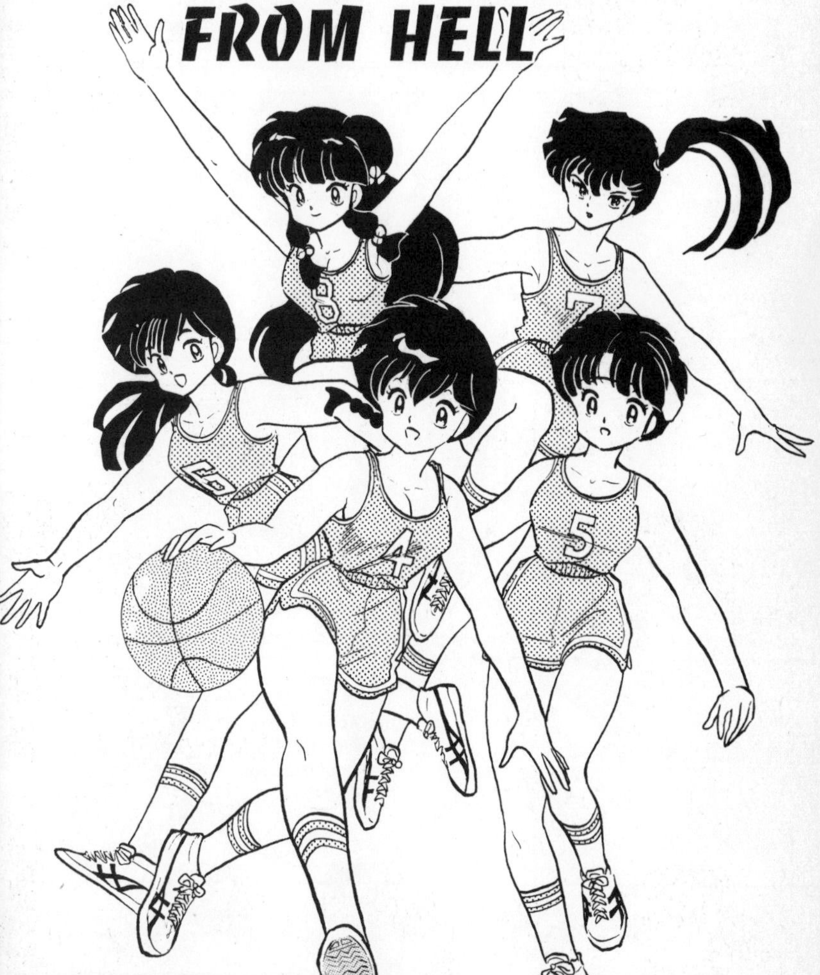

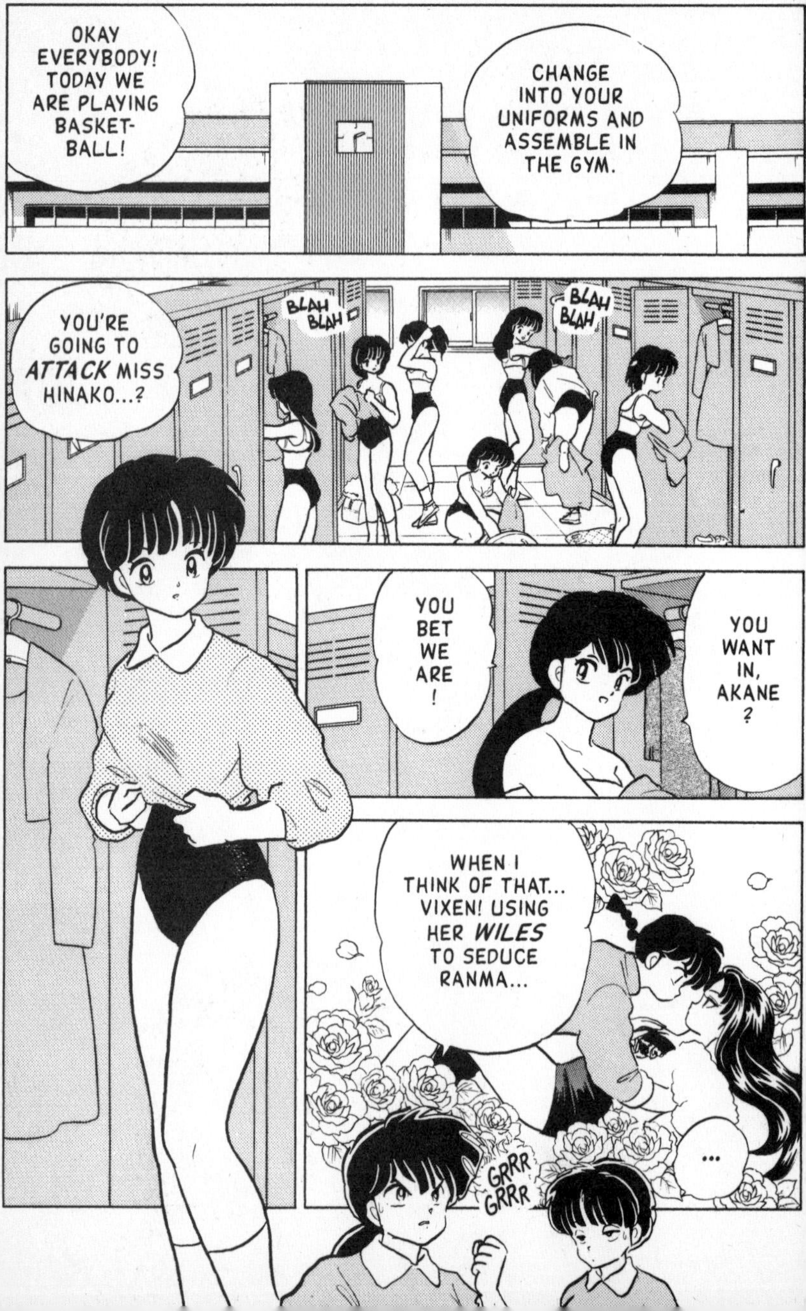
OKAY EVERYBODY! TODAY WE ARE PLAYING BASKET-BALL!
CHANGE INTO YOUR UNIFORMS AND ASSEMBLE IN THE GYM.
YOU'RE GOING TO *ATTACK* MISS HINAKO...?
BLAH BLAH
BLAH BLAH
YOU BET WE ARE!
YOU WANT IN, AKANE?
WHEN I THINK OF THAT... VIXEN! USING HER *WILES* TO SEDUCE RANMA...
GRRR GRRR
...

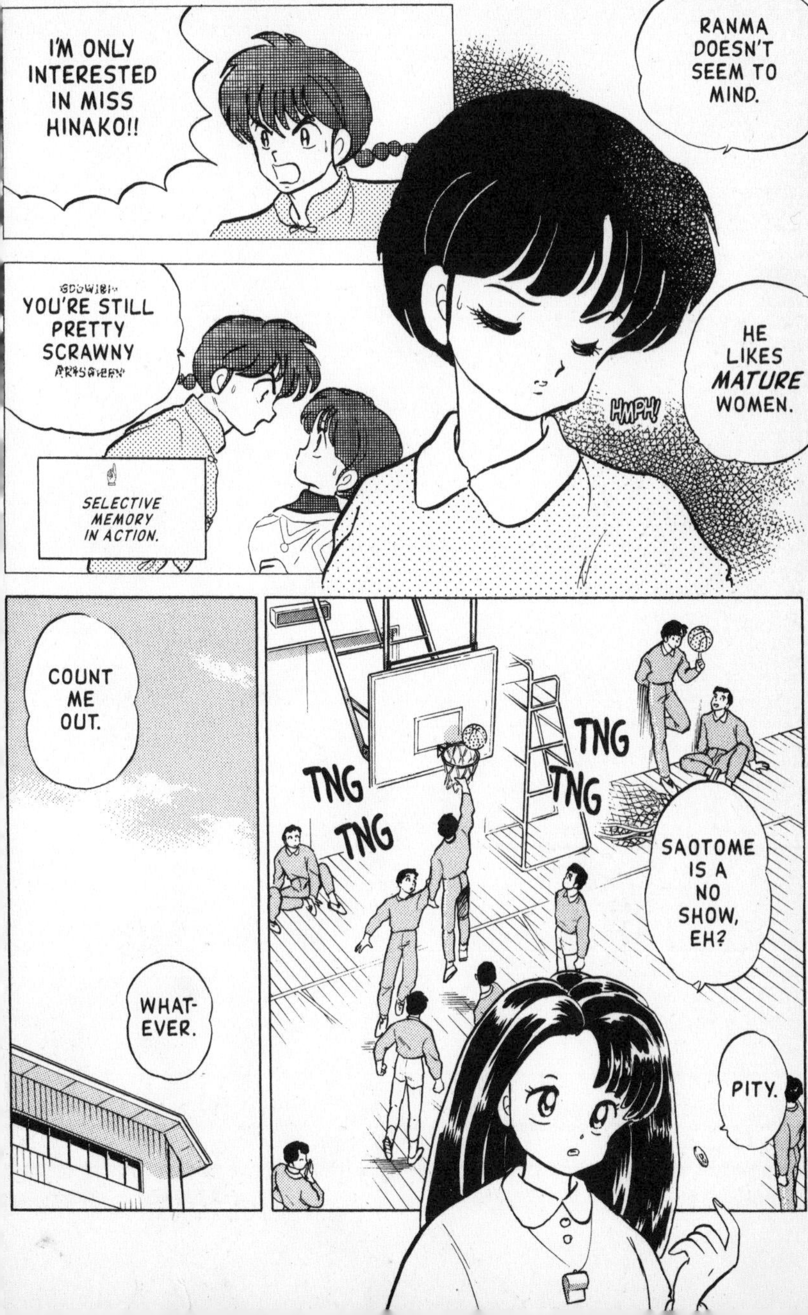
I'M ONLY INTERESTED IN MISS HINAKO!!
RANMA DOESN'T SEEM TO MIND.
YOU'RE STILL PRETTY SCRAWNY
SELECTIVE MEMORY IN ACTION.
HMPH!
HE LIKES MATURE WOMEN.
COUNT ME OUT.
WHAT-EVER.
TNG
TNG
TNG
TNG
SAOTOME IS A NO SHOW, EH?
PITY.

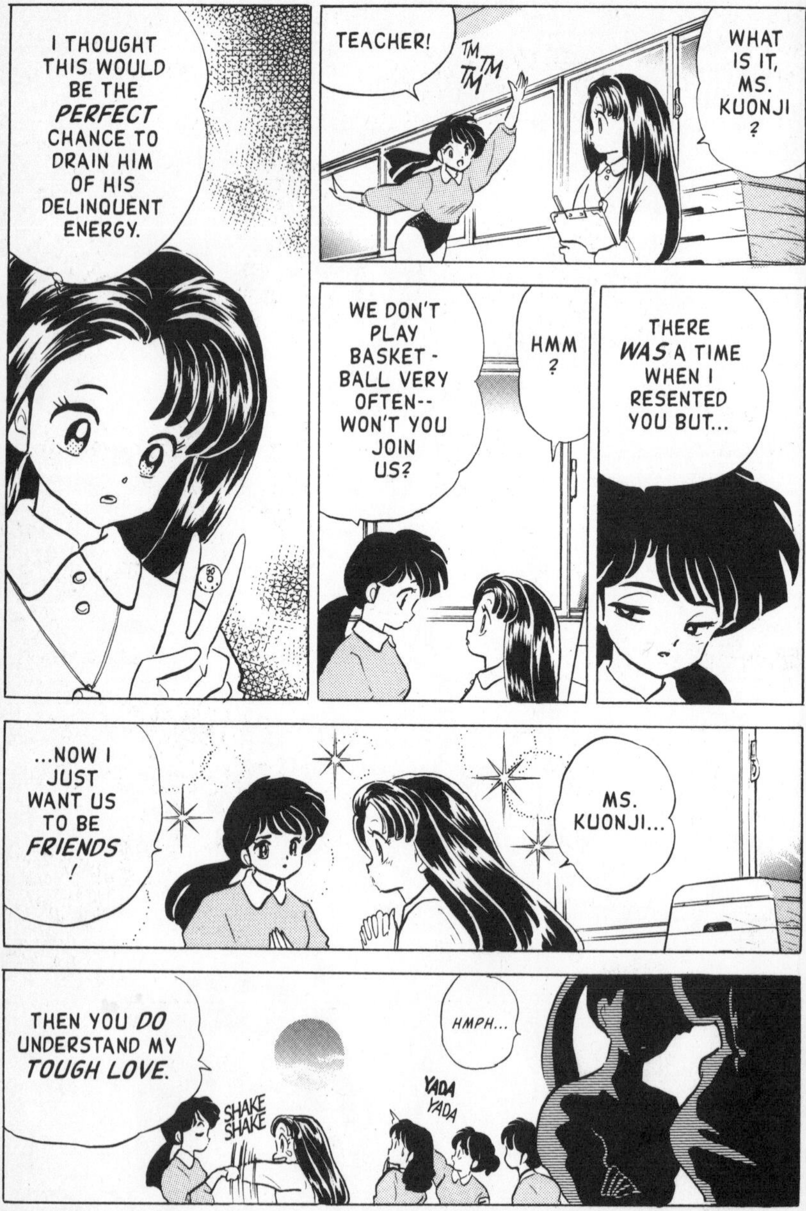
I THOUGHT THIS WOULD BE THE *PERFECT* CHANCE TO DRAIN HIM OF HIS DELINQUENT ENERGY.
TEACHER!
TM TM TM
WHAT IS IT, MS. KUONJI ?
WE DON'T PLAY BASKET - BALL VERY OFTEN-- WON'T YOU JOIN US?
HMM ?
THERE *WAS* A TIME WHEN I RESENTED YOU BUT...
...NOW I JUST WANT US TO BE *FRIENDS* !
MS. KUONJI...
THEN YOU *DO* UNDERSTAND MY *TOUGH LOVE*.
SHAKE SHAKE
HMPH...
YADA YADA

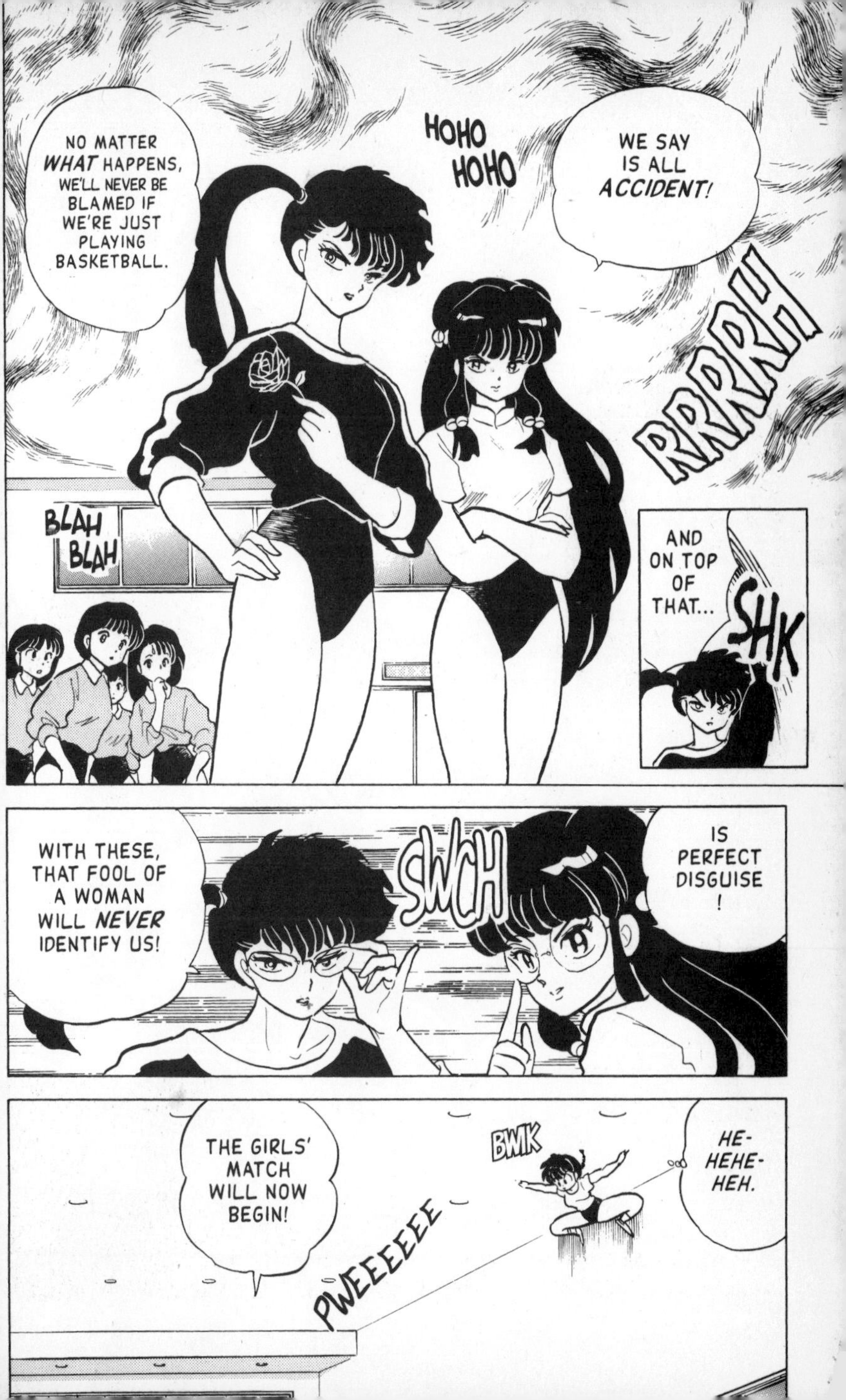
NO MATTER WHAT HAPPENS, WE'LL NEVER BE BLAMED IF WE'RE JUST PLAYING BASKETBALL.
HOHO HOHO
WE SAY IS ALL ACCIDENT!
RRRRAH
BLAH BLAH
AND ON TOP OF THAT...
SHK
WITH THESE, THAT FOOL OF A WOMAN WILL NEVER IDENTIFY US!
SWCH
IS PERFECT DISGUISE !
THE GIRLS' MATCH WILL NOW BEGIN!
BWIK
HE-HEHE-HEH.
PWEEEEEE

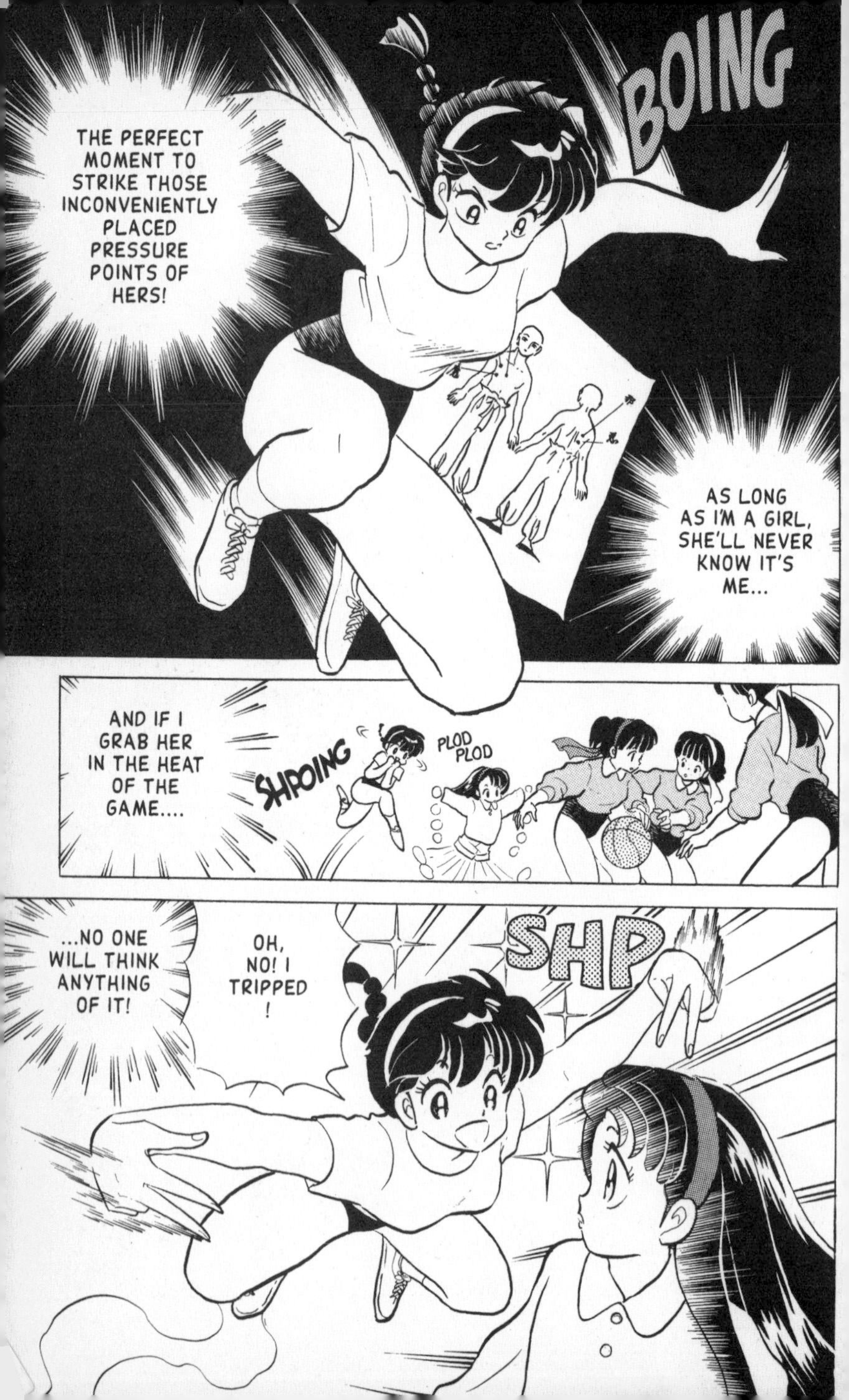
BOING
THE PERFECT MOMENT TO STRIKE THOSE INCONVENIENTLY PLACED PRESSURE POINTS OF HERS!
AS LONG AS I'M A GIRL, SHE'LL NEVER KNOW IT'S ME...
AND IF I GRAB HER IN THE HEAT OF THE GAME....
SHPOING
PLOD PLOD
...NO ONE WILL THINK ANYTHING OF IT!
OH, NO! I TRIPPED!
SHP

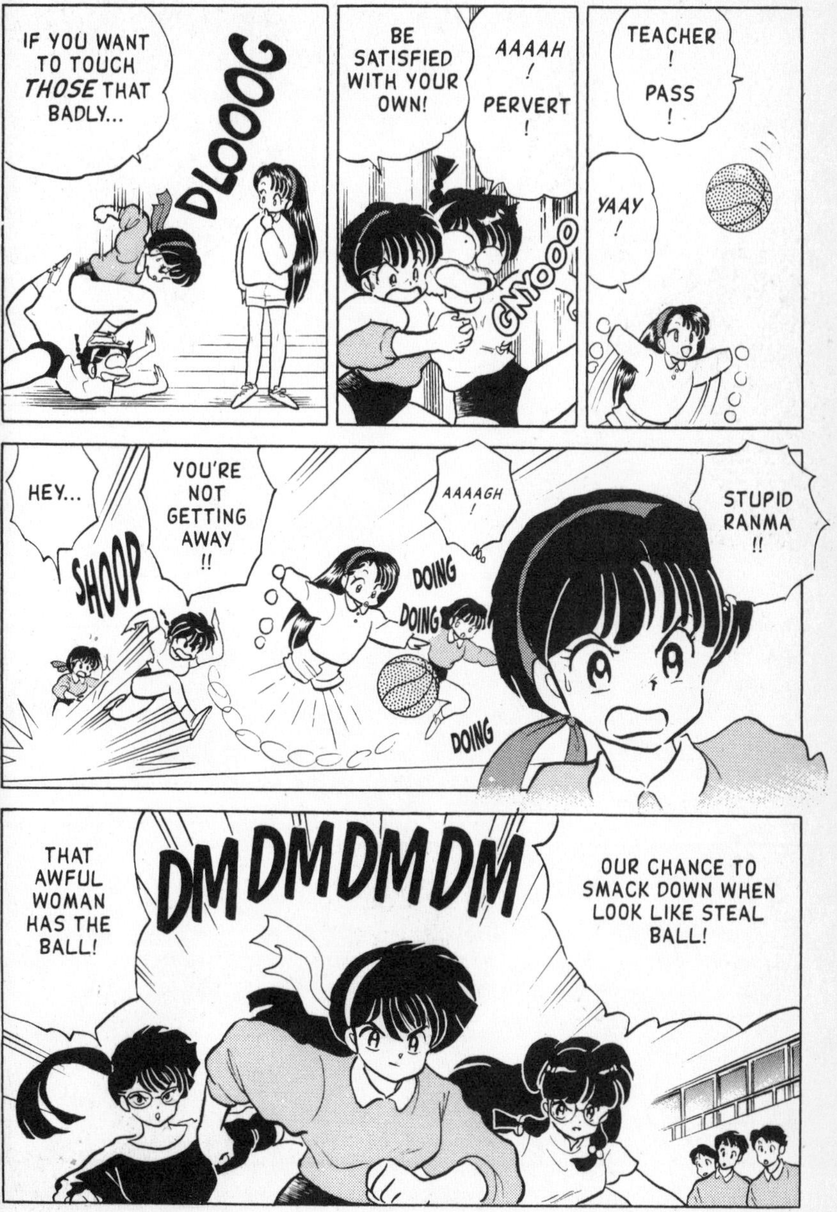
IF YOU WANT TO TOUCH *THOSE* THAT BADLY...
DLOOOG
BE SATISFIED WITH YOUR OWN!
AAAAH! PERVERT!
GNYOOO
TEACHER! PASS!
YAAY!
HEY...
SHOOP
YOU'RE NOT GETTING AWAY!!
AAAAGH!
DOING
DOING
DOING
STUPID RANMA!!
THAT AWFUL WOMAN HAS THE BALL!
DM DM DM DM DM
OUR CHANCE TO SMACK DOWN WHEN LOOK LIKE STEAL BALL!

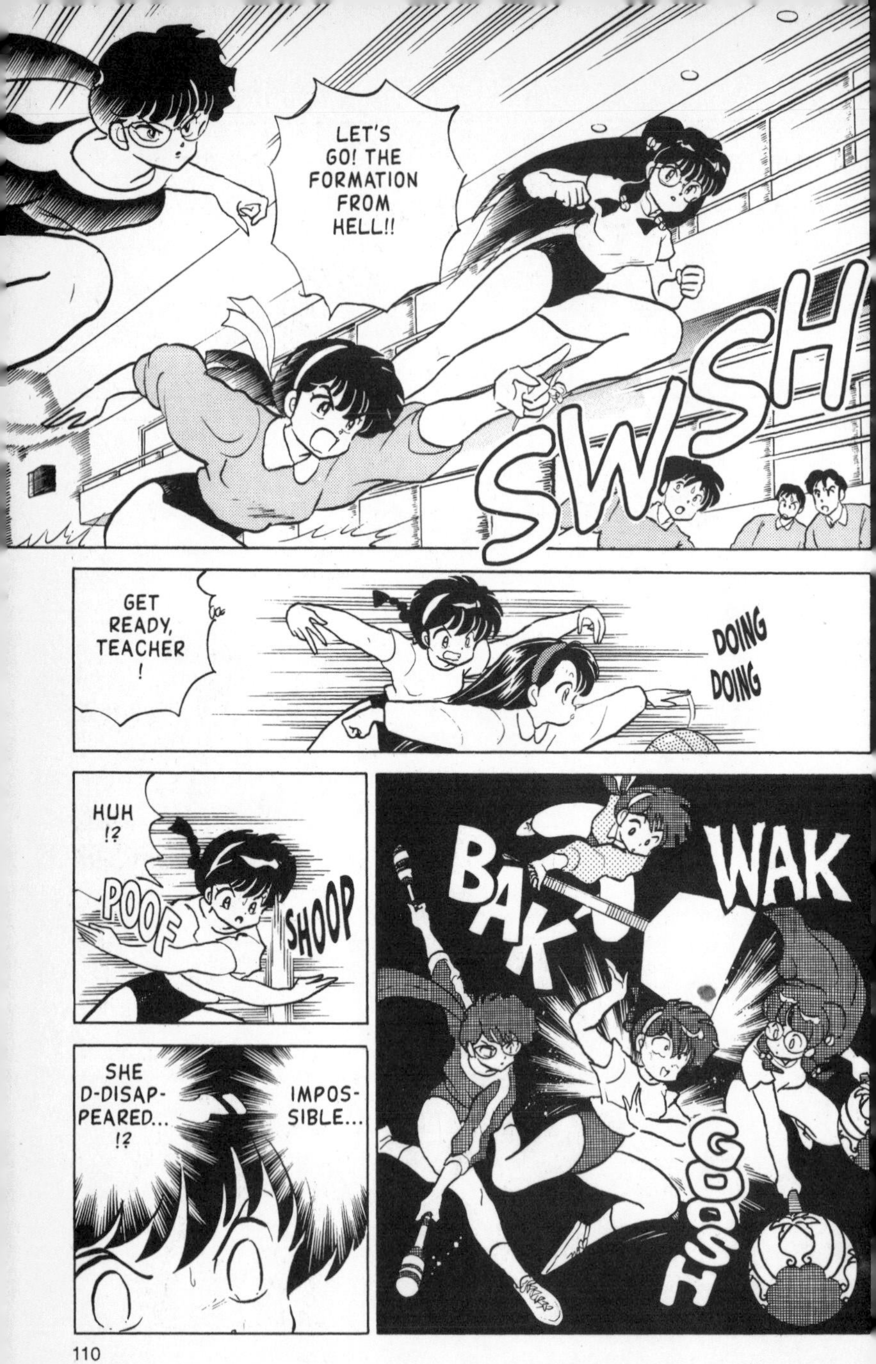
LET'S GO! THE FORMATION FROM HELL!!
SWSH
GET READY, TEACHER!
DOING DOING
HUH!?
POOF
SHOOP
SHE D-DISAPPEARED...!?
IMPOSSIBLE...
BAK
WAK
GOOSH

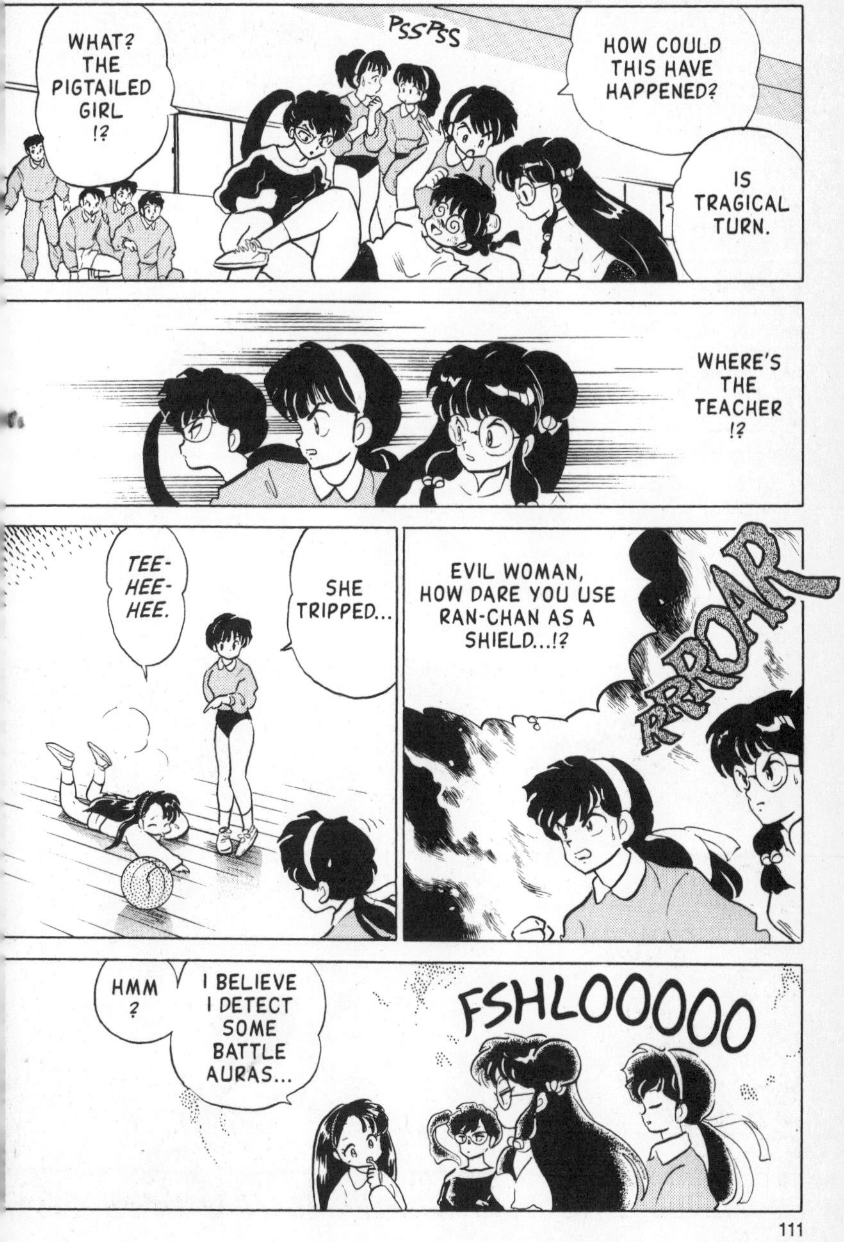
WHAT? THE PIGTAILED GIRL !?
PSSPSS
HOW COULD THIS HAVE HAPPENED?
IS TRAGICAL TURN.
WHERE'S THE TEACHER !?
TEE-HEE-HEE.
SHE TRIPPED...
EVIL WOMAN, HOW DARE YOU USE RAN-CHAN AS A SHIELD...!?
RRROAR
HMM?
I BELIEVE I DETECT SOME BATTLE AURAS...
FSHLOOOOO

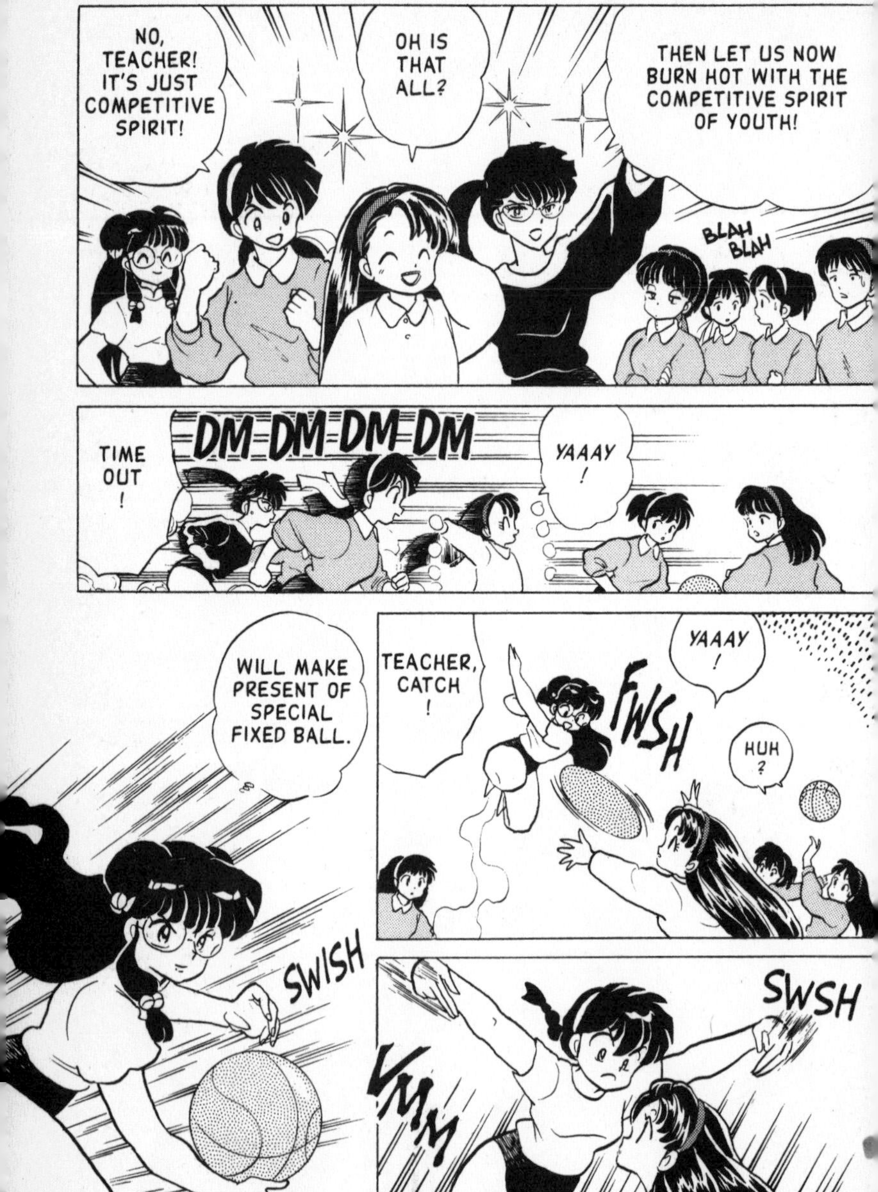
NO, TEACHER! IT'S JUST COMPETITIVE SPIRIT!
OH IS THAT ALL?
THEN LET US NOW BURN HOT WITH THE COMPETITIVE SPIRIT OF YOUTH!
BLAH BLAH
TIME OUT!
DM DM DM DM
YAAAY!
WILL MAKE PRESENT OF SPECIAL FIXED BALL.
SWISH
TEACHER, CATCH!
FWSH
YAAAY!
HUH?
VMM
SWSH

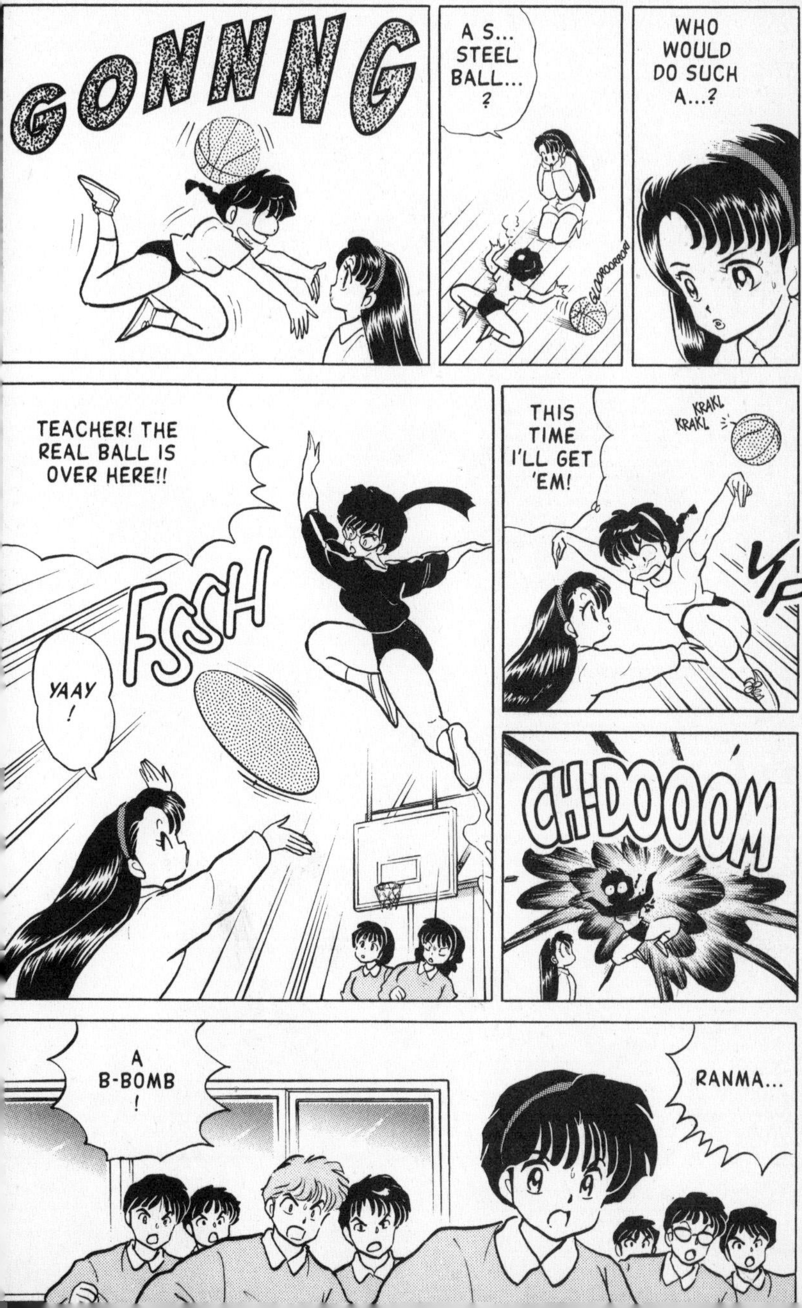
GONNNG
A S... STEEL BALL...?
GLOOROORROOR
WHO WOULD DO SUCH A...?
TEACHER! THE REAL BALL IS OVER HERE!!
FSSH
YAAY!
THIS TIME I'LL GET 'EM!
KRAKL KRAKL
YIP
CH-DOOOM
A B-BOMB!
RANMA...

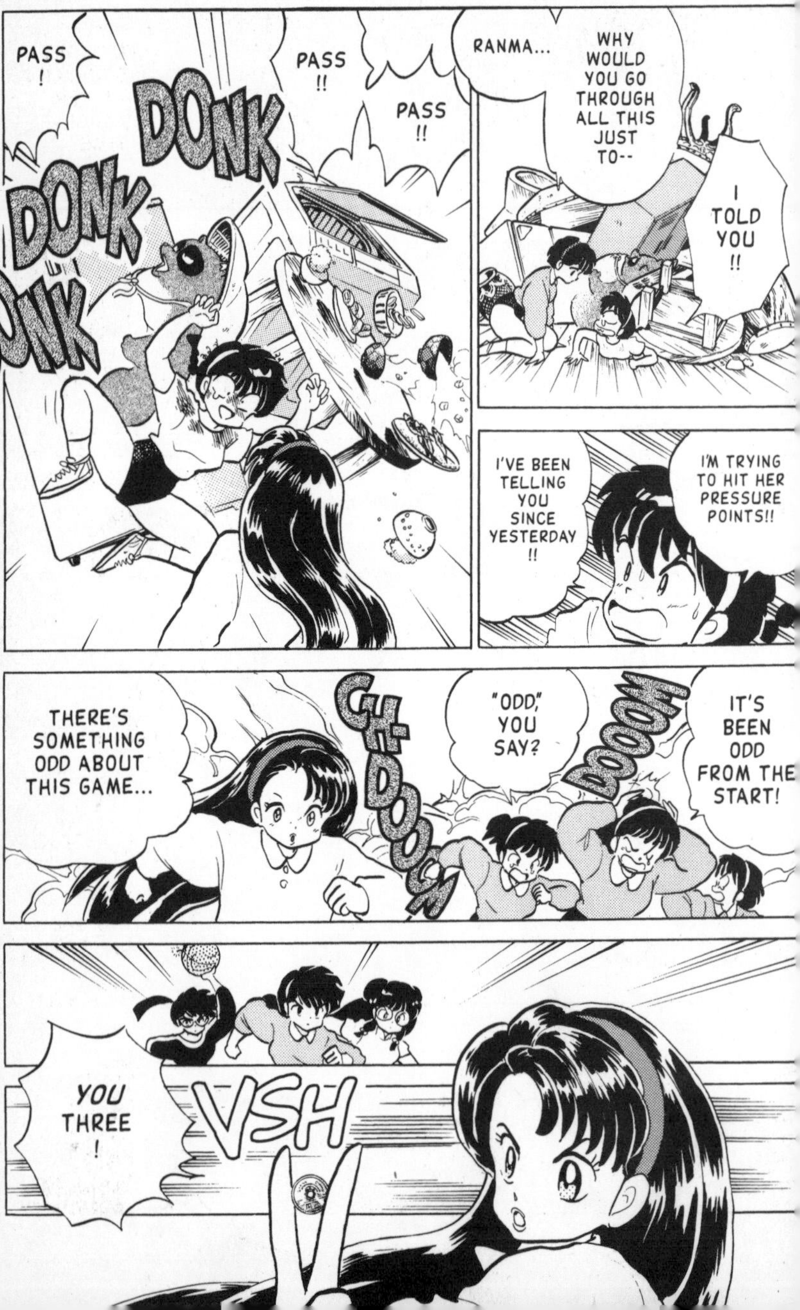
PASS !
PASS !!
PASS !!
DONK
DONK
DONK
RANMA...
WHY WOULD YOU GO THROUGH ALL THIS JUST TO--
I TOLD YOU !!
I'VE BEEN TELLING YOU SINCE YESTERDAY !!
I'M TRYING TO HIT HER PRESSURE POINTS!!
THERE'S SOMETHING ODD ABOUT THIS GAME...
CH-DOOOOM
"ODD," YOU SAY?
DOOOOM
IT'S BEEN ODD FROM THE START!
YOU THREE !
VSH

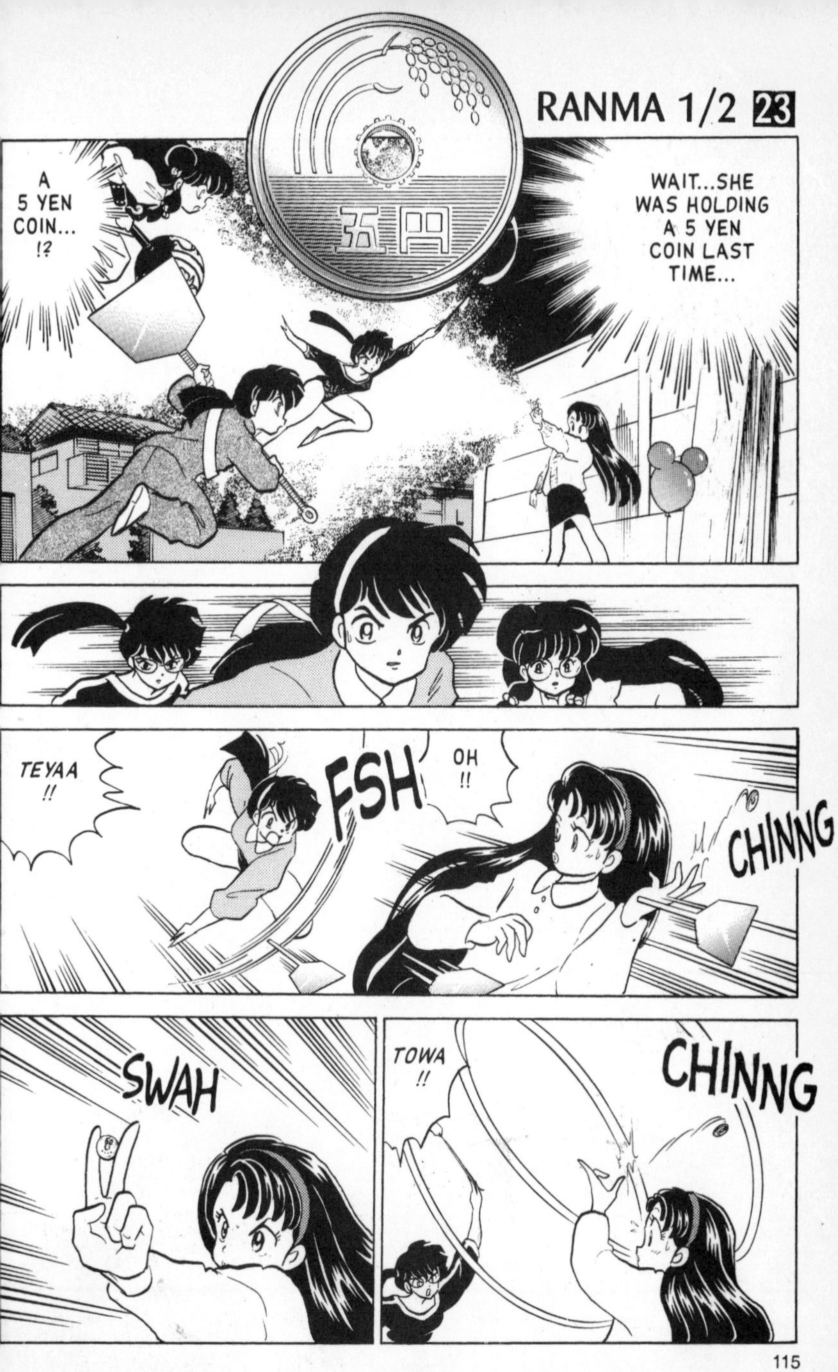
A 5 YEN COIN... !?
WAIT...SHE WAS HOLDING A 5 YEN COIN LAST TIME...
TEYAA !!
FSH
OH !!
CHINNG
SWAH
TOWA !!
CHINNG

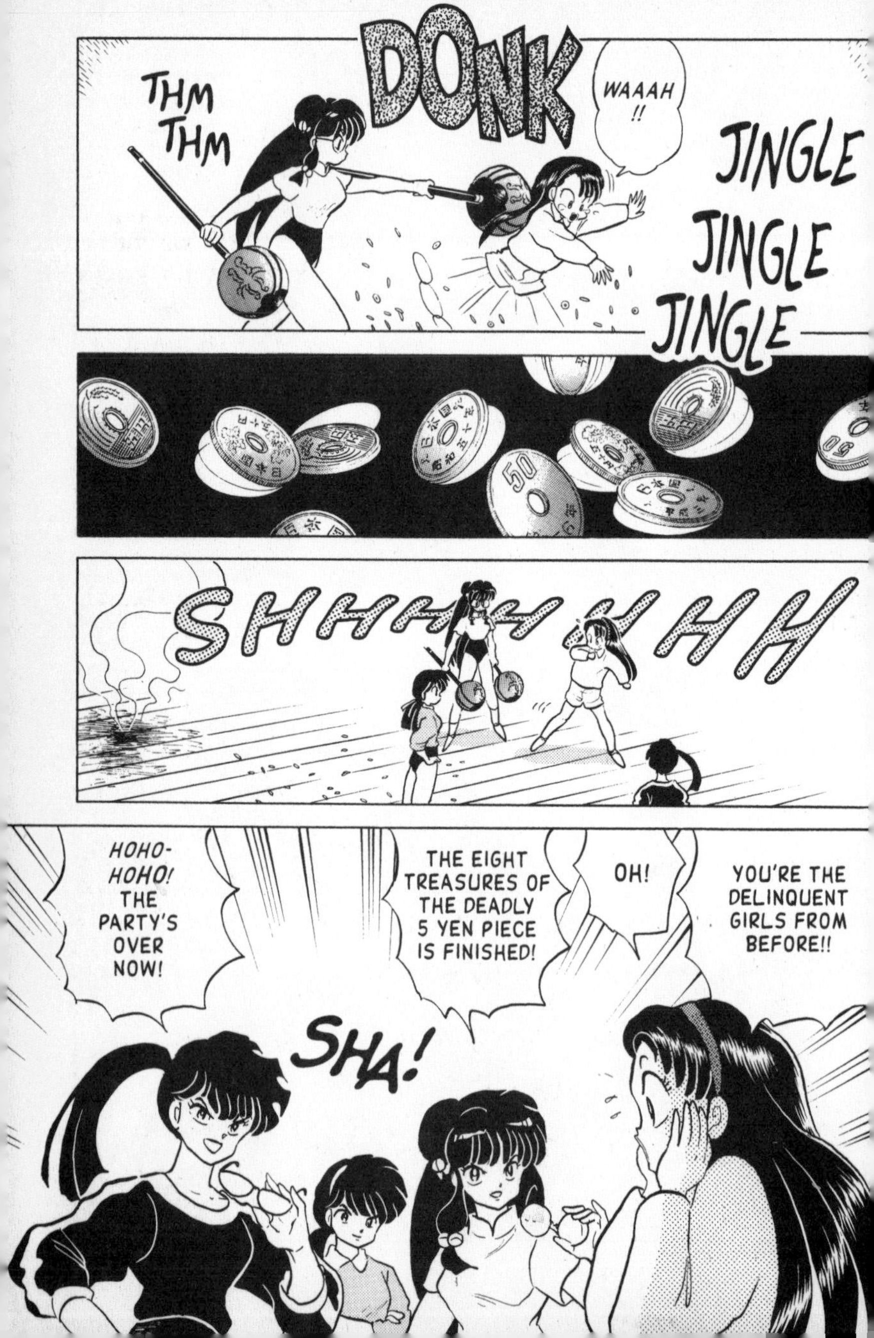
THM THM
DONK
WAAAH !!
JINGLE JINGLE JINGLE
SHHHHHHHH
HOHO-HOHO! THE PARTY'S OVER NOW!
THE EIGHT TREASURES OF THE DEADLY 5 YEN PIECE IS FINISHED!
OH!
YOU'RE THE DELINQUENT GIRLS FROM BEFORE!!
SHA!

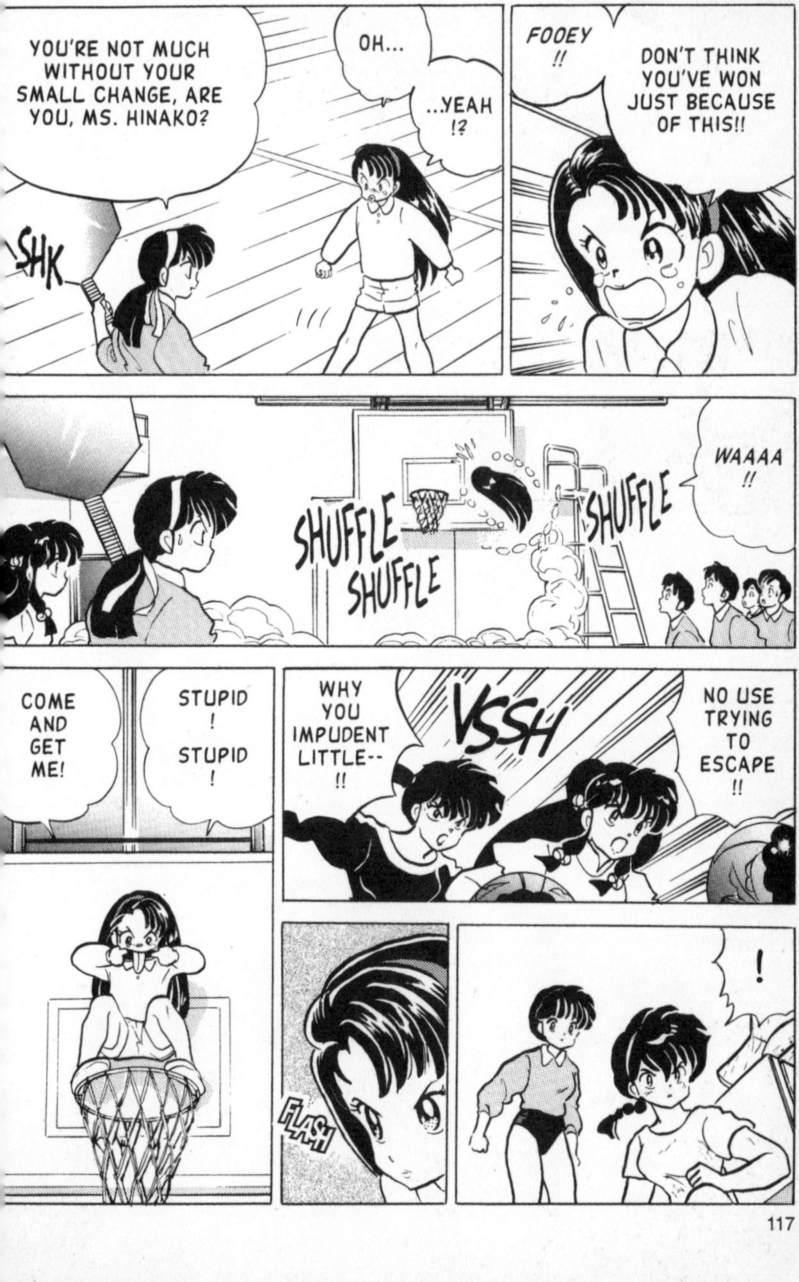
YOU'RE NOT MUCH WITHOUT YOUR SMALL CHANGE, ARE YOU, MS. HINAKO?
SHK
OH...
...YEAH !?
FOOEY !!
DON'T THINK YOU'VE WON JUST BECAUSE OF THIS!!
SHUFFLE SHUFFLE
SHUFFLE
WAAAA !!
COME AND GET ME!
STUPID ! STUPID !
WHY YOU IMPUDENT LITTLE-- !!
VSSH
NO USE TRYING TO ESCAPE !!
FLASH
!

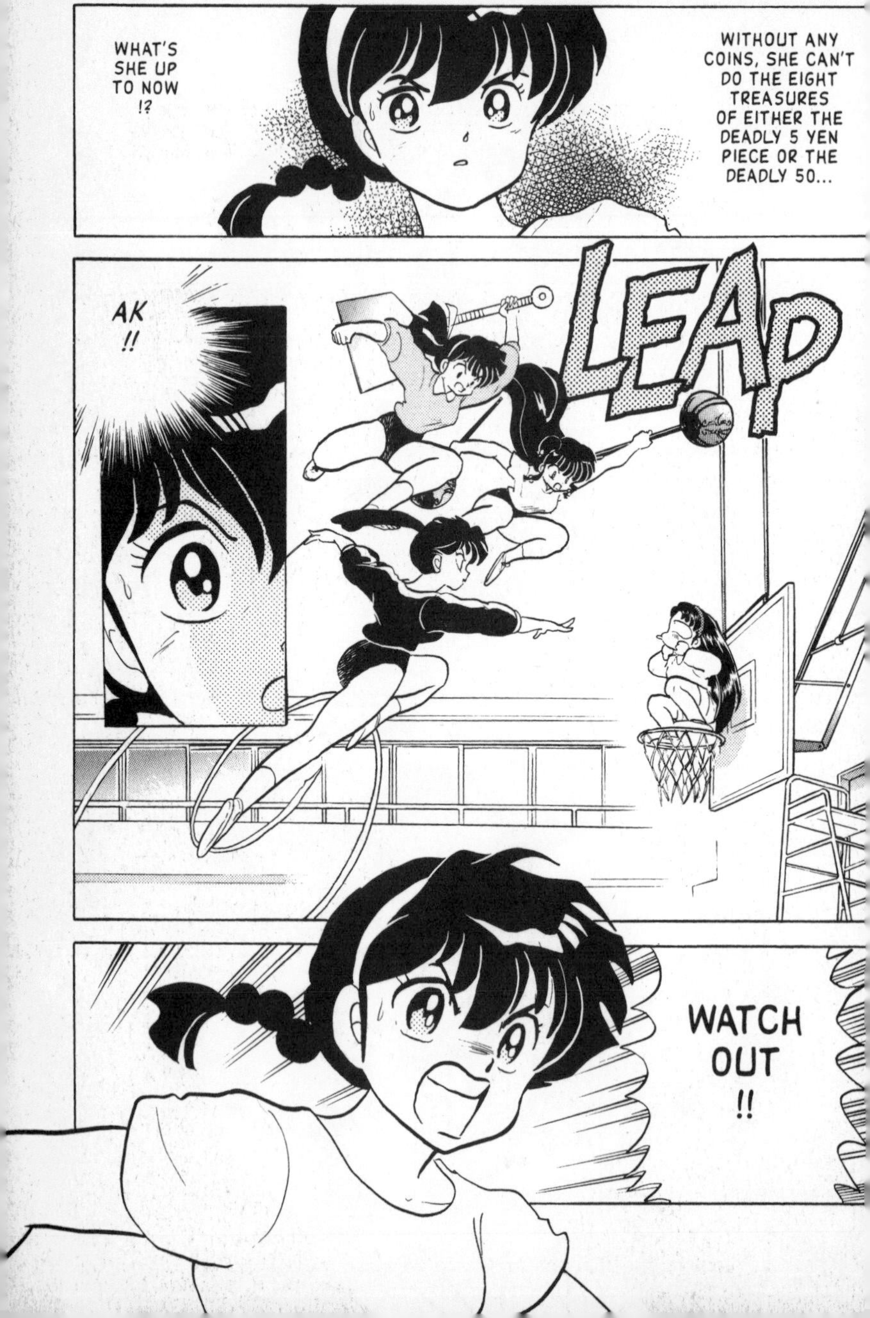
WHAT'S SHE UP TO NOW !?
WITHOUT ANY COINS, SHE CAN'T DO THE EIGHT TREASURES OF EITHER THE DEADLY 5 YEN PIECE OR THE DEADLY 50...
AK !!
LEAP
WATCH OUT !!

Part 8

THE EIGHT TREASURES CHANGE RETURN

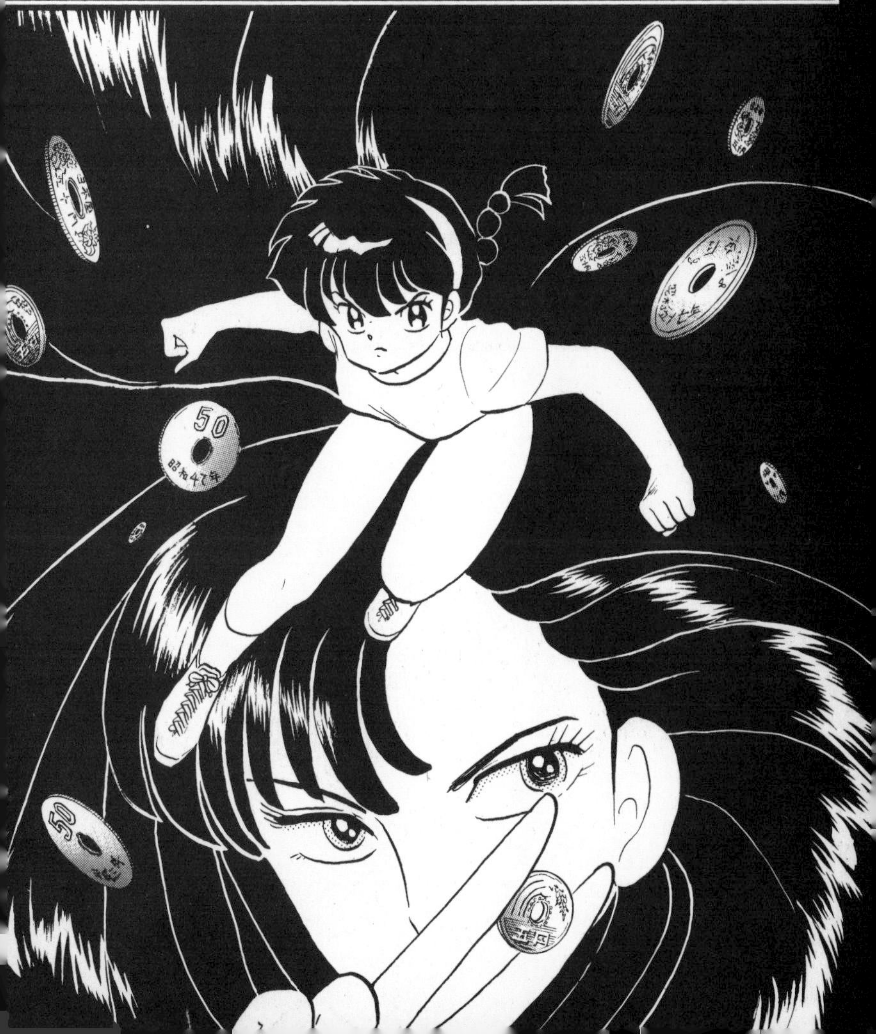

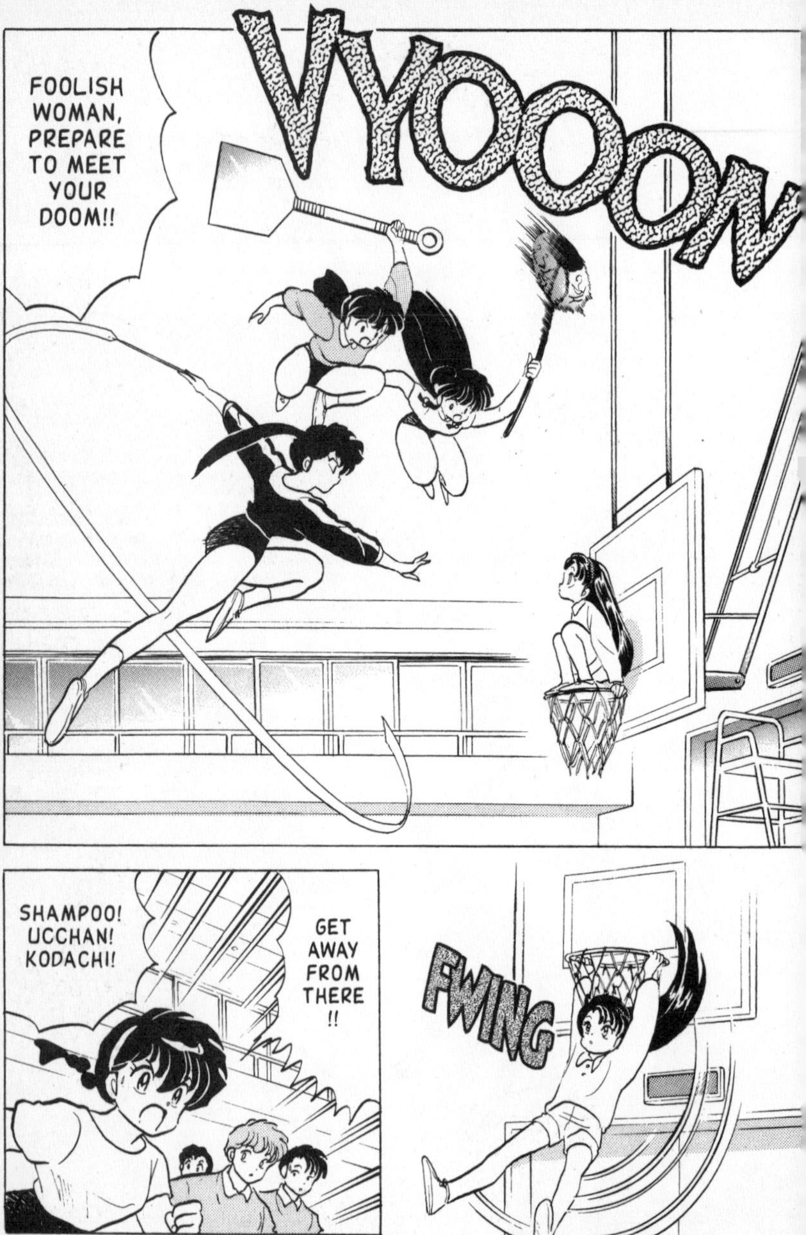
FOOLISH WOMAN, PREPARE TO MEET YOUR DOOM!!
VYOOOW
SHAMPOO! UCCHAN! KODACHI!
GET AWAY FROM THERE !!
FWING

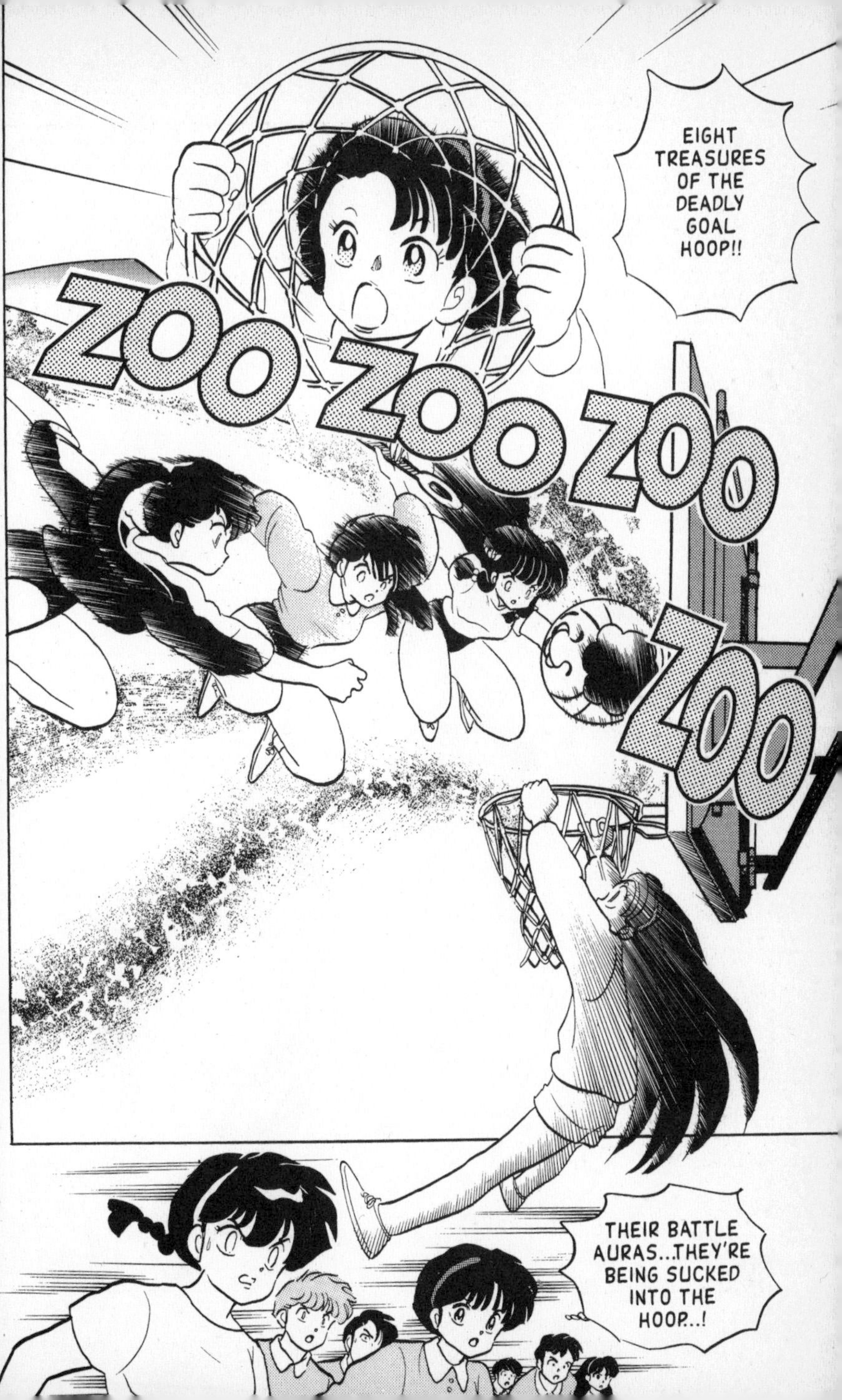
EIGHT TREASURES OF THE DEADLY GOAL HOOP!!
ZOO ZOO ZOO ZOO
THEIR BATTLE AURAS...THEY'RE BEING SUCKED INTO THE HOOP...!

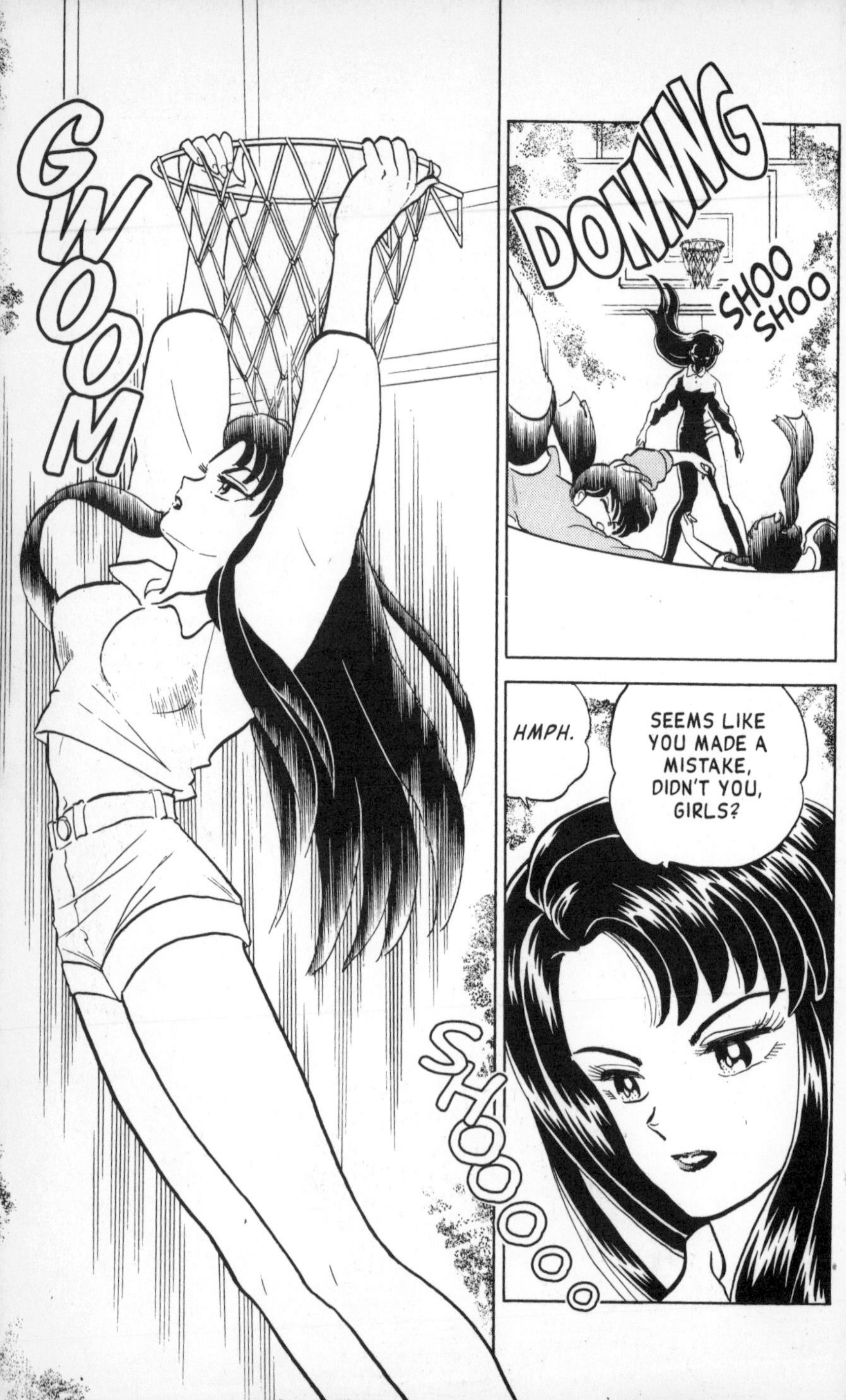
GWOOM
DONNNG
SHOO SHOO
HMPH.
SEEMS LIKE YOU MADE A MISTAKE, DIDN'T YOU, GIRLS?
SHOOOOO

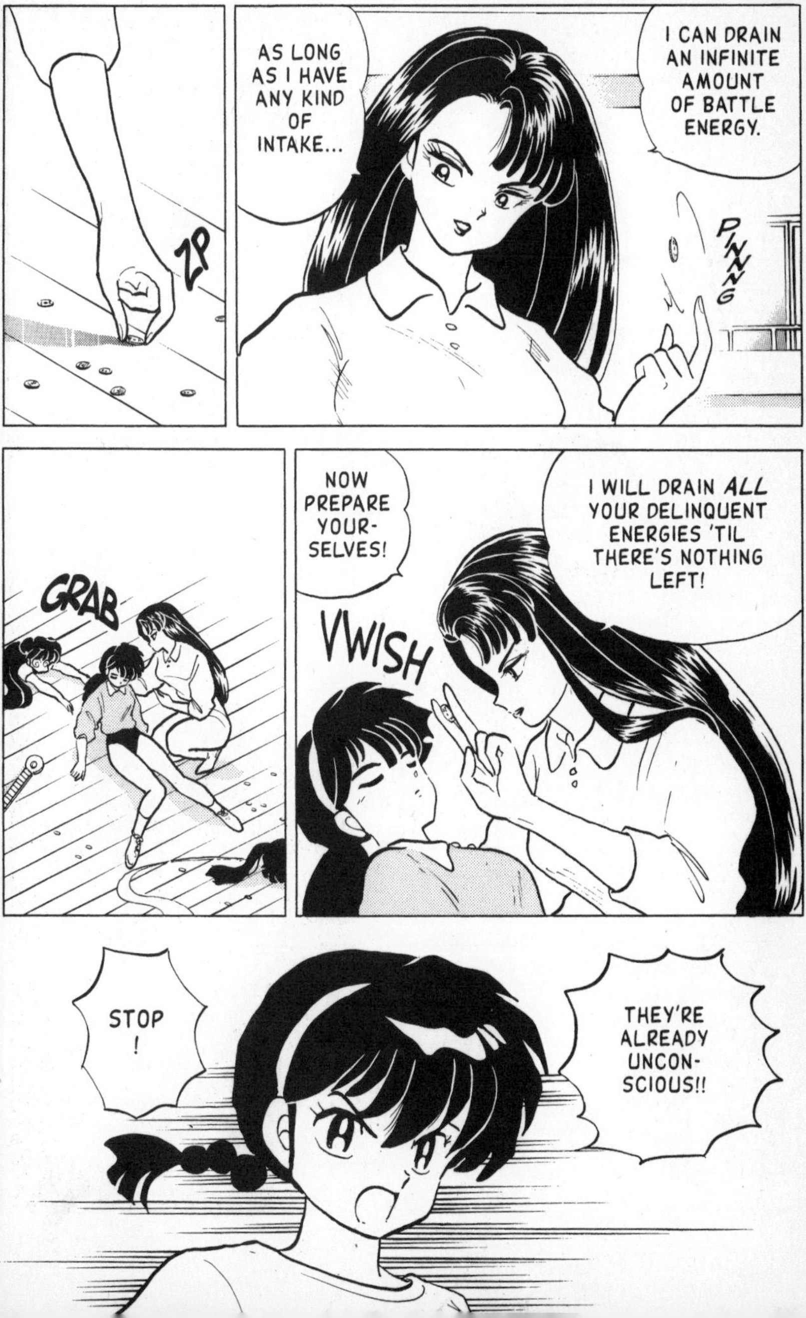
ZP
AS LONG AS I HAVE ANY KIND OF INTAKE...
I CAN DRAIN AN INFINITE AMOUNT OF BATTLE ENERGY.
PINNNG
GRAB
NOW PREPARE YOUR-SELVES!
I WILL DRAIN ALL YOUR DELINQUENT ENERGIES 'TIL THERE'S NOTHING LEFT!
VWISH
STOP!
THEY'RE ALREADY UNCON-SCIOUS!!

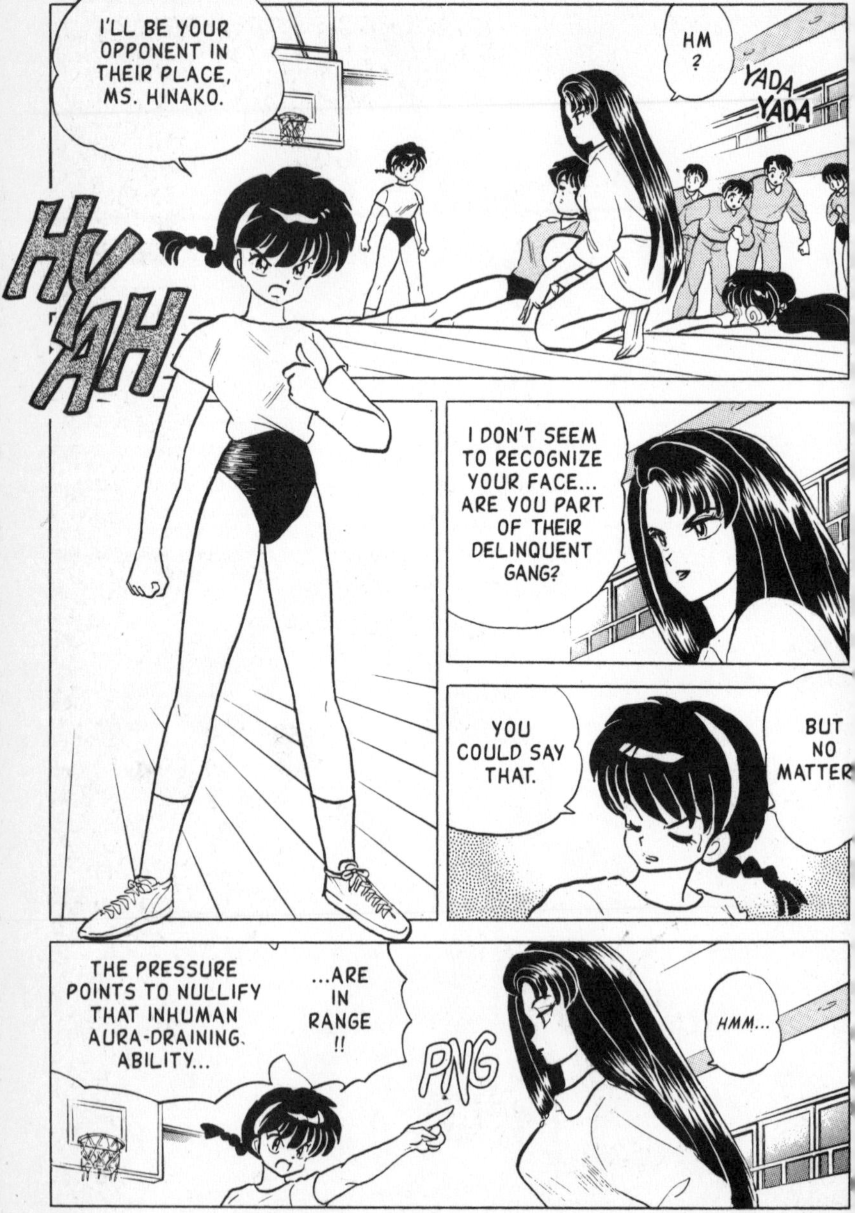
I'LL BE YOUR OPPONENT IN THEIR PLACE, MS. HINAKO.
HM ?
YADA YADA
HYAH
I DON'T SEEM TO RECOGNIZE YOUR FACE... ARE YOU PART OF THEIR DELINQUENT GANG?
YOU COULD SAY THAT.
BUT NO MATTER
THE PRESSURE POINTS TO NULLIFY THAT INHUMAN AURA-DRAINING ABILITY...
...ARE IN RANGE !!
PNG
HMM...

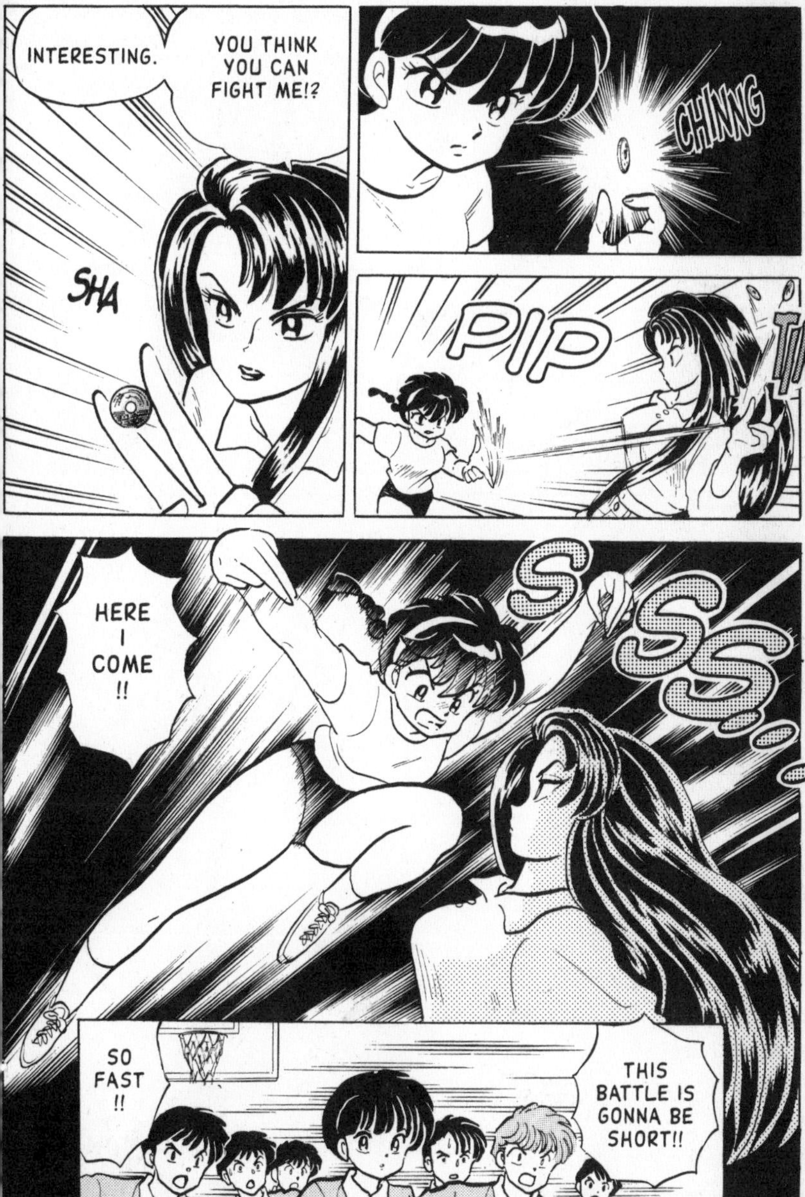
INTERESTING.
YOU THINK YOU CAN FIGHT ME!?
SHA
CHINNG
PIP
TING
HERE I COME !!
SSS...
SO FAST !!
THIS BATTLE IS GONNA BE SHORT!!

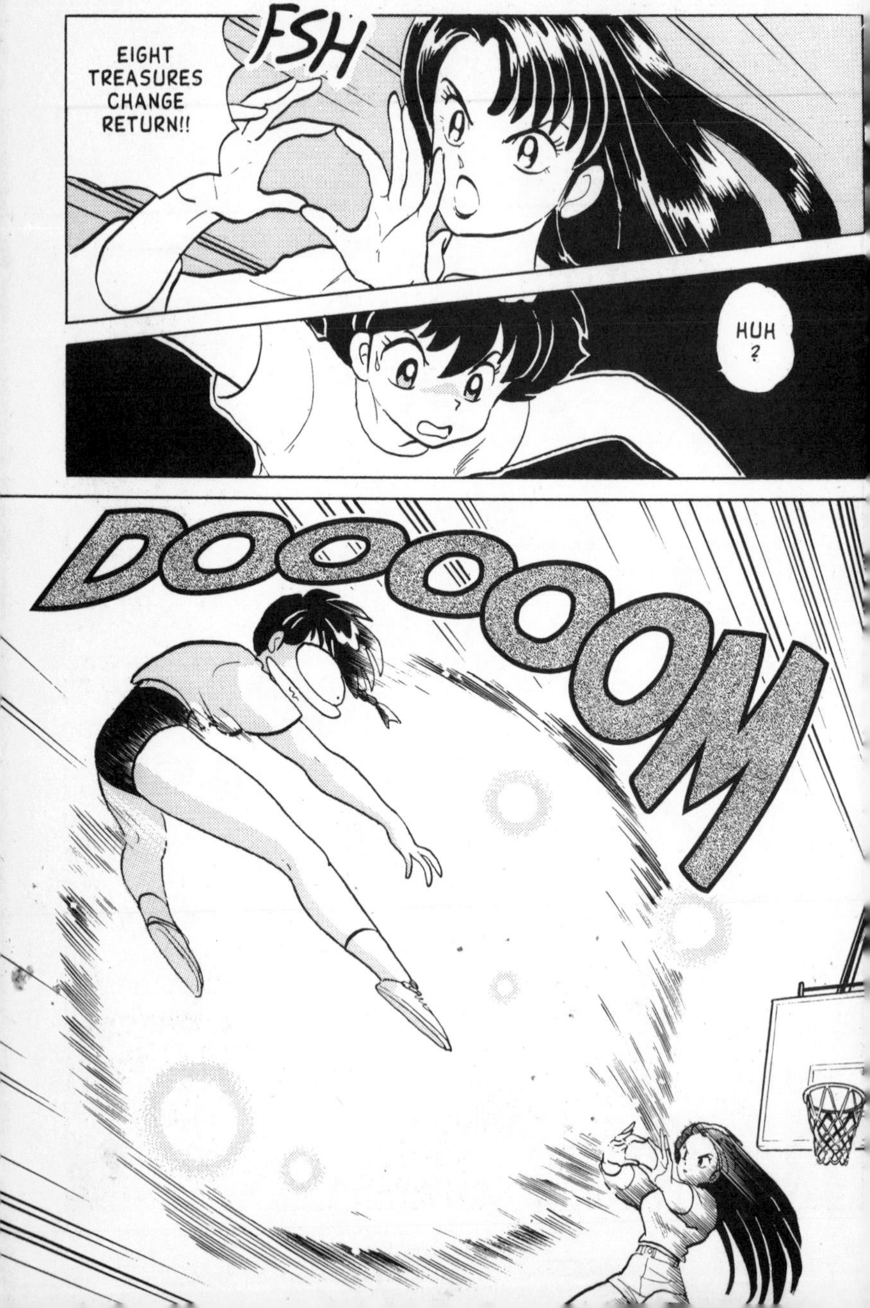
FSH
EIGHT TREASURES CHANGE RETURN!!
HUH?
DOOOOOOM

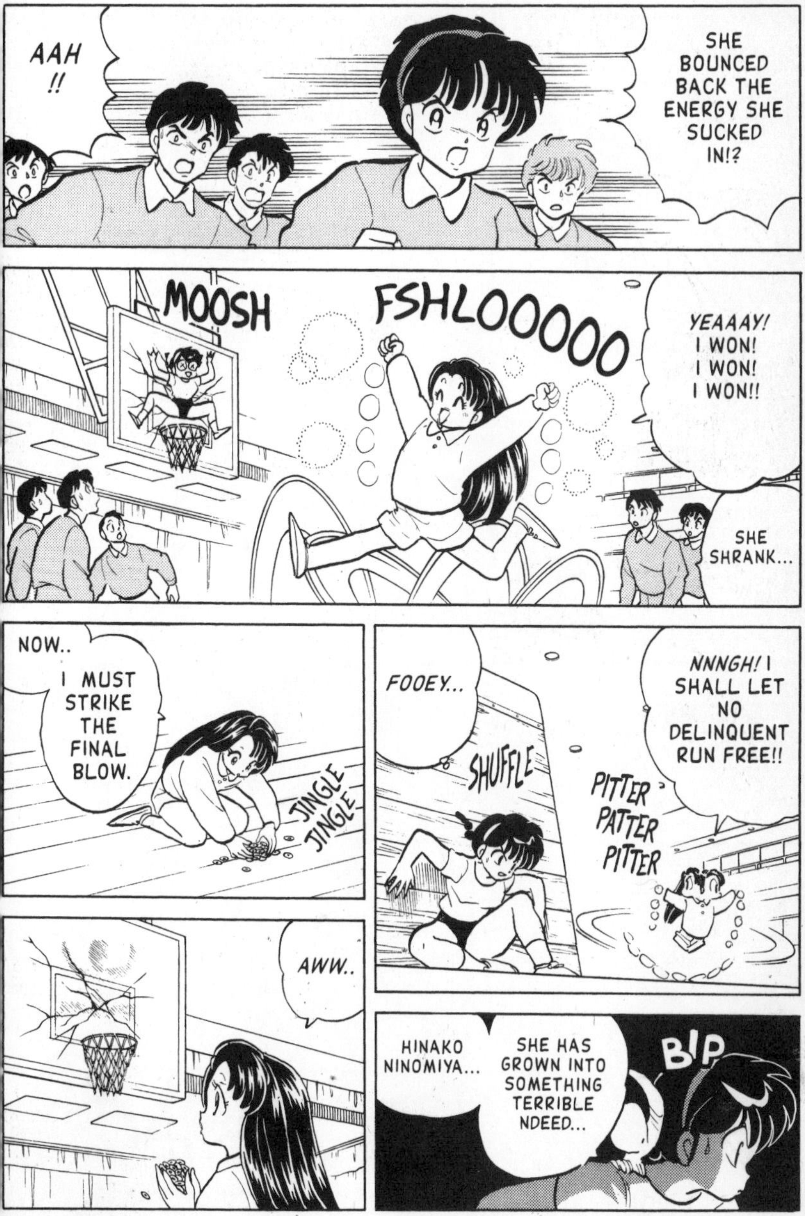
AAH !!
SHE BOUNCED BACK THE ENERGY SHE SUCKED IN!?
MOOSH
FSHLOOOOO
YEAAAY! I WON! I WON! I WON!!
SHE SHRANK...
NOW..
I MUST STRIKE THE FINAL BLOW.
JINGLE JINGLE
FOOEY...
SHUFFLE
NNNGH! I SHALL LET NO DELINQUENT RUN FREE!!
PITTER PATTER PITTER
AWW..
HINAKO NINOMIYA...
SHE HAS GROWN INTO SOMETHING TERRIBLE NDEED...
BIP

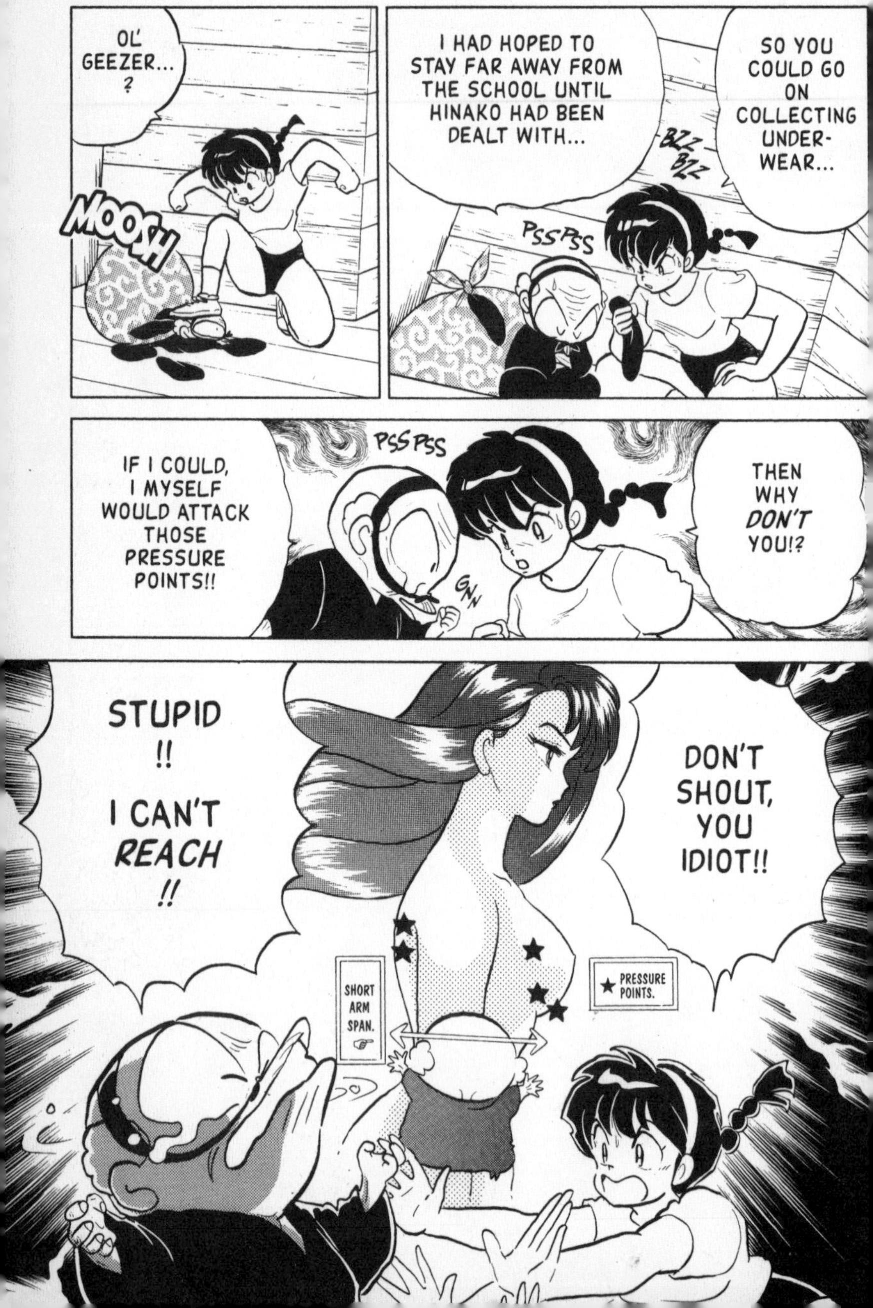
OL' GEEZER... ?
MOOSH
I HAD HOPED TO STAY FAR AWAY FROM THE SCHOOL UNTIL HINAKO HAD BEEN DEALT WITH...
SO YOU COULD GO ON COLLECTING UNDER-WEAR...
BZZ BZZ
PSS PSS
IF I COULD, I MYSELF WOULD ATTACK THOSE PRESSURE POINTS!!
PSS PSS
GNN
THEN WHY *DON'T* YOU!?
STUPID !! I CAN'T *REACH* !!
DON'T SHOUT, YOU IDIOT!!
SHORT ARM SPAN.
★ PRESSURE POINTS.

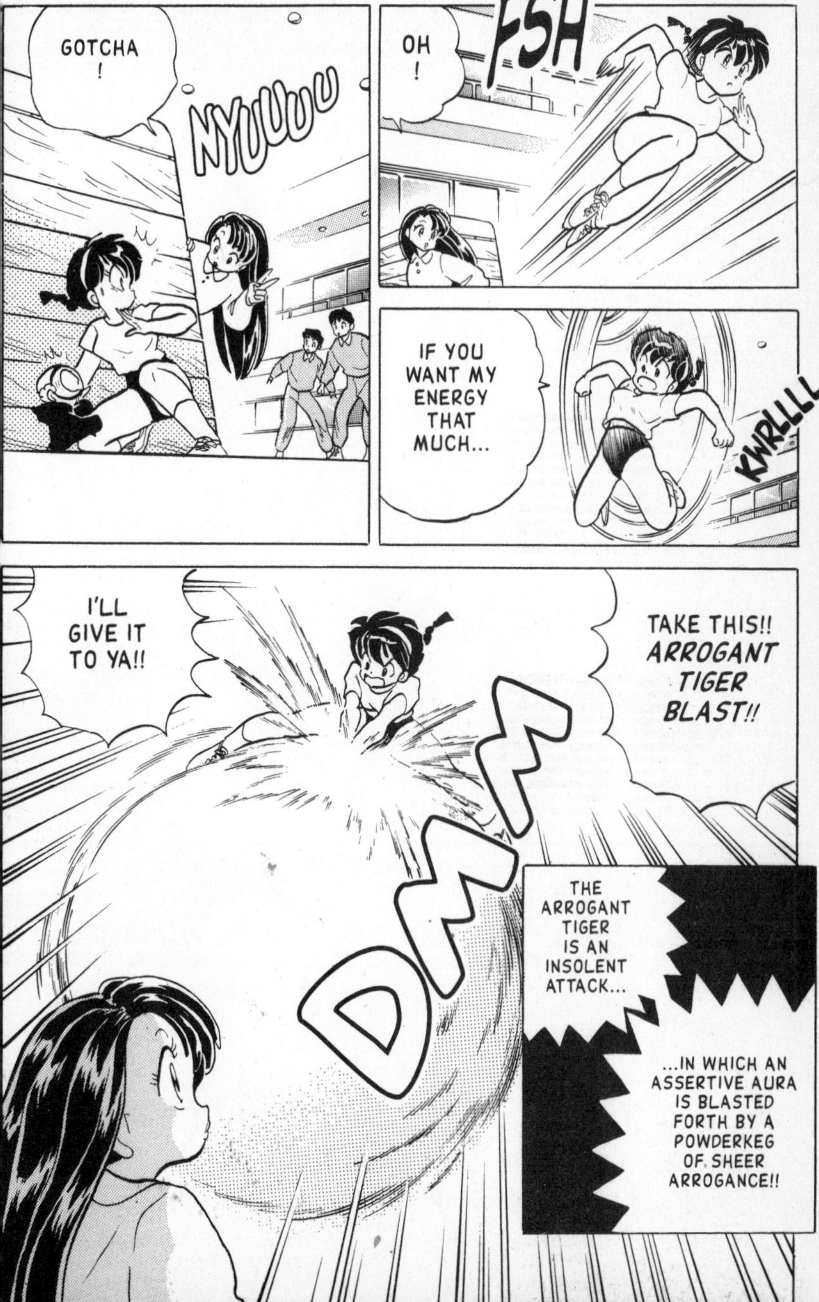
GOTCHA !
NYUUUU
OH !
FSH
IF YOU WANT MY ENERGY THAT MUCH...
KWRLLLL
I'LL GIVE IT TO YA!!
TAKE THIS!! ARROGANT TIGER BLAST!!
DMM
THE ARROGANT TIGER IS AN INSOLENT ATTACK...
...IN WHICH AN ASSERTIVE AURA IS BLASTED FORTH BY A POWDERKEG OF SHEER ARROGANCE!!

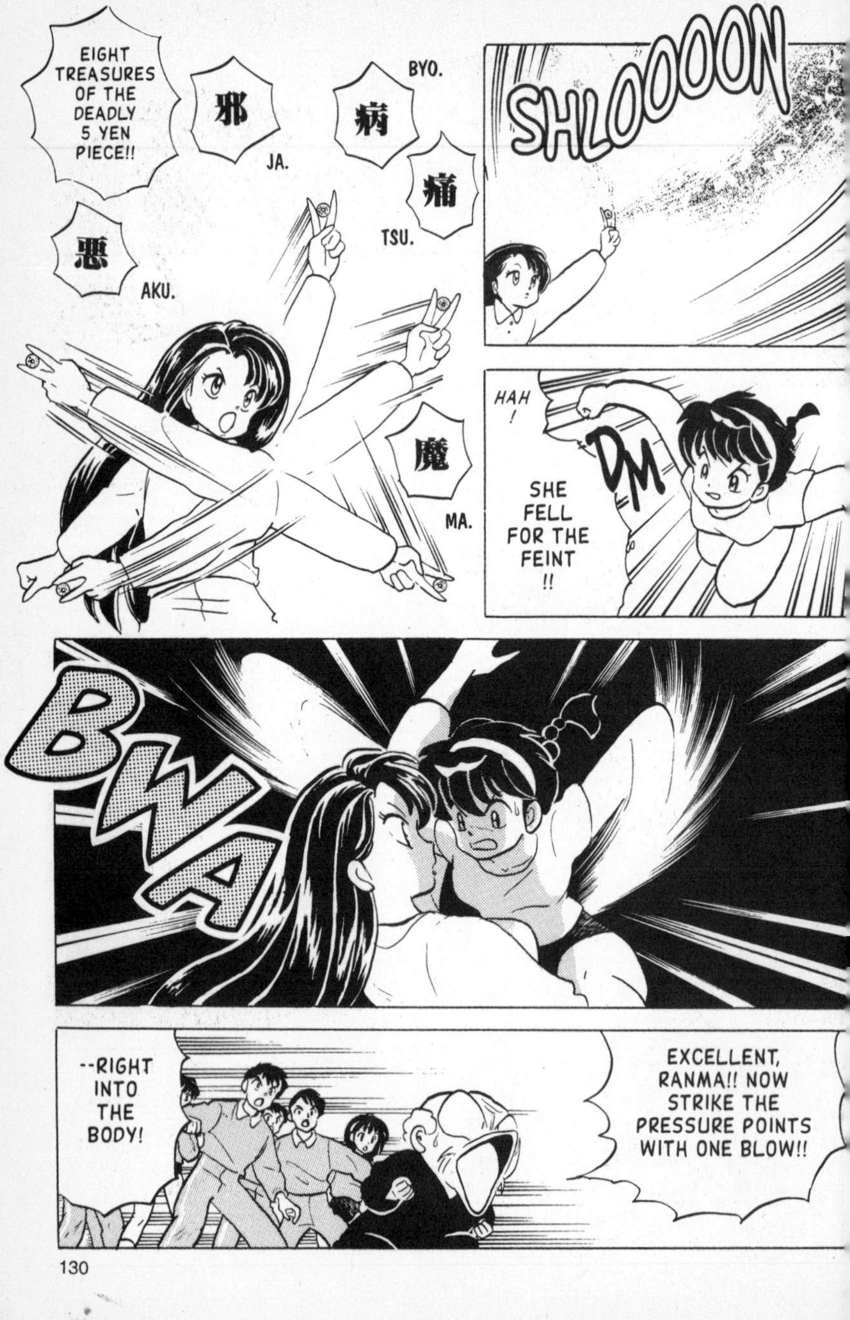
EIGHT TREASURES OF THE DEADLY 5 YEN PIECE!!
邪
JA.
病
BYO.
痛
TSU.
悪
AKU.
魔
MA.
SHLOOOON
HAH!
DM
SHE FELL FOR THE FEINT!!
BWA
--RIGHT INTO THE BODY!
EXCELLENT, RANMA!! NOW STRIKE THE PRESSURE POINTS WITH ONE BLOW!!

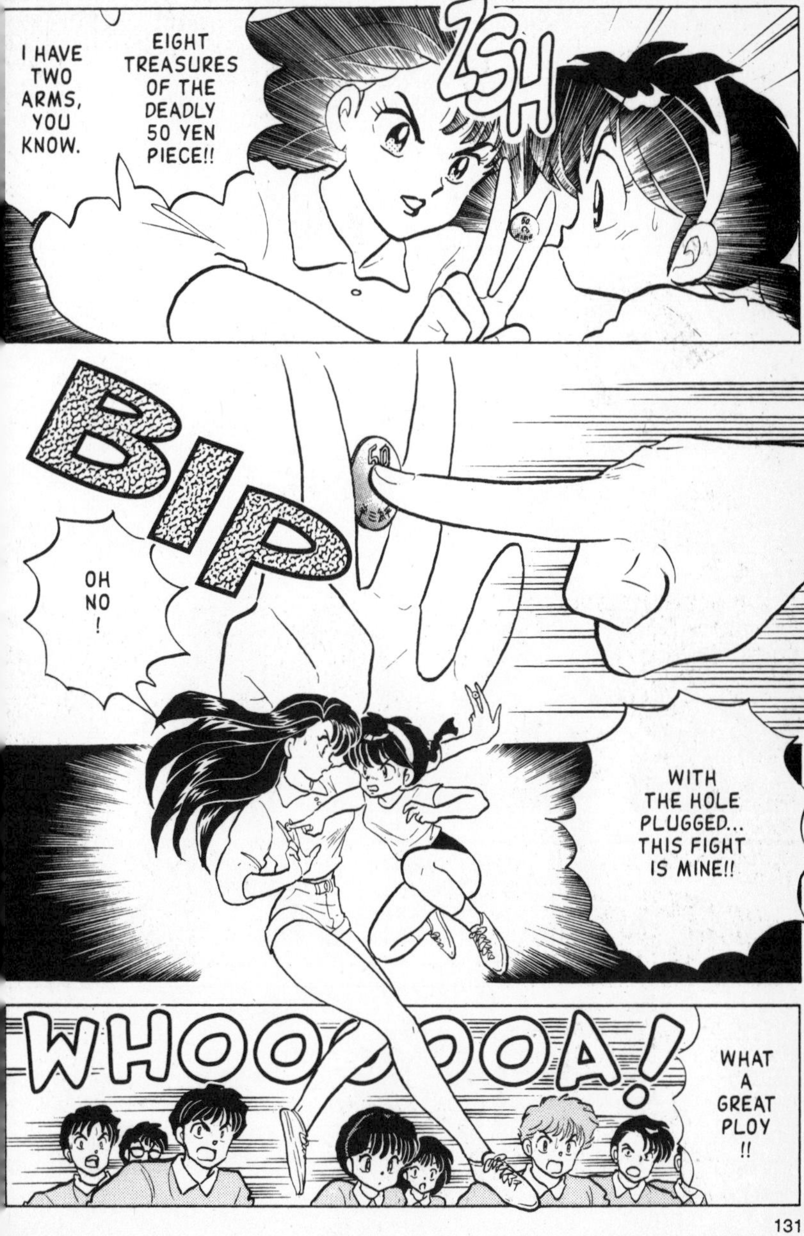
ZSH
EIGHT TREASURES OF THE DEADLY 50 YEN PIECE!!
I HAVE TWO ARMS, YOU KNOW.
BIP
OH NO !
WITH THE HOLE PLUGGED... THIS FIGHT IS MINE!!
WHAT A GREAT PLOY !!
WHOO OOA!

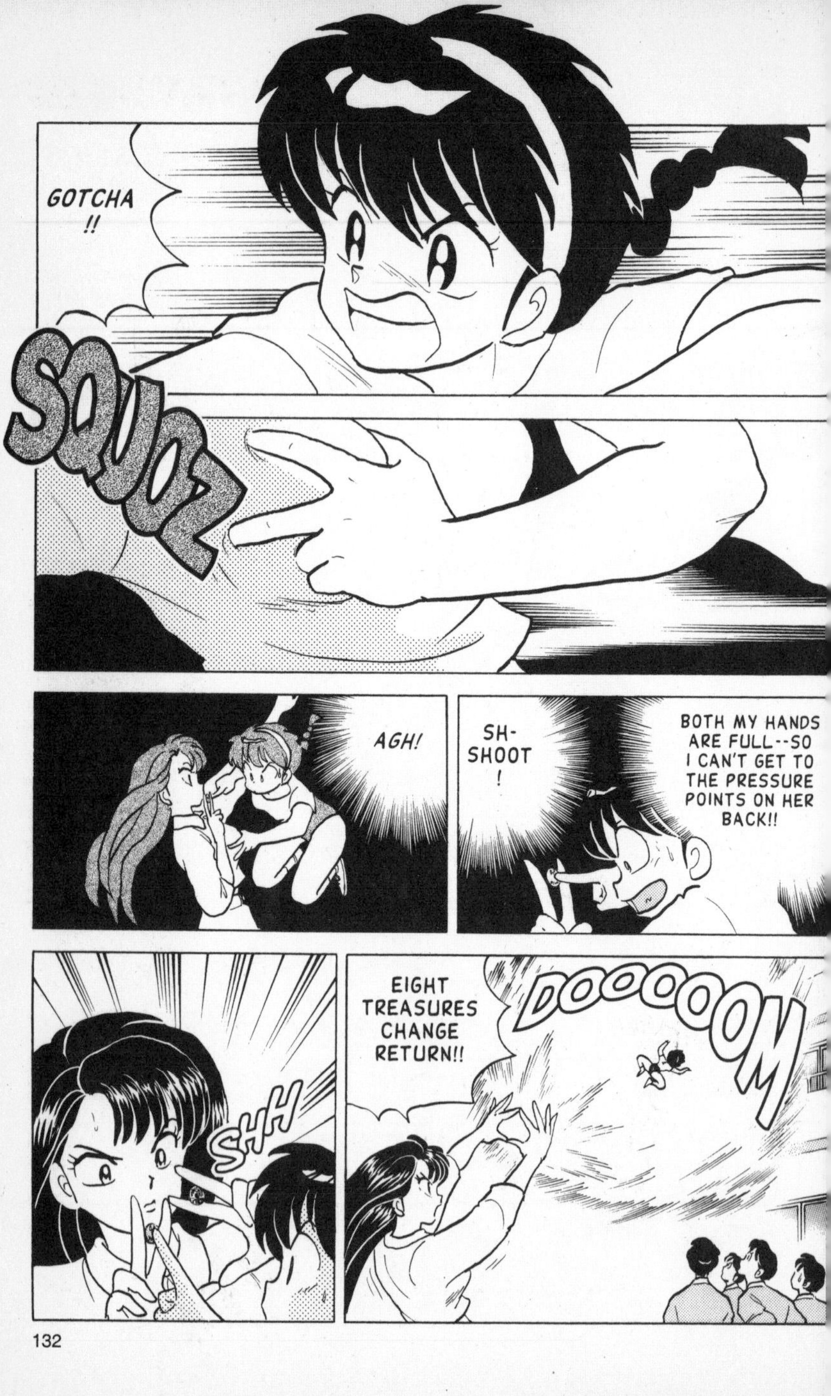
GOTCHA !!
SQUOZ
AGH!
SH-SHOOT !
BOTH MY HANDS ARE FULL--SO I CAN'T GET TO THE PRESSURE POINTS ON HER BACK!!
SHH
EIGHT TREASURES CHANGE RETURN!!
DOOOOOOM

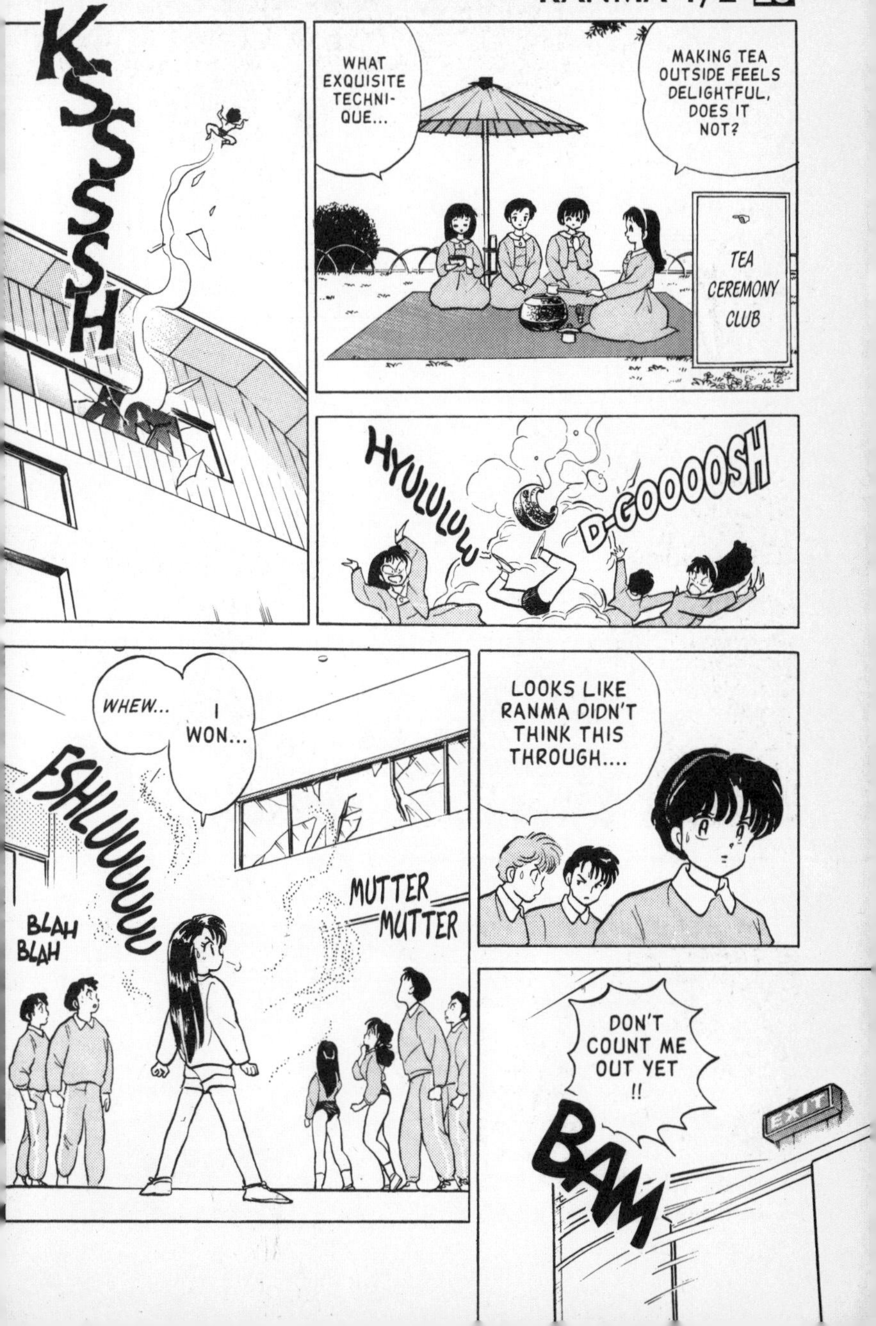
KSSSSH
WHAT EXQUISITE TECHNI-QUE...
MAKING TEA OUTSIDE FEELS DELIGHTFUL, DOES IT NOT?
TEA CEREMONY CLUB
HYULULULU
D-GOOOOOSH
WHEW... I WON...
FSHLUUUUUU
BLAH BLAH
MUTTER MUTTER
LOOKS LIKE RANMA DIDN'T THINK THIS THROUGH....
DON'T COUNT ME OUT YET !!
BAM
EXIT

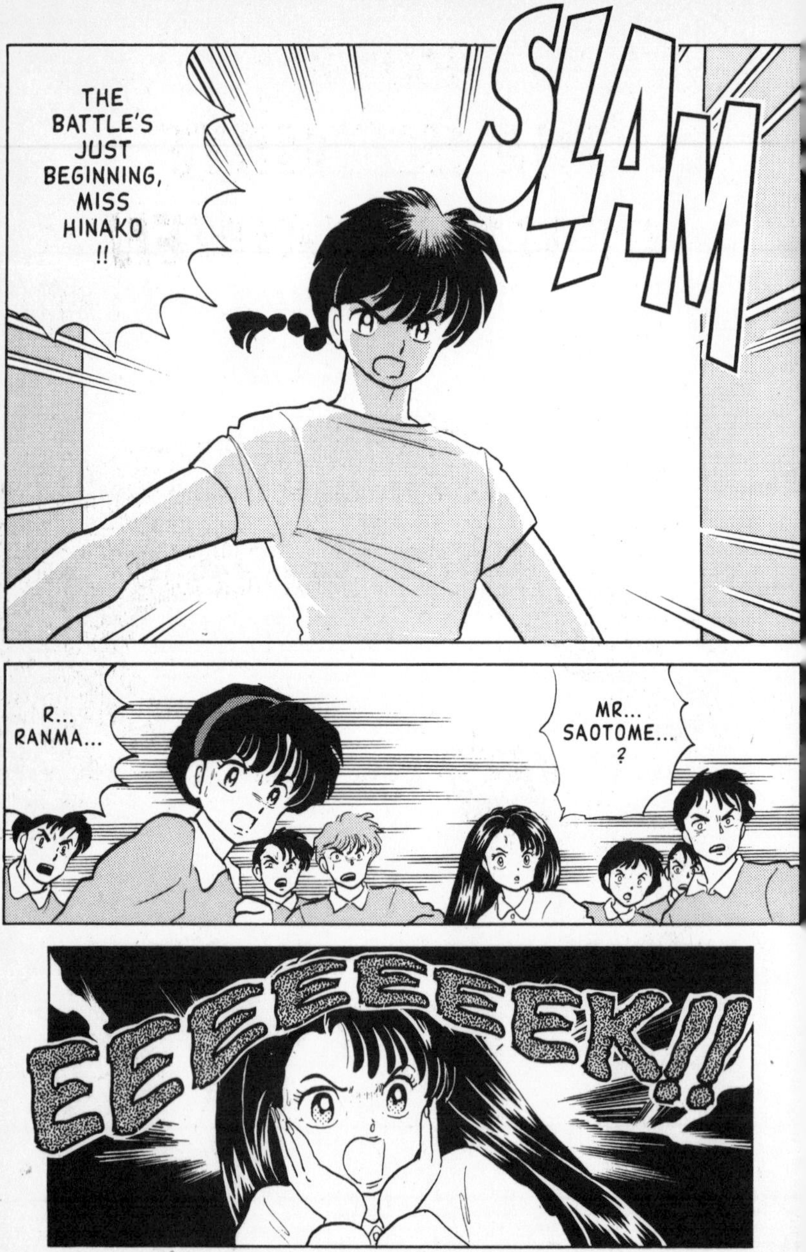
THE BATTLE'S JUST BEGINNING, MISS HINAKO !!
SLAM
R... RANMA...
MR... SAOTOME... ?
EEEEEEEK!!

Part 9

THE ULTIMATE HEALTH REGIMEN

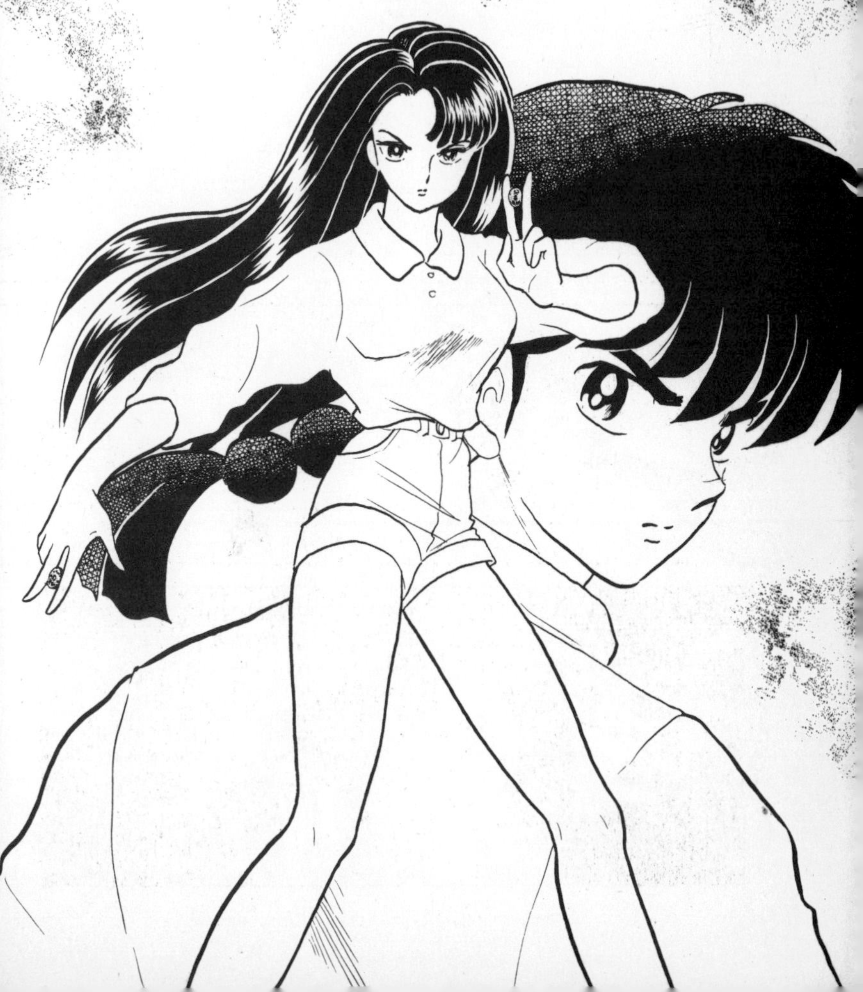

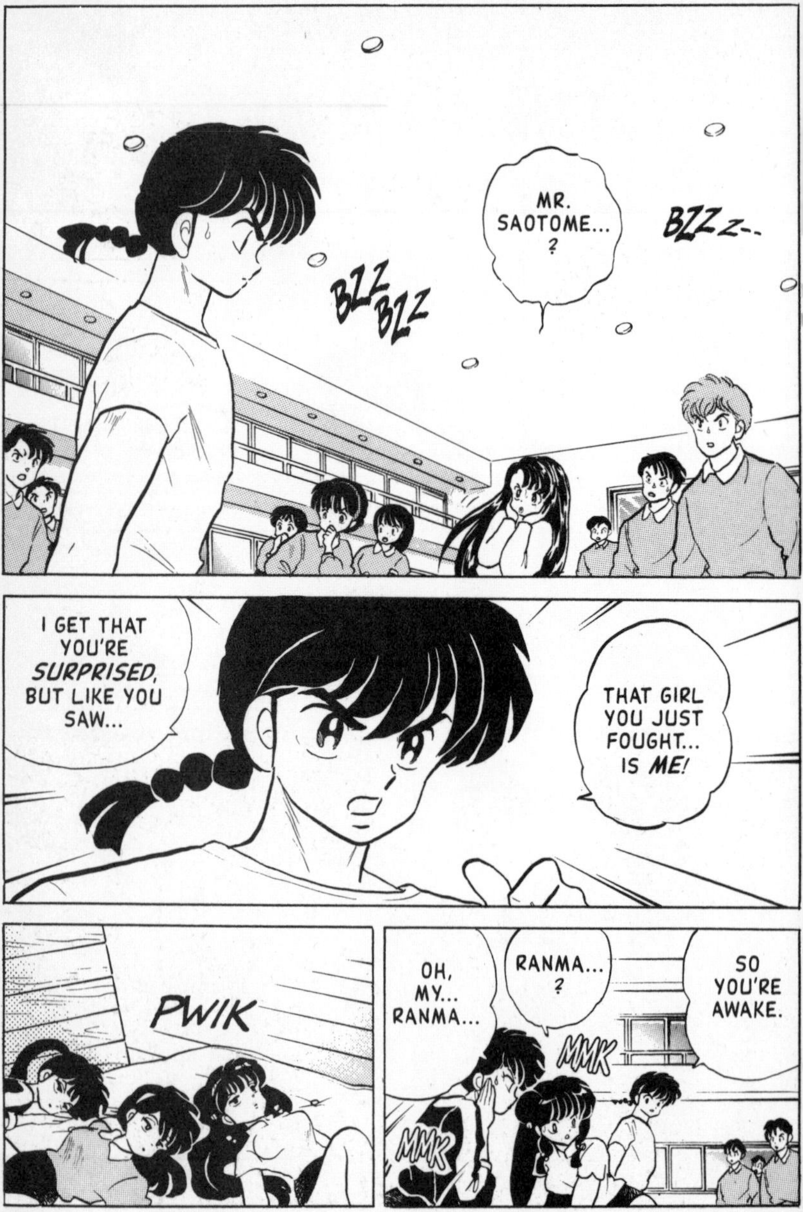
BZZ BZZ
MR. SAOTOME...?
BZZZ-..
I GET THAT YOU'RE SURPRISED, BUT LIKE YOU SAW...
THAT GIRL YOU JUST FOUGHT... IS ME!
PWIK
OH, MY... RANMA...
RANMA...?
SO YOU'RE AWAKE.
MMK
MMK

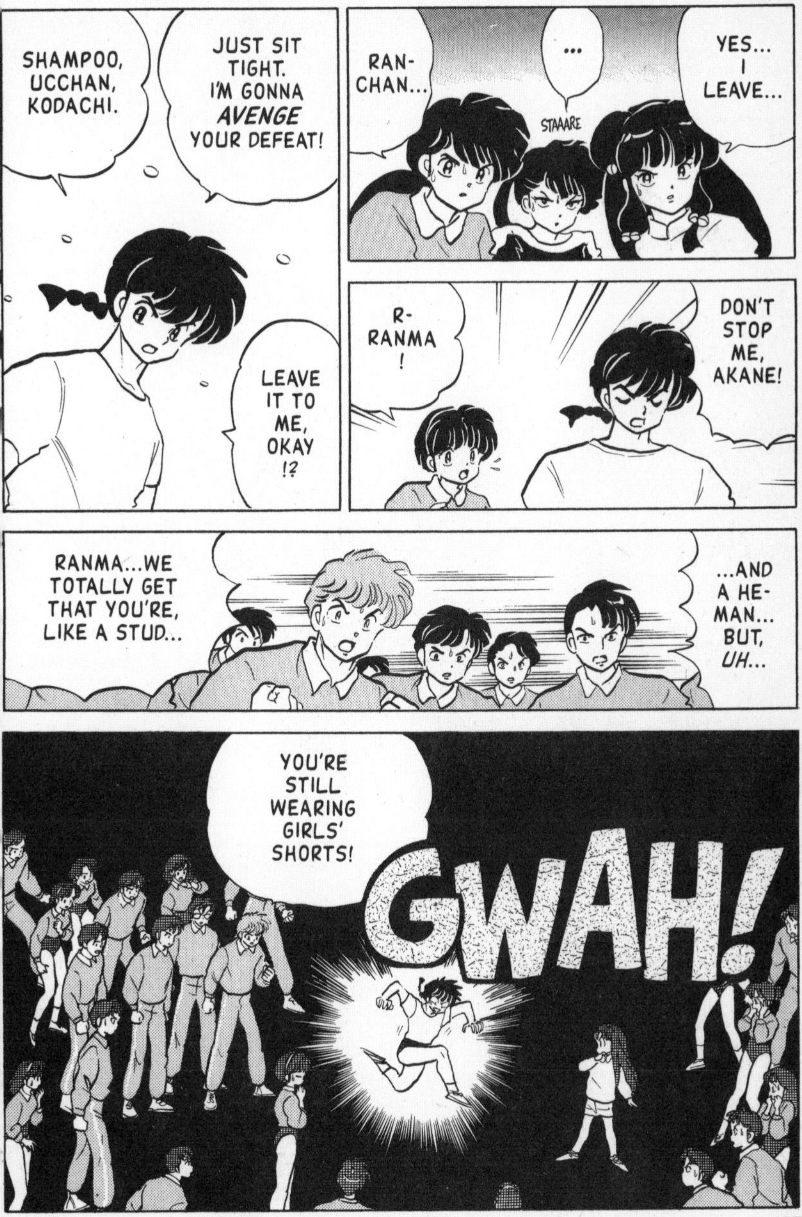
SHAMPOO, UCCHAN, KODACHI.
JUST SIT TIGHT. I'M GONNA *AVENGE* YOUR DEFEAT!
LEAVE IT TO ME, OKAY !?
RAN-CHAN...
...
STAAARE
YES... I LEAVE...
R-RANMA !
DON'T STOP ME, AKANE!
RANMA...WE TOTALLY GET THAT YOU'RE, LIKE A STUD...
...AND A HE-MAN... BUT, *UH*...
YOU'RE STILL WEARING GIRLS' SHORTS!
GWAH!

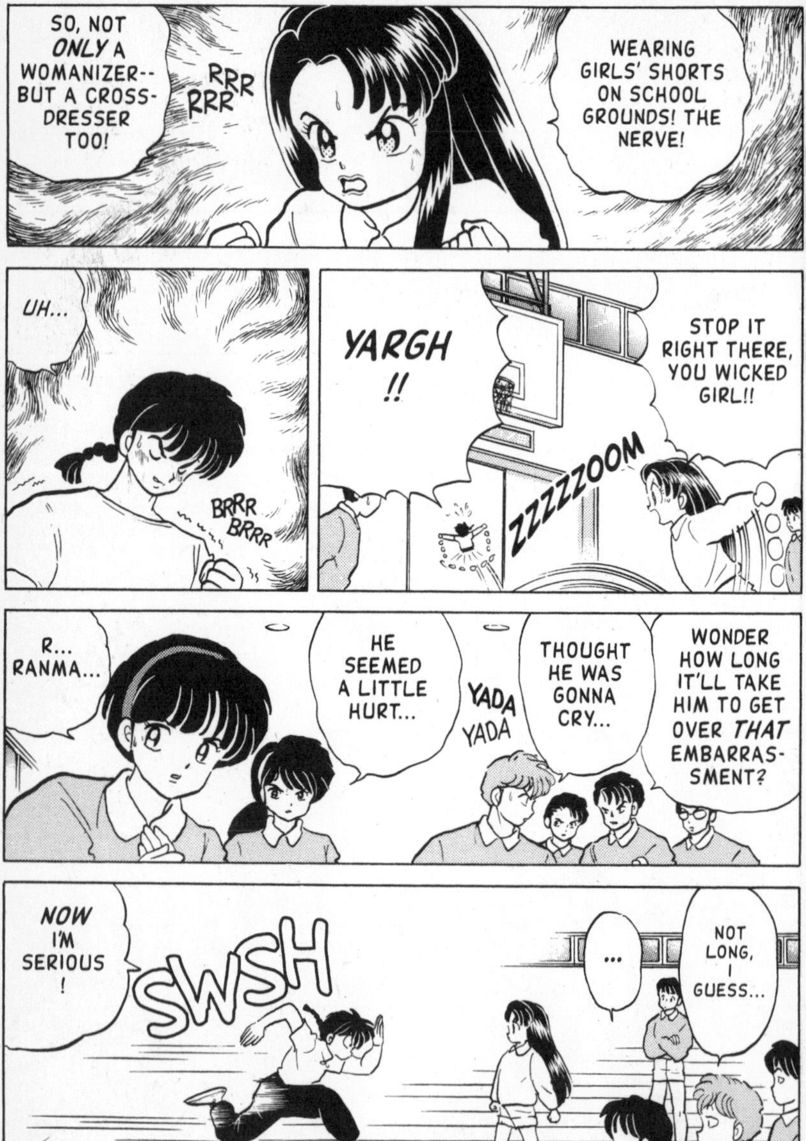
SO, NOT ONLY A WOMANIZER-- BUT A CROSS-DRESSER TOO!
RRR RRR
WEARING GIRLS' SHORTS ON SCHOOL GROUNDS! THE NERVE!
UH...
BRRR BRRR
YARGH !!
STOP IT RIGHT THERE, YOU WICKED GIRL!!
ZZZZZOOM
R... RANMA...
HE SEEMED A LITTLE HURT...
YADA YADA
THOUGHT HE WAS GONNA CRY...
WONDER HOW LONG IT'LL TAKE HIM TO GET OVER THAT EMBARRASSMENT?
NOW I'M SERIOUS!
SWSH
...
NOT LONG, I GUESS...

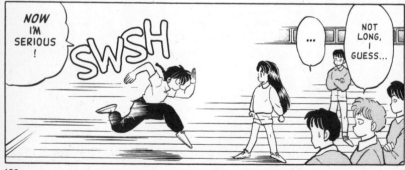

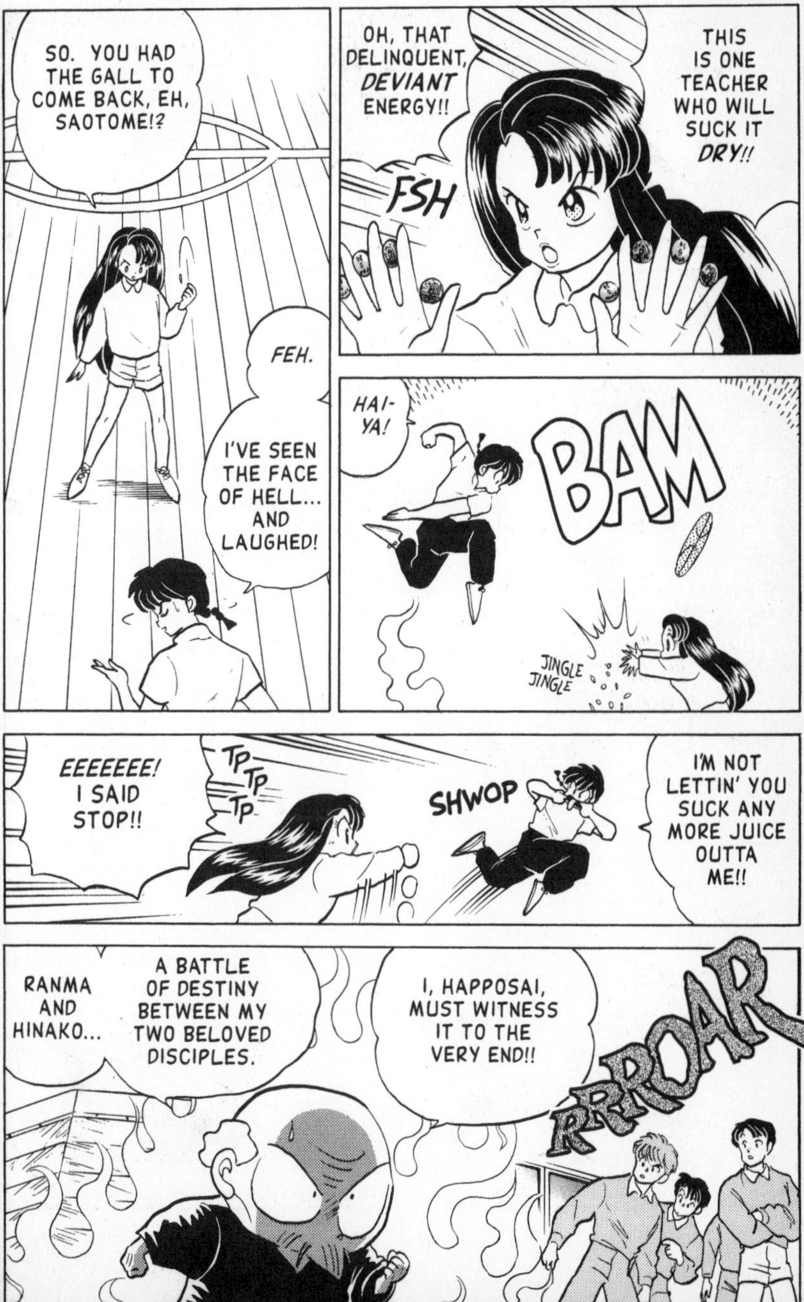
SO. YOU HAD THE GALL TO COME BACK, EH, SAOTOME!?
FEH.
I'VE SEEN THE FACE OF HELL... AND LAUGHED!
OH, THAT DELINQUENT, DEVIANT ENERGY!!
FSH
THIS IS ONE TEACHER WHO WILL SUCK IT DRY!!
HAI-YA!
BAM
JINGLE JINGLE
EEEEEEE! I SAID STOP!!
TP TP TP
SHWOP
I'M NOT LETTIN' YOU SUCK ANY MORE JUICE OUTTA ME!!
RANMA AND HINAKO...
A BATTLE OF DESTINY BETWEEN MY TWO BELOVED DISCIPLES.
I, HAPPOSAI, MUST WITNESS IT TO THE VERY END!!
RRROAR

WHAT DID YOU JUST SAY?

SO IT WAS *YOU* WHO TAUGHT HINAKO THIS ATTACK!?

BAH...

HINAKO'S EIGHT TREASURES OF THE DEADLY 5 YEN PIECE IS NO ATTACK.

IT IS THE ULTIMATE HEALTH REGIMEN WITHIN THE ANYTHING-GOES MARTIAL ARTS STYLE!

A HEALTH REGIMEN?

WHAT DO YOU MEAN?

MORE THAN 10 YEARS AGO...

ALTHOUGH HINAKO SEEMS TO HAVE COMPLETELY FORGOTTEN ABOUT IT...

WE MET FOR THE FIRST TIME AT THE MONKEY REGIONAL HOSPITAL.

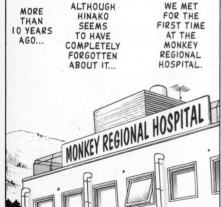

MONKEY REGIONAL HOSPITAL

SO, LITTLE GIRL, YOUR BODY IS WEAK?

THAT'S RIGHT. *KOFF KOFF.*

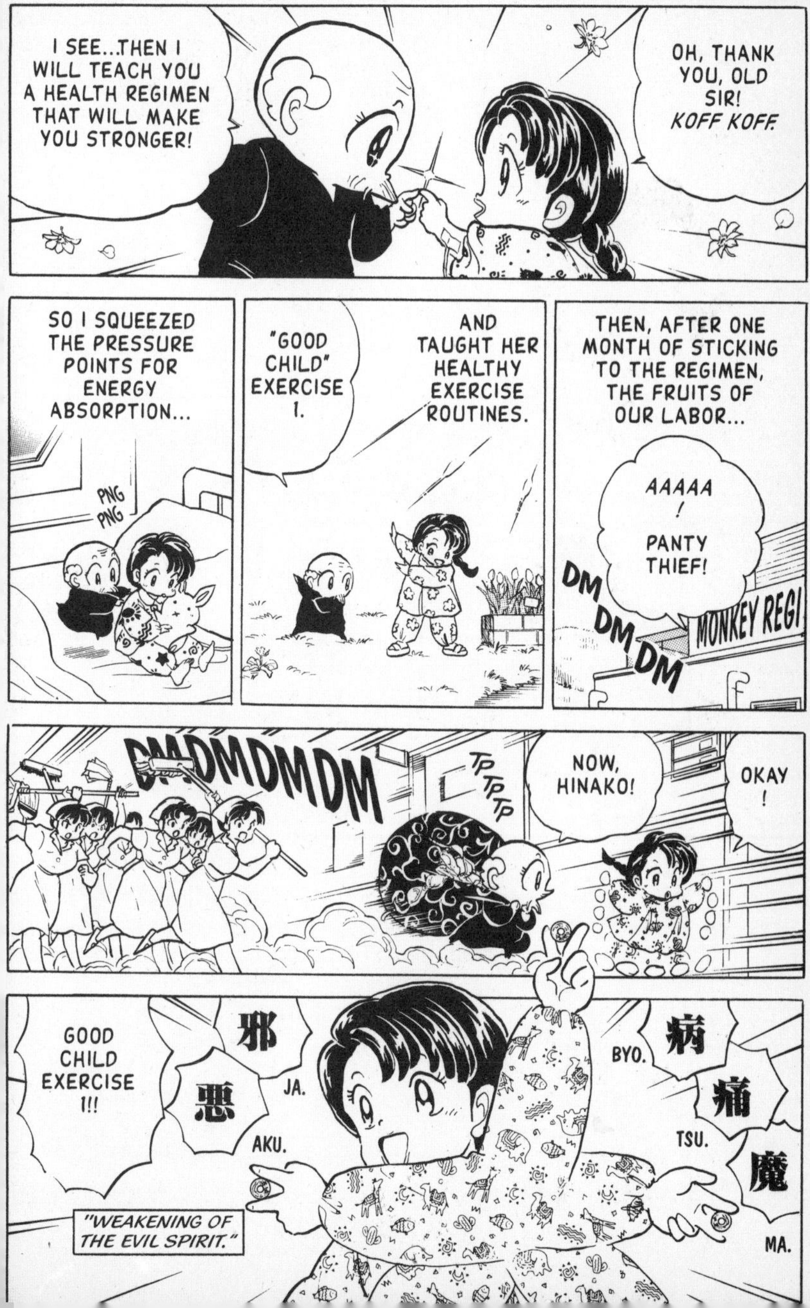
I SEE...THEN I WILL TEACH YOU A HEALTH REGIMEN THAT WILL MAKE YOU STRONGER!
OH, THANK YOU, OLD SIR! *KOFF KOFF.*
SO I SQUEEZED THE PRESSURE POINTS FOR ENERGY ABSORPTION...
PNG PNG
"GOOD CHILD" EXERCISE 1.
AND TAUGHT HER HEALTHY EXERCISE ROUTINES.
THEN, AFTER ONE MONTH OF STICKING TO THE REGIMEN, THE FRUITS OF OUR LABOR...
AAAAA! PANTY THIEF!
DM DM DM DM
MONKEY REGI
DMDMDMDM
TPTPTP
NOW, HINAKO!
OKAY!
GOOD CHILD EXERCISE 1!!!
邪 JA.
悪 AKU.
病 BYO.
痛 TSU.
魔 MA.
"WEAKENING OF THE EVIL SPIRIT."

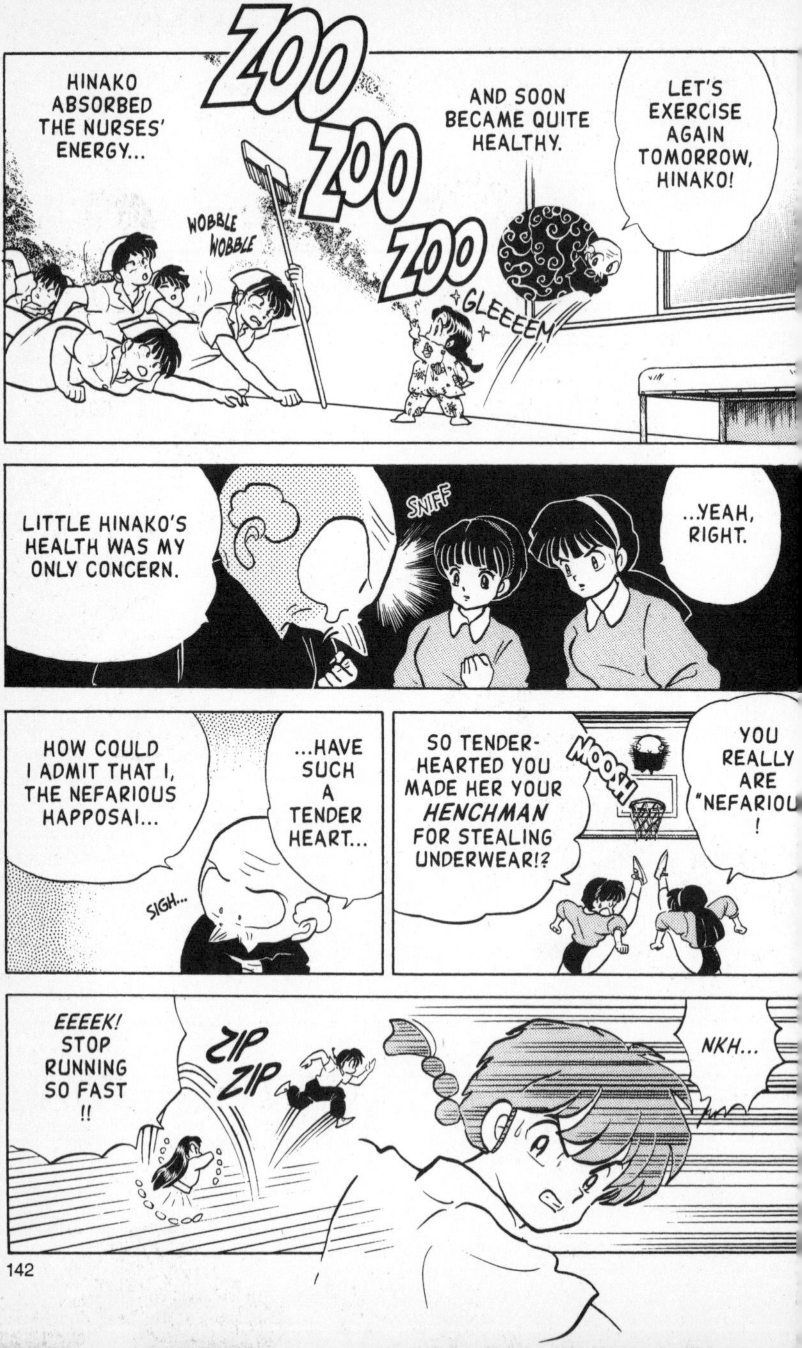

HINAKO ABSORBED THE NURSES' ENERGY...
ZOO ZOO ZOO
WOBBLE WOBBLE
AND SOON BECAME QUITE HEALTHY.
LET'S EXERCISE AGAIN TOMORROW, HINAKO!
GLEEEEEM
LITTLE HINAKO'S HEALTH WAS MY ONLY CONCERN.
SNIFF
...YEAH, RIGHT.
HOW COULD I ADMIT THAT I, THE NEFARIOUS HAPPOSAI...
...HAVE SUCH A TENDER HEART...
SIGH...
SO TENDER-HEARTED YOU MADE HER YOUR *HENCHMAN* FOR STEALING UNDERWEAR!?
WOOSH
YOU REALLY ARE "NEFARIOU
!
EEEEK! STOP RUNNING SO FAST !!
ZIP ZIP
NKH...

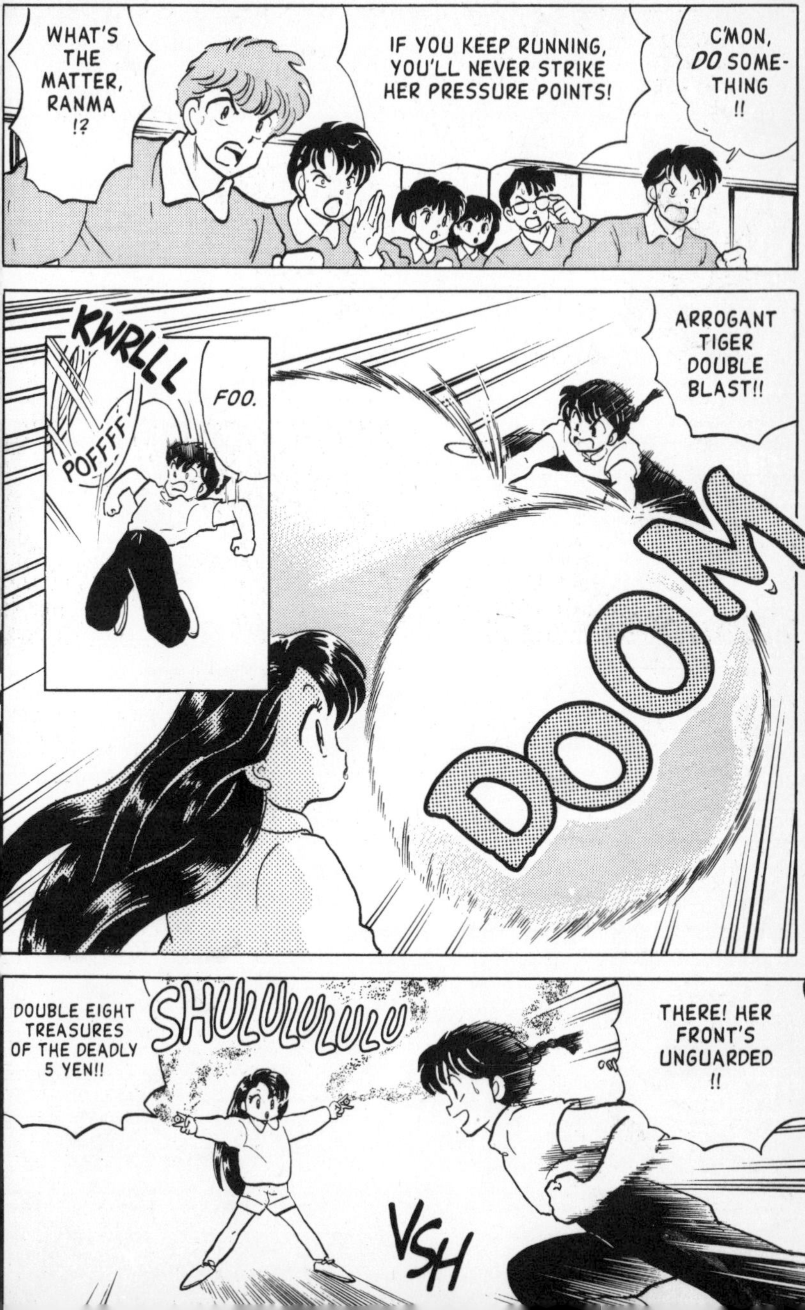
WHAT'S THE MATTER, RANMA !?
IF YOU KEEP RUNNING, YOU'LL NEVER STRIKE HER PRESSURE POINTS!
C'MON, DO SOMETHING !!
KWRLLL
FOO.
POFFFF
ARROGANT TIGER DOUBLE BLAST!!
DOOM
DOUBLE EIGHT TREASURES OF THE DEADLY 5 YEN!!
SHULULULULU
THERE! HER FRONT'S UNGUARDED !!
VSH

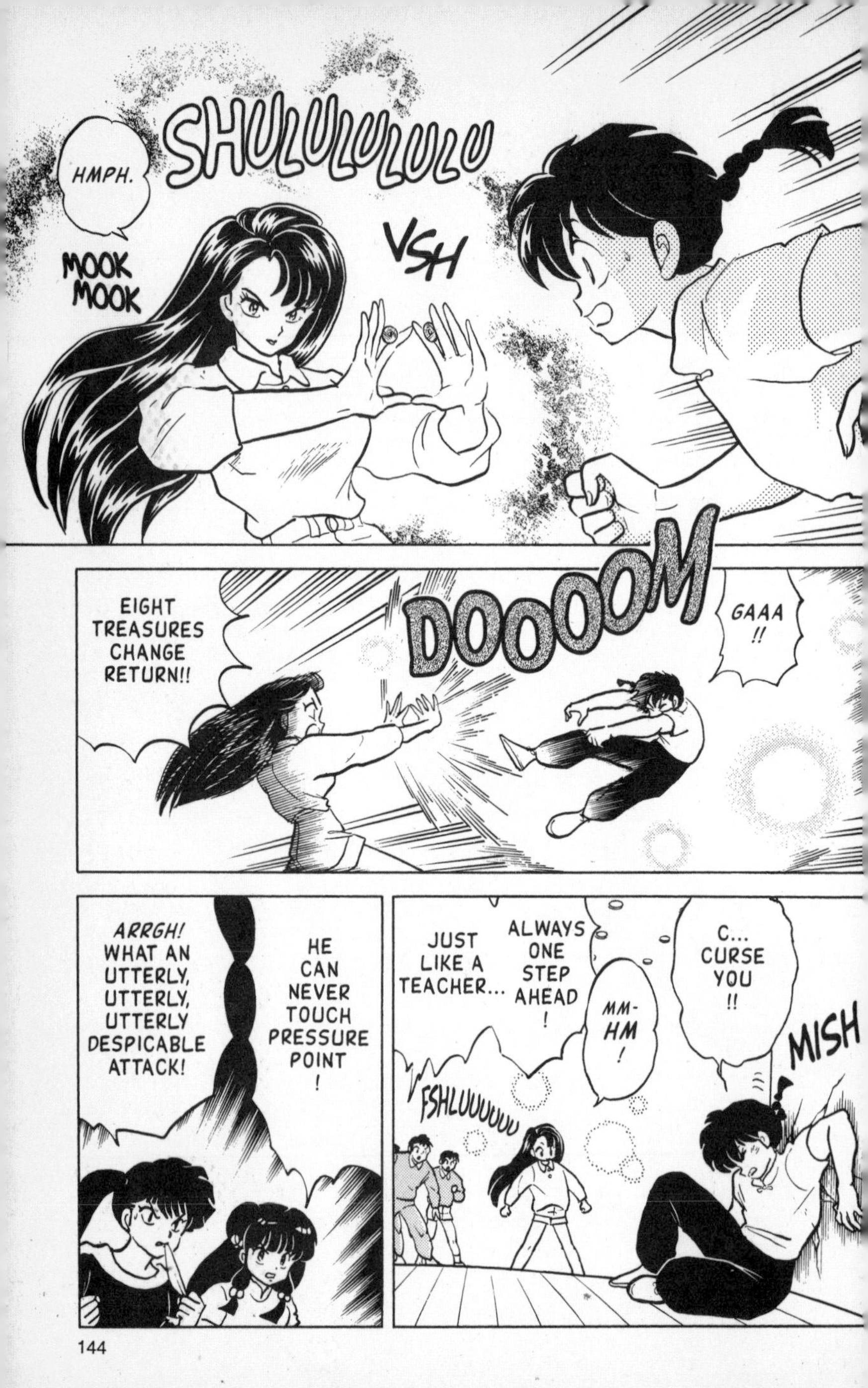

HMPH.
SHULULULULU
MOOK MOOK
VSH
EIGHT TREASURES CHANGE RETURN!!
DOOOOOM
GAAA!!
ARRGH! WHAT AN UTTERLY, UTTERLY, UTTERLY DESPICABLE ATTACK!
HE CAN NEVER TOUCH PRESSURE POINT!
JUST LIKE A TEACHER...
ALWAYS ONE STEP AHEAD!
MM-HM!
C... CURSE YOU!!
MISH
FSHLUUUUUU

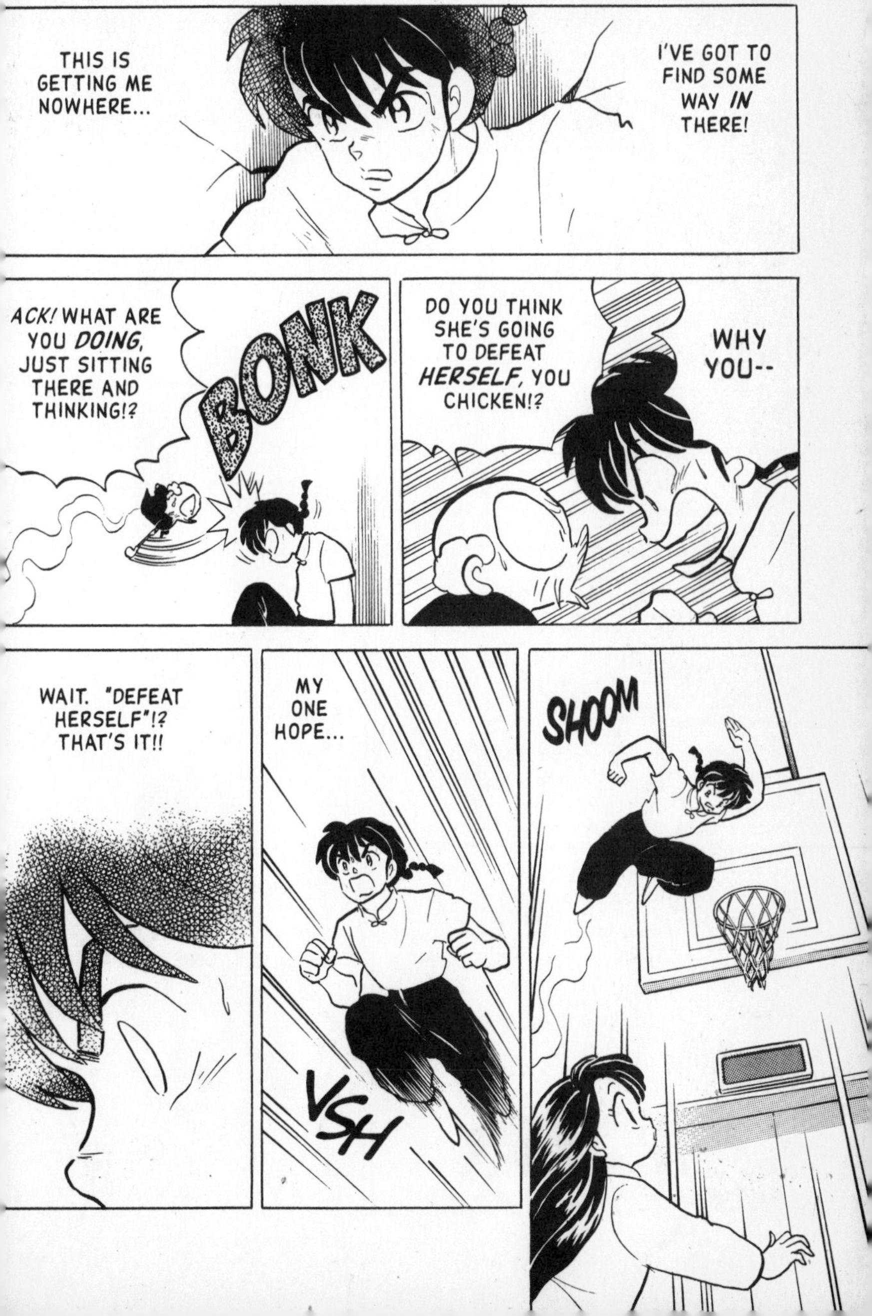
THIS IS GETTING ME NOWHERE...
I'VE GOT TO FIND SOME WAY *IN* THERE!
ACK! WHAT ARE YOU *DOING*, JUST SITTING THERE AND THINKING!?
BONK
DO YOU THINK SHE'S GOING TO DEFEAT *HERSELF*, YOU CHICKEN!?
WHY YOU--
WAIT. "DEFEAT HERSELF"!? THAT'S IT!!
MY ONE HOPE...
VSH
SHOOM

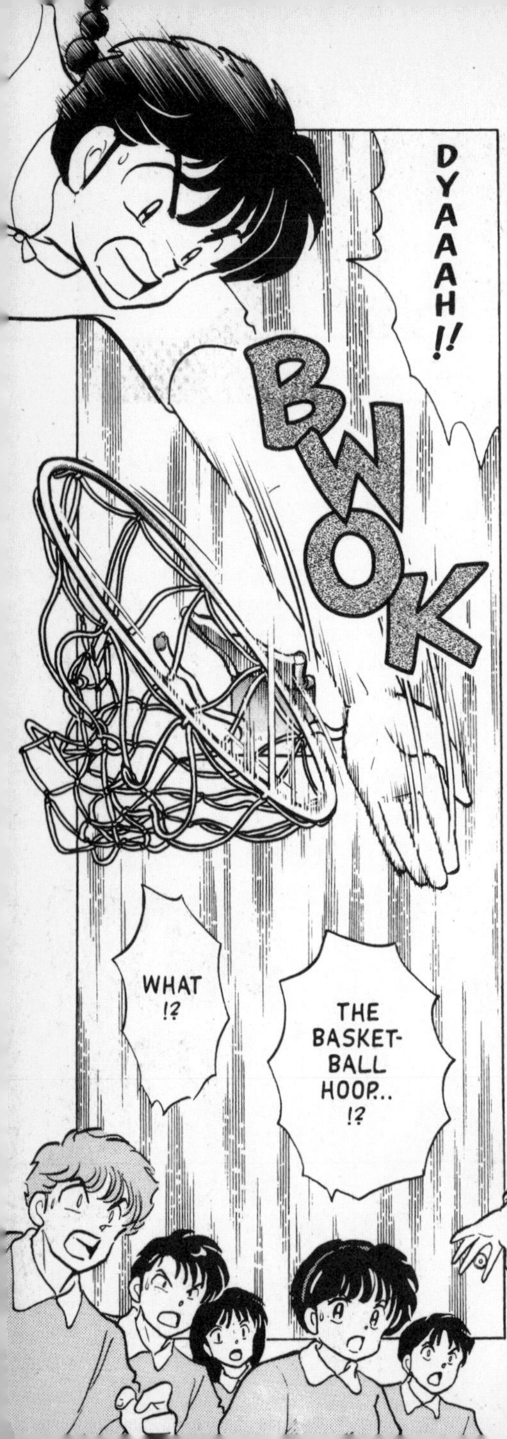
DYAAAAH!!
BWOK
WHAT!?
THE BASKET-BALL HOOP...!?
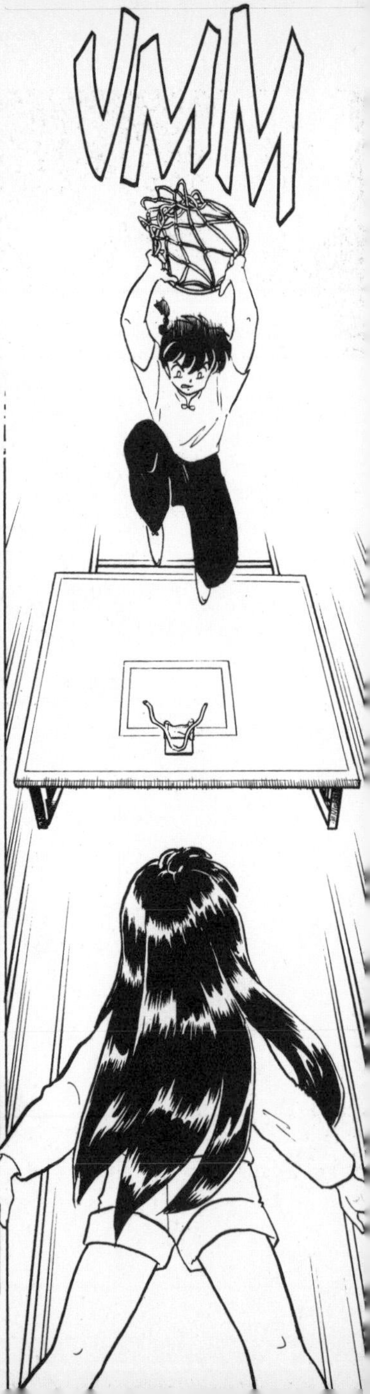
VMM

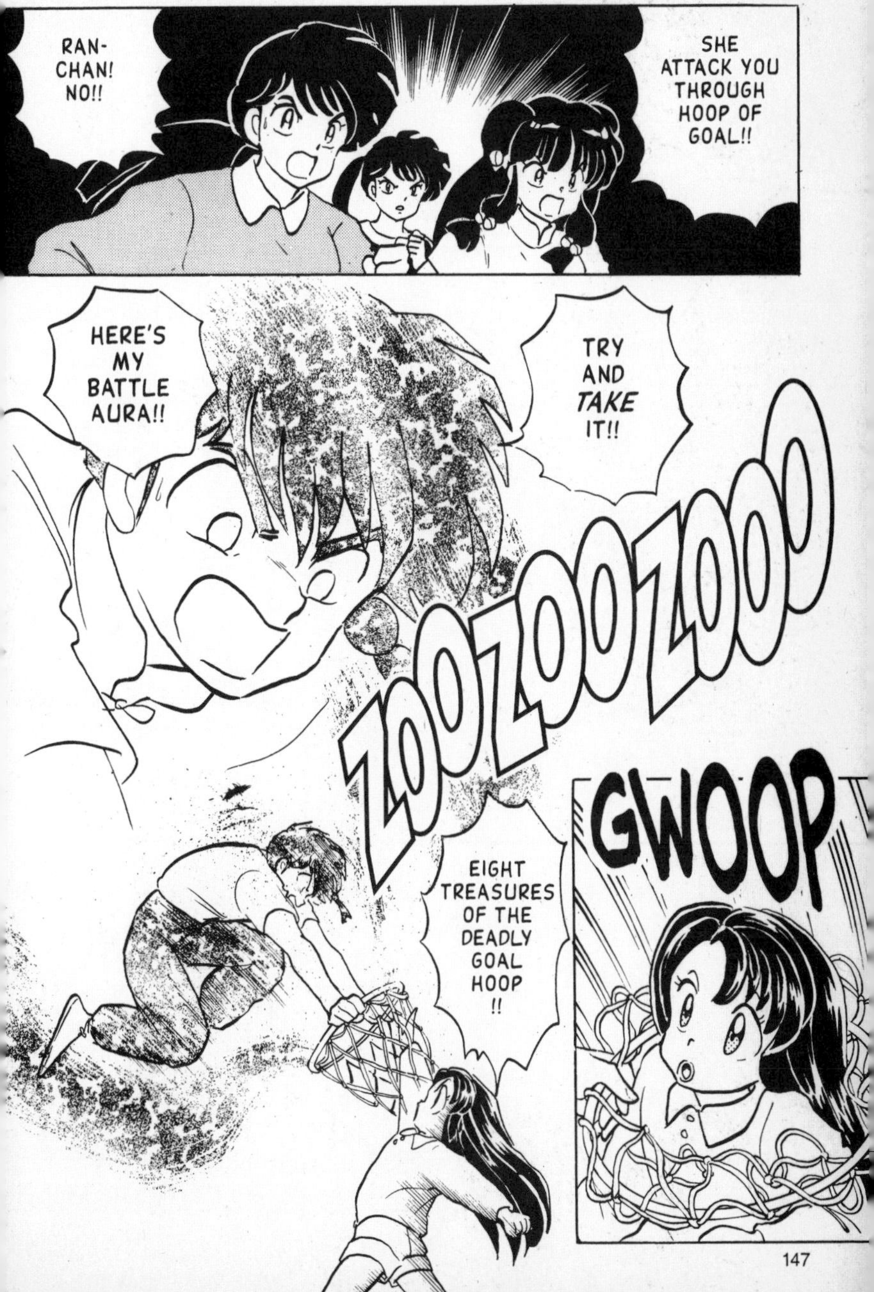
RAN-CHAN! NO!!
SHE ATTACK YOU THROUGH HOOP OF GOAL!!
HERE'S MY BATTLE AURA!!
TRY AND *TAKE* IT!!
ZOOZOOZOOO
EIGHT TREASURES OF THE DEADLY GOAL HOOP !!
GWOOP

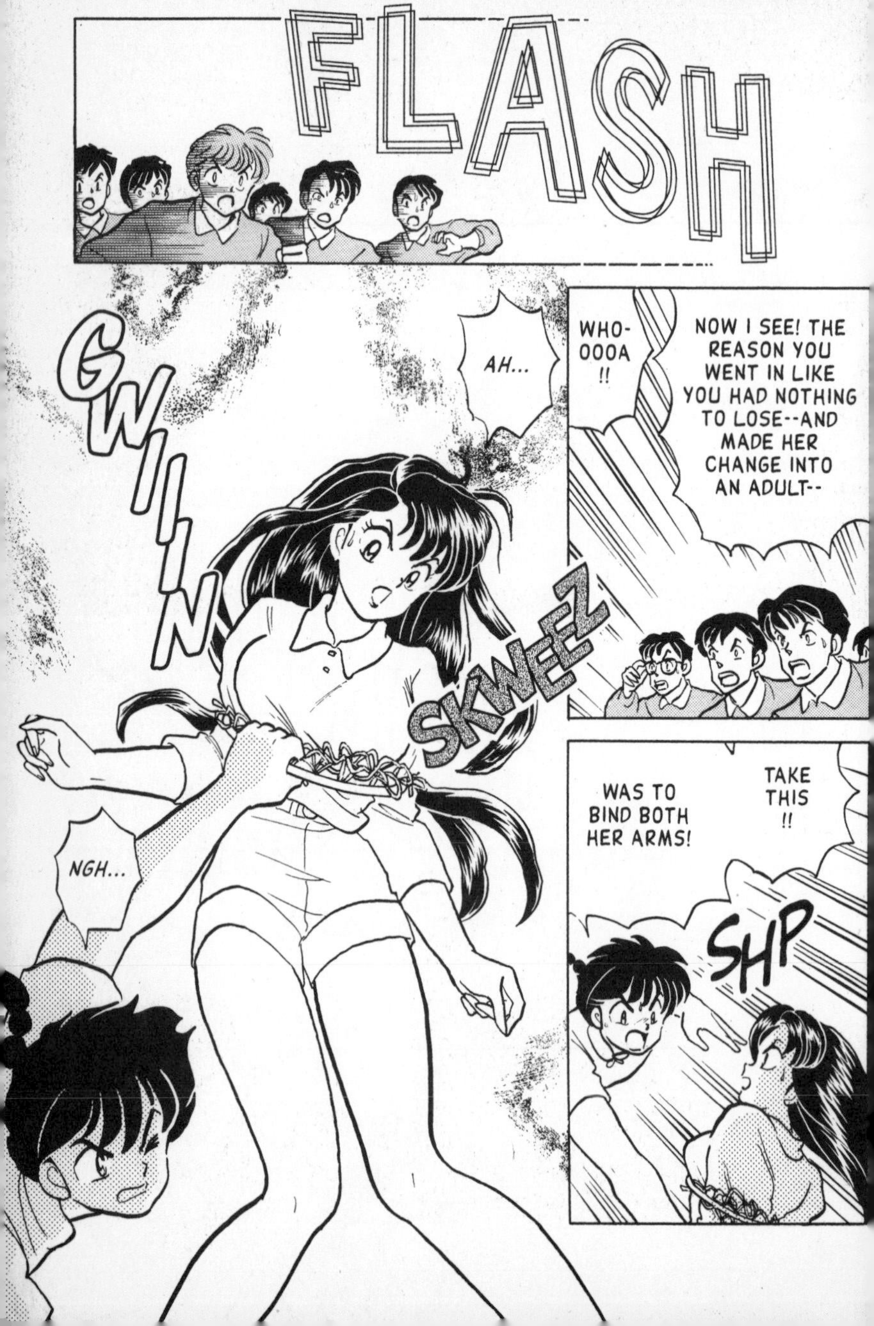
FLASH
GWIIIIN
AH...
SKWEEZ
NGH...
WHO-OOOA!!
NOW I SEE! THE REASON YOU WENT IN LIKE YOU HAD NOTHING TO LOSE--AND MADE HER CHANGE INTO AN ADULT--
WAS TO BIND BOTH HER ARMS!
TAKE THIS!!
SHP

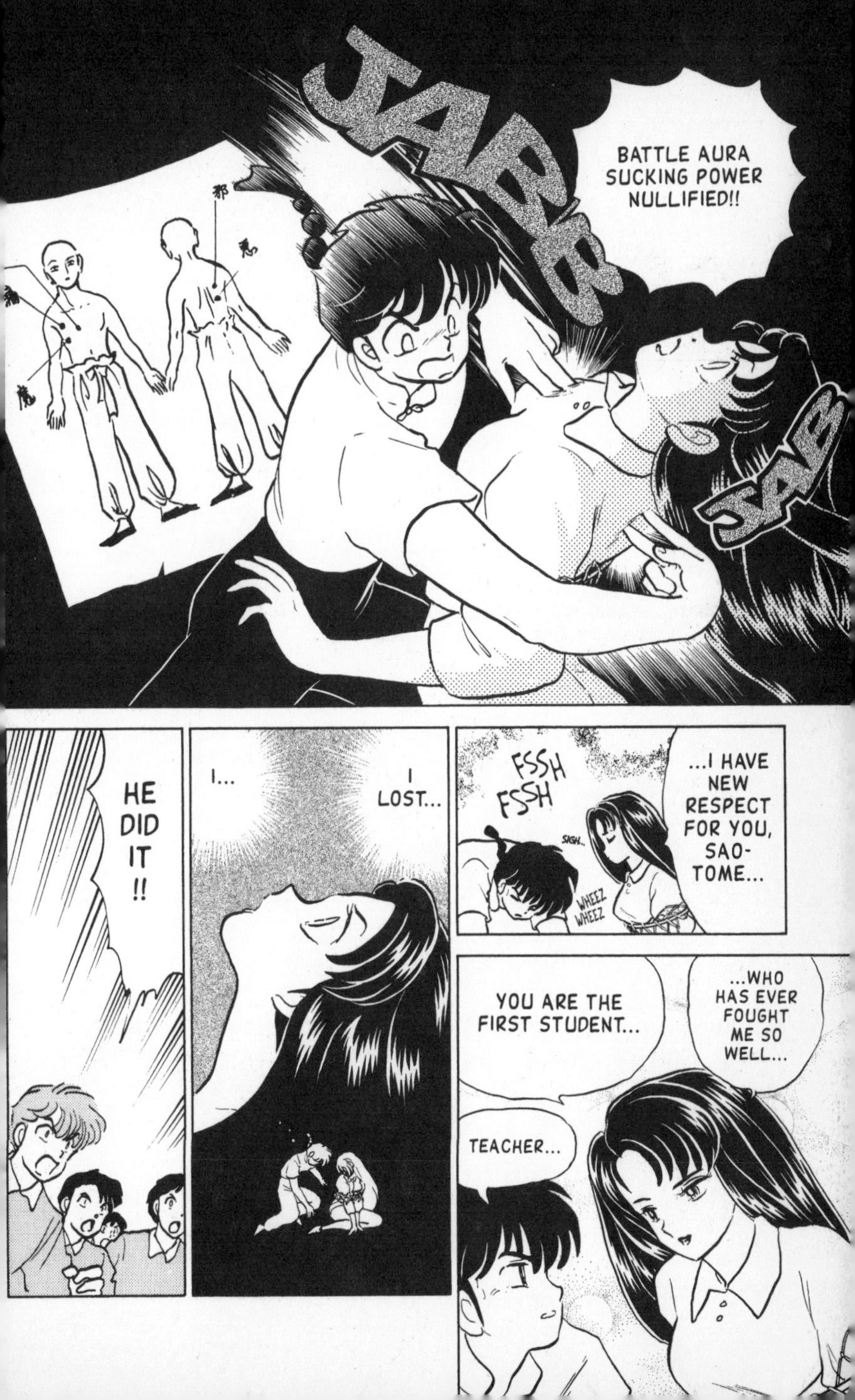
JABB
BATTLE AURA SUCKING POWER NULLIFIED!!
JAB
HE DID IT!!
I...
I LOST...
FSSH FSSH
SIGH..
WHEEZ WHEEZ
...I HAVE NEW RESPECT FOR YOU, SAO-TOME...
YOU ARE THE FIRST STUDENT...
...WHO HAS EVER FOUGHT ME SO WELL...
TEACHER...

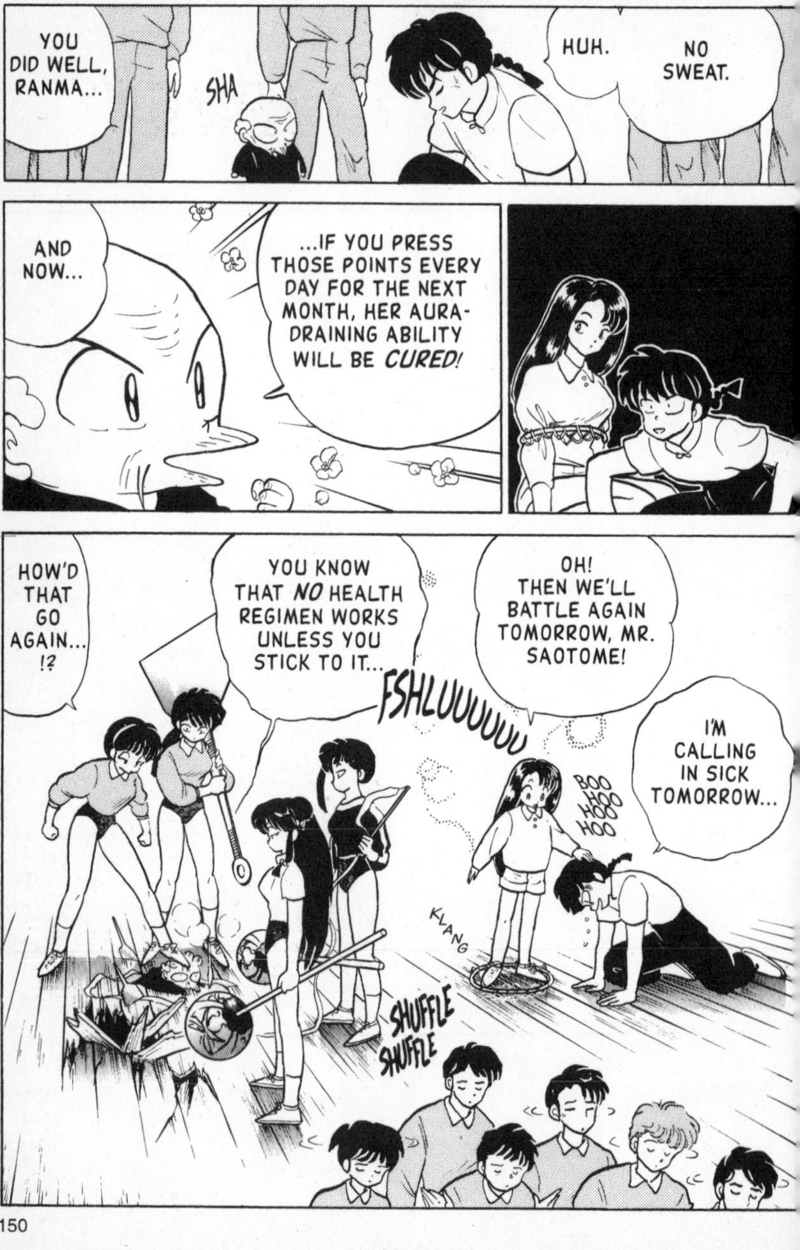
YOU DID WELL, RANMA...
SHA
HUH.
NO SWEAT.
AND NOW...
...IF YOU PRESS THOSE POINTS EVERY DAY FOR THE NEXT MONTH, HER AURA-DRAINING ABILITY WILL BE CURED!
HOW'D THAT GO AGAIN...!?
YOU KNOW THAT NO HEALTH REGIMEN WORKS UNLESS YOU STICK TO IT...
FSHLUUUUUUU
OH! THEN WE'LL BATTLE AGAIN TOMORROW, MR. SAOTOME!
I'M CALLING IN SICK TOMORROW...
BOO HOO HOO HOO
KLANG
SHUFFLE SHUFFLE

Part 10
AKANE'S JOURNEY

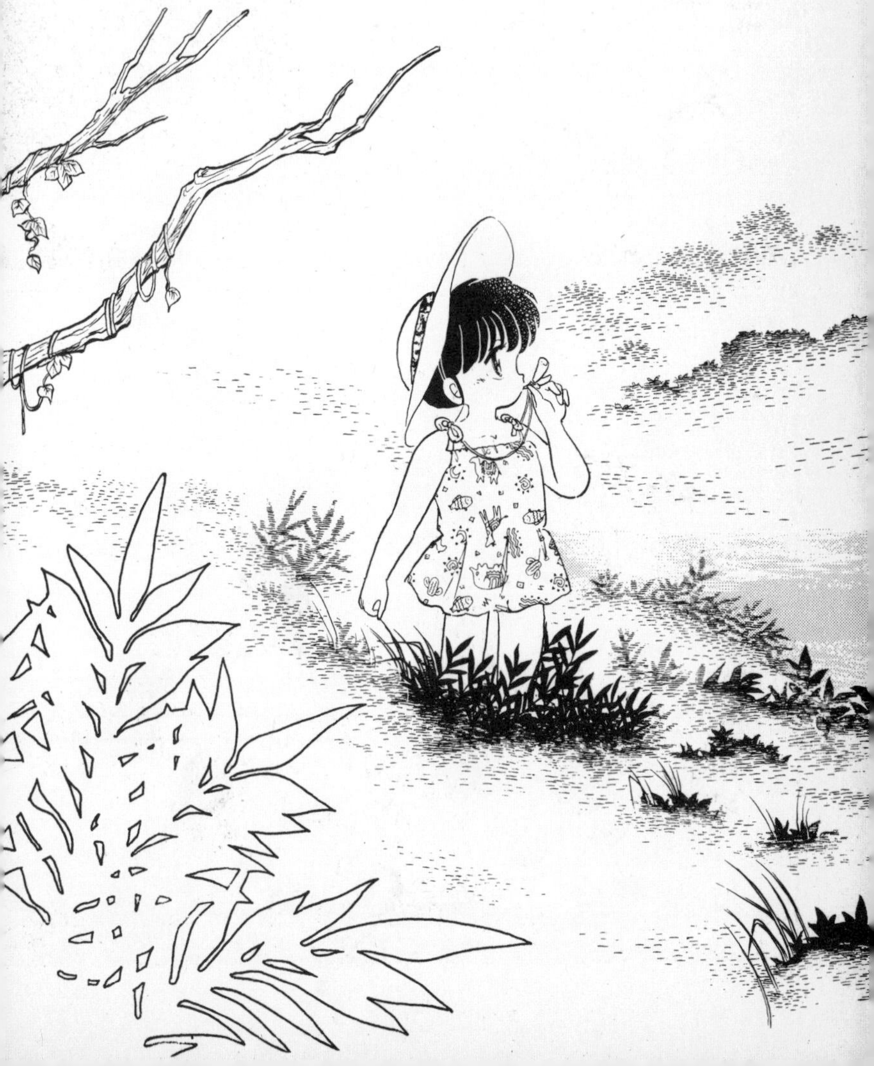

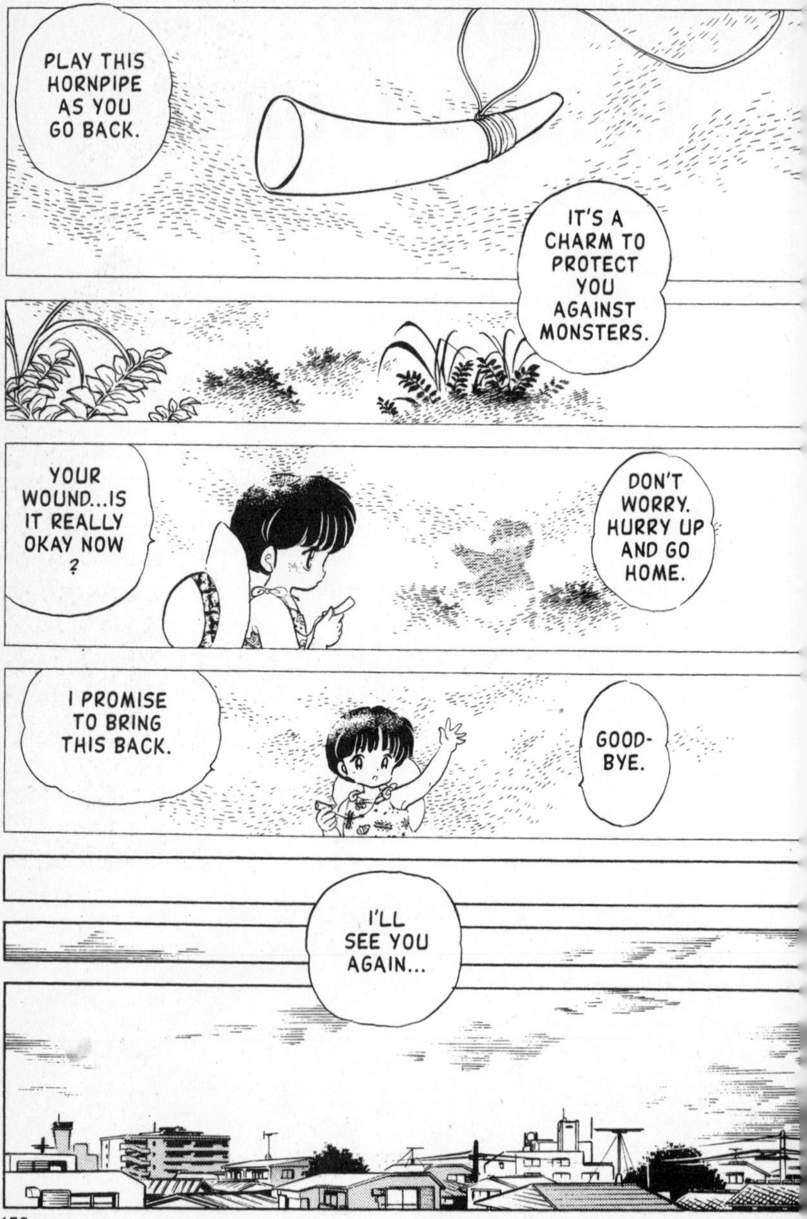

PLAY THIS HORNPIPE AS YOU GO BACK.
IT'S A CHARM TO PROTECT YOU AGAINST MONSTERS.
YOUR WOUND...IS IT REALLY OKAY NOW ?
DON'T WORRY. HURRY UP AND GO HOME.
I PROMISE TO BRING THIS BACK.
GOOD-BYE.
I'LL SEE YOU AGAIN...

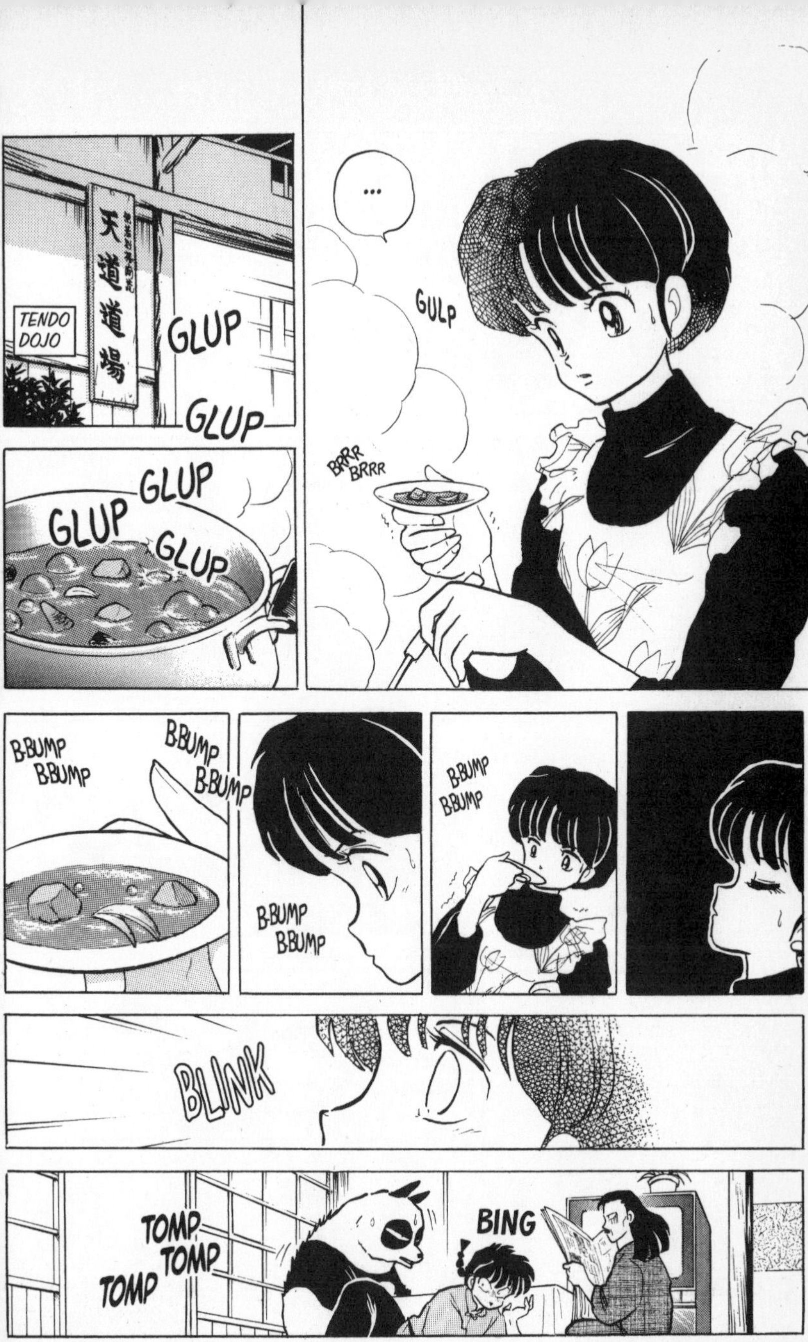

TENDO DOJO
天道道場
GLUP
GLUP
GLUP
GLUP
GLUP
...
GULP
BRRR BRRR
B-BUMP B-BUMP
B-BUMP B-BUMP
B-BUMP B-BUMP
B-BUMP B-BUMP
BLINK
TOMP TOMP TOMP
BING

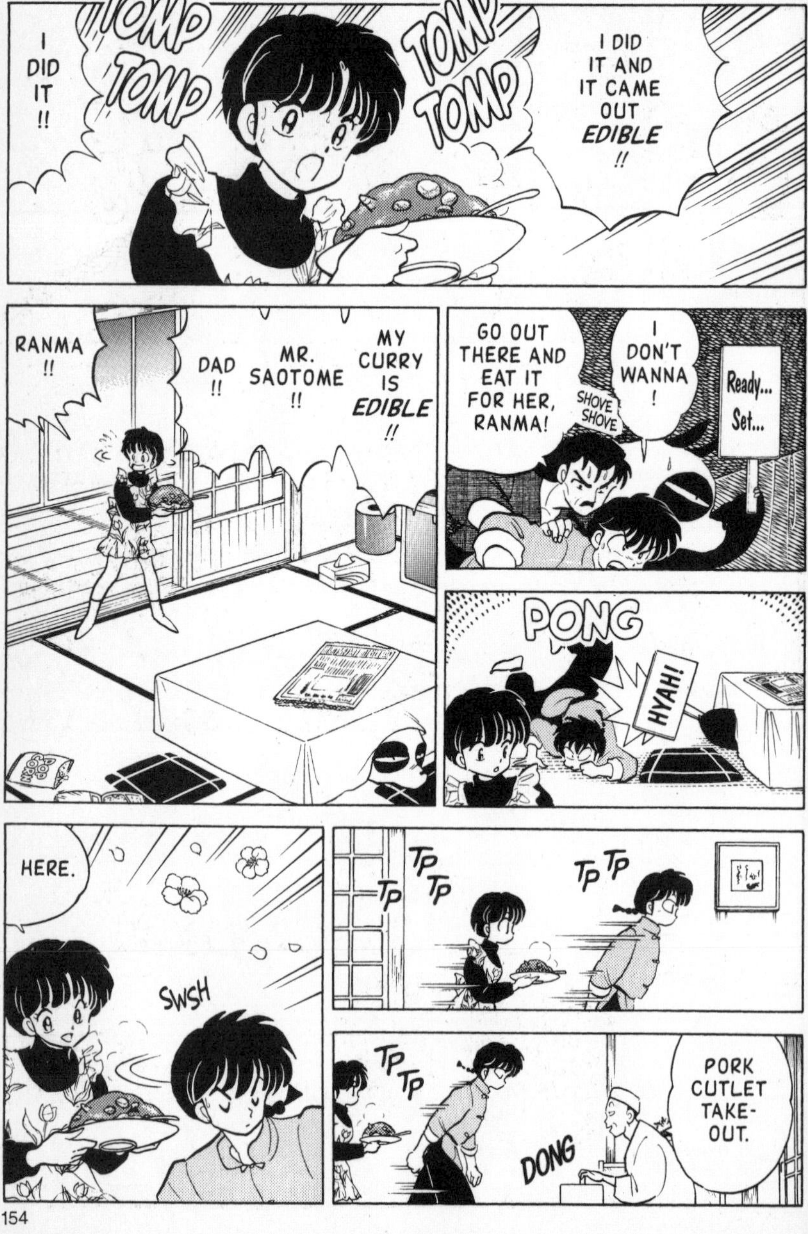
I DID IT !!
TOMP TOMP
TOMP TOMP
I DID IT AND IT CAME OUT EDIBLE !!
RANMA !!
DAD !!
MR. SAOTOME !!
MY CURRY IS EDIBLE !!
GO OUT THERE AND EAT IT FOR HER, RANMA!
SHOVE SHOVE
I DON'T WANNA !
Ready... Set...
PONG
HYAH!
HERE.
SWSH
TP TP TP
TP TP
TP TP
DONG
PORK CUTLET TAKE-OUT.

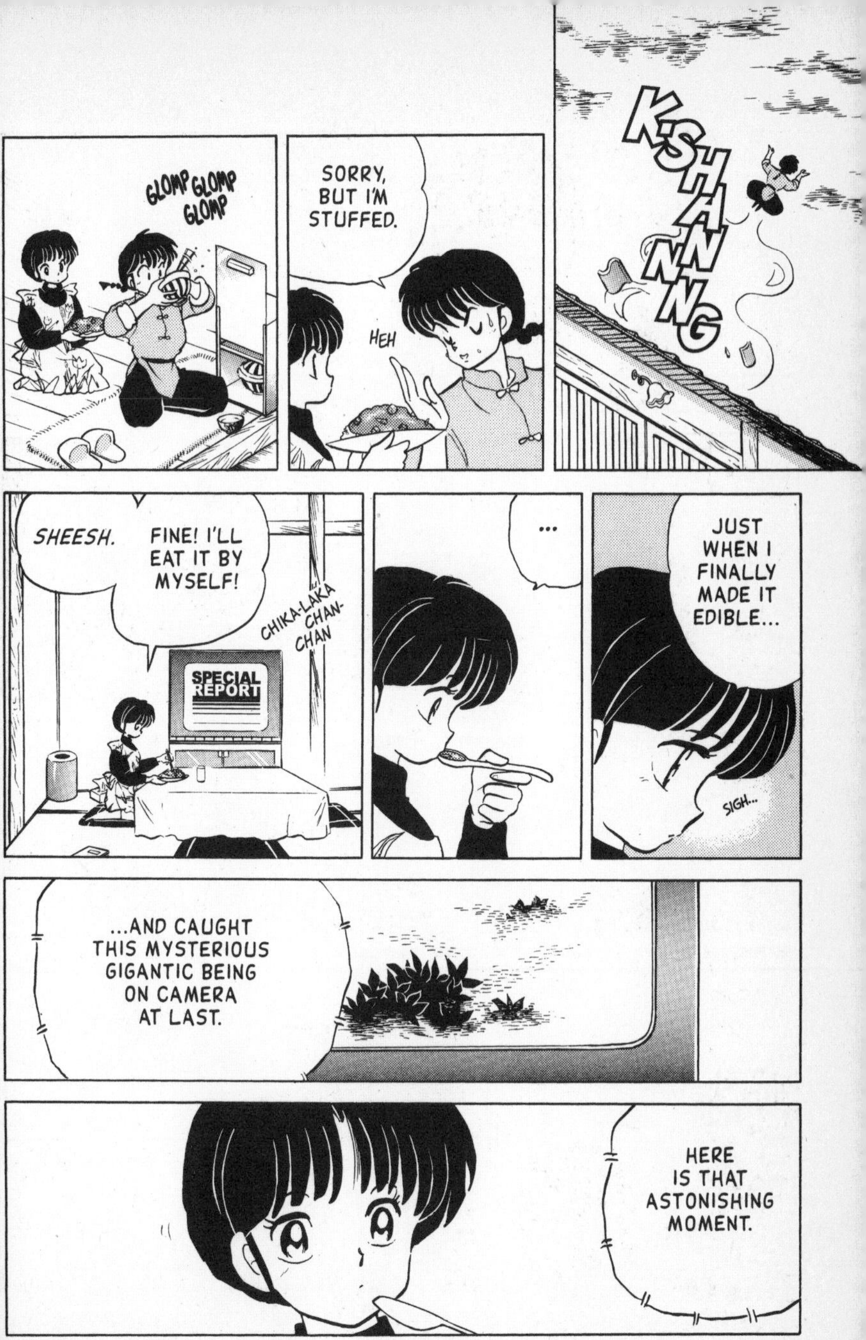
GLOMP GLOMP
GLOMP
SORRY, BUT I'M STUFFED.
HEH
K-SHANNNG
SHEESH.
FINE! I'LL EAT IT BY MYSELF!
CHIKA-LAKA CHAN-CHAN
SPECIAL REPORT
...
JUST WHEN I FINALLY MADE IT EDIBLE...
SIGH...
...AND CAUGHT THIS MYSTERIOUS GIGANTIC BEING ON CAMERA AT LAST.
HERE IS THAT ASTONISHING MOMENT.

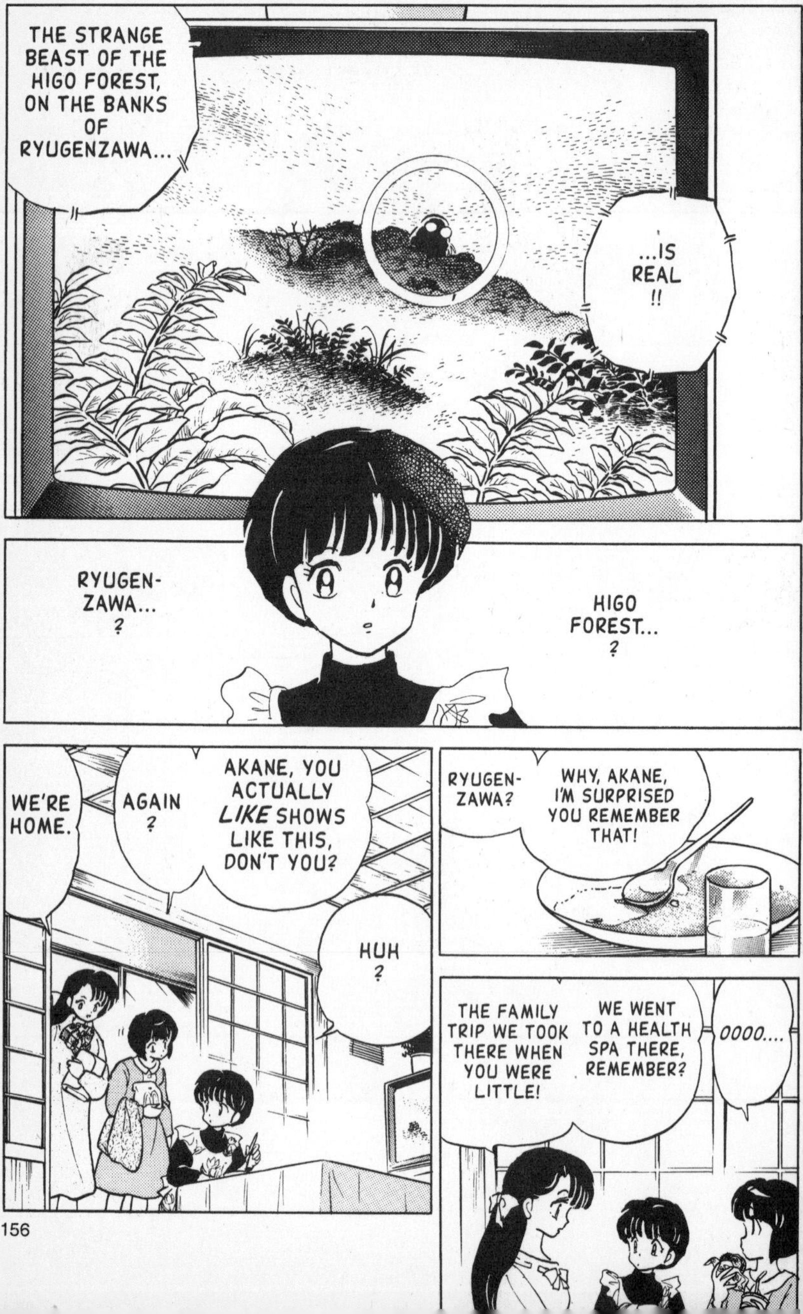
THE STRANGE BEAST OF THE HIGO FOREST, ON THE BANKS OF RYUGENZAWA...
...IS REAL !!
RYUGEN-ZAWA... ?
HIGO FOREST... ?
WE'RE HOME.
AGAIN ?
AKANE, YOU ACTUALLY *LIKE* SHOWS LIKE THIS, DON'T YOU?
HUH ?
RYUGEN-ZAWA?
WHY, AKANE, I'M SURPRISED YOU REMEMBER THAT!
THE FAMILY TRIP WE TOOK THERE WHEN YOU WERE LITTLE!
WE WENT TO A HEALTH SPA THERE, REMEMBER?
OOOO....

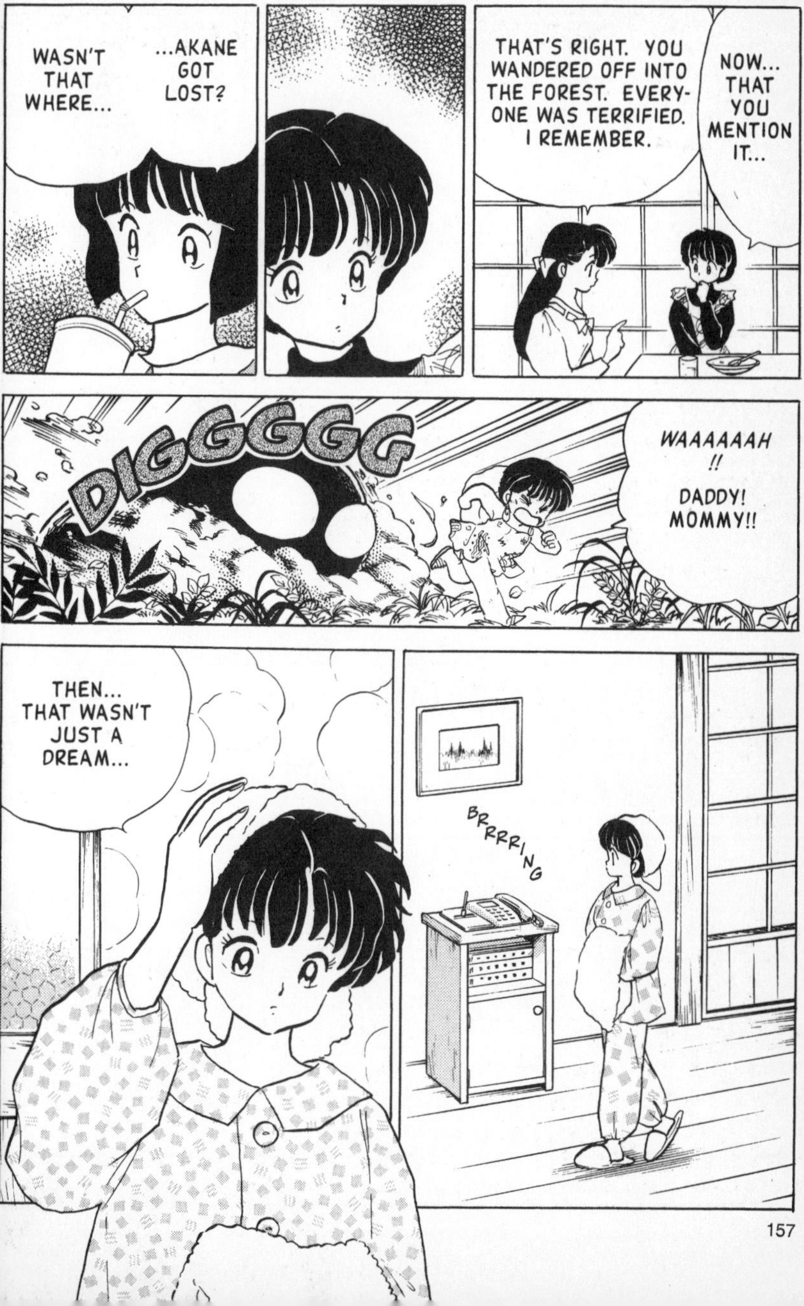
WASN'T THAT WHERE...
...AKANE GOT LOST?
THAT'S RIGHT. YOU WANDERED OFF INTO THE FOREST. EVERYONE WAS TERRIFIED. I REMEMBER.
NOW... THAT YOU MENTION IT...
DIGGGGGG
WAAAAAAH!!
DADDY! MOMMY!!
THEN... THAT WASN'T JUST A DREAM...
BRRRRING

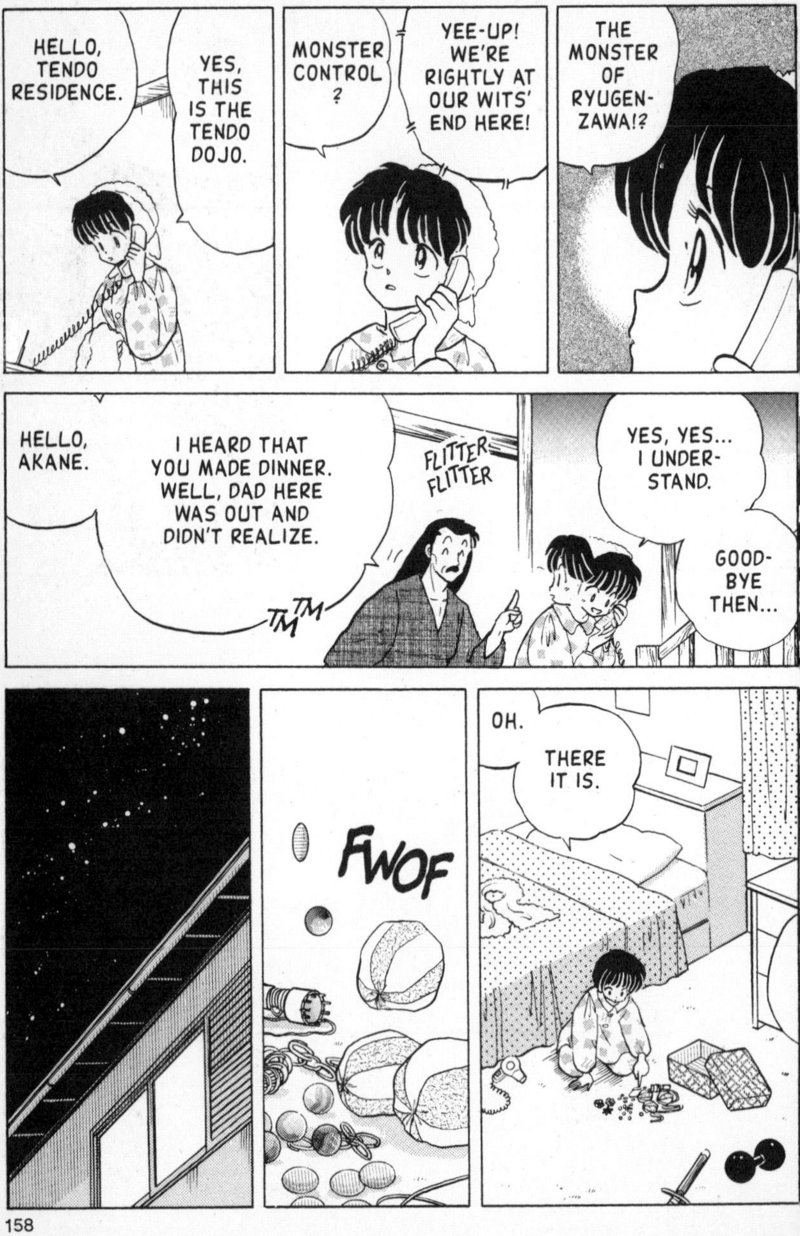
HELLO, TENDO RESIDENCE.
YES, THIS IS THE TENDO DOJO.
MONSTER CONTROL ?
YEE-UP! WE'RE RIGHTLY AT OUR WITS' END HERE!
THE MONSTER OF RYUGEN-ZAWA!?
HELLO, AKANE.
I HEARD THAT YOU MADE DINNER. WELL, DAD HERE WAS OUT AND DIDN'T REALIZE.
TM TM
FLITTER FLITTER
YES, YES... I UNDER-STAND.
GOOD-BYE THEN...
FWOF
OH.
THERE IT IS.

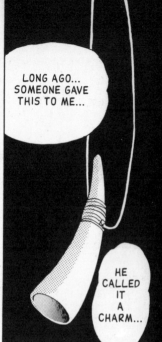

LONG AGO... SOMEONE GAVE THIS TO ME...

HE CALLED IT A CHARM...

A HORN-PIPE...

FATHER! COME QUICK!!

AKANE LEFT HOME!?

A FARE-WELL NOTE!?

I'm off to Ryugenzawa. Don't worry about me!

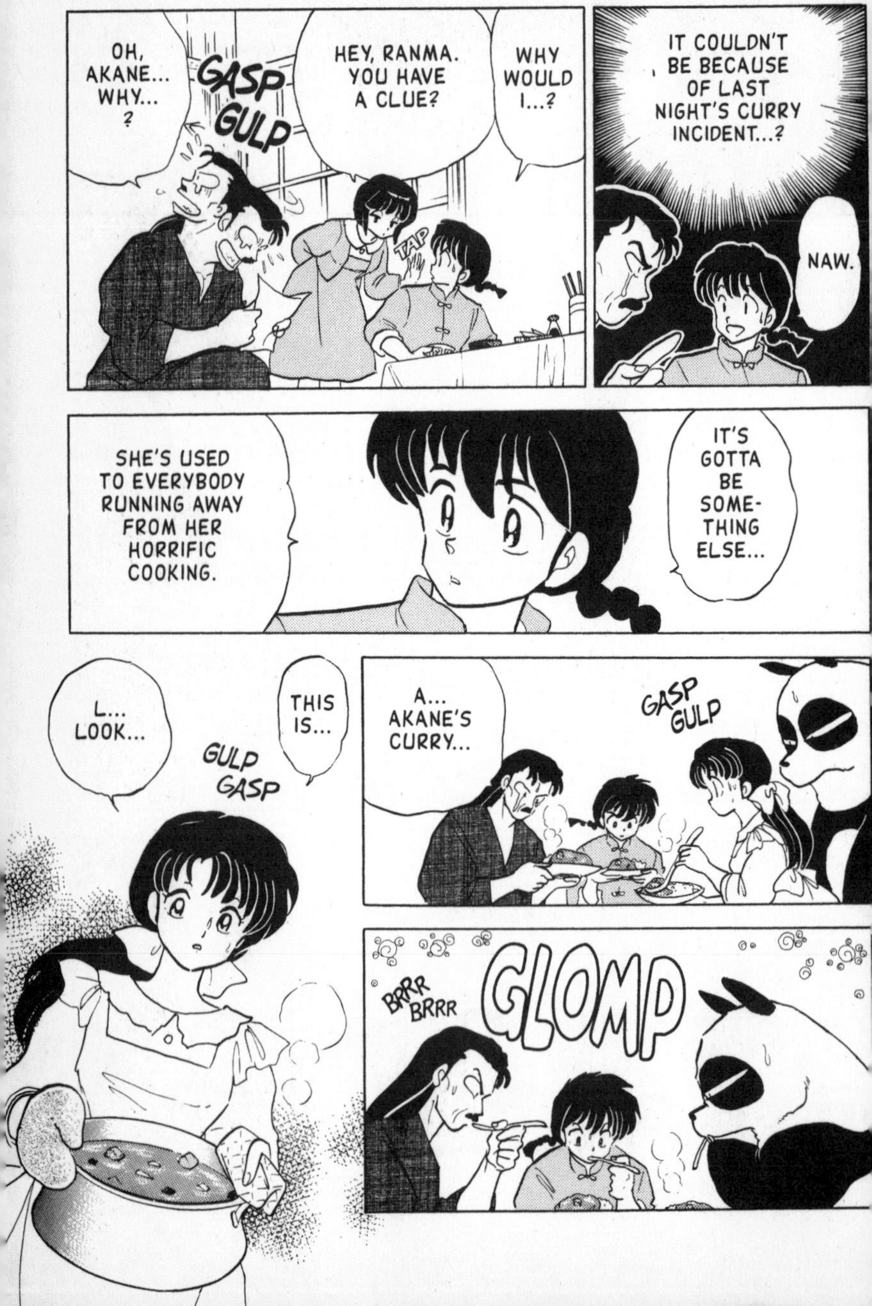

OH, AKANE... WHY...?
GASP GULP
HEY, RANMA. YOU HAVE A CLUE?
TAP
WHY WOULD I...?
IT COULDN'T BE BECAUSE OF LAST NIGHT'S CURRY INCIDENT...?
NAW.
SHE'S USED TO EVERYBODY RUNNING AWAY FROM HER HORRIFIC COOKING.
IT'S GOTTA BE SOME-THING ELSE...
L... LOOK...
THIS IS...
GULP GASP
A... AKANE'S CURRY...
GASP GULP
BRRR BRRR
GLOMP

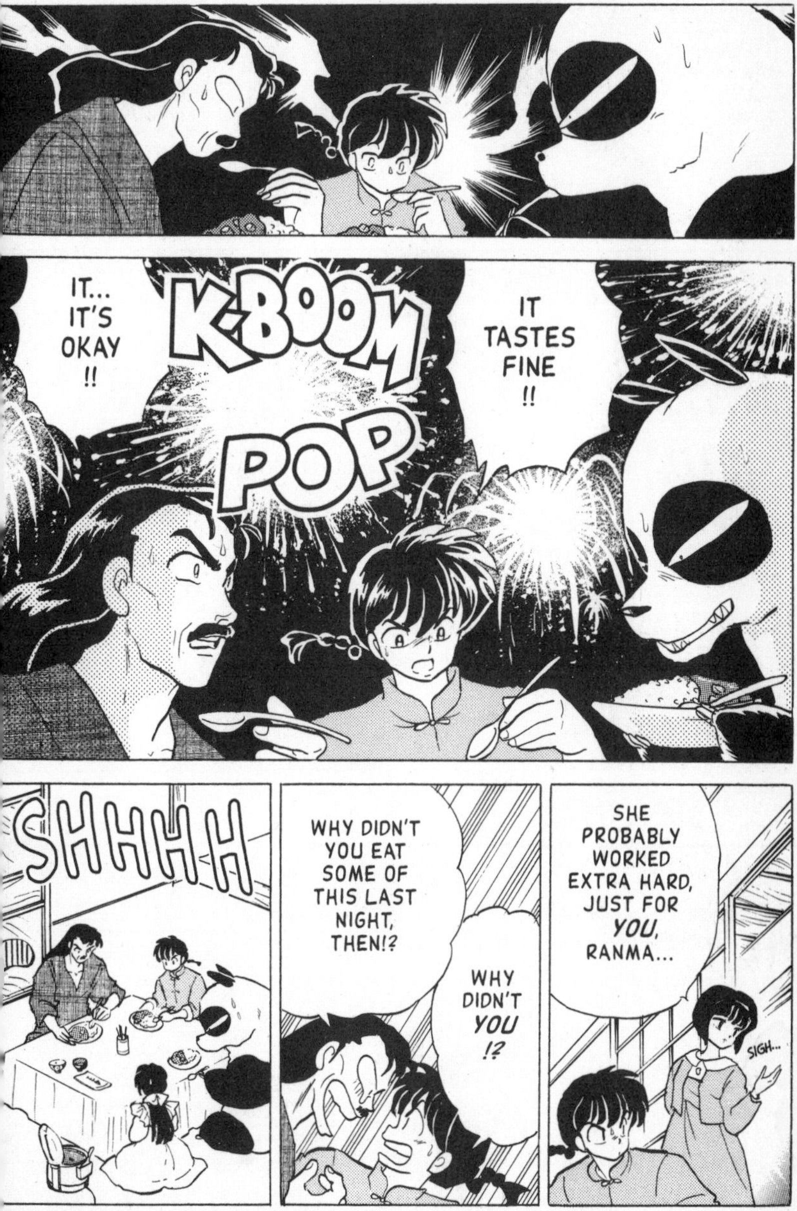
IT... IT'S OKAY !!
K-BOOM
IT TASTES FINE !!
POP
SHHHH
WHY DIDN'T YOU EAT SOME OF THIS LAST NIGHT, THEN!?
WHY DIDN'T *YOU* !?
SHE PROBABLY WORKED EXTRA HARD, JUST FOR *YOU*, RANMA...
SIGH...

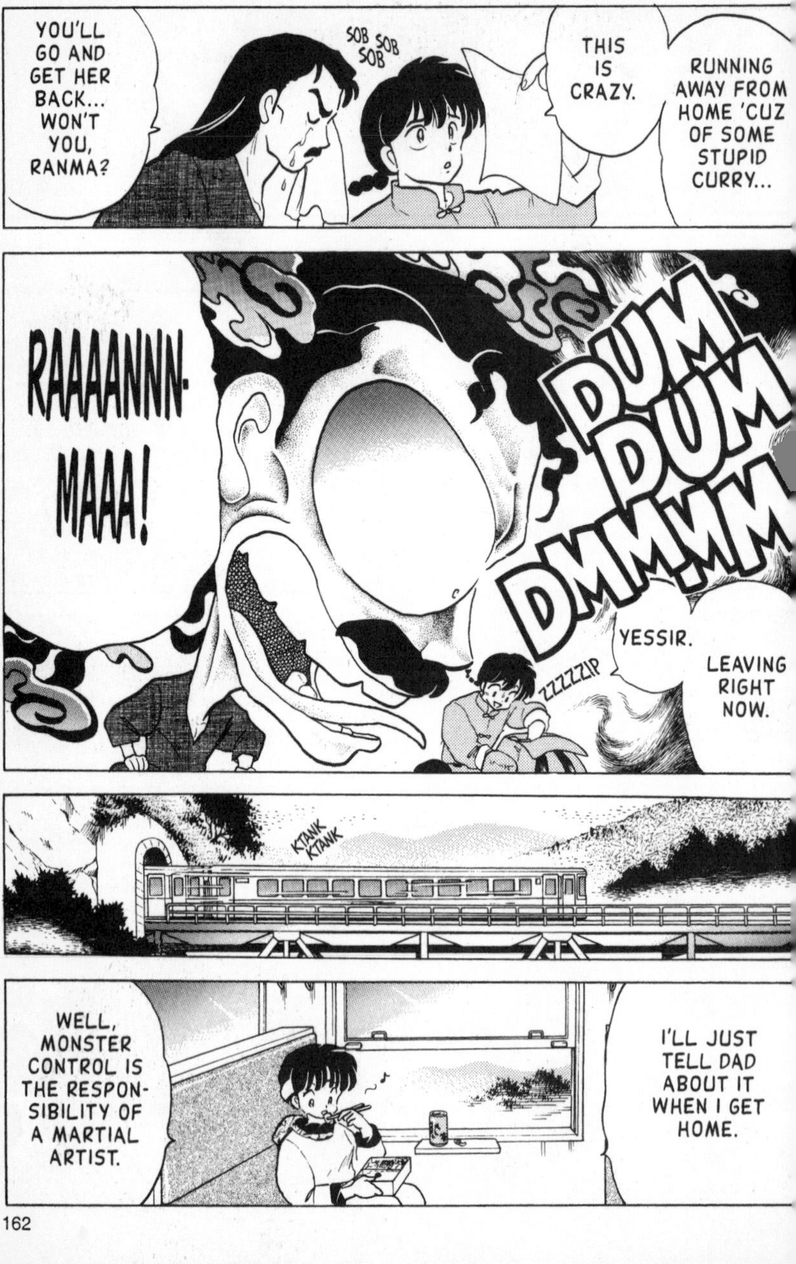
YOU'LL GO AND GET HER BACK... WON'T YOU, RANMA?
SOB SOB SOB
THIS IS CRAZY.
RUNNING AWAY FROM HOME 'CUZ OF SOME STUPID CURRY...
RAAAANNN-MAAA!
DUM DUM DMMMMM
ZZZZZZIP
YESSIR.
LEAVING RIGHT NOW.
KTANK KTANK
WELL, MONSTER CONTROL IS THE RESPON-SIBILITY OF A MARTIAL ARTIST.
I'LL JUST TELL DAD ABOUT IT WHEN I GET HOME.

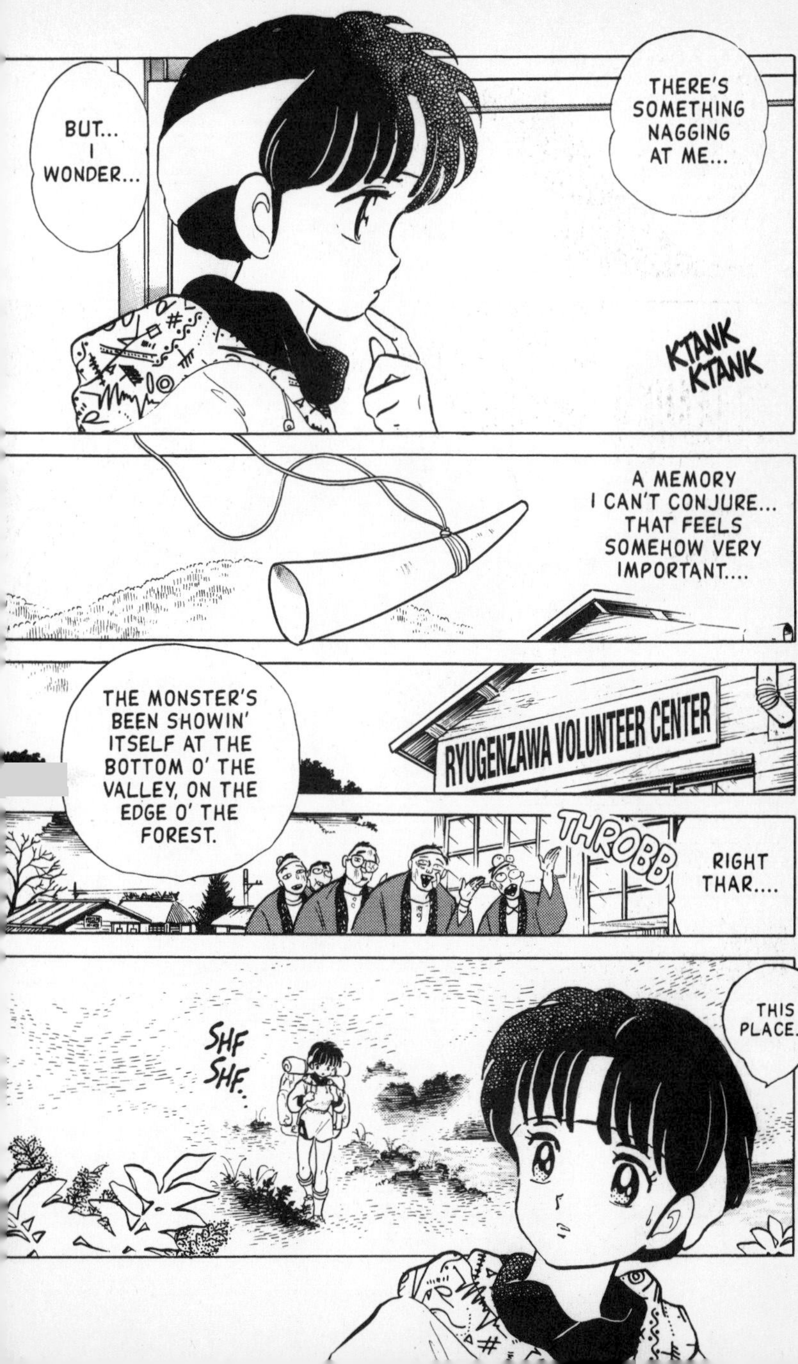
BUT... I WONDER...
THERE'S SOMETHING NAGGING AT ME...
KTANK KTANK
A MEMORY I CAN'T CONJURE... THAT FEELS SOMEHOW VERY IMPORTANT....
THE MONSTER'S BEEN SHOWIN' ITSELF AT THE BOTTOM O' THE VALLEY, ON THE EDGE O' THE FOREST.
RYUGENZAWA VOLUNTEER CENTER
THROBB
RIGHT THAR....
SHF SHF...
THIS PLACE...

I'VE *BEEN* HERE...

THIS IS WHERE I GOT LOST...

DADDY ?

DIG DIG

WAAAAAH!!

A CHARM...

TO PROTECT AGAINST MONSTERS...

YOUR WOUND...IS IT REALLY OKAY NOW ?

DON'T WORRY. HURRY UP AND GO HOME.

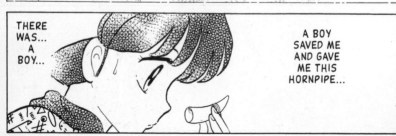

THERE WAS... A BOY...

A BOY SAVED ME AND GAVE ME THIS HORNPIPE...

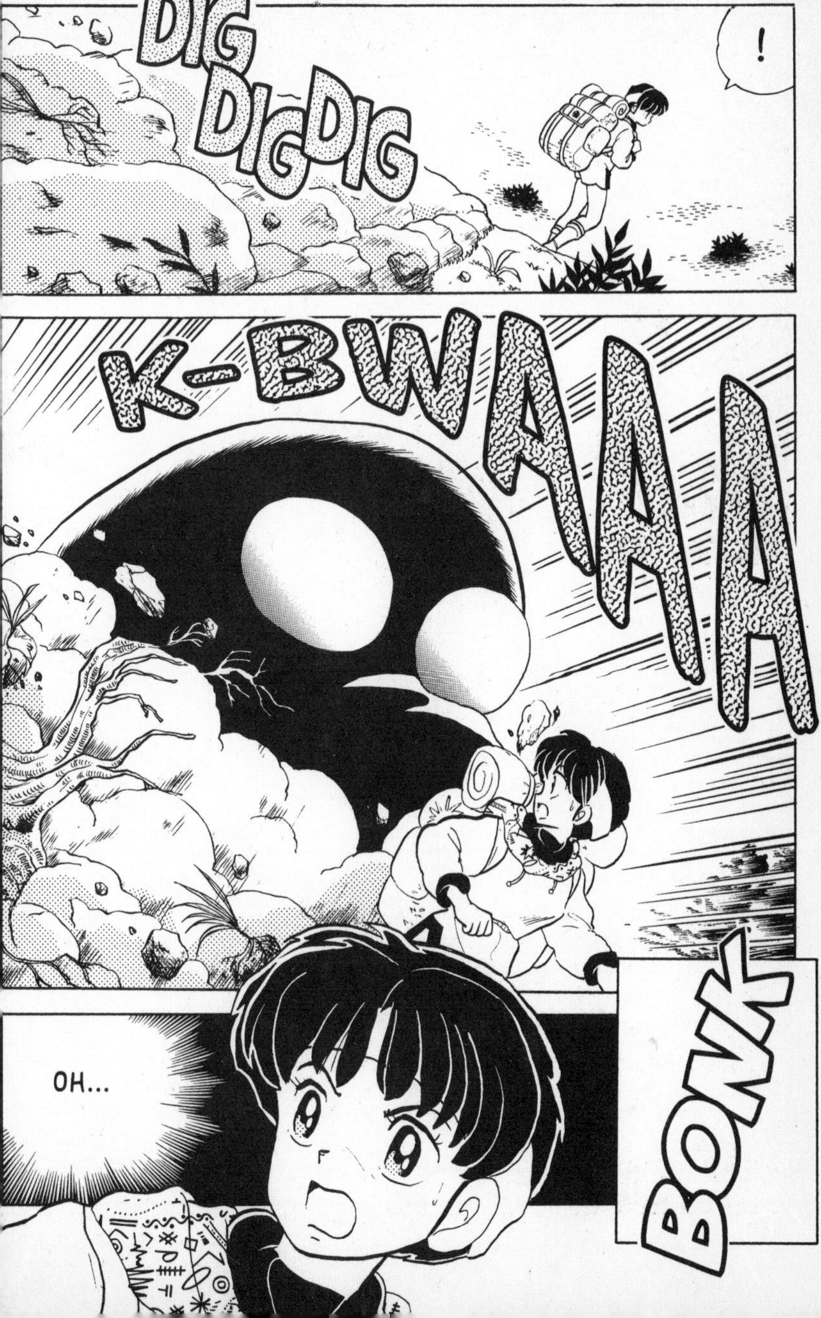
DIG
DIG DIG DIG
!
K-BWAAAA
BONK
OH...

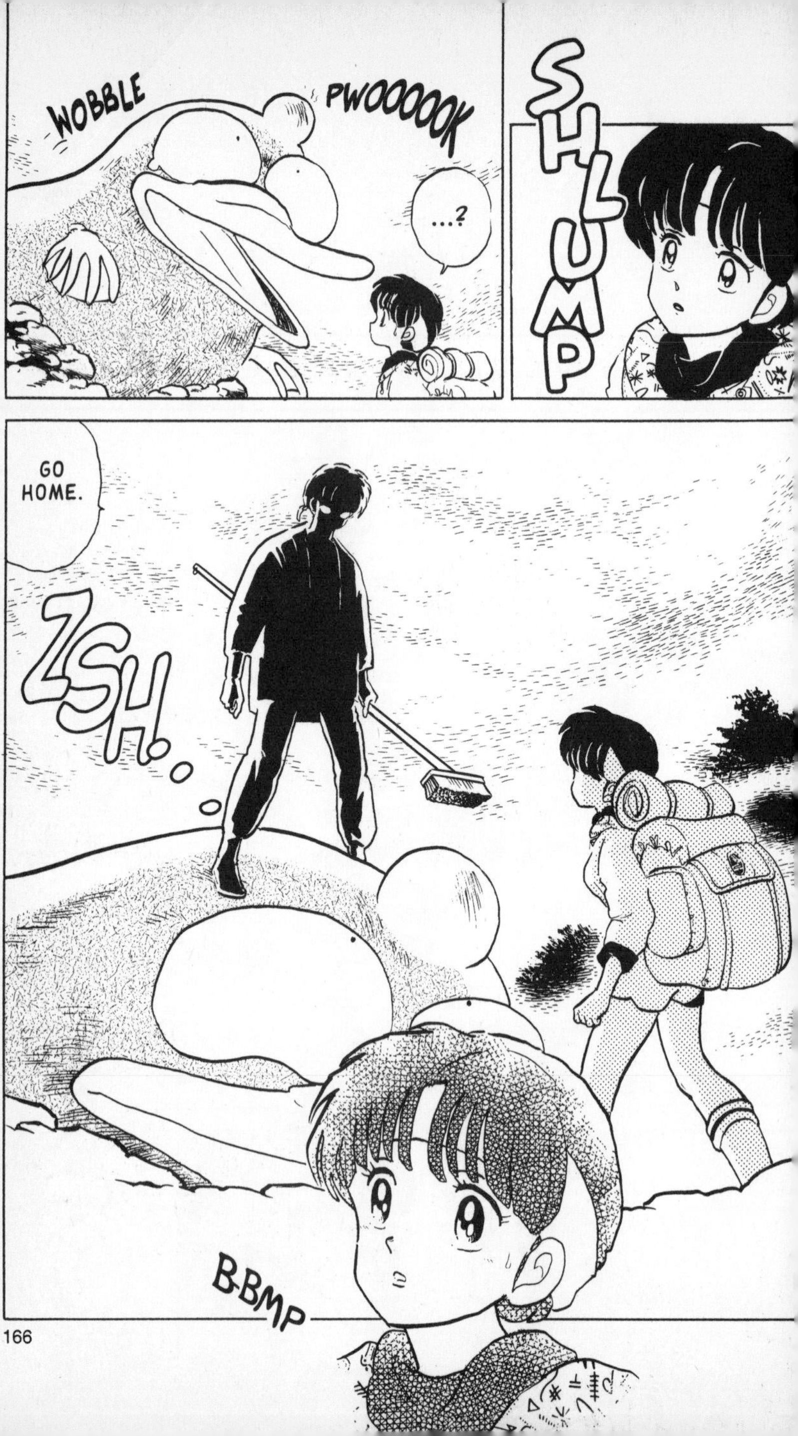
WOBBLE
PWOOOOOK
...?
SHLUMP
GO HOME.
ZSH...
B-BMP

Part 11
RECOVERED MEMORIES

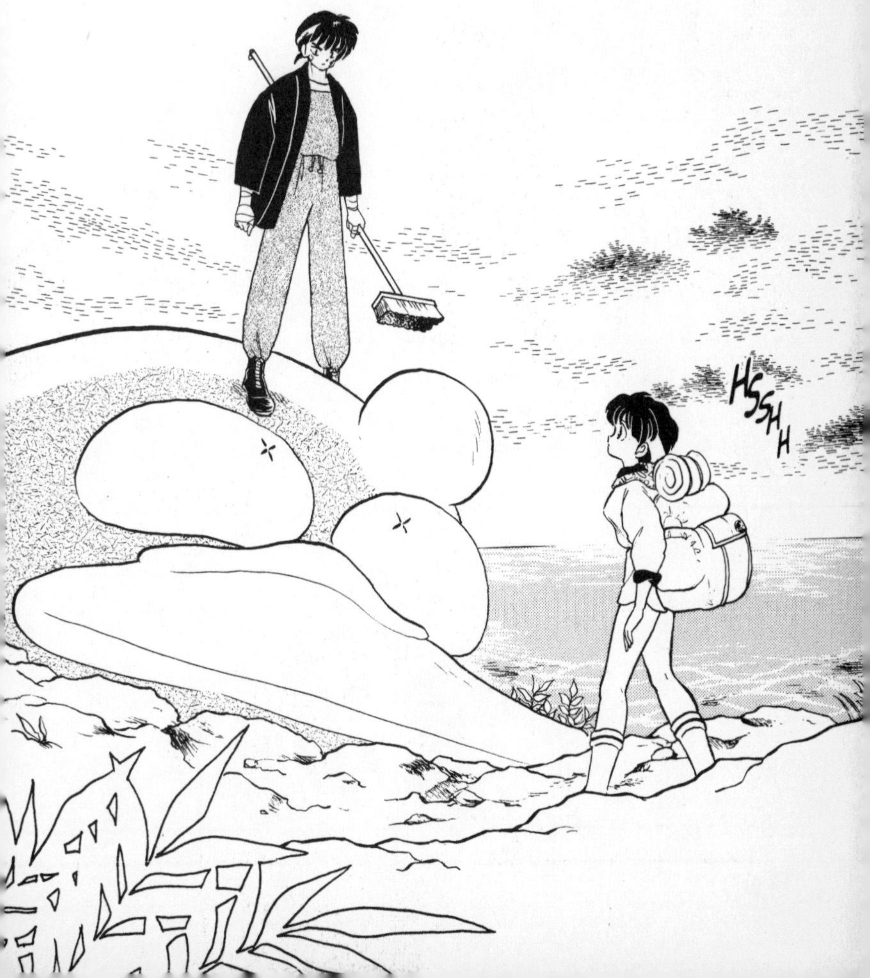
HSSHH

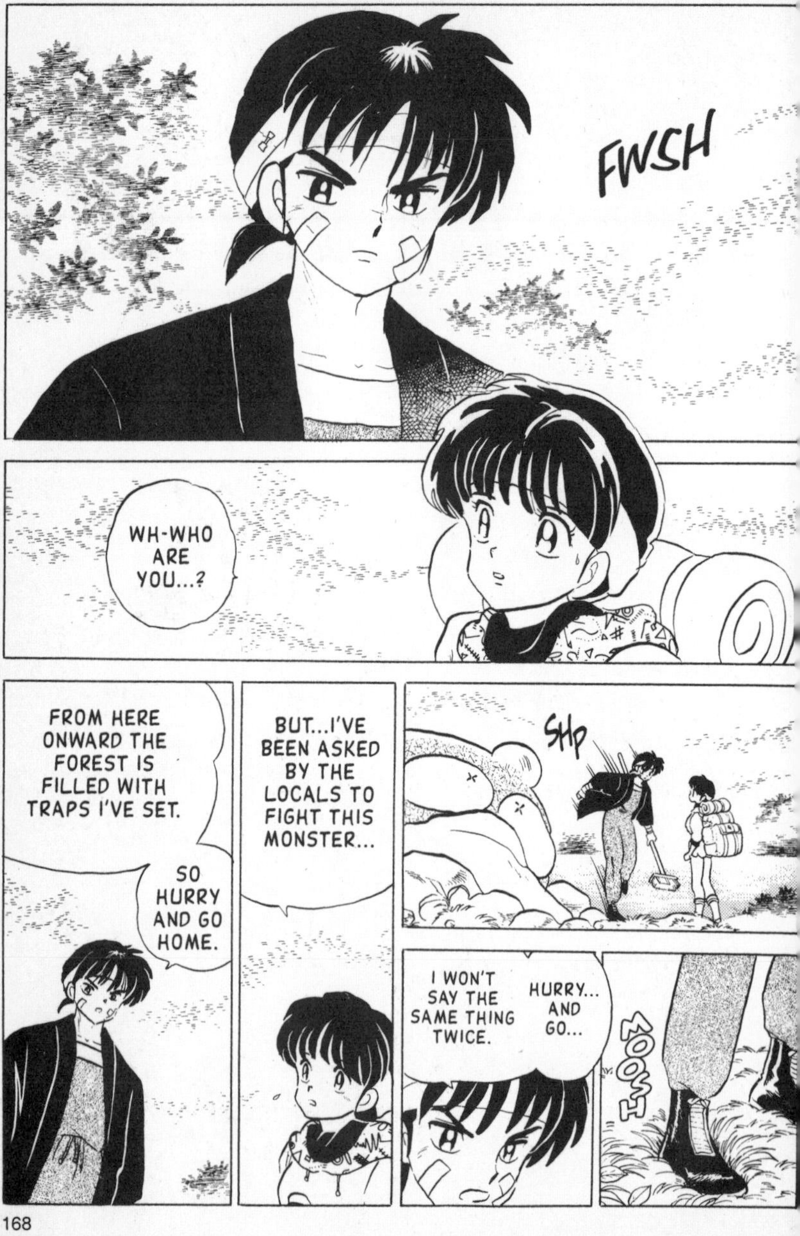
FWSH
WH-WHO ARE YOU...?
FROM HERE ONWARD THE FOREST IS FILLED WITH TRAPS I'VE SET.
SO HURRY AND GO HOME.
BUT...I'VE BEEN ASKED BY THE LOCALS TO FIGHT THIS MONSTER...
SHP
I WON'T SAY THE SAME THING TWICE.
HURRY... AND GO...
WOOSH

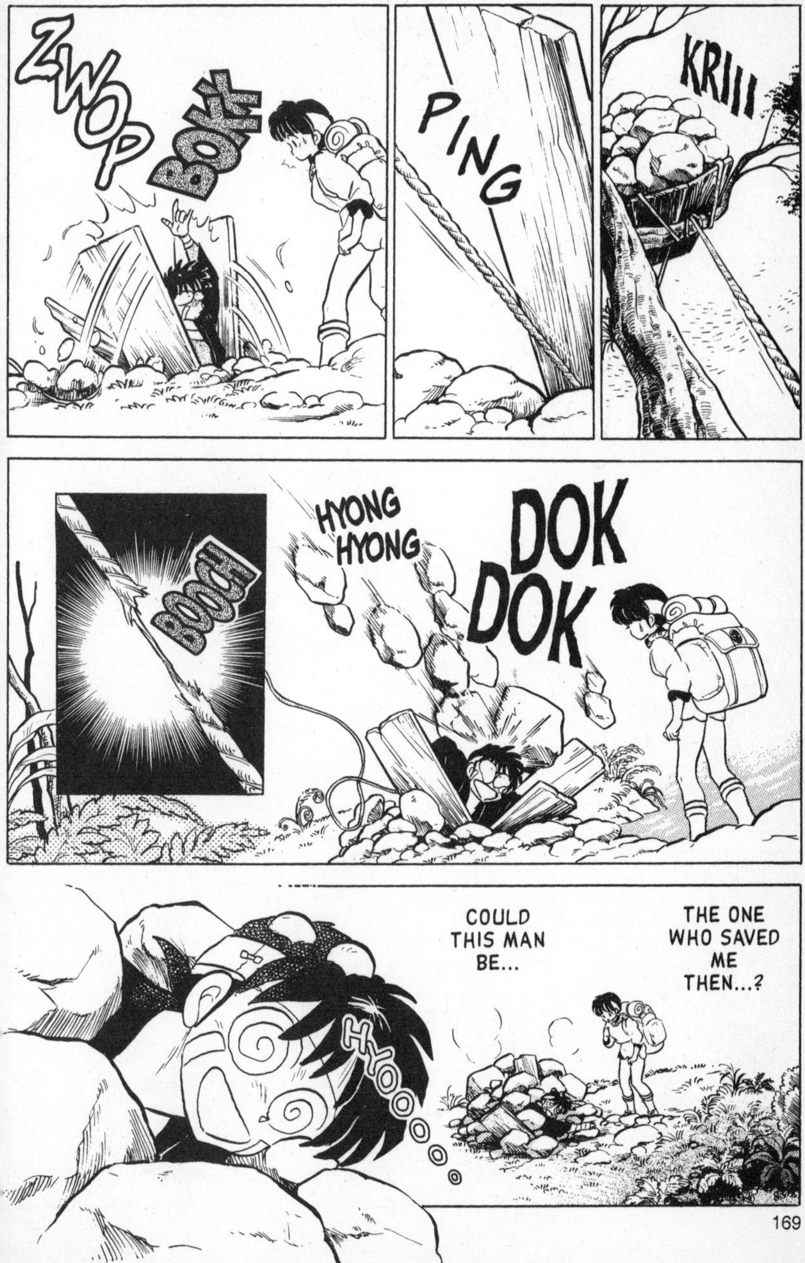
ZWOP
BOKK
PING
KRIII
BOOCH
HYONG HYONG
DOK DOK
HYOOOOO
COULD THIS MAN BE...
THE ONE WHO SAVED ME THEN...?

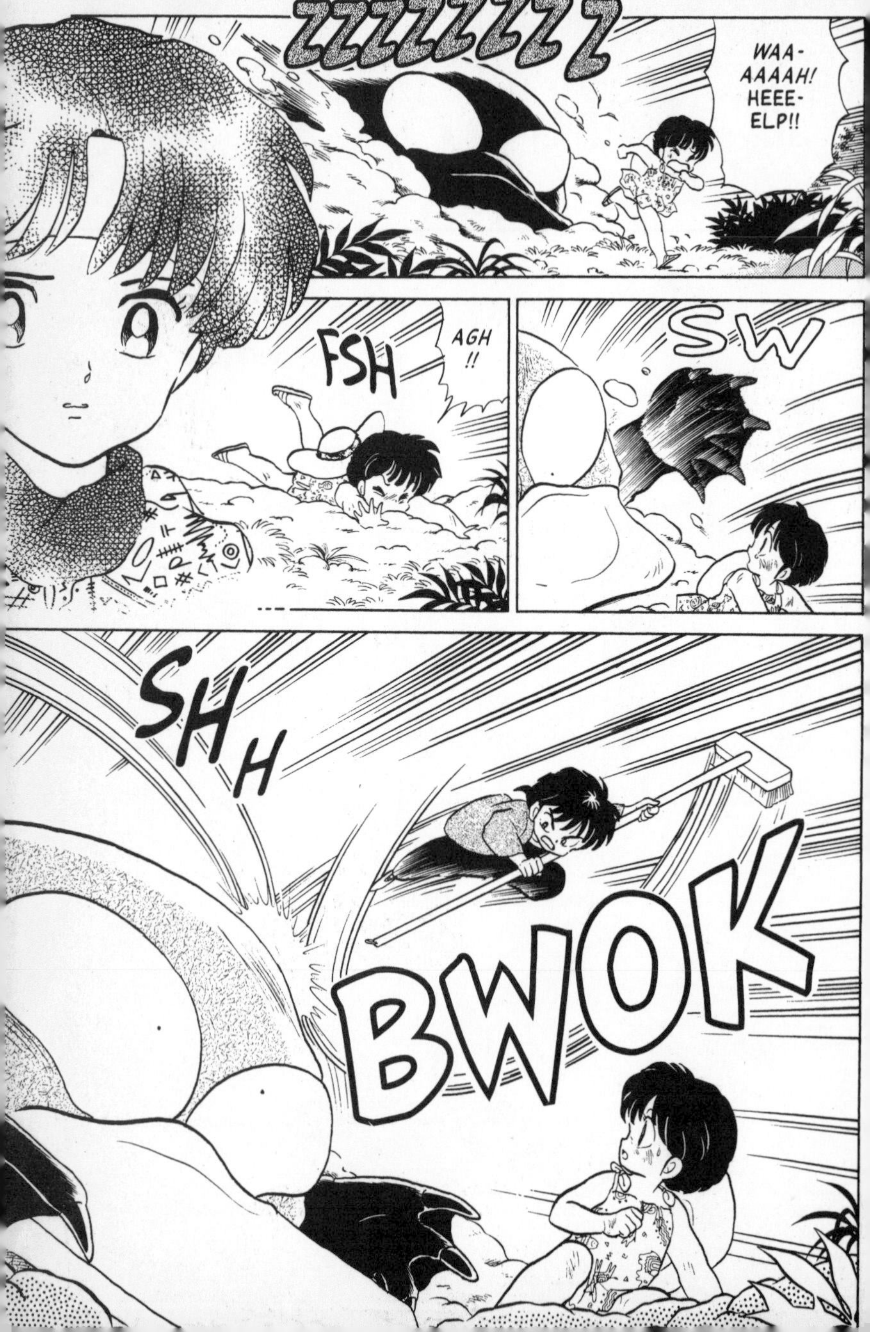
ZZZZZZZZ
WAA-
AAAAH!
HEEE-
ELP!!
FSH
AGH
!!
SW
SHH
BWOK

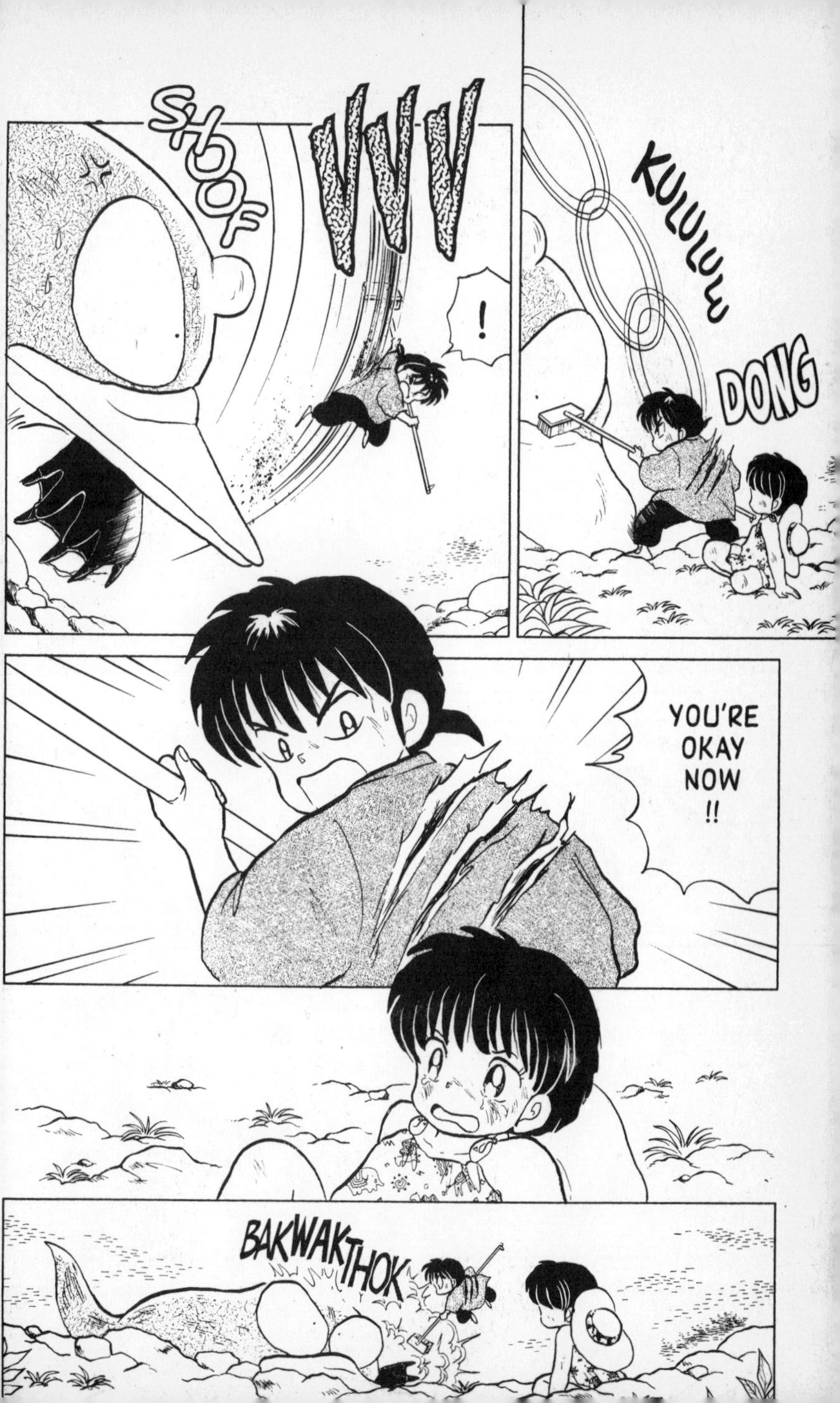SHOOF
VVV
!
KULULULU
DONG
YOU'RE OKAY NOW !!
BAKWAKTHOK

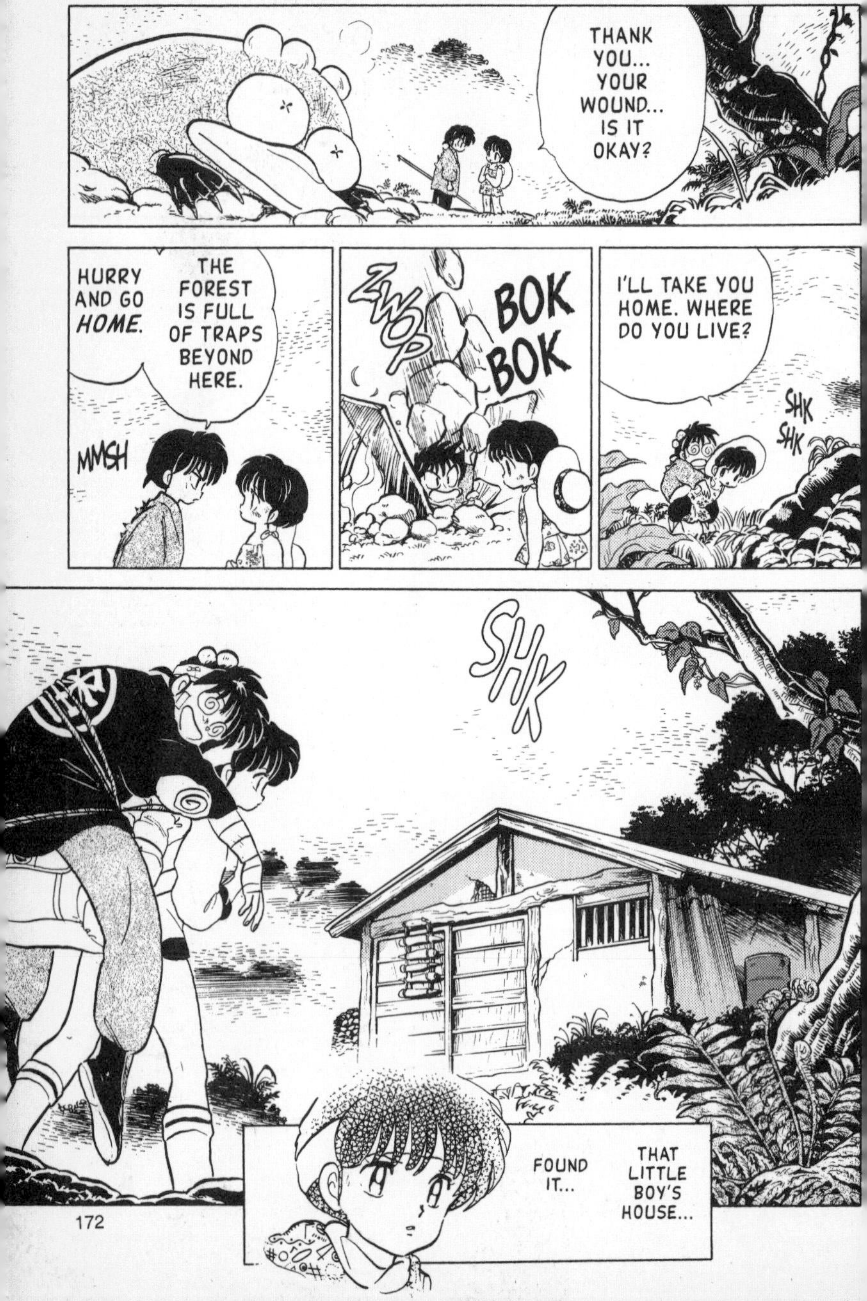
THANK YOU... YOUR WOUND... IS IT OKAY?
HURRY AND GO *HOME*.
THE FOREST IS FULL OF TRAPS BEYOND HERE.
MMSH
ZWOP
BOK BOK
I'LL TAKE YOU HOME. WHERE DO YOU LIVE?
SHK SHK
SHK
FOUND IT...
THAT LITTLE BOY'S HOUSE...

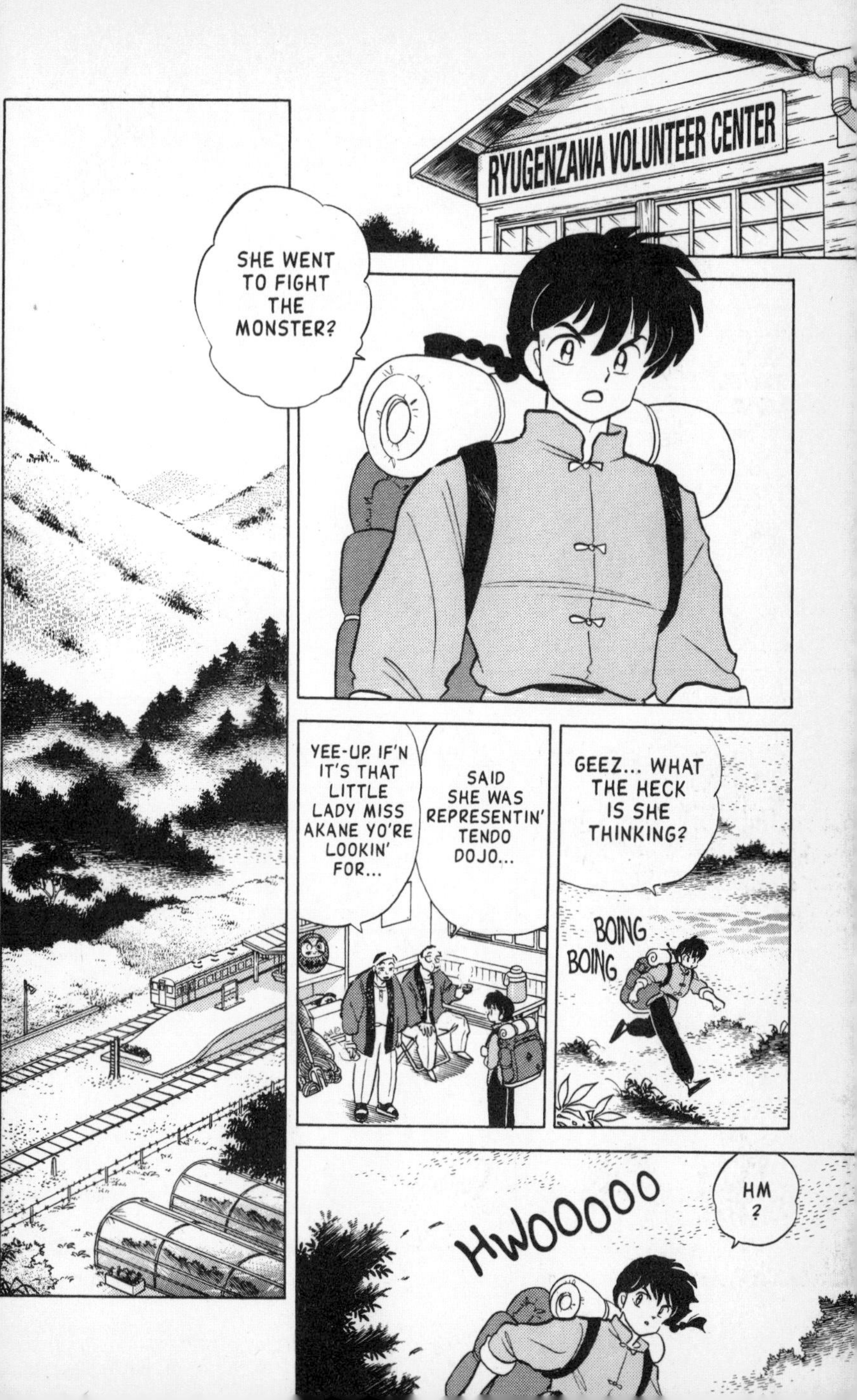
RYUGENZAWA VOLUNTEER CENTER
SHE WENT TO FIGHT THE MONSTER?
YEE-UP. IF'N IT'S THAT LITTLE LADY MISS AKANE YO'RE LOOKIN' FOR...
SAID SHE WAS REPRESENTIN' TENDO DOJO...
GEEZ... WHAT THE HECK IS SHE THINKING?
BOING
BOING
HWOOOOO
HM
?

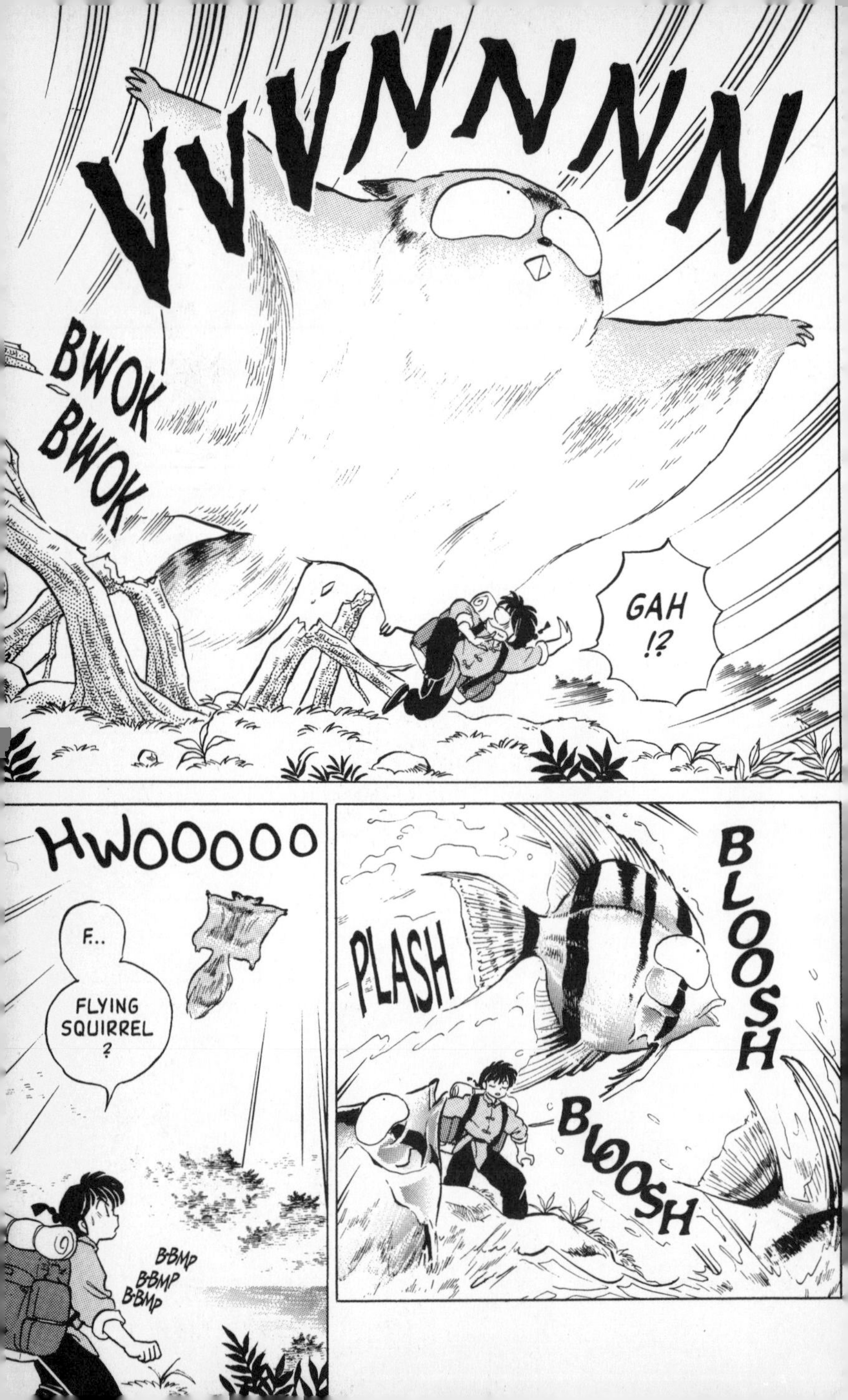
VVVNNNN
BWOK BWOK
GAH !?
HWOOOOO
F...
FLYING SQUIRREL ?
B-BMP B-BMP B-BMP
PLASH
BLOOSH
BLOOSH

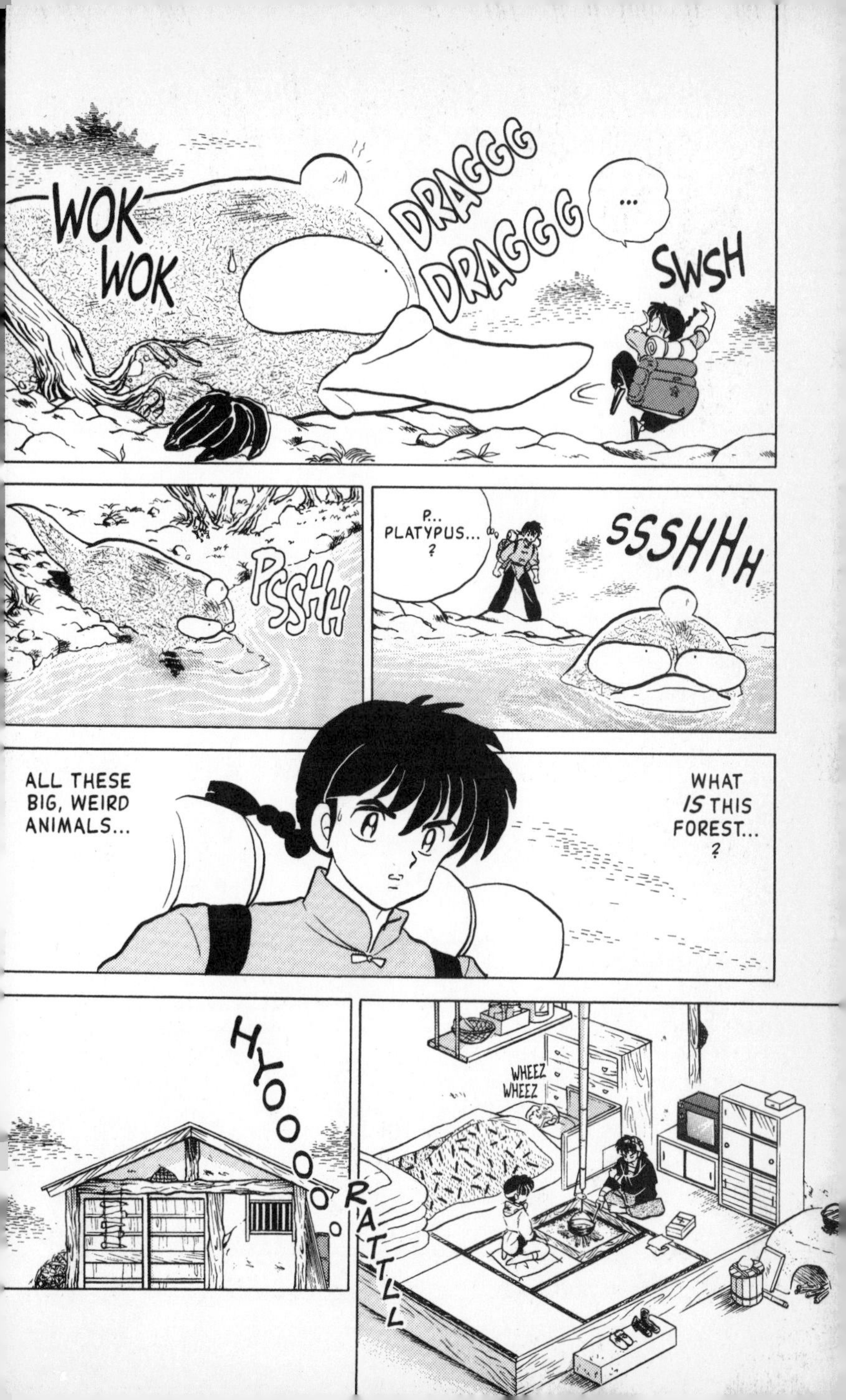
WOK
WOK
DRAGGG
DRAGGG
...
SWSH
PSSHH
P... PLATYPUS...?
SSSHHH
ALL THESE BIG, WEIRD ANIMALS...
WHAT *IS* THIS FOREST...?
HYOOOOO
RATTLL
WHEEZ WHEEZ

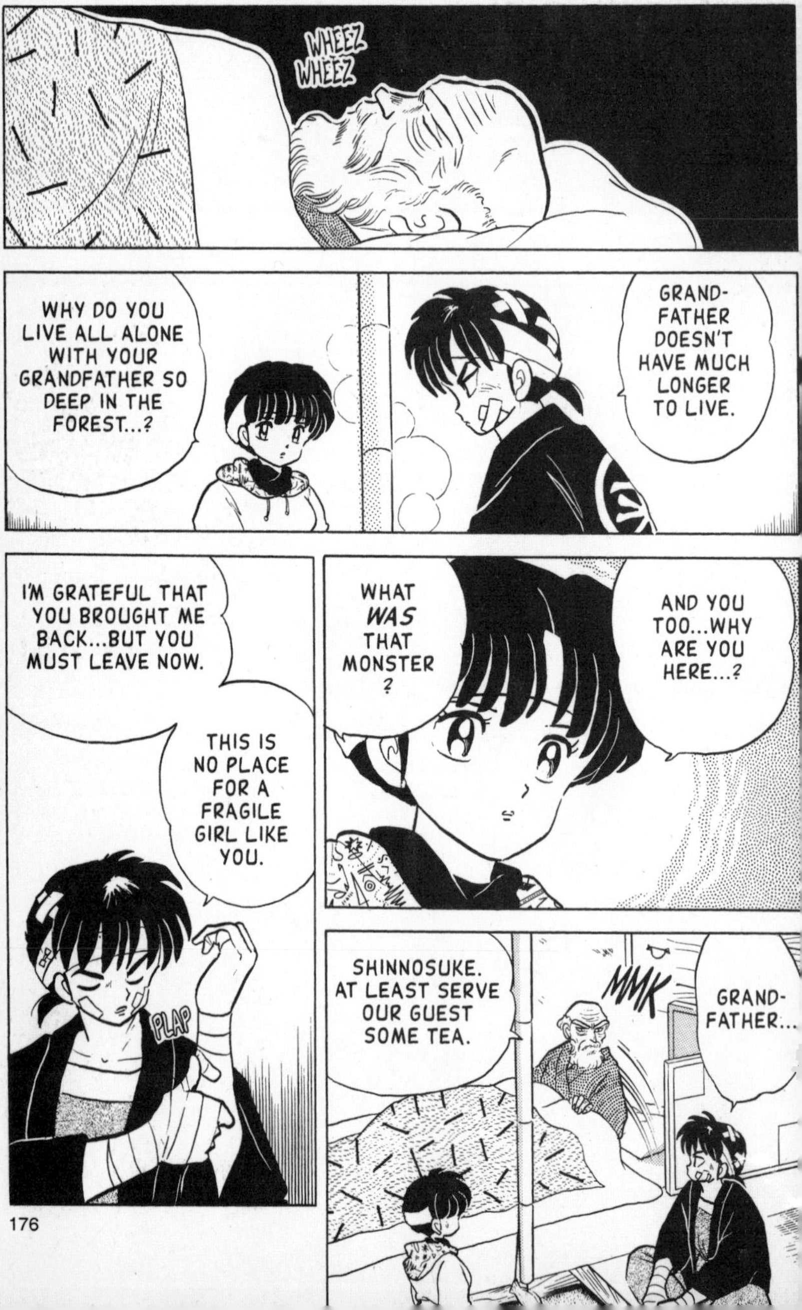

WHEEZ WHEEZ
WHY DO YOU LIVE ALL ALONE WITH YOUR GRANDFATHER SO DEEP IN THE FOREST...?
GRAND-FATHER DOESN'T HAVE MUCH LONGER TO LIVE.
I'M GRATEFUL THAT YOU BROUGHT ME BACK...BUT YOU MUST LEAVE NOW.
THIS IS NO PLACE FOR A FRAGILE GIRL LIKE YOU.
PLAP
WHAT *WAS* THAT MONSTER?
AND YOU TOO...WHY ARE YOU HERE...?
SHINNOSUKE. AT LEAST SERVE OUR GUEST SOME TEA.
MMK
GRAND-FATHER...

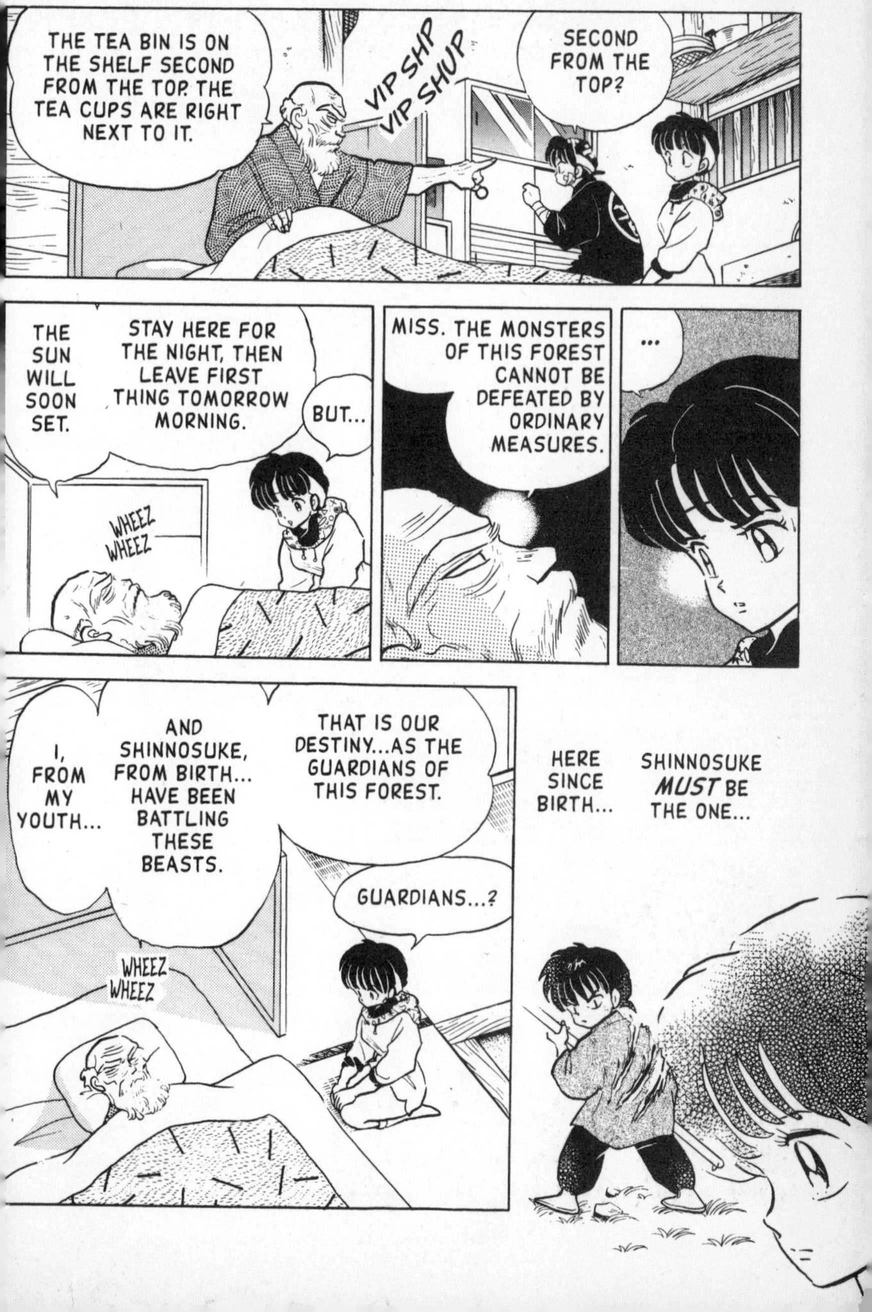
THE TEA BIN IS ON THE SHELF SECOND FROM THE TOP. THE TEA CUPS ARE RIGHT NEXT TO IT.
VIP SHP VIP SHUP
SECOND FROM THE TOP?
THE SUN WILL SOON SET.
STAY HERE FOR THE NIGHT, THEN LEAVE FIRST THING TOMORROW MORNING.
BUT...
WHEEZ WHEEZ
MISS. THE MONSTERS OF THIS FOREST CANNOT BE DEFEATED BY ORDINARY MEASURES.
...
I, FROM MY YOUTH...
AND SHINNOSUKE, FROM BIRTH... HAVE BEEN BATTLING THESE BEASTS.
THAT IS OUR DESTINY...AS THE GUARDIANS OF THIS FOREST.
GUARDIANS...?
WHEEZ WHEEZ
HERE SINCE BIRTH...
SHINNOSUKE *MUST* BE THE ONE...

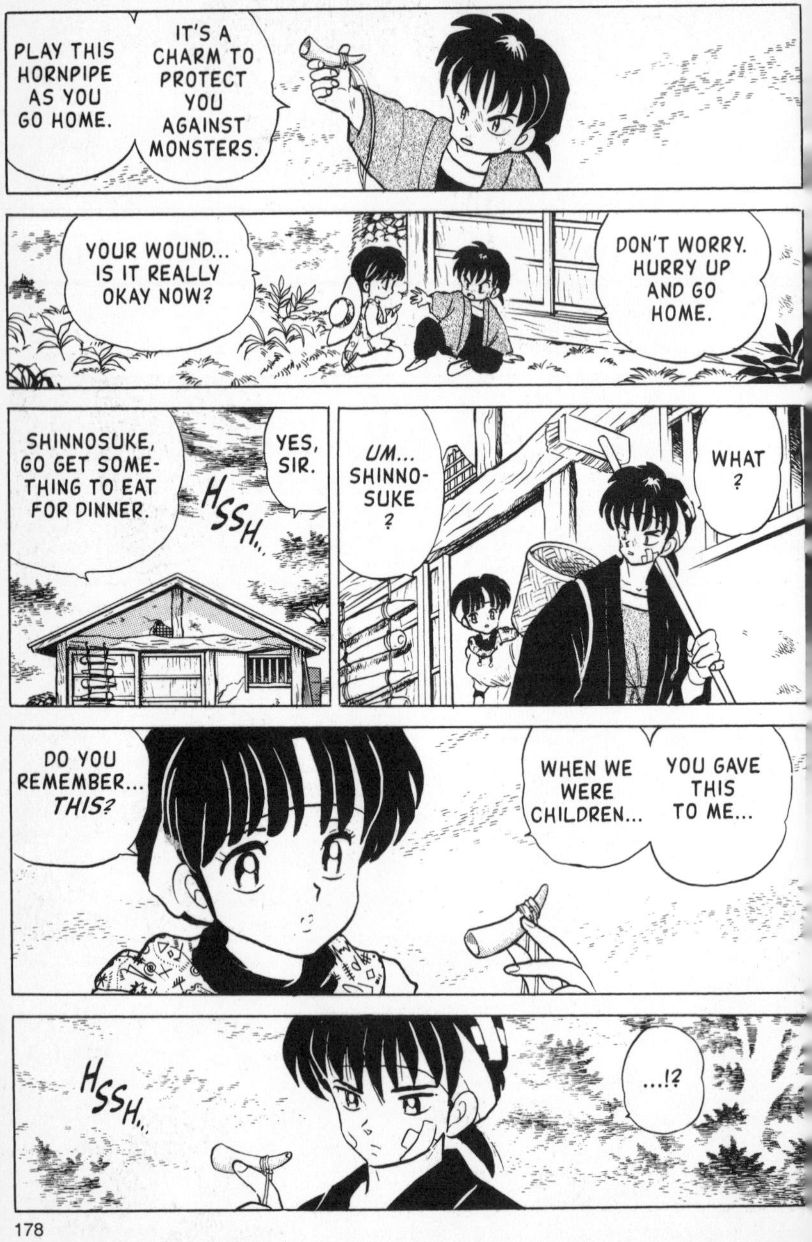
PLAY THIS HORNPIPE AS YOU GO HOME.
IT'S A CHARM TO PROTECT YOU AGAINST MONSTERS.
YOUR WOUND... IS IT REALLY OKAY NOW?
DON'T WORRY. HURRY UP AND GO HOME.
SHINNOSUKE, GO GET SOME-THING TO EAT FOR DINNER.
YES, SIR.
HSSH...
UM... SHINNO-SUKE?
WHAT?
DO YOU REMEMBER... *THIS?*
WHEN WE WERE CHILDREN...
YOU GAVE THIS TO ME...
HSSH...
...!?

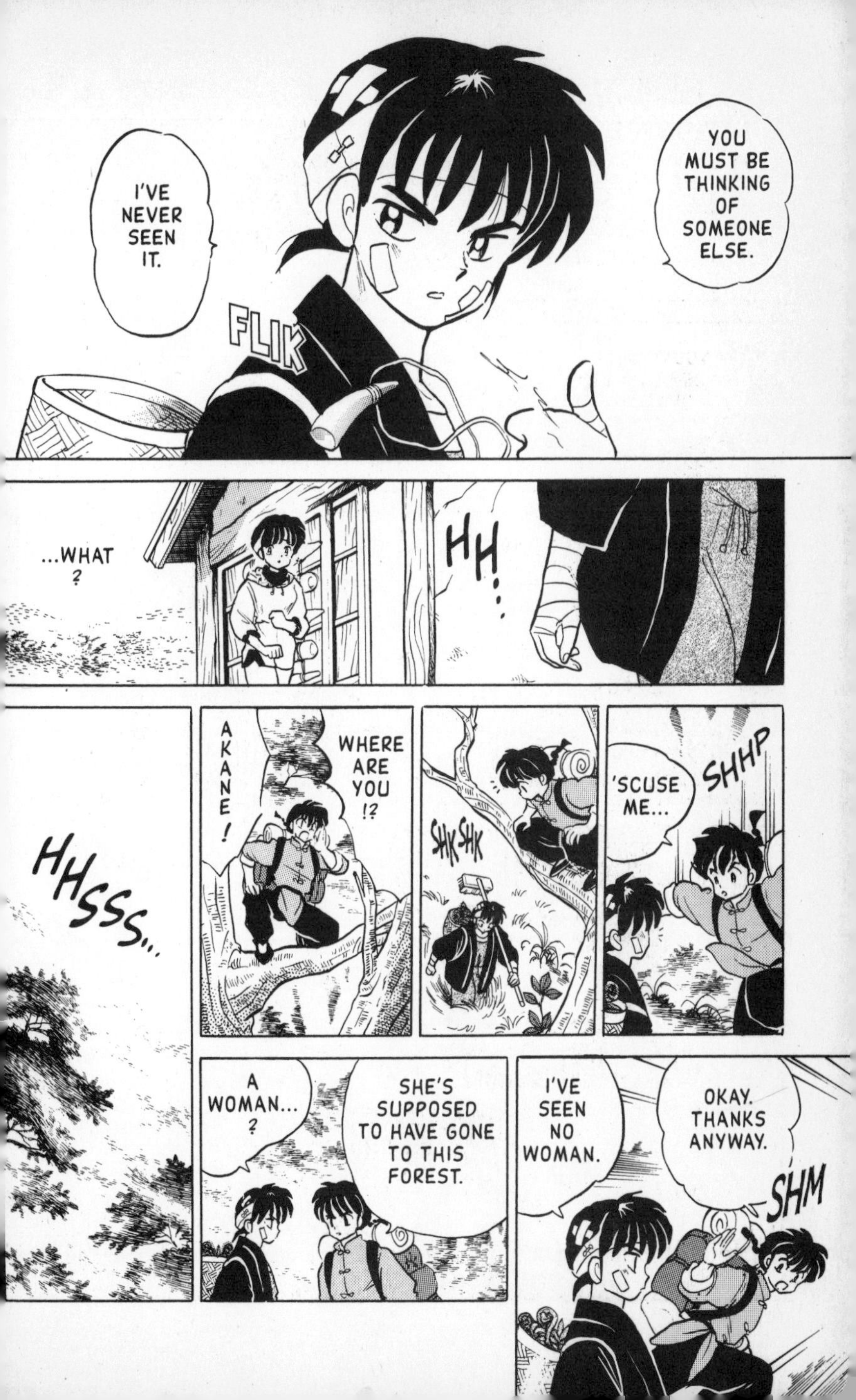

I'VE NEVER SEEN IT.
FLIK
YOU MUST BE THINKING OF SOMEONE ELSE.
...WHAT ?
HH...
HHSSS...
AKANE!
WHERE ARE YOU !?
SHK SHK
'SCUSE ME...
SHHP
A WOMAN... ?
SHE'S SUPPOSED TO HAVE GONE TO THIS FOREST.
I'VE SEEN NO WOMAN.
OKAY. THANKS ANYWAY.
SHM

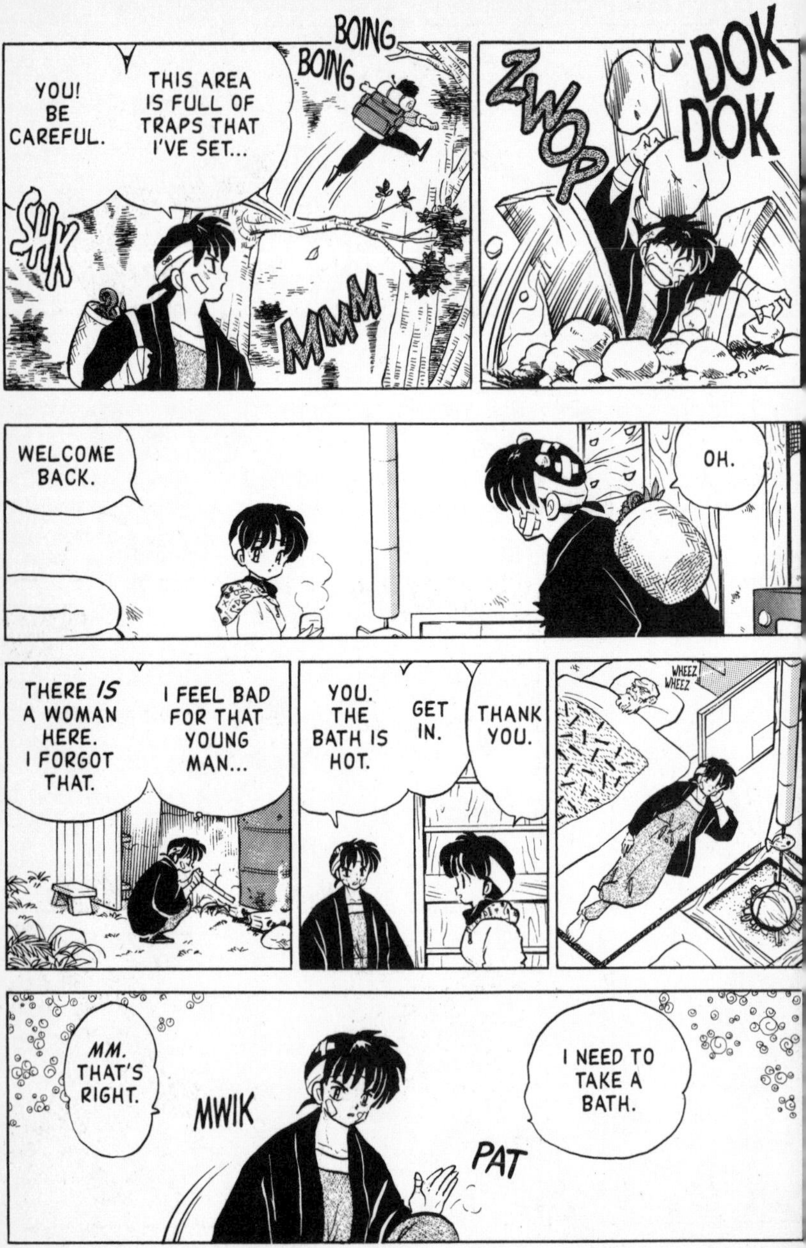
YOU! BE CAREFUL.
THIS AREA IS FULL OF TRAPS THAT I'VE SET...
SHK
BOING
BOING
MMM
ZWOP
DOK DOK
WELCOME BACK.
OH.
THERE IS A WOMAN HERE. I FORGOT THAT.
I FEEL BAD FOR THAT YOUNG MAN...
YOU. THE BATH IS HOT.
GET IN.
THANK YOU.
WHEEZ WHEEZ
MM. THAT'S RIGHT.
MWIK
I NEED TO TAKE A BATH.
PAT

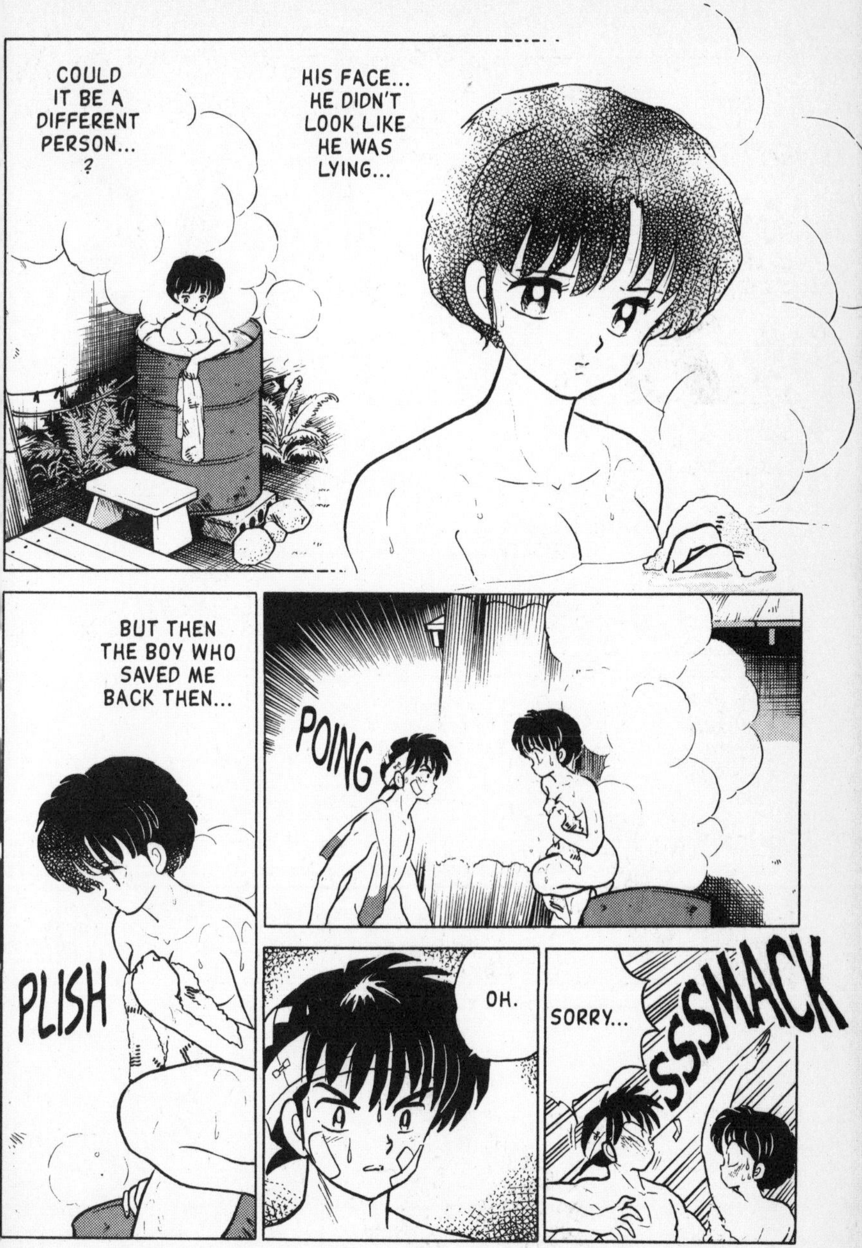
COULD IT BE A DIFFERENT PERSON...?
HIS FACE... HE DIDN'T LOOK LIKE HE WAS LYING...
BUT THEN THE BOY WHO SAVED ME BACK THEN...
PLISH
POING
OH.
SORRY...
SSSMACK

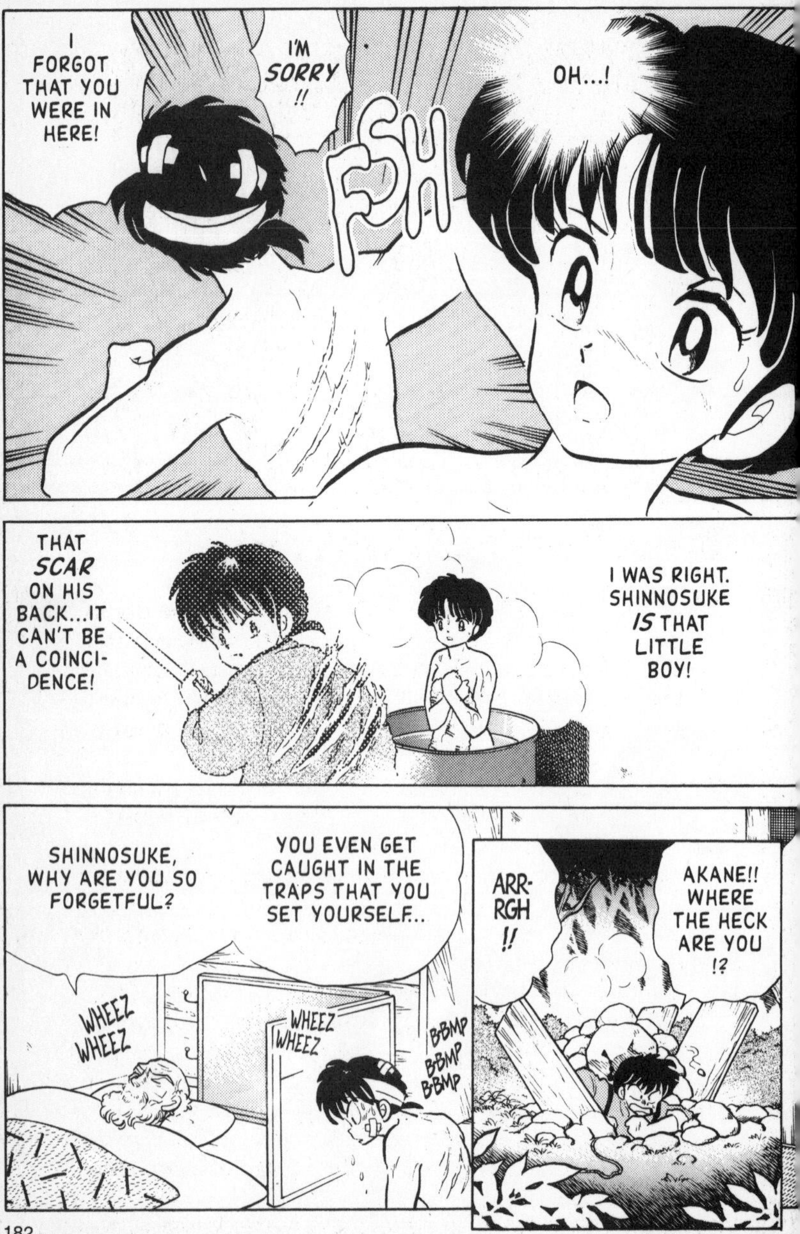
I FORGOT THAT YOU WERE IN HERE!
I'M SORRY!!
FSH
OH...!
THAT SCAR ON HIS BACK...IT CAN'T BE A COINCIDENCE!
I WAS RIGHT. SHINNOSUKE IS THAT LITTLE BOY!
SHINNOSUKE, WHY ARE YOU SO FORGETFUL?
YOU EVEN GET CAUGHT IN THE TRAPS THAT YOU SET YOURSELF...
WHEEZ WHEEZ
WHEEZ WHEEZ
B-BMP B-BMP B-BMP
ARR-RGH!!
AKANE!! WHERE THE HECK ARE YOU!?

TO BE CONTINUED!

About Rumiko Takahashi

Born in 1957 in Niigata, Japan, Rumiko Takahashi attended women's college in Tokyo, where she began studying comics with Kazuo Koike, author of *CRYING FREEMAN*. She later became an assistant to horror-manga artist Kazuo Umezu (*OROCHI*). In 1978, she won a prize in Shogakukan's annual "New Comic Artist Contest," and in that same year her boy-meets-alien comedy series *URUSEI YATSURA* began appearing in the weekly manga magazine *SHÔNEN SUNDAY*. This phenomenally successful series ran for nine years and sold over 22 million copies. Takahashi's later *RANMA 1/2* series enjoyed even greater popularity.

Takahashi is considered by many to be one of the world's most popular manga artists. With the publication of Volume 34 of her *RANMA 1/2* series in Japan, Takahashi's total sales passed *one hundred million* copies of her compiled works.

Takahashi's serial titles include *URUSEI YATSURA, RANMA 1/2, ONE-POUND GOSPEL, MAISON IKKOKU* and *INUYASHA*. Additionally, Takahashi has drawn many short stories which have been published in America under the title "Rumic Theater," and several installments of a saga known as her "Mermaid" series. Most of Takahashi's major stories have also been animated, and are widely available in translation worldwide. *INUYASHA* is her most recent serial story, first published in *SHÔNEN SUNDAY* in 1996.

EDITOR'S RECOMMENDATIONS

Did you like *Ranma 1/2*? Here's what we recommend you try next:

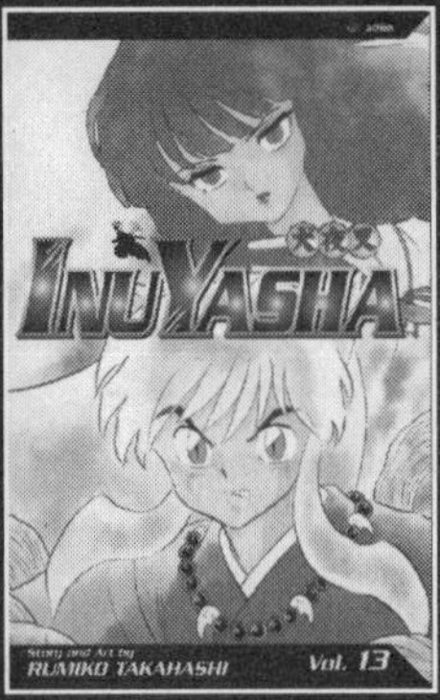

InuYasha
Story and Art by
Rumiko Takahashi
Vol. 13

© 1997 Rumiko Takahashi/Shogakukan

InuYasha is the manga serial Rumiko Takahashi began working on after she finished *Ranma 1/2*. It's a historical adventure set in ancient Japan, with romance, mystery, and horror elements.

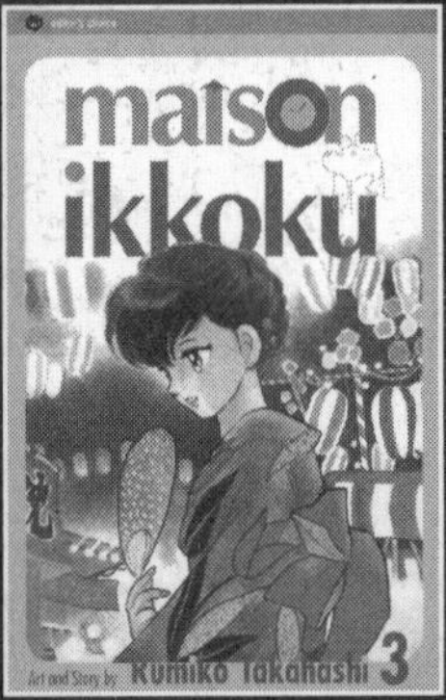

maison ikkoku
Art and Story by Rumiko Takahashi 3

© 1984 Rumiko Takahashi/Shogakukan

Maison Ikkoku is Takahashi's most romantic series. It's set in modern-day Japan, and traces the lives of the residents of a boarding house. It's intense, it's angsty, and it's one of the most absorbing manga romances ever written.

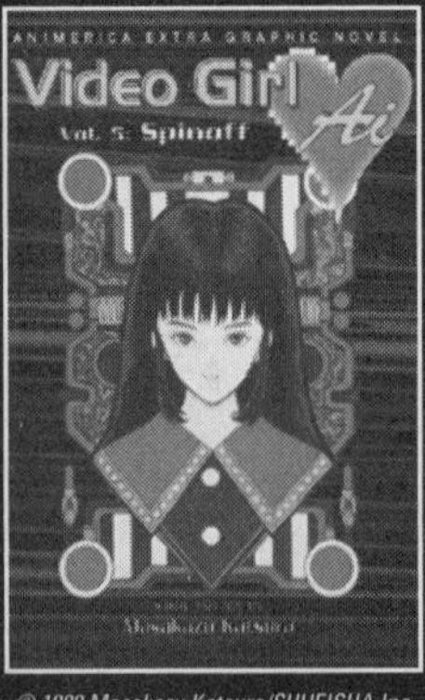

ANIMERICA EXTRA GRAPHIC NOVEL
Video Girl Ai
Vol. 5: Spinoff

© 1989 Masakazu Katsura/SHUEISHA Inc.

Video Girl Ai, by Masakazu Katsura, is a romance set in modern day Japan. Whereas *Ranma 1/2* deals with teen romances in a comedic way, *Video Girl Ai* goes for angst, and masterfully explores the feelings of first love and loss. Katsura also draws some of the most beautiful women in manga!

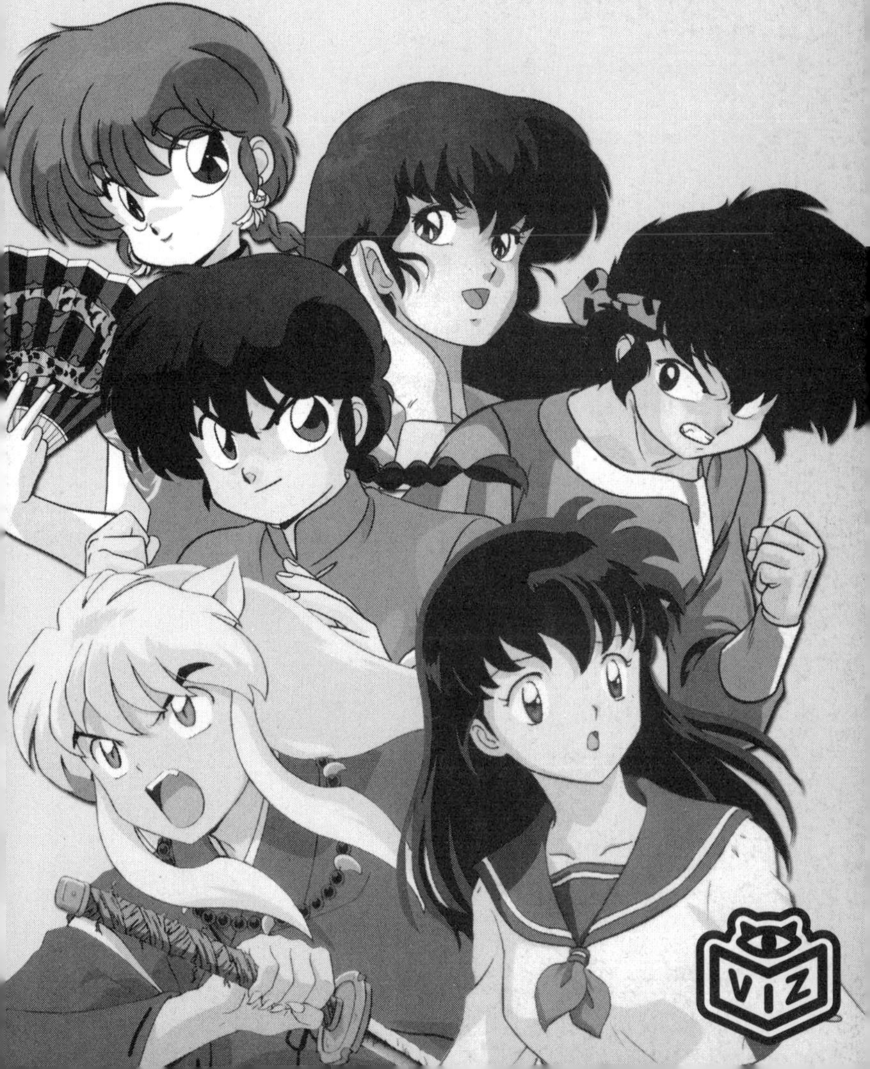

A TEST OF SKILLS...
A BATTLE OF WILLS!

Tag team players can switch between characters seamlessly!

Engage in 2 player and single player combat or tag team battles!

Launch double attacks with a team member!

From the hot new Television Show on Cartoon Network!
Based on the comic by the great manga artist, Rumiko Takahashi, Bandai is proud to present iNUYASHA for the PlayStation game console! Battle your way through the thrilling world of INUYASHA and unlock new characters for hours of pulse-pounding fighting action! Go head-to-head against a friend, or team up in tag-team and versus modes! In this fight for fun, you'll always come out the winner!

iNUYASHA
A Feudal Fairy Tale

INUYASHA Anime DVD and Manga - Now Available

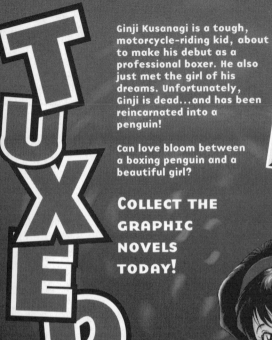

COMPLETE OUR SURVEY AND LET US KNOW WHAT YOU THINK!

☐ Please check here if you DO NOT wish to receive information or future offers from VIZ

Name: _____

Address: _____

City: _____ **State:** _____ **Zip:** _____

E-mail: _____

☐ Male ☐ Female **Date of Birth** (mm/dd/yyyy): ___ / ___ / _____ (Under 13? Parental consent required)

What race/ethnicity do you consider yourself? (please check one)

☐ Asian/Pacific Islander ☐ Black/African American ☐ Hispanic/Latino

☐ Native American/Alaskan Native ☐ White/Caucasian ☐ Other: _____

What VIZ product did you purchase? (check all that apply and indicate title purchased)

☐ DVD/VHS _____

☐ Graphic Novel _____

☐ Magazines _____

☐ Merchandise _____

Reason for purchase: (check all that apply)

☐ Special offer ☐ Favorite title ☐ Gift

☐ Recommendation ☐ Other _____

Where did you make your purchase? (please check one)

☐ Comic store ☐ Bookstore ☐ Mass/Grocery Store

☐ Newsstand ☐ Video/Video Game Store ☐ Other: _____

☐ Online (site: _____)

What other VIZ properties have you purchased/own? _____

_____

How many anime and/or manga titles have you purchased in the last year? How many were VIZ titles? (please check one from each column)

ANIME
- ☐ None
- ☐ 1-4
- ☐ 5-10
- ☐ 11+

MANGA
- ☐ None
- ☐ 1-4
- ☐ 5-10
- ☐ 11+

VIZ
- ☐ None
- ☐ 1-4
- ☐ 5-10
- ☐ 11+

I find the pricing of VIZ products to be: (please check one)

☐ Cheap   ☐ Reasonable   ☐ Expensive

What genre of manga and anime would you like to see from VIZ? (please check two)

- ☐ Adventure
- ☐ Horror
- ☐ Comic Strip
- ☐ Romance
- ☐ Detective
- ☐ Sci-Fi/Fantasy
- ☐ Fighting
- ☐ Sports

What do you think of VIZ's new look?

☐ Love It   ☐ It's OK   ☐ Hate It   ☐ Didn't Notice   ☐ No Opinion

THANK YOU! Please send the completed form to:

NJW Research
42 Catharine St.
Poughkeepsie, NY 12601

All information provided will be used for internal purposes only. We promise not to sell or otherwise divulge your information.